EURIPIDES

ANDROMACHE

EURIPIDES

ANDROMACHE

EDITED WITH
INTRODUCTION AND COMMENTARY
BY

P. T. STEVENS

OXFORD
AT THE CLARENDON PRESS

Oxford University Press, Walton Street, Oxford OX2 6DP
London New York Toronto
Delhi Bombay Calcutta Madras Karachi
Kuala Lumpur Singapore Hong Kong Tokyo
Nairobi Dar es Salaam Cape Town
Melbourne Auckland

and associated companies in
Beirut Berlin Ibadan Mexico City Nicosia

Published in the United States
by Oxford University Press, New York

First published 1971
First issued in paperback 1984

British Library Cataloguing in Publication Data

Euripides
Andromache.
I. Title II. Stevens, P.T.
882'.01 PA3973.A6

ISBN 0-19-872118-8

Printed in Great Britain
by Antony Rowe Ltd.
Chippenham

PREFACE

THIS edition of the *Andromache* does not aim at providing all the help needed by those reading a Greek play for the first time, though I am well aware of the value and importance of such editions. It is intended chiefly for the more advanced students at undergraduate and postgraduate level, and I hope it may also be of some use to older scholars. The Commentary is chiefly concerned with interpreting the text of the play, but on the ground that students should be encouraged to think of any Greek text as a window opening on the world of antiquity, I have sometimes carried discussion of points of interest in language, thought, dramatic conventions, and other matters beyond what is strictly needed for the understanding of this particular play.

As in most editions in this series, the text and apparatus criticus are reprinted from the Oxford Classical Text by G. Murray. The reasons for this need not be repeated here, and I think the advantages of this procedure outweigh the objections. There are inevitably some passages, discussed in the Commentary, where I have indicated that Murray's text seems to me unacceptable and others where I have doubts about it.

This edition naturally owes much to the work of previous editors and commentators. Among modern editions those of F. Bornmann, A. Garzya, and J. C. Kamerbeek have proved particularly useful, and my obligations to them and to others are not of course limited to passages where it seemed appropriate to make specific acknowledgements. Finally, it gives me much pleasure to record my gratitude to several scholars who have generously given me their help and encouragement. The first among these is the late Miss A. M. Dale, who read part of my manuscript and in addition to giving me the benefit of her expertise in metrical matters made many penetrating criticisms. She did not, however, see any of the Commentary in final form and has no responsibility for anything in it, except where her name is specifically mentioned. Professor T. B. L. Webster and Professor Hugh Lloyd-Jones also read parts of the manuscript and made many valuable suggestions. I am also grateful to Professor P. E. Corbett and Mr. J. N. Coldstream for advice on archaeological questions. Lastly I should like to thank the Clarendon Press Reader not only for the correction of minor errors, but also for many acute comments and valuable criticisms.

P. T. S.

Bedford College, London
October 1970

CONTENTS

INTRODUCTION

1. *The Legend before Euripides*

OWING to the loss of most of the poems of the Epic Cycle and much early lyric poetry, a loss only partly made good by later allusions and post-classical summaries, we cannot be sure in what forms the legendary material reached the tragic dramatists of the fifth century. At any rate the chief characters in *Andromache* apart from Hermione, to whom there are only brief references, are familiar figures in epic tradition.

Neoptolemus is only mentioned once in the *Iliad* (19. 327), as son of Achilles; in the *Odyssey* his return from Troy is alluded to in 3. 189; he is mentioned in 4. 5 as prospective husband of Hermione; and in 11. 506–36 Odysseus delights the shade of Achilles by an enthusiastic account of his son's prowess at Troy. He is also prominent in later Epic as one who played a major part in the last stage of the fighting at Troy and in the capture of the city. Here he is presented as a ruthless figure: it was he who killed the old king Priam, either dragging him from the altar where he had taken refuge[1] or killing him at the altar itself;[2] in *Ilias Parva*[3] it was he who cast the child Astyanax down from the walls of Troy, though in *Iliou Persis* this act is ascribed to Odysseus. Another strand of tradition, concerning Neoptolemus' subsequent visit to Delphi and his death, is first recorded for us in Pindar and Pherecydes of Athens. In Pindar, *Paean* 6, dated about 490 B.C., it is said that he did not escape from Apollo, who had sworn that he who slew the aged Priam at the altar should not reach old age. So the god slew him in his precinct, while he was striving with the attendants over the established dues. In this paean, composed for performance at Delphi, we

[1] Pausanias 10. 27. 1 ff.
[2] *Iliou Persis* ap. Procl.
[3] Kinkel, fr. 18.

probably have the current Delphic version.[1] In *Nemean* 7, however, composed for Sogenes of Aegina, Pindar adopted, or invented, a different version, in which Neoptolemus on his return from Troy ruled for a short time as king in Molossia, where his descendants were destined to rule for ever. Then he went to Delphi with rich offerings for the god from the spoils of Troy, but while involved in a quarrel concerning the flesh of victims he was killed, to the great grief of the Delphians, and was buried there. No blame attached to Neoptolemus and his death occurred almost by accident, perhaps even θείᾳ τύχῃ, since he thus fulfilled the decree of fate that one of the Aeacidae should dwell for ever beside the temple of the god. A third version, probably derived from some epic source, is given by Pherecydes,[2] in which the reason for Neoptolemus' visit to Delphi is to consult the oracle about children, since Hermione has so far proved barren. His death is again said to have occurred during a dispute with the Delphians concerning the sacrificial meats.

Hermione is mentioned in Homer as the only child of Menelaus and Helen; in Hesiod fr. 99 (Rz.) and perhaps in *Cypria* they have two; so also in S. *El.* 539. In *Odyssey* 4. 4 ff. we hear that Menelaus is making preparations for her marriage to Neoptolemus, in accordance with a promise made during the war at Troy. That she inherited something of her mother's loveliness is indicated in *Od.* 4. 13–14, in Hesiod fr. 96 (Rz.), and perhaps in a fragment of Sappho.[3]

Andromache is presented in the *Iliad* as the loyal and loving wife of Hector, whom in *Il.* 22 she sees dragged behind the chariot of Achilles. Even at her first appearance in *Il.* 6 she is invested with special pathos through her own and Hector's presentiment of the fate in store for her and her son. It was also part of the epic tradition that Andromache was allotted

[1] The proverbial expression Νεοπτολέμειος τίσις (Paus. 4. 17. 4) suggests that this was the best-known version. See further S. L. Radt, *Pindars zweiter und sechster Paian*, pp. 155 ff.

[2] F. Jacoby, *FGH* 1, 78, 64a.

[3] See Page, *Sappho and Alcaeus*, p. 139; so also in later tradition, e.g. Prop. 1. 4. 6.

to Neoptolemus as part of his share of the spoils of Troy,[1] and probably that she bore him children.[2] Her subsequent marriage to Helenus may also belong to epic tradition.[3]

The remaining characters, Menelaus, Peleus, and Orestes, are of course famous legendary figures. There is no evidence extant that in the earlier tradition Peleus and Orestes were associated with the Neoptolemus–Hermione story, though the betrothal of Hermione to Orestes, apparently used by Sophocles in his *Hermione* and by Philocles and Theognis as well as by Euripides, may well be derived from some epic source. Menelaus is presented in the Homeric poems as a heroic figure,[4] and so is Orestes as far as the few slight indications go.[5] The very different presentation in Tragedy, especially of Menelaus, is not peculiar to this play or to Euripides, nor are these the only Homeric heroes to be degraded in the fifth century.[6] In each case there may be a special reason, e.g. that Menelaus was a Spartan, but there would be more general reasons such as changes in the climate of thought[7] and the fact that Tragedy needs stronger contrasts between characters than Epic, e.g. in this play between Peleus and Menelaus.

II. *The Legend in Fifth-century Tragedy*

In the fifth century several plays were concerned wholly or partly with the same legendary material as *Andromache*. In the *Hermione* of Sophocles, of which practically nothing

[1] *Ilias Parva*, fr. 18 Kinkel.

[2] See schol. on *Andr.* 24.

[3] Virgil's account in *Aen.* 3. 293 ff. does not seem to be derived from Eur., but perhaps from a common source.

[4] See note on 456–7.

[5] In *Od.* 1. 30 he is τηλεκλυτός and in 298–300 he is held up as an example to Telemachus.

[6] Some have suggested that the process may have begun in post-Homeric Epic, but there is no reliable indication of this. For a rehabilitation of Menelaus in the fourth century see Isoc. 12. 72 Μενέλαον τὸν διὰ σωφροσύνην καὶ δικαιοσύνην μόνον ἀξιωθέντα Διὸς γενέσθαι κηδεστήν.

[7] See, for example, on reasons for the growth of hostility to Odysseus, Stanford, *The Ulysses Theme*, pp. 90–102.

survives, we learn from the brief summary of Eustathius that Hermione was first given to Orestes[1] by Tyndareus, her grandfather, while Menelaus was away at Troy, and was later taken from him and given to Neoptolemus in accordance with a promise made at Troy, presumably by Menelaus. Subsequently while Neoptolemus was on a visit to Delphi to claim satisfaction from Apollo for the death of his father, Achilles, he was killed by Machaireus, and Hermione was then restored to Orestes and bore him a son, Tisamenos. A. C. Pearson (Sophocles, *Fragments*, I. 141–3) rightly notes that this is our only explicit evidence for the plot, and if so, his own observation that 'the plot of this play proceeds on parallel lines to that of Euripides' *Andromache*' seems rather too sweeping: there is nothing to show what part, if any, was played by Andromache or Peleus, and it cannot be assumed that Orestes was directly responsible for the death of Neoptolemus. It is likely that a play of Sophocles would be more favourable to Apollo and Delphi than our play, and Ovid's treatment of the story in *Her. Ep.* 8, where Hermione is represented as forcibly abducted by Neoptolemus and begging her former lover, Orestes, to rescue her, may be partly indebted to the Sophoclean play; so also perhaps the *Hermione* of Pacuvius, of which few fragments survive. Attempts at reconstruction are, however, extremely conjectural. If Sophocles' play were extant it would certainly be interesting and perhaps illuminating to compare the treatment of characters and the working out of the plot; but as it is I doubt whether speculations about what Sophocles may have done[2] can contribute anything of value to our understanding of the Euripidean play. Of other contemporary plays concerned with the same material we know only that according to the scholiast on *Andr.* 32 the tragic dramatists Philocles and

[1] ἐκδοθῆναι would normally, but perhaps not inevitably, imply that the marriage took place.

[2] See T. Zieliński, *Tragodoumenon Libri Tres*, pp. 114 ff., with criticism by A. Koerte in *Phil. Woch.*, 47 (1927), 577 ff. and reply by Zieliński in *Eos*, 31 (1928), 1–39; W. H. Friedrich, *Euripides und Diphilos*, pp. 47–9.

Theognis refer to Hermione as first betrothed or given in marriage (προεκδοθῆναι) to Orestes by Tyndareus, and, when already pregnant by him, given by Menelaus to Neoptolemus. There is no evidence to indicate whether either of the relevant plays or the *Hermione* of Sophocles was produced before or after *Andromache*.

III. *The* Andromache *of Euripides: Structure and Theme*

Before considering the plot structure and interpretation of Euripides' play it will be useful to note how he diverges from or chooses between traditional accounts. In the first part he started with two well-established data, that Hermione was the wife and Andromache the slave of Neoptolemus. He assumed the existence of a single child of Andromache by her master and took from Pherecydes or his source the barrenness of Hermione. On the basis of these facts he almost certainly invented the whole sequence in which the relationship between the two women is worked out, the jealousy of Hermione leading to an attempt to kill Andromache and her child, a plot that is foiled by the last-minute intervention of Peleus. Andromache, a minor figure in post-Homeric epic, is thus brought into prominence, though her role is mainly passive, and everything is calculated to win sympathy for her and to present in the most unfavourable light Hermione and her father, who in the scene with Andromache is treacherous and brutal, in the scene with Peleus blustering and cowardly. In the second part, it is now Menelaus who is represented as first promising Hermione to Orestes and then using her as a bribe to secure the help of Neoptolemus. This is different from the Sophoclean version and more discreditable to Menelaus; but we do not know which version came first or whether either of them was traditional. The responsibility of Orestes for the death of Neoptolemus may also be an innovation by Euripides. In any case there are considerable changes in the presentation of Neoptolemus and the manner of his death. There is no suggestion here of the ruthless Neoptolemus of epic tradition.[1] To Andromache he is the master with whom she must lie perforce, and she reproaches him as absent when she and their child are in danger; but she does not seem to feel enmity against him[2] and assumes that he will return to protect or avenge them.[3] Both Sophocles and Euripides refer to a visit of Neoptolemus to Delphi to seek satisfaction from Apollo for his father's death, a motive which may be a fifth-century invention. At any rate Euripides has invented the second visit in which he seeks to atone for his presumption, and it is during this second visit that he is killed. The whole account of his death, the details of which are probably invented by Euripides, is so contrived as to bring the maximum discredit upon Delphi and Orestes; everything is calculated to present him as a simple and brave warrior and Orestes as an unscrupulous schemer. A minor innovation is that after his death his body is brought to Phthia, the scene of the play, so that Peleus and the chorus can lament over it, though it must later be sent back again to Delphi, where the supposed site of his burial was probably well known.[4]

Euripides has so shaped his plot[5] that in the first part Andromache is the centre of interest. She speaks the opening monologue: she is continuously present from the beginning up to 463, including the parodos (throughout which the Chorus are directly addressing her) and the first stasimon, and is again present from 501 to 765: the action of this part of the play is primarily concerned with her peril and rescue

[1] Contrast *Hec.* 23 αὐτὸς (sc. Priam) . . . σφαγεὶς Ἀχίλλεως παιδὸς ἐκ μιαιφόνου.

[2] See notes on 341 and 416.

[3] See 268–9 and 339–43.

[4] See Pind. *Nem.* 7. 62; Paus. 10. 24. 5.

[5] I have not provided a detailed account of the plot, since in any case discussion of a play, though conventionally called an 'introduction', assumes in fact some knowledge of it. Anyone who comes fresh to the play should of course begin by reading it and forming his own impressions before considering these or any other general observations.

by Peleus. The threat to her life arises from the jealousy and hatred of Hermione, the causes of which are explained in the prologue and amplified in the confrontation of Andromache and Hermione in the first epeisodion. In this scene interest is thus divided between the two women, but in the next epeisodion Hermione is either not present[1] or at any rate does not speak, and the opposition is now between Andromache and Menelaus.

After 765 Andromache either does not appear again,[2] or if she is present from 1047 to the end she has nothing to say or do. In the third epeisodion (802–1008) it is Hermione, almost hysterical with fear about the consequences of her unsuccessful schemes against the life of Andromache and her child, who becomes the main centre of interest; though when Orestes, a more famous legendary figure, suddenly appears at 881 as her rescuer and the deadly enemy of Neoptolemus, he may perhaps steal the limelight.

In the last part of the play from 1047 onwards Hermione does not appear again, and apart from two brief allusions is never mentioned. Our direct concern is now mainly with the fortunes of the House of Aeacus: we are absorbed in the exciting narrative of the death of Neoptolemus at Delphi, victim of Orestes and Phoebus Apollo, and in contemplating Peleus overcome with sorrow and despair, till his divine consort Thetis appears to comfort him with the promise of immortality for himself and glory for his descendants.

The play thus falls into three parts. Between each part and the next there is certainly a clear causal connection: the plight of Hermione in part two is the result of her share in the proceedings of part one, and her rescue by Orestes involves his guarantee to dispose of Neoptolemus, whose death becomes the subject of part three. Thus I think it is going too far to say that 'the play falls feebly and mysteriously to pieces'.[3] All the same there is a striking shift of interest after 765 away from the fortunes of Andromache to those of Hermione, and

[1] See note on 268 ff. [2] See note on 1047.

[3] D. W. Lucas, *The Greek Tragic Poets* (2nd ed., 1959), p. 182.

again after 992 away from Hermione to Neoptolemus. The last scenes have on the face of it only a tenuous connection with the initial pathos and peril of Andromache, a connection that is not greatly strengthened by the brief allusion in the epilogue to her subsequent fate or even by her silent presence, if she is on stage. *Andromache* is not of course the only Attic tragedy which exhibits such shifts of interest and falls into two or more parts. *Heracles*, for instance, has a similar tripartite structure, and the sudden appearance of Orestes in *Andromache* is comparable with the unexpected and unprepared entrance of Iris,[1] initiating a new phase of the action unrelated to the previous scenes.[2] There are other plays in which the causal framework is there, as in *Andromache*, but there is a shift of interest, as from Phaedra to Hippolytus, from Deianira to Heracles. In fact the dramatists allow this sort of thing to happen fairly often,[3] though they could surely have prevented it—sufficiently often to suggest that neither they nor their audiences can have attached much importance to what modern critics are inclined to consider a structural weakness. On the other hand, in many plays which in varying degrees and in different ways may be said to lack unity on Aristotelian canons we can see that there is unity of another kind, derived perhaps from a dominant character or from an idea. Is *Andromache*, then, merely a dramatization of episodes traditional or invented, calculated to stir excitement, anger, and pity and linked together by a superficially adequate causal connection,[4] or is there

[1] The speech of Iris in 822 ff. has been described as a sort of second prologue; the same might be said of the speech of Orestes, esp. *Andr.* 966 ff., where for the benefit of the spectators he gives the background of his feud with Neoptolemus.

[2] Unless of course, without encouragement from Euripides, we ascribe the madness of Heracles to pathological causes.

[3] On the frequency of plays of the 'diptych' type in Sophocles and Euripides see A. J. A. Waldock, *Sophocles the Dramatist*, pp. 54 ff., though I do not find convincing his argument that the nature of Attic tragedy made this frequency inevitable.

[4] This may indeed be all that some of the audience would look for

a character or a theme which inspired the choice of material and manner of presentation, and which gives to the play its own form of inner dramatic unity?

It is characteristic of Euripides to take a bald fact in the epic tradition, such as the handing over of Andromache to Neoptolemus as his slave, and to imagine what her feelings would be and ask what effect the introduction of such a woman into the household might have. The fact that he was probably the first to dramatize this aspect of the situation confirms his special interest,[1] and some have thought of Hermione, others of Andromache, others of the clash between them as the main centre of interest. Thus for A. Garzya[2] the heart of the drama is a study of feminine psychology as exhibited in Hermione's relations with her husband and her husband's mistress, in her plot against her rival, its failure, and her despair and remorse. He thinks of her as a tragic figure, essentially innocent and caught in the net of a situation that is too much for her inexperience. On this view we might perhaps have expected that the play would have been entitled *Hermione*. In any case this estimate of Hermione seems to me much too favourable,[3] and my impression is that the dramatist has made no effort to enlist our sympathy on her behalf. Moreover there is nothing here to account for the form of the play, since from 274 to 801 Hermione is absent from the scene[4] (though she is often referred to), and after 1062 she is both out of sight and out of mind.

and all that they could be expected to be aware of, but it would not follow that Euripides meant and hoped to convey no more than this.

[1] W. Schmid (*Gesch. der gr. Lit.* 7. 1. 3. 1, 397 ff.) puts *Andromache* in his group of plays concerned with problems of love and marriage, together with *Medea*, *Hippolytus*, *Stheneboea*, and others; chronologically it is nearer to *Hecuba* and *Supplices*, but in any case we should not allow any system of grouping, by date or theme, to have too much influence on the interpretation of each play.

[2] *Dioniso*, 1952, pp. 104–21; Euripide, *Andromaca* (2nd ed., 1963), Introduzione.

[3] See notes on 805 and 825.

[4] Garzya thinks she may be present during the first stasimon and the following epeisodion (274–463), but see note on 268 ff.

H. Erbse in an interesting paper[1] takes the play to be primarily about Andromache, as the title might lead us to expect.[2] There is no doubt that the pathos of her position, her danger and last-minute rescue form the centre of interest in the first part of the play. After 765 she has no further part in the action, but Erbse maintains that she still dominates the play, in the sense that she has set a standard by which others are measured, and that though she is now a slave her inner greatness continues to show up the essential weakness or baseness of her enemies.[3] He also believes that she returns with Peleus at 1047 and is present as a silent figure for the rest of the play;[4] moreover, though she does not speak, he takes her silence in the scene where Peleus laments over the body of Neoptolemus to be in effect a bitter condemnation of the dead man, 'who sacked Troy, took her by force and then abandoned her to the malice of Hermione, and who thus deserves no word of lamentation or affection from her'.

There is some truth in this: in particular there is no doubt that our judgement of Hermione is influenced by the comparison with Andromache. Yet even before Andromache leaves the stage, in the greater part of the rescue scene the main interest is in the clash between Peleus and Menelaus, with Andromache as merely the bone of contention; and in the following scenes Erbse seems to me to exaggerate the extent to which the spectator's reactions to what he sees before him will continue to be determined by his thoughts of Andromache. It is just possible that Andromache is present from 1047, but if so I cannot believe that the audience were

[1] 'Euripides' *Andromache*', *Hermes*, 94 (1966), 276–97 (= *Euripides, Wege der Forschung*, 89. 275–304).

[2] Greek tragedies are not character studies, but when a play is named after a single character, it is he or she who is generally the chief point of reference for the action.

[3] See also Kamerbeek, *Mnem.* 11 (1943), 62: 'Sa figure (sc. Andromache) domine réellement, grâce au contraste avec Hermione, la scène entre Hermione et la nourrice, et au sens figuré elle n'est non plus absente de la scène entre Hermione et Oreste.'

[4] See note on 1047.

expected to read so much into the silence of a κωφὸν πρόσωπον. Also Erbse's interpretation of her silence seems to me inconsistent with the impression of Neoptolemus in the rest of the play and with such indications as we have of Andromache's feelings towards him.[1] Nor do the choral odes lend much support, since references to Andromache in them are brief and incidental.[2] Finally in the epilogue, out of thirty-three lines in which Thetis rounds off the play and ties up loose ends, three lines,[3] addressed to Peleus, suffice to ordain the fate of Andromache.

Others[4] have taken the purpose of the play to be political, and think that its interest lies in the changing fortunes of the House of Peleus, represented by the son of Neoptolemus and Andromache, who is destined to be the ancestor of Tharyps, king of the Molossians and now an ally of Athens, by Peleus himself, and by Neoptolemus, who is constantly referred to and whose dead body lies before us in the last scenes of the play. On this view, however, apart from other objections, the emphasis in earlier scenes on Hermione and her relations with Andromache seems to be almost pointless.

Rather more promising at first sight is Kitto's interpretation,[5] that this tragedy is 'not incidentally, but fundamentally, a violent attack on the Spartan mind, on *Machtpolitik*: in particular on three Spartan qualities, arrogance, treachery, and criminal ruthlessness. These are portrayed in three separate characters, Hermione, Menelaus, and Orestes, and in two separate actions.' We are indeed often reminded that Hermione and Menelaus are Spartans and the audience might be expected to draw its own conclusions. The condemnation of Spartan brutality and treachery, which is implicit in the manner in which the conduct of Spartans is here presented,

[1] See notes on 341 and 416.

[2] See 302–3, 489, 1041–2 with notes ad locc. In the second stasimon on the dangers of rivalry the Chorus are at least as much interested in Hermione.

[3] See 1243–5.

[4] See D. S. Robertson in *CR* 37 (1923), 58–60; R. Goossens, *Euripide et Athènes*, pp. 376–410.

[5] *Greek Tragedy* (3rd ed., 1961), p. 228.

is made explicit chiefly in the words of Andromache in 437 and in her scornful denunciation in 445 ff., compared with which Peleus' tirade against the immodesty of Spartan girls is rather trivial. No doubt when the audience heard these accusations they would think of contemporary examples of Spartan ways.[1] On the other hand most of Andromache's speech is appropriate to its dramatic context; on her own account she has every reason to say things that an angry Athenian in about 425 B.C. might also be inclined to say. Her quarrel is strictly speaking with individuals, but it is natural for her in such circumstances to generalize and say 'So this is your Spartan code' and 'You Spartans are all liars and cheats.'[2] But of course dramatic relevance does not preclude contemporary reference. In the third part of the play it is not clear that Orestes would naturally be taken as representing another facet of Spartan villainy. He is related to Menelaus, but he is himself referred to as an Argive,[3] and there is no suggestion that he too exemplifies Spartan characteristics. If then the Sparta motif is dropped after 765 it is less likely to be the central idea of the play. Moreover if the play was intended as not only incidentally but fundamentally an attack on the Spartan mind, we might have expected this to be reflected in at least one of the choral songs.

[1] See note on 445–53.

[2] It therefore seems to me surprising that D. W. Lucas (op. cit., p. 187) should write: 'Two savage outbursts on the perfidy and private immorality of Spartans disfigure the *Andromache*, and suggest that the years of the plague and the Spartan devastation of Attica had put an unbearable strain on the sanity even of Euripides.' Wilamowitz, *Hermes*, 60 (1925), 295, takes a similar view, and Pohlenz called the play a hymn of hate (*Gr. Tr.*, p. 304). Yet in *Hecuba*, composed within a year or two of this play, there is no trace of anti-Spartan sentiment, though it could have been introduced, e.g. at 450. (It is surely perverse to see, with K. W. Müller, an allusion to Sphacteria in 650–1, since this would ruin the effect of the ode.)

[3] See 1032, but the text is doubtful. In 1075, a line omitted in some MSS., he is referred to as *Μυκηναῖος ξένος*. Cf. *Or.* 1660 *Ἄργους δ' Ὀρέστην, Μενέλεως, ἔα κρατεῖν.*

The theme to which the first and last of the four stasima are in fact devoted is the Trojan war, the ἀρχὴ κακῶν, and the bitter consequences for victors and vanquished alike. The same constant reference back pervades the dialogue and speeches from the first lines of the prologue to the words of Thetis in 1251–2. It is indeed natural that Andromache should keep harping on the past, that Hector and Troy should be the constant burden of her speech and song, but it is not any less significant for that. Again, in the agon between Peleus and Menelaus both of them constantly look back, Peleus condemning the wanton Helen as the unworthy cause of it all and scornfully rejecting Menelaus' claims to renown. From beginning to end the Trojan war is kept too prominently before us to be regarded as a mere background, and Aldrich may be right in holding that here, as perhaps in *Hecuba* and certainly in *Troades*, the real theme of the play is the disastrous war, its trivial origin, and its tragic aftermath.[1] Andromache opens the play, and it is rightly named after her, not because she is the 'heroine' in the usual theatrical sense, but because, widowed, orphaned, and enslaved, she more than anyone brings together in her person the woes of the conquered city, and now finds that her own life and that of her child is threatened. Menelaus in contrast represents the ὕβρις of the victor. He is portrayed here as without any redeeming qualities: he set war afoot for unworthy and selfish reasons; he shirked the actual fighting but now boasts that he is the conqueror of Troy. He is the type that survives a war and profits by it, when the truly heroic figures such as Hector and Achilles are dead. Hermione belongs to the victorious side and is partly a cause of the miseries of Andromache, but partly also herself a victim of the war, used by Menelaus as a bribe to Neoptolemus and then deserted when their joint schemes end in failure. Orestes took no part in the war, but he is shown as one whose life was

[1] See Keith M. Aldrich, *The Andromache of Euripides*, University of Nebraska Studies, N.S. 25, 1961, to whose valuable essay I am indebted here and at several points in the Commentary.

blighted and his character warped by the sequence of events that began with the sacrifice of Iphigeneia at Aulis and culminated in the dread command of Apollo, of which the chorus sing in horror and incredulity in the fourth stasimon. He has committed one murder by divine bidding, and now he plans another for reasons of revenge and self-interest. Finally Neoptolemus, presented as impetuous but brave and honourable, a true son of Achilles, falls a victim to treachery and slander, and the play proper ends with Peleus, a survival from an earlier and more heroic age,[1] mourning over his grandson: 'Would that he had perished beneath the walls of Ilium by the banks of Simois.'[2] The last part of the play thus puts the finishing touch to the picture of what in the end the Great War really meant, in terms of the misery and degradation that marked its aftermath. *τοιαῦθ' ὁ τλήμων πόλεμος ἐξεργάζεται.*

It is, I think, at least possible that some such idea was in the mind of Euripides, and that it was partly this that led him to dramatize this sequence of events and influenced his handling of the traditional material. Thus, for example, the selection of the tradition most favourable to Neoptolemus and the whole account of the manner of his death were not designed primarily as an attack on Apollo and Delphi, but to make us see his death not as just retribution but as a final outrage. From this point of view the play has a certain unity of conception and every scene can be said to make some contribution to the total effect. It is, moreover, a theme which, like that of *Troades*, is suitable for, and perhaps calls for, episodic treatment. It must be admitted, however, that if the theme indicated was never altogether absent from Euripides' mind, there were times when other interests were

[1] This is brought out in the reference to some of his exploits in 790–801.

[2] Kamerbeek (who takes a rather different view of the play as a whole) writes of Neoptolemus: . . . 'son corps est porté sur la scène, symbole de la corruption dont la guerre de Troie est la cause, corruption dont l'action souvent terre à terre de la pièce est l'expression préméditée' (*Mnem.* 11 (1943), 67).

admitted and given disproportionate emphasis. In particular his interest in the marital problems of Hermione and her relationship with Andromache led him to develop this aspect of the situation for its own sake beyond the requirements of his theme. His treatment of this episode also enabled him to provide *more suo* scenes of pathos and self-sacrifice and the excitement of a last-minute rescue, and these, together with the anti-Sparta and anti-Delphi colouring, may have been intended to increase the popular appeal. At any rate the result is a play that has, I think, been underestimated by many scholars, though in comparison with *Troades*, which has a similar theme and is completely episodic, it lacks the single-minded concentration of the later play, where every scene is composed only to illustrate the theme and every choral ode gives it direct expression.

IV. *Date and Place of Production*

The surviving fragment of the second (Aristophanic) Hypothesis unfortunately does not include the indication of date. The only ancient testimony is the comment of a scholiast on 445, with reference to Andromache's denunciation of Spartan treachery: *ταῦτα ἐπὶ τῷ Ἀνδρομάχης προσχήματί φησιν Εὐριπίδης λοιδορούμενος τοῖς Σπαρτιάταις διὰ τὸν ἐνεστῶτα πόλεμον. καὶ γὰρ δὴ καὶ παρεσπονδήκεσαν πρὸς Ἀθηναίους, καθάπερ οἱ περὶ τὸν Φιλόχορον ἀναγράφουσιν. εἰλικρινῶς δὲ τοὺς τοῦ δράματος χρόνους οὐκ ἔστι λαβεῖν· οὐ δεδίδακται γὰρ Ἀθήνησιν. ὁ δὲ Καλλίμαχος ἐπιγραφῆναί φησι τῇ τραγῳδίᾳ Δημοκράτην . . . φαίνεται δὲ γεγραμμένον τὸ δρᾶμα ἐν ἀρχαῖς τοῦ Πελοποννησιακοῦ πολέμου.* The value of this evidence for dating is limited. It is unlikely that the commentators[1] from whom the note is derived had any evidence apart from the text that Euripides is using Andromache as his mouthpiece, or that there is a reference to a breach of truce; Philochorus is cited

[1] For an attempt to distinguish in this passage the contributions of three different scholars and to identify two of them see Bergk, *Hermes*, 18 (1883), 487 ff.

as authority for the existence of a breach, not for its connection with this passage. If there is such a reference it could be to the opening hostilities in 431,[1] as ἐν ἀρχαῖς[2] seems to imply, but there could as well or better be an allusion to 423, when Athens claimed that Brasidas acted in contravention of the one year's truce, or to accusations of Spartan bad faith after the Peace of Nicias in 421. In fact, as far as explicit or implicit condemnation of Sparta is concerned, the play might have been composed at any time during the Archidamian War or in subsequent years, and we cannot safely assume allusions to this or that specific example of Spartan brutality or bad faith.

It has been urged that Andromache's bitter complaint ἀδίκως εὐτυχεῖτ' ἀν' Ἑλλάδα (449) and Peleus' grudging admission of Spartan military renown in 724–5 would have sounded inappropriate about the time of the Spartan disaster on Sphacteria in the autumn of 425 and the consequent blow to her military reputation. This would also apply shortly after the Peace of 421, when, according to Thucydides,[3] Spartan prestige was at low ebb. These considerations, for what they are worth, would suggest either March 425 or earlier, or about 423–2, when the achievements of Brasidas must have done something to restore Spartan prestige. The later date is supported by those who think of the play partly or chiefly in terms of propaganda, and stressing the general anti-Spartan colouring, the reference of Peleus to Spartan interference in Phthia,[4] the ignominious retreat of Menelaus,

[1] In Thuc. 7. 18. 2 the Spartan admission ἐν γὰρ τῷ προτέρῳ πολέμῳ (i.e. the Archidamian War) σφέτερον τὸ παρανόμημα μᾶλλον γενέσθαι refers partly to the Theban attack on Plataea.

[2] It is possible that the statement in the last sentence is based on some genuine external evidence, but it sounds more like an inference from the play itself. ἐν ἀρχαῖς is rather vague and could perhaps cover the first five years or so.

[3] Thuc. 5. 28. 2 κατὰ γὰρ τὸν χρόνον τοῦτον ἥ τε Λακεδαίμων μάλιστα δὴ κακῶς ἤκουσε καὶ ὑπερώφθη διὰ τὰς ξυμφοράς . . .

[4] *Andr.* 581–2 πῶς; ἢ τὸν ἁμὸν οἶκον οἰκήσεις μολὼν
δεῦρ'; οὐχ ἅλις σοι τῶν κατὰ Σπάρτην κρατεῖν;

and the complimentary reference to the kings of Molossia, regard it as an attempt to counteract the impression made by a real Spartan in that part of Greece.[1] This involves the further assumption that the play was written for performance in one or more of the towns of northern Greece.[2] The reference to the kings of Molossia has also been related to the visit to Athens of the young king, Tharyps, and the grant to him of Athenian citizenship.[3] The date of this is not known, except that it must be after 429, when the Molossians were hostile to Athens.[4]

I am, however, sceptical about the extent of Euripides' preoccupation with diplomacy and propaganda, and consequently about the reliability of many alleged topical allusions. I am not of course denying that here and elsewhere in Euripides we find current events and ideas reflected. It is clear that sometimes the legendary wars prefigure the war in which Athens was engaged, that when, for instance, the dramatist writes of Ἑλλὰς δοριμανής he is not thinking only of the past. There is no doubt too that patriotic sentiments frequently find expression in Euripides, as in other tragic dramatists, and that they have at times inspired specific allusions to historical events. In *Andromache*, given that condemnation of certain Spartans and of Delphi is required by the theme, it is natural that it should also be coloured by contemporary impressions. In 693 ff. Peleus' championship of the common soldier sounds like an echo of current discussion. See also the introductory note on the second stasimon for a possible allusion giving 430 as a *terminus post quem*. In 733–5 πόλις τις has been identified as Argos and as Mantineia, with implications for dating, both of which conflict with metrical evidence. I do not however think it necessary here to

[1] See R. Goossens, *Euripide et Athènes*, pp. 387–94 and 401–10.

[2] See below, p. 21.

[3] *IG* 2. 115 = Ditt. *Syll.* 228. It is not, however, certain that this reference has any topical significance; Euripides is following a tradition already known to Pindar (*Nem.* 7. 38 ff.).

[4] Thuc. 2. 80.

examine these possibilities, since the circumstantial air of the description may be due to Menelaus' desire to make his excuse sound plausible, and there is no certainty that Euripides has any particular city in mind. In general I believe that topical allusions in this play are too vague and uncertain to provide reliable evidence for a specific date, and that evidence of this kind is compatible with any date between 430 and 421.

The range is narrowed if we can trust metrical evidence, which is more objective and may well be a better guide. The most reliable metrical statistics are of course derived from the iambic trimeters, and it has long been recognized that some indication of the order in which the plays of Euripides were composed can be derived from the degree of freedom with which resolutions are admitted; and since the dates of eight of the seventeen extant plays (and of some others) are fixed by reliable external evidence,[1] an approximate date for the other nine can generally be inferred from metrical evidence. The two most useful publications are T. Zieliński's *Tragodoumenon: II De Trimetri Euripidei Evolutione* in 1925 and E. B. Ceadel's paper 'Tragic Trimeters in Euripides' in *CQ* 35 (1941), 66–89. The basis of their calculations is somewhat different: Zieliński's work is by no means superseded, and his criteria are in some respects a more accurate measure of these metrical variations.[2] In any case, for our present purpose the difference between their results is not significant. Both sets of figures indicate that *Andromache*, *Hecuba*, and

[1] These are generally dates of production, whereas metrical evidence refers of course to order of composition; but it is usually assumed that plays were composed shortly before production. Plays for the March festival must presumably have been ready before the end of the previous year.

[2] For an account of the different methods of calculation see Ritchie, *Authenticity of the Rhesus*, pp. 260–70, and for the best appreciation of Zieliński's criteria see A. M. Dale (ed.), *Helen*, pp. xxiv–xxviii. Ceadel's exclusion of proper names may be an over-simplification, since Eur. himself seems to have taken them into account; certainly in early plays where a resolution is (so to speak) forced on him by a proper name, he avoids another resolution in the same line, but in later plays he does not.

Supplices are close together and as a group should be placed several years after *Hippolytus* (428) and well before *Troades* (415). They also agree in placing *Andromache* first, though the differences are far less than between the group as a whole and earlier and later plays, and their significance should not be overestimated. *Hecuba* can safely be assigned on other evidence to 425 or 424, probably the latter;[1] dates commonly given for *Supplices* on historical grounds vary from 424 to 422.[2] Thus for *Andromache* a date about 425 seems to accord best with the metrical evidence, though a year or two earlier or later could not be ruled out.

Other metrical and stylistic evidence of a less systematic nature is discussed by Garzya,[3] e.g. rarity of antilabe, absence of trochaic tetrameters, predilection for dactylic and dactylo-epitrite rhythms,[4] which merely suggest a fairly early date, and greater freedom in the associations of dochmiacs, which, as far as it goes, suggests a date after 428. There is at any rate no contradiction between these slighter indications and the evidence of the trimeters. Thus Murray's note, below the list of dramatis personae in OCT, 'Actam esse intra annos 430–424 Andromacham arguunt numeri' is a little misleading; Murray is apparently following Wilamowitz, *Analecta Euripidea*, p. 148.

On the whole, then, a date about 425 is highly probable, but in the absence of any conclusive evidence, there remains a margin of doubt.

As regards the place of production our only evidence is the bare statement of the scholiast, who gives no indication of his

[1] After 426, because *Hec.* 458 ff. is almost certainly an allusion to the festival at Delos, first celebrated after the purification in 426/5 (Thuc. 3. 104), and before 423, when *Hec.* 172 is closely parodied in Ar. *Nub.* 1165.

[2] See Zuntz, *Political Plays of Euripides*, pp. 88–93; H. Grégoire, *Euripides*, Budé ed. 3, pp. 94–8.

[3] See A. Garzya, 'Intorno all'Andromaca di Euripide', *Giornale ital. di filologia*, 5 (1952), 346–66.

[4] Kranz, *Stasimon*, p. 182, links *Andr.* with *Med.*, *Hcld.*, and *Hipp.* on these grounds. On p. 175 he actually dates *Andr.* about 440 on the style of choral odes, but does not substantiate this.

source. Wilamowitz,[1] cited by Murray (in the note immediately before the text), seems to assume that it is merely an inference from the absence of an *Andromache* of Euripides from the didascalia; and from the statement attributed to Callimachus[2] he concludes that *Andromache* was produced in Athens but not by Euripides. But there may, for all we know, have been other grounds for the scholiast's assertion, and production of the play by the otherwise unknown Democrates is rather more plausible if it was also produced in some city other than Athens. If we do not reject this possibility we then have to ask where it was produced and why not in Athens.

Page favours Argos,[3] and links this with his theory that the elegiacs in 103–6 belong to a Dorian tradition of elegiac lament, centred at Argos, of which no other examples have survived. If this is true it would not in itself be an adequate reason for producing the play at Argos, and the connection with the Argive Timocrates rests on a conjectural emendation. Moreover the presentation in this play of the Argive representative, Orestes, is an objection to production at Argos. Page is, I think, too indulgent to Orestes. He has indeed a genuine grievance against Neoptolemus; but when we reflect that he certainly did not act alone against his rival, but first stirred up by slander the mass hostility of the Delphians and then either was one of the company who lay in wait for Neoptolemus and attacked him when he was standing unsuspecting in the temple of Apollo at the altar of the god, or, worse still, set the plot afoot and left others to strike the blow,[4] can we agree that all this is 'amply justified as a crime passionel' or believe that Euripides expected his audience to see that there was no real harm in Orestes, compared with Menelaus? Garzya[5] follows Delebecque[6] in holding that the

[1] *Analecta Euripidea*, p. 148. [2] Pfeiffer, 1, fr. 451.
[3] *Greek Poetry and Life*, pp. 206–30: cf. note on 103 ff.
[4] See note on 1008.
[5] *Giornale ital. di fil.* 5 (1952), 346 ff.
[6] *Euripide et la guerre du Péloponnèse*, 200–1.

play was actually composed for performance in Athens at the Great Dionysia of 421, but that after it was written and when plays were being selected for production, negotiations for the Peace of Nicias were under way and the anti-Spartan effect of this play (whatever its intention) led to its rejection as diplomatically unfortunate. Euripides then arranged for its production by a local friend in a town of northern Greece, where as an 'unofficial production' it would have less significance, and in view of its content might have some popular appeal. This involves a date which, though not quite ruled out by metrical evidence, is certainly rather late. In any case this is a matter of speculation, and I doubt whether we have sufficient evidence to reach any firm conclusion.

v. *The Text*[1]

At the end of the fifth century texts of most, if not all, of the plays of Euripides were probably in existence. In the fourth century, when Euripides became the most popular of the fifth-century dramatists, copies would be multiplied and in the absence of any check these were exposed to the danger of deliberate changes, omissions, and additions by actors, as well as other hazards. An example of such interference with the text of *Andromache* is referred to by the scholiast on verse 7 and there are other probable examples, e.g. 330–2, 668–77, 1254. It was evidently this sort of interference that prompted the decree sponsored by Lycurgus about 330 B.C., that a standard version of the plays of the three great tragedians should be established, and that henceforward performances

[1] This section makes no new contribution to the history of the text and is merely a brief outline of stages in the transmission, keeping in the main to views which now seem to be fairly widely accepted. What we know or conjecture in this field is now based mainly on the researches of Turyn, *The Byzantine Manuscript Tradition of the Tragedies of Euripides* (1957), and Zuntz, *An Inquiry into the Transmission of the Plays of Euripides* (1965). See also Di Benedetto, *La tradizione manoscritta euripidea* (1965), Page, *Actors' Interpolations in Greek Tragedy*, and Barrett's Introduction to *Hippolytus*, pp. 45–81.

should conform to this text.[1] This would, however, do little to repair damage already done, and there is no guarantee that the decree was or long remained effective. The next and most important landmark in the history of the text is the great Alexandrian edition of the plays of the three major tragedians, generally and reasonably ascribed to Aristophanes of Byzantium[2] about the end of the third century B.C. The basis of this was presumably the Lycurgan text, which had been acquired by the Library of the Museum. Other manuscripts were probably collated, though as Aristophanes seems to have edited some three hundred tragedies as well as Homer, Hesiod, and much lyric poetry, he can hardly have given very prolonged personal attention to the text of any particular play. This edition is the ancestor of our medieval manuscripts, and if a few passages in papyri of the centuries following Aristophanes are a fair indication, it looks as though these manuscripts, in spite of all the hazards of transmission over a period of nearly a thousand years, including transliteration from uncial to minuscule script, are closer to the text of Aristophanes than we might have expected. The Alexandrian scholars not only produced texts superior to most others in existence (as may be inferred from a comparison of some pre-Alexandrian papyri with the medieval manuscripts),[3] but established probably for the first time a tradition of respect for the precise wording of classical texts which must have done something to counteract the tendency to gradual corruption. On the other hand the sources available for Aristophanes were of course imperfect, and in accordance with the usual practice of Alexandrian scholars his text would include variants and interpolations found in the tradition, with critical signs to warn readers: when these signs were lost variants might not be distinguishable from the main text.

[1] See R. Pfeiffer, *History of Classical Scholarship*, p. 82.

[2] For a recent and excellent appraisal of his place in the history of scholarship see R. Pfeiffer, op. cit., pp. 171–209.

[3] See for example Snell on the Strasbourg Papyrus in *Hermes, Einzelschriften*, Heft 5 (1937), 49 ff., esp. 78.

Moreover we cannot assume that this new edition involved the disappearance of earlier and inferior texts.

In the following centuries the plays of Euripides continued to be studied; the text was copied, each play on a separate papyrus roll, and commentaries were written, not on the same roll as the text. As the codex gradually took the place of the roll, a process nearly completed in the course of the fourth century A.D., extracts from various commentaries began to be copied on to the wider margins of the codex. From these marginal annotations are derived the scholia in our medieval manuscripts. From these comments it is sometimes possible to infer the readings in the manuscripts for which they were originally composed, and which must have been earlier, sometimes much earlier, than the manuscripts in which they are now preserved.[1] Soon after the Alexandrian period it appears that a gradual process of selection began, in the sense that some plays of Euripides were more widely known and copied than others, and eventually in the third century A.D. a definitive selection of ten plays was made. These were *Hecuba*, *Orestes*, *Phoenissae*, *Hippolytus*, *Medea*, *Andromache*, *Alcestis*, *Rhesus*, *Troades*, and *Bacchae*. It is not easy to discern any one principle accounting for the choice of all these and the exclusion of the other eight extant plays. The inclusion of *Rhesus* suggests that school requirements influenced the choice (as is generally supposed), but other factors such as general popularity and opportunities for actors may also have been at work. At any rate after about 250 we find no reference to plays outside the selection. Only the selected plays are found in our earliest manuscripts; only these plays are provided with scholia, and only these plays would have survived the Dark Ages, had not a codex containing the *Hecuba* (also in the selection) and eight other plays, evidently part of a complete edition arranged alphabetically, come into the possession of some Byzantine scholar who copied these plays, together with the plays of the selection (but without the marginal notes) on to a manuscript

[1] See, for example, notes on 181 and 323.

which is the ancestor of our codex Laurentianus, dated early in the fourteenth century.

There are thus two main branches in the manuscript tradition for *Andromache* and the other selected plays: one represented by the earlier medieval manuscripts M A V B (twelfth and thirteenth centuries), H (the Jerusalem palimpsest, perhaps tenth century),*[1] and the Ambrosian fragment (Ambr. = codex Ambrosianus, twelfth or thirteenth century, containing Homeric scholia in which *Andr.* 1–102 are quoted); the other by the later manuscripts L (Laurentianus) and P (Palatinus), both fourteenth century. All these manuscripts are in cursive script; transliterations from the earlier uncial (majuscule) to cursive (minuscule) script were made about the beginning of the tenth century. As regards the relationship between manuscripts, there is a general tendency for M A V B to form a group contrasted with L P, but there has been extensive contamination, and there is considerable variation between plays. In *Andromache*, for instance, there are numerous disagreements between L and P, where one or other agrees with some of the other group, and there are fairly common coincidences in error in V and L and more in V and P. The relationship of L and P also varies: in the 'alphabetic' plays Zuntz has now firmly and finally established that P is a copy of L and thus, generally speaking, has no independent value, but in the selected plays it is not. Its quality varies in different plays, and it looks as though for these plays the scribe of P abandoned L in favour of a variety of annotated manuscripts. In view of widespread contamination (underestimated by Turyn) it seems likely that any detailed stemma or precise classification will impose a bogus clarity on an essentially complex situation. In practice it seems to be advisable to consider the readings of medieval manuscripts on their merits.*

The three chief later, and generally speaking inferior, manuscripts are Haun. (Hauniensis 417, fifteenth century), which in *Andromache* seems to be derived from V, O (Laurent.

[1] An asterisk directs attention to the Addenda.

xxxi. 10), and D (Laurent. xxxi. 15). The last two are fourteenth-century manuscripts and in *Andromache* are copied from B; they are thus useful as representing the older tradition in 957–1215, which are missing in B.

In addition to these manuscripts, a number of short passages of the text are preserved on papyri whose date ranges from iii B.C. to viii A.D. These are Pap. Paris. 2 (Pack 160)[1] iii–ii B.C. v. 205; Ox. Pap. 22. 2335 ii A.D. vv. 954–82, 983–1022; Ox. Pap. 31. 2543 ii A.D. vv. 346–68; Pap. Rendel Harris 39 (Pack 278) iii A.D. vv. 907–14; Ox. Pap. 3. 449 (Pack 277) iii A.D. vv. 5–6, 8–28, 30–6, 39–48; Pap. Berol. 13418 (Pack 280) v A.D. vv. 1134–42, 1164–72 (published by G. Manteuffel in *J. of Jurid. Pap.* 2 (1948), 84 ff.); Pap. Russ. Georg. 1. 8 (Pack 279) viii A.D. vv. 957–9, 988–90, 1239–42, 1273–6. These papyri are all of course much earlier than our earliest manuscripts, but in general they do not differ from them greatly, and when they do differ their readings are not necessarily superior; they may have been more carelessly copied. These papyrus fragments do not solve any of the main textual problems of the play, but sometimes serve to confirm this or that manuscript reading, and are discussed where relevant in the Commentary.

Some further evidence for the text is provided by quotations in anthologies and elsewhere, e.g. the anthology compiled by Stobaeus, probably in v A.D., and from the *gnomologia*, which contain lines excerpted from manuscripts of the selection plays, e.g. the *Gnomològium Vatopedianum*, of which the twelfth-century A.D. manuscript is older than most medieval manuscripts of Euripides. The readings derived from these *gnomologia* do not in fact add very much to our knowledge of the text, but these too sometimes provide confirmatory evidence.[2]

[1] R. A. Pack, *The Greek and Roman Literary Texts from Graeco-Roman Egypt*, 2nd ed., Ann Arbor, 1965. See also C. Prato, 'Il contributo dei papiri al testo dei tragici greci', *Studi italiani di filologia classica*, 36 (1964), 5–19, 57–60.

[2] See note on 181. These *gnomologia* have recently been discussed and

VI. *The Hypotheses*

Of the two hypotheses to *Andromache* preserved in our manuscripts, the first belongs to a type prefixed to many plays of Euripides. Nearly half of it consists of a competent summary of the situation at the beginning of the play, as described in the opening monologue of Andromache, and the rest is a succinct account of the action, lucid and prosaic, keeping to the bare facts and making no attempt to indicate how the dramatist has presented them. For example the Chorus is ignored and there is no mention of the long and brilliant messenger speech: after referring to the plot against Neoptolemus the writer merely continues 'and men appeared bearing the body of the murdered man'. These summaries provide no help to readers of the plays, and it now seems to be established that they were taken from an independent collection of 'Tales from Euripides',[1] composed perhaps in the first century B.C., for the benefit of those whose interest was in the plots rather than the plays. These summaries are usually correct, though there may be omissions. In line 12 the words might be taken to mean that the plot against Neoptolemus was not laid until after Orestes appeared in Phthia, which is erroneous, but this may not be the writer's intention. The last sentence, which is at variance with the text (1257–8) and contains an odd construction with οἰκεῖν, has been suspected of being an interpolation.

The second hypothesis also belongs to a common and quite

collated. See G. A. Longman, '*Gnomologium Vatopedianum*, The Euripidean Section', *CQ* 9 (1959), 129–41, and on *Gnomologium Barberinianum* and *Escorialense* see K. Matthiessen, *Hermes*, 93 (1965), 148–58, and 94 (1966), 398–410.

[1] This was suggested by Wilamowitz, *Anal. Eur.*, p. 183 and later confirmed by papyrus fragments: see Gallavotti, *Riv. fil.* 61 (1933), 177 ff., and for detailed discussion and references G. Zuntz, *Political Plays of Euripides*, pp. 129–52. See also for later additions to knowledge Ox. Pap. 27. 2455; 31. 2534, 2544; and Coles and Barns, 'Fragments of Dramatic Hypotheses', in *CQ* 15 (1965), 52–7.

different type, generally and plausibly ascribed to the famous Alexandrian scholar, Aristophanes of Byzantium. These are prefaces, not arguments, and were presumably prefixed to his editions of the plays. For Euripides only nine have survived and these are not complete, but comparison of the fragments suggests that in complete form they followed a fairly regular pattern[1] and contained concise information on plot, previous treatment, place of action, composition of the chorus, speaker of the prologue, date of production, result of competition, together with brief critical comments. For us the most valuable information is the date and result of the competition, which would be derived ultimately from official records, but in the preface to *Andromache* both these items are missing.

In the critical comments on this play the phrase τὸ δὲ δρᾶμα τῶν δευτέρων has been variously interpreted. Elsewhere in hypotheses the phrase τὸ δὲ δρᾶμα followed by a genitive is clearly an appraisal of value and always in fact laudatory. So S. *Ant.* τὸ μὲν δρᾶμα τῶν καλλίστων Σοφοκλέους; S. *OC* τὸ δὲ δρᾶμα τῶν θαυμαστῶν; E. *Or.* τὸ δὲ δρᾶμα τῶν ἐπὶ σκηνῆς εὐδοκιμούντων. In Comedy the expression τὸ δὲ δρᾶμα τῶν εὖ σφόδρα πεποιημένων, or a close variant, is found in the following hypotheses to plays of Aristophanes: *Ach.*, *Eq.*, *Nub.* iii, *Av.* i, *Ra.* i and iii. The closest parallel is, however, in the hypothesis to E. *Hipp.* τὸ δὲ δρᾶμα τῶν πρώτων, and analogy suggests that this and τῶν δευτέρων are also appraisals of value, and tells against Garzya's tentative suggestion that τῶν δευτέρων may refer to some 'second group' in a chronological sense. Welcker and Hermann took τῶν δευτέρων to mean that *Andromache* won the second prize. Against this is that the official order was regularly indicated by πρῶτος (or ἐνίκα) . . . δεύτερος . . . τρίτος . . . followed by the dramatists' names. Nevertheless in value judgements it would be difficult to dissociate πρώτων and δευτέρων from the familiar classification. It may be a coincidence that τῶν πρώτων is in fact used of *Hipp.*, part of a tetralogy to which the first prize was

[1] For a more detailed account see Page (ed.), *Medea*, Intr. liii–lv.

awarded, as already recorded in the same hypothesis and by the usual formula; but perhaps these phrases could be used to describe a single play[1] as being of first- or second-prize quality. If so, *τῶν δευτέρων* would not be a term of depreciation, as many scholars now assume, and our word 'second-rate' is a misleading translation. A complimentary expression would be in line with similar expressions elsewhere and more consistent with the detailed comments which follow in this hypothesis and are all favourable.[2]

[1] We have no information about the fate of *Andromache* and do not know with what other plays, if any, it was produced, or where. For the possibility that *Kresphontes* belonged to the same production see T. B. L. Webster, *The Tragedies of Euripides*, p. 137.

[2] That is if, with almost all editors, we accept *οὐ κακῶς* in the penultimate sentence. *οὐ καλῶς*, the reading of V L P, seems out of line and probably involves emending *ὑποφαίνουσα*.

SIGLA

M = cod. Marcianus 471 saec. xii
A = cod. Parisinus 2712 saec. xiii
B = cod. Parisinus 2713 saec. xii vel xiii
V = cod. Vaticanus 909 saec. xiii

L = cod. Laurentianus xxxii. 2 saec. xiv ineuntis
P = cod. Palatinus 287 et Laurentianus 172 saec. xiv

Π = fragmenta papyracea diversa
K = fragmentum Berolinense a Kirchhoffio editum
H = codex Hierosolymitanus xxxvi, rescriptus
Ambr. = fragmenta Ambrosiana ab Angelo Maio edita

Σ = Scholia a Schwartzio ex codicibus M B V Nap. maximam partem edita: *Σ*V, *Σ*B, et similia scholia in uno tantum codice inventa

Raro citantur:

O = Laurentianus xxxi. 10, saec. xiv (?)
D = Laurentianus xxxi. 15, saec. xiv
F = Marcianus 468, saec. xiv
N = Marcianus 470, saec. xv
Nap. = Neapolitanus II F 41, saec. xv
Haun. = Hauniensis 417, saec. xv
Apogr. Paris. = apographa codicis L Parisina; quae sunt (1) cod. Parisinus 2887, 2888, saec. xvi; et (2) cod. Par. 2817, eiusdem fere aetatis

L^1 V^1 similibus designantur cuiusque codicis prima manus se ipsa corrigens vel scholia scribens; L^2 V^2 similibus secunda manus; litteris minusculis (*l*, *v*, *b*) manus recentiores correctrices
Notis codd. et rell. (= reliqui), *nullos praeter* M A B V L P *respeximus*
γρ. = *γράφεται*, i.e. varia lectio in libris aut scholiis memorata

ΑΝΔΡΟΜΑΧΗ

ΥΠΟΘΕΣΙΣ ΑΝΔΡΟΜΑΧΗΣ

I

Νεοπτόλεμος ἐν τῇ Τροίᾳ γέρας λαβὼν τὴν Ἀνδρομάχην, τὴν Ἕκτορος γυναῖκα, παῖδα ἔτεκεν ἐξ αὐτῆς. ὕστερον δὲ ἐπέγημεν Ἑρμιόνην, τὴν Μενελάου θυγατέρα. δίκας δὲ πρῶτον ᾐτηκὼς τῆς Ἀχιλλέως ἀναιρέσεως τὸν ἐν Δελφοῖς Ἀπόλλωνα, πάλιν ἀπῆλθεν ἐπὶ τὸ χρηστήριον μετανοήσας, ἵνα τὸν θεὸν ἐξιλάσηται. ζηλοτύπως δ' ἔχουσα πρὸς τὴν Ἀνδρομάχην ἡ βασιλὶς ἐβουλεύετο κατ' αὐτῆς θάνατον, μεταπεμψαμένη τὸν Μενέλαον· ἡ δὲ τὸ παιδίον μὲν ὑπεξέθηκεν, αὐτὴ δὲ κατέφυγεν ἐπὶ τὸ ἱερὸν τῆς Θέτιδος. οἱ δὲ περὶ τὸν Μενέλαον καὶ τὸ παιδίον ἀνεῦρον καὶ ἐκείνην ἀπατήσαντες ἤγειραν. καὶ σφάττειν μέλλοντες ἀμφοτέρους ἐκωλύθησαν Πηλέως ἐπιφανέντος. Μενέλαος μὲν οὖν ἀπῆλθεν εἰς Σπάρτην, Ἑρμιόνη δὲ μετενόησεν εὐλαβηθεῖσα τὴν παρουσίαν τοῦ Νεοπτολέμου. παραγενόμενος δὲ ὁ Ὀρέστης ταύτην μὲν ἀπήγαγε πείσας, Νεοπτολέμῳ δὲ ἐπεβούλευσεν· ὃν καὶ φονευθέντα παρῆσαν οἱ φέροντες. Πηλεῖ δὲ μέλλοντι τὸν νεκρὸν θρηνεῖν Θέτις ἐπιφανεῖσα τοῦτον μὲν ἐπέταξεν ἐν Δελφοῖς θάψαι, τὴν δὲ Ἀνδρομάχην εἰς Μολοσσοὺς ἀποστεῖλαι μετὰ τοῦ παιδός, αὐτὸν δὲ ἀθανασίαν προσδέχεσθαι. τυχὼν δὲ αὐτῆς εἰς μακάρων νήσους ᾤκησεν.

II

. . . ἡ μὲν σκηνὴ τοῦ δράματος ὑποκεῖται ἐν Φθίᾳ, ὁ δὲ χορὸς συνέστηκεν ἐκ Φθιωτίδων γυναικῶν. προλογίζει δὲ Ἀνδρομάχη. τὸ

Argumentum et Dram. Pers. om. L, add. L[2]   1 τὴν τοῦ Ἕκτορος V   3 πρῶτον] πρότερον Lascaris   9 ἀπαντήσαντες V   ἀνήγειραν L[2]   13 πείσας] εἰς Σπάρτην P   ὃν] οἳ M V B N. Aliquid deesse iudicat Schwartz   15 θάψαι ex μένειν correx. V   16 ἀπέστειλε codd. (V?) : corr. Lascaris et Musurus   17 τυχόντα δὲ . . . οἰκήσειν Hermann

Caput secundum fragmentum videtur esse argumenti Aristophanei : omissum est in M B O   18 ὑποκεῖται Wilamowitz : κεῖται codd.   19 συνέστηκεν L P : om. M N V A δὲ δρᾶμα τῶν δευτέρων. ὁ πρόλογος σαφῶς καὶ εὐλόγως εἰρημένος. ἔτι δὲ καὶ τὰ ἐλεγεῖα τὰ ἐν τῷ θρήνῳ τῆς Ἀνδρομάχης. ἐν τῷ δευτέρῳ μέρει ῥῆσις Ἑρμιόνης τὸ βασιλικὸν ὑποφαίνουσα, καὶ ὁ πρὸς Ἀνδρομάχην λόγος οὐ κακῶς ἔχων· εὖ δὲ καὶ ὁ Πηλεὺς ὁ τὴν Ἀνδρομάχην ἀφελόμενος.

1 ὁ (ante πρόλογος) om. codd, add. Lascaris 2 ἔτι δὲ Hermann : ἔστι δὲ codd. (εὖ δὲ Trendelenburg) 3 τῆς Ἑρμ. A ὑφαίνουσα V N L P: corr. Lascaris (ἐμφαίνουσα Musurus; non ut vid. A) 4 οὐ καλῶς V L P, quo recepto οὐ φαίνουσα supra Bergk

ΤΑ ΤΟΥ ΔΡΑΜΑΤΟΣ ΠΡΟΣΩΠΑ

ΑΝΔΡΟΜΑΧΗ
ΘΕΡΑΠΑΙΝΑ
ΧΟΡΟΣ
ΕΡΜΙΟΝΗ
ΜΕΝΕΛΑΟΣ
ΠΑΙΣ ΑΝΔΡΟΜΑΧΗΣ
ΠΗΛΕΥΣ
ΤΡΟΦΟΣ
ΟΡΕΣΤΗΣ
ΑΓΓΕΛΟΣ
ΘΕΤΙΣ

Sic L[2] (deest L) nisi quod *θεράπων* dat pro *τροφός* (cf. ad vv. 802, 851) et, cum rell. omnibus, Μολοττός pro Παῖς Ἀνδρομάχης; cf. Dram. Pers. Alc. et Helid. et Paus. i. 11. Ordinem rell. praebent alii alium. Θέτις omissa in M V. In Ambr. extat: *ἀνδρομάχη. θεράπαινα. ἑρμιόνη μενέλαος. τροφός. μολοττός*: reliqua evanida

Actam esse intra annos 430–424 Andromacham arguunt numeri. Cf. Σ. 445. *εἰλικρινῶς δὲ τοὺς τοῦ δράματος χρόνους οὐκ ἔστι λαβεῖν· οὐ δεδίδακται γὰρ Ἀθήνησιν. Ὁ δὲ Καλλίμαχος ἐπιγραφῆναί φησι τῇ τραγῳδίᾳ Δημοκράτην* (*Τιμοκράτην* Bergk) . . . *φαίνεται δὲ γεγραμμένον τὸ δρᾶμα ἐν ἀρχαῖς τοῦ Πελοποννησιακοῦ πολέμου.* Cum Timocrates Argivus carmina Euripidi scripsisse dicatur (Vit. Eur. cap. 1) fortasse Argis actam fuisse hanc fabulam coniecit Nauck (vol. i. p. xviii, editionis Eurip.) ('Immo; nulla fuit in Didascaliis Andromacha Euripidis: ergo aut extra Athenas, quod vix credibile, docta est, aut sub alieno nomine: at exemplum alieno nomine inscriptum invenit Callimachus: hoc igitur verum.' Wilamowitz)

Codices M A V L P: B (desunt 957–1215): Ambr. (vv. 1–120): palimpsestus H (vv. 81–169, 793–849, 906–1006, 1071–1118): vv. 5–48 Π, fragmenta valde mutila: sunt etiam vv. 1284–1288 in Pap. Hibeh. 25: raro memorantur O D Haun. Saepius dissident L et P. Accedunt Scholia.

ΑΝΔΡΟΜΑΧΗ

ΑΝΔΡΟΜΑΧΗ

Ἀσιάτιδος γῆς σχῆμα, Θηβαία πόλι,
ὅθεν ποθ' ἕδνων σὺν πολυχρύσῳ χλιδῇ
Πριάμου τύραννον ἑστίαν ἀφικόμην
δάμαρ δοθεῖσα παιδοποιὸς Ἕκτορι,
ζηλωτὸς ἔν γε τῷ πρὶν Ἀνδρομάχη χρόνῳ,
νῦν δ', εἴ τις ἄλλη, δυστυχεστάτη γυνή·
[ἐμοῦ πέφυκεν ἢ γενήσεταί ποτε]
ἥτις πόσιν μὲν Ἕκτορ' ἐξ Ἀχιλλέως
θανόντ' ἐσεῖδον, παῖδά θ' ὃν τίκτω πόσει
ῥιφθέντα πύργων Ἀστυάνακτ' ἀπ' ὀρθίων,
ἐπεὶ τὸ Τροίας εἷλον Ἕλληνες πέδον·
αὐτὴ δὲ δούλη τῶν ἐλευθερωτάτων
οἴκων νομισθεῖσ' Ἑλλάδ' εἰσαφικόμην
τῷ νησιώτῃ Νεοπτολέμῳ δορὸς γέρας
δοθεῖσα λείας Τρωικῆς ἐξαίρετον.
Φθίας δὲ τῆσδε καὶ πόλεως Φαρσαλίας
σύγχορτα ναίω πεδί', ἵν' ἡ θαλασσία
Πηλεῖ ξυνῴκει χωρὶς ἀνθρώπων Θέτις
φεύγουσ' ὅμιλον· Θεσσαλὸς δέ νιν λεὼς
Θετίδειον αὐδᾷ θεᾶς χάριν νυμφευμάτων.

1 *πόλι* L : *πτόλι* M A B : *πόλις* V P 6 *οὔτις* V (corr. V²) Haun. *l*. Cf. sq. 7 om. Π : *οἱ ὑποκριταὶ τὸν ἴαμβον προσέθηκαν ὑπονοήσαντες εἶναι τὴν γραφὴν δὴ τίς . . . καὶ ἀντὶ τοῦ συγκριτικοῦ τὸ δυστυχεστάτη* Σ 9 *ἐπεῖδον* Naber θ'] δ' A V 10 *ῥιφθέντα* L P : *ῥιφέντα* rell. Π 17 initium diversum, ut videtur, in Π

ἔνθ' οἶκον ἔσχε τόνδε παῖς Ἀχιλλέως,
Πηλέα δ' ἀνάσσειν γῆς ἐᾷ Φαρσαλίας,
ζῶντος γέροντος σκῆπτρον οὐ θέλων λαβεῖν.
κἀγὼ δόμοις τοῖσδ' ἄρσεν' ἐντίκτω κόρον,
πλαθεῖσ' Ἀχιλλέως παιδί, δεσπότῃ γ' ἐμῷ.
  καὶ πρὶν μὲν ἐν κακοῖσι κειμένην ὅμως
ἐλπίς μ' ἀεὶ προσῆγε σωθέντος τέκνου
ἀλκήν τιν' εὑρεῖν κἀπικούρησιν κακῶν·
ἐπεὶ δὲ τὴν Λάκαιναν Ἑρμιόνην γαμεῖ
τοὐμὸν παρώσας δεσπότης δοῦλον λέχος,
κακοῖς πρὸς αὐτῆς σχετλίοις ἐλαύνομαι.
λέγει γὰρ ὥς νιν φαρμάκοις κεκρυμμένοις
τίθημ' ἄπαιδα καὶ πόσει μισουμένην,
αὐτὴ δὲ ναίειν οἶκον ἀντ' αὐτῆς θέλω
τόνδ', ἐκβαλοῦσα λέκτρα τἀκείνης βίᾳ·
ἁγὼ τὸ πρῶτον οὐχ ἑκοῦσ' ἐδεξάμην,
νῦν δ' ἐκλέλοιπα· Ζεὺς τάδ' εἰδείη μέγας,
ὡς οὐχ ἑκοῦσα τῷδ' ἐκοινώθην λέχει.
ἀλλ' οὔ σφε πείθω, βούλεται δέ με κτανεῖν,
πατήρ τε θυγατρὶ Μενέλεως συνδρᾷ τάδε.
καὶ νῦν κατ' οἴκους ἔστ', ἀπὸ Σπάρτης μολὼν
ἐπ' αὐτὸ τοῦτο· δειματουμένη δ' ἐγὼ
δόμων πάροικον Θέτιδος εἰς ἀνάκτορον
θάσσω τόδ' ἐλθοῦσ', ἤν με κωλύσῃ θανεῖν.
Πηλεύς τε γάρ νιν ἔκγονοί τε Πηλέως
σέβουσιν, ἑρμήνευμα Νηρῇδος γάμων.
ὃς δ' ἔστι παῖς μοι μόνος, ὑπεκπέμπω λάθρᾳ

23 om. M 24 ἄρσενα τίκτω L : ἄρσεν' ἕνα τ. Barnes. cl. Σ ἰδίως ἕνα φησὶ παῖδα γενέσθαι 25 πλασθεῖσ' V P γ' Brunck : τ' codd. : δ' Elmsley 27 μ' ἄελπτος ἦγε Rutherford : προῆγε Reiske σωθέντος] τ]εχθέντ[ος Π 28 κἀπικούφισιν Elmsley δόμων B O (γρ. κακῶν B) 29-31 om. V spatio vacuo relicto : add. *v* 36 πρόσθεν A V (corr. V[2]) 37 τά γ' A V 40 Μενέλαος Ambr. A V (non notatur amplius) 41 ἀπὸ πάτρας B O 43 δόμον primitus A V P, correxerunt V P πάροικον suprascr. ων A 44 ἄν με P

ἄλλους ἐς οἴκους, μὴ θάνῃ φοβουμένη.
ὁ γὰρ φυτεύσας αὐτὸν οὔτ' ἐμοὶ πάρα
προσωφελῆσαι, παιδί τ' οὐδέν ἐστ', ἀπὼν
Δελφῶν κατ' αἶαν, ἔνθα Λοξίᾳ δίκην
δίδωσι μανίας, ᾗ ποτ' εἰς Πυθὼ μολὼν
ᾔτησε Φοῖβον πατρὸς οὗ κτείνει δίκην,
εἴ πως τὰ πρόσθε σφάλματ' ἐξαιτούμενος
θεὸν παράσχοιτ' εἰς τὸ λοιπὸν εὐμενῆ.

ΘΕΡΑΠΑΙΝΑ

δέσποιν'—ἐγώ τοι τοὔνομ' οὐ φεύγω τόδε
καλεῖν σ', ἐπείπερ καὶ κατ' οἶκον ἠξίουν
τὸν σόν, τὸ Τροίας ἡνίκ' ᾠκοῦμεν πέδον,
εὔνους δὲ καὶ σοὶ ζῶντί τ' ἦ τῷ σῷ πόσει,
καὶ νῦν φέρουσά σοι νέους ἥκω λόγους,
φόβῳ μέν, εἴ τις δεσποτῶν αἰσθήσεται,
οἴκτῳ δὲ τῷ σῷ· δεινὰ γὰρ βουλεύεται
Μενέλαος εἰς σὲ παῖς θ', ἅ σοι φυλακτέα.

Αν. ὦ φιλτάτη σύνδουλε—σύνδουλος γὰρ εἶ
τῇ πρόσθ' ἀνάσσῃ τῇδε, νῦν δὲ δυστυχεῖ—
τί δρῶσι; ποίας μηχανὰς πλέκουσιν αὖ,
κτεῖναι θέλοντες τὴν παναθλίαν ἐμέ;

Θε. τὸν παῖδά σου μέλλουσιν, ὦ δύστηνε σύ,
κτείνειν, ὃν ἔξω δωμάτων ὑπεξέθου.

Αν. οἴμοι· πέπυσται τὸν ἐμὸν ἔκθετον γόνον;
πόθεν ποτ'; ὦ δύστηνος, ὡς ἀπωλόμην.

Θε. οὐκ οἶδ', ἐκείνων δ' ᾐσθόμην ἐγὼ τάδε·
φροῦδος δ' ἐπ' αὐτὸν Μενέλεως δόμων ἄπο.

52 ᾗ Reiske: ἣν codd. et Σ ποτ' A V² L: τότ' rell. 53 κτείνει Ambr. M V B L Σ: τίνει A P γρ. Σ: 'κτίνει D *b*: 'κτίνειν Hermann (οὐκτίνειν = οἱ ἐκτίνειν Badham) 57 σ' om. L 58 τὸ σὸν γρ. Σ (et primitus A) 59 δ' ἐκεῖ σοὶ Badham ἦν codd. 63 παῖδά θ' V: παῖδ' Ambr. B O 65 τῇδε om. L: add. *l* 66 αὖ om. L: πλέκουσι νῦν P: δὴ suprascr. A 70 πέπυσται codd. et Σ: πέπυσθε Ludv. Dindorf 73 ante 70 transp. Radermacher 72 ἐκεῖνον ut vid L: ἐκ τούτου videtur reddere Σ 73 ἐπ' αὐτὸ Ambr. (-τον Σ)

Αν. ἀπωλόμην ἄρ᾽. ὦ τέκνον, κτενοῦσί σε
δισσοὶ λαβόντες γῦπες· ὁ δὲ κεκλημένος
πατὴρ ἔτ᾽ ἐν Δελφοῖσι τυγχάνει μένων.
Θε. δοκῶ γὰρ οὐκ ἂν ὧδέ σ᾽ ἂν πράσσειν κακῶς
κείνου παρόντος· νῦν δ᾽ ἔρημος εἶ φίλων.
Αν. οὐδ᾽ ἀμφὶ Πηλέως ἦλθεν, ὡς ἥξοι, φάτις;
Θε. γέρων ἐκεῖνος ὥστε σ᾽ ὠφελεῖν παρών.
Αν. καὶ μὴν ἔπεμψ᾽ ἐπ᾽ αὐτὸν οὐχ ἅπαξ μόνον.
Θε. μῶν οὖν δοκεῖς σου φροντίσαι τιν᾽ ἀγγέλων;
Αν. πόθεν; θέλεις οὖν ἄγγελος σύ μοι μολεῖν;
Θε. τί δῆτα φήσω χρόνιος οὖσ᾽ ἐκ δωμάτων;
Αν. πολλὰς ἂν εὕροις μηχανάς· γυνὴ γὰρ εἶ.
Θε. κίνδυνος· Ἑρμιόνη γὰρ οὐ σμικρὸν φύλαξ.
Αν. ὁρᾷς; ἀπαυδᾷς ἐν κακοῖς φίλοισι σοῖς.
Θε. οὐ δῆτα· μηδὲν τοῦτ᾽ ὀνειδίσῃς ἐμοί.
ἀλλ᾽ εἶμ᾽, ἐπεί τοι κοὐ περίβλεπτος βίος
δούλης γυναικός, ἤν τι καὶ πάθω κακόν.
Αν. χώρει νυν· ἡμεῖς δ᾽, οἷσπερ ἐγκείμεσθ᾽ ἀεὶ
θρήνοισι καὶ γόοισι καὶ δακρύμασι,
πρὸς αἰθέρ᾽ ἐκτενοῦμεν· ἐμπέφυκε γὰρ
γυναιξὶ τέρψις τῶν παρεστώτων κακῶν
ἀνὰ στόμ᾽ ἀεὶ καὶ διὰ γλώσσης ἔχειν.
πάρεστι δ᾽ οὐχ ἓν ἀλλὰ πολλά μοι στένειν,
πόλιν πατρῴαν τὸν θανόντα θ᾽ Ἕκτορα
στερρόν τε τὸν ἐμὸν δαίμον᾽ ᾧ συνεζύγην
δούλειον ἦμαρ εἰσπεσοῦσ᾽ ἀναξίως.
χρὴ δ᾽ οὔποτ᾽ εἰπεῖν οὐδέν᾽ ὄλβιον βροτῶν,
πρὶν ἂν θανόντος τὴν τελευταίαν ἴδῃς
ὅπως περάσας ἡμέραν ἥξει κάτω.

77 οὐκ ἂν] οὐδὲν Σ (Ottobonensis) et Haun. 79 ἥξει V 80 γέρων γ᾽ L 82 δοκεῖς σου Ambr. M V²: δοκεῖ σου L: δοκεῖ σοι rell. 83 μολεῖν σύ μοι B O P, ob accentum 86 σμικρὸν φύλαξ Kirchhoff: σμικρὸν φίλον Ambr.: σμικρὰ φύλαξ rell. et Orion. Etym. p. 26 89 κατ᾽ ἐνίους δὲ γράφεται χωρὶς τοῦ ΟΥ . . . ἐν εἰρωνείᾳ Σ 94 τέρψις] μέμψεις Herwerden, cl. Plat. Legg. 684 D 100 Χορ. praef. M

Ἰλίῳ αἰπεινᾷ Πάρις οὐ γάμον ἀλλά τιν᾽ ἄταν
ἠγάγετ᾽ εὐναίαν εἰς θαλάμους Ἑλέναν.
ἇς ἕνεκ᾽, ὦ Τροία, δορὶ καὶ πυρὶ δηιάλωτον
εἷλέ σ᾽ ὁ χιλιόναυς Ἑλλάδος ὠκὺς Ἄρης
καὶ τὸν ἐμὸν μελέας πόσιν Ἕκτορα, τὸν περὶ τείχη
εἵλκυσε διφρεύων παῖς ἁλίας Θέτιδος·
αὐτὰ δ᾽ ἐκ θαλάμων ἀγόμαν ἐπὶ θῖνα θαλάσσας,
δουλοσύναν στυγερὰν ἀμφιβαλοῦσα κάρᾳ.
πολλὰ δὲ δάκρυά μοι κατέβα χροός, ἀνίκ᾽ ἔλειπον
ἄστυ τε καὶ θαλάμους καὶ πόσιν ἐν κονίαις.
ὤμοι ἐγὼ μελέα, τί μ᾽ ἐχρῆν ἔτι φέγγος ὁρᾶσθαι
Ἑρμιόνας δούλαν; ἇς ὕπο τειρομένα
πρὸς τόδ᾽ ἄγαλμα θεᾶς ἱκέτις περὶ χεῖρε βαλοῦσα
τάκομαι ὡς πετρίνα πιδακόεσσα λιβάς.

ΧΟΡΟΣ

ὦ γύναι, ἃ Θέτιδος δάπεδον καὶ ἀνάκτορα θάσσεις [στρ.
δαρὸν οὐδὲ λείπεις,
Φθιὰς ὅμως ἔμολον ποτὶ σὰν Ἀσιήτιδα γένναν,
εἴ τί σοι δυναίμαν
ἄκος τῶν δυσλύτων πόνων τεμεῖν,
οἳ σὲ καὶ Ἑρμιόναν ἔριδι στυγερᾷ συνέκλῃσαν,
τλάμον᾽ †ἀμφὶ λέκτρων
διδύμων ἐπίκοινον ἐοῦσαν
ἀμφὶ† παῖδ᾽ Ἀχιλλέως.

103 ἀνδρ praef. M L 104 Ἑλένην P 105 ὦ Τροία* M (ὦ Τροῖαι M²): Τροίαν V (corr. V²) δὴ ἁλωτὸν M A V B (corr. V²) 107 τείχει A 109 αὐτὴ P *v* ἄγομαι V B θαλάσσας V: θαλάσσης rell. 111 ἔλιπον codd.: corr. L² P² 114 Ἑρμιόνης et ἧς P 117 ἀνάκτορον L 118 δηρὸν P 119 Ἀσιάτιδα L: γένναν (γέναν M) suspectum. Fortasse Ἀσιάτιδ᾽ ἰωάν 121 τεμεῖν πόνων B D O: τεμεῖν periit in L: εὑρεῖν *l* et sic interpretatur Σ (alter Σ habuit τεμεῖν). Fortasse τετμεῖν habuit (ἄκος post πόνων transp. P) 123 τλάμονα M A B V: τλάμων L. Locus nondum emendatus ἀμφὶ λεχῶν P 125 Ἀχιλῆος V (-εω suprascr. V²): Ἀχιλλῆος A B

γνῶθι τύχαν, λόγισαι τὸ παρὸν κακὸν εἰς ὅπερ ἥκεις. [ἀντ.
δεσπόταις ἁμιλλᾷ
Ἰλιὰς οὖσα κόρα Λακεδαίμονος ἐγγενέτῃσιν;
λεῖπε δεξίμηλον
δόμον τᾶς ποντίας θεοῦ. τί σοι
καιρὸς ἀτυζομένᾳ δέμας αἰκέλιον καταλείβειν
δεσποτῶν ἀνάγκαις;
τὸ κρατοῦν δέ σ' ἔπεισι. τί μόχθον
οὐδὲν οὖσα μοχθεῖς;

ἀλλ' ἴθι λεῖπε θεᾶς Νηρηίδος ἀγλαὸν ἕδραν, [στρ.
γνῶθι δ' οὖσ' ἐπὶ ξένας
δμωὶς ἐπ' ἀλλοτρίας
πόλεος, ἔνθ' οὐ φίλων τιν' εἰσορᾷς
σῶν, ὦ δυστυχεστάτα,
παντάλαινα νύμφα.

οἰκτροτάτα γὰρ ἔμοιγ' ἔμολες, γύναι Ἰλιάς, οἴκους [ἀντ.
δεσποτῶν ἐμῶν· φόβῳ δ'
ἡσυχίαν ἄγομεν—
τὸ δὲ σὸν οἴκτῳ φέρουσα τυγχάνω—
μὴ παῖς τᾶς Διὸς κόρας
σοί μ' εὖ φρονοῦσαν εἰδῇ.

. . . .

. . . .

126 τ' ἄπορον κακὸν Wecklein 128 ἐγγενέτῃσιν] ἐγγ. M A V B Σ : ἐκγ. L P : -τησι L B O : -ταισι rell. 130 ποντίου L θεᾶς (suprascr. οῦ P) L P τίς σοι codd. : corr. Musgrave 131 ἀεικέλιον codd. 132 ἀνάγκῃ V Haun. (corr. V²) 133 κρατοῦν A V L Σ : κράτος rell. V² δέ σ' ἔπεισι e Σ (κατά σου ἐλεύσονται) Hermann : δέ σε πείσει codd. et γρ. Σ 137 ἐπ'] fortasse ἀπ' (ἐπ' Σ) 138 πόλεως codd. : corr. Hermann φίλον L 140 τάλαινα P : ὦ παντάλαινα L² : πασᾶν, τάλαινα Wilamowitz 142 δεσποτῶν δ' ἐ. φ. codd. et Σ : δὲ transposuit Nauck 144 οἴκτῳ] σκότῳ Badham 146 σοί del. Hartung εἰδῇ Musgrave : ἴδῃ codd. (A in ras.) et Σ Post v. 146 hiatum statuit Musgrave, cf. v. 154 : contra Matthiaeus censet reginam comitibus suis colloquentem progredi

ΕΡΜΙΟΝΗ

κόσμον μὲν ἀμφὶ κρατὶ χρυσέας χλιδῆς
στολμόν τε χρωτὸς τόνδε ποικίλων πέπλων
οὐ τῶν Ἀχιλλέως οὐδὲ Πηλέως ἄπο
δόμων ἀπαρχὰς δεῦρ' ἔχουσ' ἀφικόμην,
ἀλλ' ἐκ Λακαίνης Σπαρτιάτιδος χθονὸς
Μενέλαος ἡμῖν ταῦτα δωρεῖται πατὴρ
πολλοῖς σὺν ἕδνοις, ὥστ' ἐλευθεροστομεῖν.
ὑμᾶς μὲν οὖν τοῖσδ' ἀνταμείβομαι λόγοις·
 σὺ δ' οὖσα δούλη καὶ δορίκτητος γυνὴ
δόμους κατασχεῖν ἐκβαλοῦσ' ἡμᾶς θέλεις
τούσδε, στυγοῦμαι δ' ἀνδρὶ φαρμάκοισι σοῖς,
νηδὺς δ' ἀκύμων διὰ σέ μοι διόλλυται·
δεινὴ γὰρ ἠπειρῶτις εἰς τὰ τοιάδε
ψυχὴ γυναικῶν· ὧν ἐπισχήσω σ' ἐγώ,
κοὐδέν σ' ὀνήσει δῶμα Νηρῇδος τόδε,
οὐ βωμὸς οὐδὲ ναός, ἀλλὰ κατθανῇ.
ἢν δ' οὖν βροτῶν τίς σ' ἢ θεῶν σῷσαι θέλῃ,
δεῖ σ' ἀντὶ τῶν πρὶν ὀλβίων φρονημάτων
πτῆξαι ταπεινὴν προσπεσεῖν τ' ἐμὸν γόνυ,
σαίρειν τε δῶμα τοὐμὸν ἐκ χρυσηλάτων
τευχέων χερὶ σπείρουσαν Ἀχελῴου δρόσον,
γνῶναί θ' ἵν' εἶ γῆς. οὐ γάρ ἐσθ' Ἕκτωρ τάδε,
οὐ Πρίαμος οὐδὲ χρυσός, ἀλλ' Ἑλλὰς πόλις.
εἰς τοῦτο δ' ἥκεις ἀμαθίας, δύστηνε σύ,
ἣ παιδὶ πατρός, ὃς σὸν ὤλεσεν πόσιν,
τολμᾷς ξυνεύδειν καὶ τέκν' αὐθέντου πάρα
τίκτειν. τοιοῦτον πᾶν τὸ βάρβαρον γένος·

148 *στόλον* L B *τῶνδε* A V P 151 *ἀλλ' οὐκ* Nauck 154 *τοῖσδ'* L (non *l*): *τοιοῖσδ'* rell. (*ἀμείβομαι* P O) 159 fortasse *ἠπειρῶτις* 160 *ψυχὴ* etiam Σ, ni fallor: *ψύχη* Verrall 163 *θεῶν τις σ' ἢ βροτῶν* P (*τί σ'* M: *τίς* A) 165 *προυσπεσεῖν* M 167 *χερὶ σπείρασαν* L (corr. *l*): *περὶ σπείρουσαν* P 168 *ἵνα ἣ γῆς* V B: *ἵνα γῆς* A 169 *οὐδὲ χρυσός* codd. et Σ: cf. Tro. 995 173 *τοιοῦτο* M A V

πατήρ τε θυγατρὶ παῖς τε μητρὶ μίγνυται
κόρη τ' ἀδελφῷ, διὰ φόνου δ' οἱ φίλτατοι
χωροῦσι, καὶ τῶνδ' οὐδὲν ἐξείργει νόμος.
ἃ μὴ παρ' ἡμᾶς εἴσφερ'· οὐδὲ γὰρ καλὸν
δυοῖν γυναικοῖν ἄνδρ' ἕν' ἡνίας ἔχειν,
ἀλλ' εἰς μίαν βλέποντες εὐναίαν Κύπριν
στέργουσιν, ὅστις μὴ κακῶς οἰκεῖν θέλει.
Χο. ἐπίφθονόν τοι χρῆμα θηλείας φρενὸς
καὶ ξυγγάμοισι δυσμενὲς μάλιστ' ἀεί.
Αν. φεῦ φεῦ·
κακόν γε θνητοῖς τὸ νέον ἔν τε τῷ νέῳ
τὸ μὴ δίκαιον ὅστις ἀνθρώπων ἔχει.
ἐγὼ δὲ ταρβῶ μὴ τὸ δουλεύειν μέ σοι
λόγων ἀπώσῃ πόλλ' ἔχουσαν ἔνδικα,
ἢν δ' αὖ κρατήσω, μὴ 'πὶ τῷδ' ὄφλω βλάβην·
οἱ γὰρ πνέοντες μεγάλα τοὺς κρείσσους λόγους
πικρῶς φέρουσι τῶν ἐλασσόνων ὕπο·
ὅμως δ' ἐμαυτὴν οὐ προδοῦσ' ἁλώσομαι.
εἴπ', ὦ νεᾶνι, τῷ σ' ἐχεγγύῳ λόγῳ
πεισθεῖσ' ἀπωθῶ γνησίων νυμφευμάτων;
ὡς ἡ Λάκαινα τῶν Φρυγῶν μείων πόλις,
τύχῃ θ' ὑπερθεῖ, κἄμ' ἐλευθέραν ὁρᾷς;
ἢ τῷ νέῳ τε καὶ σφριγῶντι σώματι
πόλεώς τε μεγέθει καὶ φίλοις ἐπηρμένη
οἶκον κατασχεῖν τὸν σὸν ἀντὶ σοῦ θέλω;
πότερον ἵν' αὐτὴ παῖδας ἀντὶ σοῦ τέκω
δούλους ἐμαυτῇ τ' ἀθλίαν ἐφολκίδα;
ἢ τοὺς ἐμούς τις παῖδας ἐξανέξεται

180 θέλει Haun. et cod. optimus Stob. 74. 9: θέλοι codd. 181 τοι Dobree: τι codd. θηλείας φρενὸς Σ et Stob. 73. 18: θηλειῶν ἔφυ codd. et fortasse alter Σ 184 ἐν δὲ Stob. 52. 1 190 ἄπο Hermann 194 τῆς Φρυγῶν Scaliger 195 τύχῃ fere codd: τύχη B: τῇ εὐδαιμονίᾳ ὑπερβάλλει (leg. -ῃ?) Σ videtur ὑπερθέῃ scribendum esse, nam persona secunda passivi praes. indic. est: ὑπερθεῖ τἄμ', ἐλευθέραν θ' Lenting ἐλεύθερον B 197 πλούτου τε Brunck 200 τ'] γ' Hermann

Φθίας τυράννους ὄντας, ἣν σὺ μὴ τέκῃς;
φιλοῦσι γάρ μ' Ἕλληνες Ἕκτορός τ' ἄπο;
αὐτή τ' ἀμαυρὰ κοὐ τύραννος ἦ Φρυγῶν;
οὐκ ἐξ ἐμῶν σε φαρμάκων στυγεῖ πόσις,
ἀλλ' εἰ ξυνεῖναι μὴ 'πιτηδεία κυρεῖς.
φίλτρον δὲ καὶ τόδ'· οὐ τὸ κάλλος, ὦ γύναι,
ἀλλ' ἀρεταὶ τέρπουσι τοὺς ξυνευνέτας.
σὺ δ' ἤν τι κνισθῇς, ἡ Λάκαινα μὲν πόλις
μέγ' ἐστί, τὴν δὲ Σκῦρον οὐδαμοῦ τίθης·
πλουτεῖς δ' ἐν οὐ πλουτοῦσι· Μενέλεως δέ σοι
μείζων 'Αχιλλέως. ταῦτά τοί σ' ἔχθει πόσις.
χρὴ γὰρ γυναῖκα, κἂν κακῷ πόσει δοθῇ,
στέργειν, ἅμιλλάν τ' οὐκ ἔχειν φρονήματος.
εἰ δ' ἀμφὶ Θρῄκην χιόνι τὴν κατάρρυτον
τύραννον ἔσχες ἄνδρ', ἵν' ἐν μέρει λέχος
δίδωσι πολλαῖς εἷς ἀνὴρ κοινούμενος,
ἔκτεινας ἂν τάσδ'; εἶτ' ἀπληστίαν λέχους
πάσαις γυναιξὶ προστιθεῖσ' ἂν ηὑρέθης.
αἰσχρόν γε· καίτοι χείρον' ἀρσένων νόσον
ταύτην νοσοῦμεν, ἀλλὰ προὔστημεν καλῶς.
ὦ φίλταθ' Ἕκτορ, ἀλλ' ἐγὼ τὴν σὴν χάριν
σοὶ καὶ ξυνήρων, εἴ τί σε σφάλλοι Κύπρις,
καὶ μαστὸν ἤδη πολλάκις νόθοισι σοῖς
ἐπέσχον, ἵνα σοι μηδὲν ἐνδοίην πικρόν.
καὶ ταῦτα δρῶσα τῇ ἀρετῇ προσηγόμην
πόσιν· σὺ δ' οὐδὲ ῥανίδ' ὑπαιθρίας δρόσου
τῷ σῷ προσίζειν ἀνδρὶ δειμαίνουσ' ἐᾷς.
μὴ τὴν τεκοῦσαν τῇ φιλανδρίᾳ, γύναι,
ζήτει παρελθεῖν· τῶν κακῶν γὰρ μητέρων

204 ἦν codd. 217 κοινούμενος Λ V P Σ (κοιμ. V[2]) : κοιμώμενος M L B O 220 ἀνθρώπων L B O. Fortasse αἰσχρόν γ'· ἐπεὶ κεὶ legendum 221 προσταῖμεν Hermann : fortasse ποῦ 'σθ' ἡμῖν καλῶς; Vv. 220, 221 delet Hirzel 223 σφαλλοι A et primitus L : σφάλοι rell. 224 ἤδη] αὐτὴ Nauck 230 γὰρ] δὲ Elmsley

φεύγειν τρόπους χρὴ τέκν', ⟨ὅσ⟩οις ἔνεστι νοῦς.
Χο. δέσποιν', ὅσον σοι ῥᾳδίως προσίσταται,
τοσόνδε πείθου τῇδε συμβῆναι λόγοις.
Ερ. τί σεμνομυθεῖς κεἰς ἀγῶν' ἔρχῃ λόγων,
ὡς δὴ σὺ σώφρων, τἀμὰ δ' οὐχὶ σώφρονα;
Αν. οὔκουν ἐφ' οἷς γε νῦν καθέστηκας λόγοις.
Ερ. ὁ νοῦς ὁ σός μοι μὴ ξυνοικοίη, γύναι.
Αν. νέα πέφυκας καὶ λέγεις αἰσχρῶν πέρι.
Ερ. σὺ δ' οὐ λέγεις γε, δρᾷς δέ μ' εἰς ὅσον δύνῃ.
Αν. οὐκ αὖ σιωπῇ Κύπριδος ἀλγήσεις πέρι;
Ερ. τί δ'; οὐ γυναιξὶ ταῦτα πρῶτα πανταχοῦ;
Αν. [ναί,]
καλῶς γε χρωμέναισιν· εἰ δὲ μή, οὐ καλά.
Ερ. οὐ βαρβάρων νόμοισιν οἰκοῦμεν πόλιν.
Αν. κἀκεῖ τά γ' αἰσχρὰ κἀνθάδ' αἰσχύνην ἔχει.
Ερ. σοφὴ σοφὴ σύ· κατθανεῖν δ' ὅμως σε δεῖ.
Αν. ὁρᾷς ἄγαλμα Θέτιδος εἰς σ' ἀποβλέπον;
Ερ. μισοῦν γε πατρίδα σὴν Ἀχιλλέως φόνῳ.
Αν. Ἑλένη νιν ὤλεσ', οὐκ ἐγώ, μήτηρ δὲ σή.
Ερ. ἦ καὶ πρόσω γὰρ τῶν ἐμῶν ψαύσεις κακῶν;
Αν. ἰδοὺ σιωπῶ κἀπιλάζυμαι στόμα.
Ερ. ἐκεῖνο λέξον, οὗπερ εἵνεκ' ἐστάλην.
Αν. λέγω σ' ἐγὼ νοῦν οὐκ ἔχειν ὅσον σε δεῖ.
Ερ. λείψεις τόδ' ἁγνὸν τέμενος ἐναλίας θεοῦ;
Αν. εἰ μὴ θανοῦμαί γ'· εἰ δὲ μή, οὐ λείψω ποτέ.
Ερ. ὡς τοῦτ' ἄραρε, κοὐ μενῶ πόσιν μολεῖν.
Αν. ἀλλ' οὐδ' ἐγὼ μὴν πρόσθεν ἐκδώσω μέ σοι.

231 τέκν' ὅσοις *l*: τέκν' οἷς codd. (τέκνα οἷς M B O): τέκν' αἷς Stob. 74. 21: παῖδας αἷς olim Nauck 232 παρίσταται P 239 δύνᾳ Porson 240 αὖ A: αὐ M: ἂν rell. 241 πρῶτα ταῦτα L B O πανταχῇ P 242 ναί om. P καλά] καλῶς L B O 244 τάδ' P O 246 ἐπιβλέπον A (ἀποβλέπων M: ἀποβλέπ** L, -ον L²) 248 Ἑλένη νιν] Ἑλένην M et primitus L 251 οὗπερ ἕνεκ' ἐνθάδ' ἱκάνω V, ἐστάλην suprascr. V¹: οὗπερ ἐνθάδ' ἱκάνω A, suprascr. γρ. ἕνεκ' ἐστάλην A¹. Cf. Med. 668 ἕνεκ' etiam P: εἵνεκ' Haun.: οὕνεκ' rell. ut solent 252 οἷόν σε Nauck

Ερ. πῦρ σοι προσοίσω, κοὐ τὸ σὸν προσκέψομαι—
Αν. σὺ δ' οὖν κάταιθε· θεοὶ γὰρ εἴσονται τάδε.
Ερ. καὶ χρωτὶ δεινῶν τραυμάτων ἀλγηδόνας.
Αν. σφάζ', αἱμάτου θεᾶς βωμόν, ἣ μέτεισί σε.
Ερ. ὦ βάρβαρον σὺ θρέμμα καὶ σκληρὸν θράσος,
ἐγκαρτερεῖς δὴ θάνατον; ἀλλ' ἐγώ σ' ἕδρας
ἐκ τῆσδ' ἑκοῦσαν ἐξαναστήσω τάχα·
τοιόνδ' ἔχω σου δέλεαρ. ἀλλὰ γὰρ λόγους
κρύψω, τὸ δ' ἔργον αὐτὸ σημανεῖ τάχα.
κάθησ' ἑδραία· καὶ γὰρ εἰ πέριξ σ' ἔχοι
τηκτὸς μόλυβδος, ἐξαναστήσω σ' ἐγὼ
πρὶν ᾧ πέποιθας παῖδ' Ἀχιλλέως μολεῖν.
Αν. πέποιθα. δεινὸν δ' ἑρπετῶν μὲν ἀγρίων
ἄκη βροτοῖσι θεῶν καταστῆσαί τινα·
ὃ δ' ἔστ' ἐχίδνης καὶ πυρὸς περαιτέρω,
οὐδεὶς γυναικὸς φάρμακ' ἐξηύρηκέ πω
κακῆς· τοσοῦτόν ἐσμεν ἀνθρώποις κακόν.

Χο. Ἦ μεγάλων ἀχέων ἄρ' ὑπῆρξεν, ὅτ' Ἰδαίαν [στρ. α
ἐς νάπαν ἦλθ' ὁ Μαί-
ας τε καὶ Διὸς τόκος,
τρίπωλον ἅρμα δαιμόνων
ἄγων τὸ καλλιζυγές,
ἔριδι στυγερᾷ κεκορυθμένον εὐμορφίας
σταθμοὺς ἐπὶ βούτα,
βοτῆρά τ' ἀμφὶ μονότροπον νεανίαν
ἔρημόν θ'
ἑστιοῦχον αὐλάν.

258 τόδε A 260 αἵματος P 266 σ' om. A P ἔχοι Bruhn: ἔχει codd. 268 ᾧ] ὃν P 270 καταστῆσαι *p* Σ et Stob. 73. 19: ἐγκαταστῆσαι codd. (βροτοῖς P) 271 ὃ Dobree: ἃ codd. et Σ 273 τοιοῦτον P. Versum videtur non habuisse Σ 276 ἦλθεν ὁ codd.: corr. *l* (ἦλθεν et v. 286 νίψαντ' Wecklein) τέκος M: γόνος P 279 ἀγλαΐας olim Headlam. Cf. v. 289 280 βούτας Schoene, cl. Hip. 537 (τὰς ποιμενικὰς ἐπαύλεις B[1] in margine) 281 τ' om. A L (add. *l*)

ταὶ δ' ἐπεὶ ὑλόκομον νάπος ἤλυθον οὐρειᾶν [ἀντ. α
πιδάκων νίψαν αἰ-
γλᾶντα σώματα ῥοαῖς,
ἔβαν δὲ Πριαμίδαν ὑπερ-
βολαῖς λόγων δυσφρόνων
παραβαλλόμεναι, δολίοις ⟨δ'⟩ ἕλε Κύπρις λόγοις,
τερπνοῖς μὲν ἀκοῦσαι,
πικρὰν δὲ σύγχυσιν βίου Φρυγῶν πόλει
ταλαίνᾳ
περγάμοις τε Τροίας.

ἀλλ' εἴθ' ὑπὲρ κεφαλὰν ἔβαλεν κακὸν [στρ. β
ἁ τεκοῦσά νιν [Πάριν]
πρὶν Ἰδαῖ-
ον κατοικίσαι λέπας·
ὅτε νιν παρὰ θεσπεσίῳ δάφνᾳ
βόασε Κασάνδρα κτανεῖν,
μεγάλαν Πριάμου πόλεως λώβαν.
τίν' οὐκ ἐπῆλθε, ποῖον οὐκ ἐλίσσετο
δαμογερόν-
των βρέφος φονεύειν;

οὔτ' ἂν ἐπ' Ἰλιάσι ζυγὸν ἤλυθε [ἀντ. β
δούλιον, σύ τ' ἂν γύναι,
τυράννων

285 *νίψαν* Hermann : *νίψαντο* LP : *ἔνιψαν* BO : *ἔνιψάν τ'* MA : *ἐνίψαν*** *τ'* V *αἰγλάεντα* codd. 287 *δὲ*] *τε* P 288 *δυσφόρων* P et *γρ.* Σ (*δ' εὐφρόνων* Hermann). Fortasse *πόθων δυσφόρων* 289 *Κύπρις εἷλε λόγοις δολίοις* codd. (*Κύπρις δ'* V²: *Κύπρις* * L : *δὲ Κύπρις* BO) : correxi (*λόγοις αἰόλοις* vel *αἱμύλοις* Musgrave) 290 Fortasse *τέρψιν* 291 *βίου* ante *σύγχυσιν*, et *ταλαίνᾳ* post *Τροίας* habet A 292 *τάλαιναν* M 293 *εἴθε δ'* *l* : malim *εἴθ' ἄρ'* *κεφαλᾶς* P 294 *Πάριν* corruptum : *μόρον* Hermann, ex Σ qui *ἔβαλε θάνατον* : malim *μύσος* vel *τέρας*. Cf. Aesch. Choeph. v. 98 sq. 295 *κατοικίσαι* M² V *l* : *κατοικῆσαι* rell. 296 *περὶ* P 301 *οὔ τἂν* Kirchhoff *ἦλθε* A V 302 *δούλιον* V : *δούλειον* rell. (*ζυγὸς . . . δούλειος* P *l*) *σύ τ' ἂν* Pflugk : *οὔτ' ἂν σὺ* codd. et Σ 303 *τύραννον* P : *τυράννων τάσδ'* L (*τάνδ'* *l*)

ἔσχες ἂν δόμων ἕδρας·
παρέλυσε δ' ἂν Ἑλλάδος ἀλγεινοὺς
†μόχθους οὓς ἀμφὶ Τροίαν†
δεκέτεις ἀλάληντο νέοι λόγχαις.
λέχη τ' ἔρημ' ἂν οὔποτ' ἐξελείπετο,
καὶ τεκέων
ὀρφανοὶ γέροντες.

ΜΕΝΕΛΑΟΣ

ἥκω λαβὼν σὸν παῖδ', ὃν εἰς ἄλλους δόμους
λάθρᾳ θυγατρὸς τῆς ἐμῆς ὑπεξέθου.
σὲ μὲν γὰρ ηὔχεις θεᾶς βρέτας σῴσειν τόδε,
τοῦτον δὲ τοὺς κρύψαντας· ἀλλ' ἐφηυρέθης
ἧσσον φρονοῦσα τοῦδε Μενέλεω, γύναι.
κεἰ μὴ τόδ' ἐκλιποῦσ' ἐρημώσεις πέδον,
ὅδ' ἀντὶ τοῦ σοῦ σώματος σφαγήσεται.
ταῦτ' οὖν λογίζου, πότερα κατθανεῖν θέλεις
ἢ τόνδ' ὀλέσθαι σῆς ἁμαρτίας ὕπερ,
ἣν εἰς ἔμ' εἴς τε παῖδ' ἐμὴν ἁμαρτάνεις.
Αν. ὦ δόξα δόξα, μυρίοισι δὴ βροτῶν
οὐδὲν γεγῶσι βίοτον ὤγκωσας μέγαν.
εὔκλεια δ' οἷς μὲν ἔστ' ἀληθείας ὕπο,
εὐδαιμονίζω· τοὺς δ' ὑπὸ ψευδῶν, ἔχειν
οὐκ ἀξιώσω, πλὴν τύχῃ φρονεῖν δοκεῖν.
σὺ δὴ στρατηγῶν λογάσιν Ἑλλήνων ποτὲ
Τροίαν ἀφείλου Πρίαμον, ὧδε φαῦλος ὤν;
ὅστις θυγατρὸς ἀντίπαιδος ἐκ λόγων
τοσόνδ' ἔπνευσας, καὶ γυναικὶ δυστυχεῖ

303 *δόμον* M V (corr. M² V²) : *δόμους* A *ἕδραν* V P *l* 305 *πόνους* P *l* (et fort. Σ) : v. corruptus : *πόνους, ὅτ' ἀμφὶ Τρωΐαις* Hermann : *οὓς ἀμφὶ Τρωΐαν μόγους* (malim *πόνους*) Headlam 306 *δεκέτεις* A L : *δέκ' ἔτ' εἶσ* (*ἔτη εἶσ* V²) rell. ut vid. *ὀλόληντο* V 307 *οὔποτ'* M B L : *οὐπώποτ'* A V : *οὐκ ἂν* P 311, 312 *σὺ μὲν . . . καὶ κρύψαντες* P 311 *σῶσαι* codd. : corr. Dobree 316 *πότερον* L 320 *μέγα* A V : corr. V² 322 *ἔχει* Hirzel 323 *δοκεῖν φρονεῖν* corr. *l* *πλὴν ὅσον τύχῃ δοκεῖν* post Dobraeum Wecklein. De Σ incertum 324 *Ἀργείων* V

δούλῃ κατέστης εἰς ἀγῶν'; οὐκ ἀξιῶ
οὔτ' οὖν σὲ Τροίας οὔτε σοῦ Τροίαν ἔτι.
[ἔξωθέν εἰσιν οἱ δοκοῦντες εὖ φρονεῖν
λαμπροί, τὰ δ' ἔνδον πᾶσιν ἀνθρώποις ἴσοι,
πλὴν εἴ τι πλούτῳ· τοῦτο δ' ἰσχύει μέγα.]
Μενέλαε, φέρε δὴ διαπεράνωμεν λόγους·
τέθνηκα τῇ σῇ θυγατρὶ καί μ' ἀπώλεσε·
μιαιφόνον μὲν οὐκέτ' ἂν φύγοι μύσος.
ἐν τοῖς δὲ πολλοῖς καὶ σὺ τόνδ' ἀγωνιῇ
φόνον· τὸ συνδρῶν γάρ σ' ἀναγκάσει χρέος.
ἢν δ' οὖν ἐγὼ μὲν μὴ θανεῖν ὑπεκδράμω,
τὸν παῖδά μου κτενεῖτε; κᾆτα πῶς πατὴρ
τέκνου θανόντος ῥᾳδίως ἀνέξεται;
οὐχ ὧδ' ἄνανδρον αὐτὸν ἡ Τροία καλεῖ·
ἀλλ' εἶσιν οἷ χρή—Πηλέως γὰρ ἄξια
πατρός τ' Ἀχιλλέως ἔργα δρῶν φανήσεται—
ὤσει δὲ σὴν παῖδ' ἐκ δόμων· σὺ δ' ἐκδιδοὺς
ἄλλῳ τί λέξεις; πότερον ὡς κακὸν πόσιν
φεύγει τὸ ταύτης σῶφρον; ἀλλὰ πεύσεται.
γαμεῖ δὲ τίς νιν; ἤ σφ' ἄνανδρον ἐν δόμοις
χήραν καθέξεις πολιόν; ὦ τλήμων ἀνήρ,
κακῶν τοσούτων οὐχ ὁρᾷς ἐπιρροάς;
πόσας ἂν εὐνὰς θυγατέρ' ἠδικημένην
βούλοι' ἂν εὑρεῖν ἢ παθεῖν ἁγὼ λέγω;
οὐ χρὴ 'πὶ μικροῖς μεγάλα πορσύνειν κακὰ
οὐδ', εἰ γυναῖκές ἐσμεν ἀτηρὸν κακόν,
ἄνδρας γυναιξὶν ἐξομοιοῦσθαι φύσιν.
ἡμεῖς γὰρ εἰ σὴν παῖδα φαρμακεύομεν
καὶ νηδὺν ἐξαμβλοῦμεν, ὡς αὐτὴ λέγει,

330–332 Δίδυμος μέμφεται τούτοις Σ: ut Menandreos citat Stob. 104. 14 εὐτυχεῖν legens pro εὖ φρονεῖν 333 suspectus: versum eicit Wilamowitz, εἶεν eius loco ponens 334 δὴ σῇ Reiske 337 Sic codd. et Σ 342 Fortasse τ' ἄρ' ἄξια vel τ' ἐπάξια 346 πεύσεται Kiehl: ψεύσεται codd. et Σ: ἀλλ' ἐψεύσεται Porson 348 ἀνήρ Dindorf: ἄνερ codd. (τλῆμον MAV) 350 πόσας δ' LP 351 βούλοιμ' M

ἑκόντες οὐκ ἄκοντες, οὐδὲ βώμιοι
πίτνοντες, αὐτοὶ τὴν δίκην ὑφέξομεν
ἐν σοῖσι γαμβροῖς, οἷσιν οὐκ ἐλάσσονα
βλάβην ὀφείλω προστιθεῖσ' ἀπαιδίαν.
ἡμεῖς μὲν οὖν τοιοίδε· τῆς δὲ σῆς φρενὸς—
ἕν σου δέδοικα· διὰ γυναικείαν ἔριν
καὶ τὴν τάλαιναν ὤλεσας Φρυγῶν πόλιν.
Χο. ἄγαν ἔλεξας ὡς γυνὴ πρὸς ἄρσενας,
καί σου τὸ σῶφρον ἐξετόξευσεν φρενός.
Με. γύναι, τάδ' ἐστὶ σμικρὰ καὶ μοναρχίας
οὐκ ἄξι', ὡς φῄς, τῆς ἐμῆς οὐδ' Ἑλλάδος.
εὖ δ' ἴσθ', ὅτου τις τυγχάνει χρείαν ἔχων,
τοῦτ' ἔσθ' ἑκάστῳ μεῖζον ἢ Τροίαν ἑλεῖν.
κἀγὼ θυγατρί—μεγάλα γὰρ κρίνω τάδε,
λέχους στέρεσθαι—σύμμαχος καθίσταμαι.
τὰ μὲν γὰρ ἄλλα δεύτερ' ἂν πάσχοι γυνή,
ἀνδρὸς δ' ἁμαρτάνουσ' ἁμαρτάνει βίου.
δούλων δ' ἐκεῖνον τῶν ἐμῶν ἄρχειν χρεὼν
καὶ τῶν ἐκείνου τοὺς ἐμούς, ἡμᾶς τε πρός·
φίλων γὰρ οὐδὲν ἴδιον, οἵτινες φίλοι
ὀρθῶς πεφύκασ', ἀλλὰ κοινὰ χρήματα.
μένων δὲ τοὺς ἀπόντας, εἰ μὴ θήσομαι
τἄμ' ὡς ἄριστα, φαῦλός εἰμι κοὐ σοφός.
ἀλλ' ἐξανίστω τῶνδ' ἀνακτόρων θεᾶς·
ὡς, ἢν θάνῃς σύ, παῖς ὅδ' ἐκφεύγει μόρον,
σοῦ δ' οὐ θελούσης κατθανεῖν, τόνδε κτενῶ.
δυοῖν δ' ἀνάγκη θατέρῳ λιπεῖν βίον.

357 οἱ βώμιοι videtur habuisse Σ 358 πίπτοντες B O αὐτῇ Kirchhoff 360 ἀπαιδίαν A L P γρ. B γρ. V: ἀβουλίαν M V B O (ἀκυμίαν Headlam) 362 ἕν σου etiam Σ: ἕν που Scaliger 363 Δίδυμος μέμφεται πᾶσι (τρισὶ Verrall) τούτοις Σ πόλιν Φρυγῶν A 365 ἐξετόξευσας Seager 372 πάσχοι Haun. et v. l. in P: πάσχῃ rell. (ἂν πάσχῃ Musgrave): πάσχῃ -ει et -οι codices Stobaei 74. 23 383 ἀνάγκη L P[2] γρ. Σ V: ἀνάγκαιν ἢ (ex ἀνάγκαιν suprascripto ἀνάγκη orta) fere rell. (ἀνάγκιν P)

Αν. οἴμοι, πικρὰν κλήρωσιν αἵρεσίν τέ μοι
βίου καθίστης· καὶ λαχοῦσά γ' ἀθλία
καὶ μὴ λαχοῦσα δυστυχὴς καθίσταμαι.
ὦ μεγάλα πράσσων αἰτίας μικρᾶς πέρι,
πιθοῦ· τί καίνεις μ'; ἀντὶ τοῦ; ποίαν πόλιν
προύδωκα; τίνα σῶν ἔκτανον παίδων ἐγώ;
ποῖον δ' ἔπρησα δῶμ'; ἐκοιμήθην βίᾳ
σὺν δεσπόταισι· κᾆτ' ἔμ', οὐ κεῖνον κτενεῖς,
τὸν αἴτιον τῶνδ', ἀλλὰ τὴν ἀρχὴν ἀφεὶς
πρὸς τὴν τελευτὴν ὑστέραν οὖσαν φέρῃ;
οἴμοι κακῶν τῶνδ', ὦ τάλαιν' ἐμὴ πατρίς,
ὡς δεινὰ πάσχω. τί δέ με καὶ τεκεῖν ἐχρῆν
ἄχθος τ' ἐπ' ἄχθει τῷδε προσθέσθαι διπλοῦν;
[ἀτὰρ τί ταῦτα δύρομαι, τὰ δ' ἐν ποσὶν
οὐκ ἐξικμάζω καὶ λογίζομαι κακά;]
ἥτις σφαγὰς μὲν Ἕκτορος τροχηλάτους
κατεῖδον οἰκτρῶς τ' Ἴλιον πυρούμενον,
αὐτὴ δὲ δούλη ναῦς ἐπ' Ἀργείων ἔβην
κόμης ἐπισπασθεῖσ'· ἐπεὶ δ' ἀφικόμην
Φθίαν, φονεῦσιν Ἕκτορος νυμφεύομαι.
τί δῆτ' ἐμοὶ ζῆν ἡδύ; πρὸς τί χρὴ βλέπειν;
πρὸς τὰς παρούσας ἢ παρελθούσας τύχας;
εἷς παῖς ὅδ' ἦν μοι λοιπὸς ὀφθαλμὸς βίου·
τοῦτον κτενεῖν μέλλουσιν οἷς δοκεῖ τάδε.
οὐ δῆτα τοὐμοῦ γ' εἵνεκ' ἀθλίου βίου·
ἐν τῷδε μὲν γὰρ ἐλπίς, εἰ σωθήσεται,
ἐμοὶ δ' ὄνειδος μὴ θανεῖν ὑπὲρ τέκνου.

384 γέ μοι M   385 καὶ] εἰ Kirchhoff   γ'] τ' Hermann et fortasse Σ   Vv. 397, 398 et 404, 405 invicem transposuit Musgrave : vv. 406–410 ante 399 Hirzel : vv. 399-405 seclusit Bruhn, Hartung vv. 397–398   397 ταῦτ' ὀδύρομαι codd. et Σ : corr. Porson   398 ἐξικμάζω codd. et Σ : ἐξιχμάζω Rutherford : ἐκλίκμαζω Madvig   399 τροχηλάτου M O (non B)   402 ἀποσπασθεῖσ' L P   406 λοιπὸν L   407 κτενεῖν P : κτανεῖν rell.   408 εἵνεκ' P : οὕνεκ' rell.

ἰδοὺ προλείπω βωμὸν ἥδε χειρία
σφάζειν φονεύειν, δεῖν, ἀπαρτῆσαι δέρην.
ὦ τέκνον, ἡ τεκοῦσά σ', ὡς σὺ μὴ θάνῃς,
στείχω πρὸς Ἅιδην· ἢν δ' ὑπεκδράμῃς μόρον,
μέμνησο μητρός, οἷα τλᾶσ' ἀπωλόμην,
καὶ πατρὶ τῷ σῷ διὰ φιλημάτων ἰὼν
δάκρυά τε λείβων καὶ περιπτύσσων χέρας
λέγ' οἷ' ἔπραξα. πᾶσι δ' ἀνθρώποις ἄρ' ἦν
ψυχὴ τέκν'· ὅστις δ' αὔτ' ἄπειρος ὢν ψέγει,
ἧσσον μὲν ἀλγεῖ, δυστυχῶν δ' εὐδαιμονεῖ.
Χο. ᾤκτιρ' ἀκούσασ'· οἰκτρὰ γὰρ τὰ δυστυχῆ
βροτοῖς ἅπασι, κἂν θυραῖος ὢν κυρῇ.
εἰς ξύμβασιν δὲ χρῆν σε παῖδα σὴν ἄγειν,
Μενέλαε, καὶ τήνδ', ὡς ἀπαλλαχθῇ πόνων.
Με. λάβεσθέ μοι τῆσδ', ἀμφελίξαντες χέρας,
δμῶες· λόγους γὰρ οὐ φίλους ἀκούσεται.
ἐγώ σ', ἵν' ἁγνὸν βωμὸν ἐκλίποις θεᾶς,
προύτεινα παιδὸς θάνατον, ᾧ σ' ὑπήγαγον
εἰς χεῖρας ἐλθεῖν τὰς ἐμὰς ἐπὶ σφαγήν.
καὶ τἀμφὶ σοῦ μὲν ὧδ' ἔχοντ' ἐπίστασο·
τὰ δ' ἀμφὶ παιδὸς τοῦδε παῖς ἐμὴ κρινεῖ,
ἤν τε κτανεῖν νιν ἤν τε μὴ κτανεῖν θέλῃ.
ἀλλ' ἕρπ' ἐς οἴκους τούσδ', ἵν' εἰς ἐλευθέρους
δούλη γεγῶσα μήποθ' ὑβρίζειν μάθῃς.
Αν. οἴμοι· δόλῳ μ' ὑπῆλθες, ἠπατήμεθα.
Με. κήρυσσ' ἅπασιν· οὐ γὰρ ἐξαρνούμεθα.
Αν. ἦ ταῦτ' ἐν ὑμῖν τοῖς παρ' Εὐρώτᾳ σοφά;
Με. καὶ τοῖς γε Τροίᾳ, τοὺς παθόντας ἀντιδρᾶν.

414 μόρον] μόνος L 419 ψέγει M A V B P Σ: λέγει L et Stob. 76. 3 423 παῖδα σὴν Kirchhoff: σὴν παῖδ' M V L: σήν γε παῖδ' A: καὶ σὴν παῖδ' P: σὴν παῖδ' ἐξάγειν B O: σήν τε παῖδ' Elmsley 426 οὐκ ἀκ. φίλ. B O, propter accentum 427 ἔγωγ' Lobeck (et V[2]). Fortasse εἰδὼς ἐκλίποις Brunck: ἐκλίπῃς V L P (ἐλίπῃς V): ἐκλείπῃ M B: ἐκλίπῃ A O, quo recepto legendum foret ᾧ σφ' 432 νιν om. M B O μὴ κτανεῖν L V[2]: κτεῖναι P: κτείνειν M A V B O 434 μηκέθ' Paley 438 γε l (τε L): γ' ἐν P O: τ' ἐν A V B: ἐν M

Αν. τὰ θεῖα δ' οὐ θεῖ' οὐδ' ἔχειν ἡγῇ δίκην;
Με. ὅταν τάδ' ᾖ, τότ' οἴσομεν· σὲ δὲ κτενῶ.
Αν. ἦ καὶ νεοσσὸν τόνδ', ὑπὸ πτερῶν σπάσας;
Με. οὐ δῆτα· θυγατρὶ δ', ἢν θέλῃ, δώσω κτανεῖν.
Αν. οἴμοι· τί δῆτά σ' οὐ καταστένω, τέκνον;
Με. οὔκουν θρασεῖά γ' αὐτὸν ἐλπὶς ἀναμένει.
Αν. ὦ πᾶσιν ἀνθρώποισιν ἔχθιστοι βροτῶν
Σπάρτης ἔνοικοι, δόλια βουλευτήρια,
ψευδῶν ἄνακτες, μηχανορράφοι κακῶν,
ἑλικτὰ κοὐδὲν ὑγιές, ἀλλὰ πᾶν πέριξ
φρονοῦντες, ἀδίκως εὐτυχεῖτ' ἀν' Ἑλλάδα.
τί δ' οὐκ ἐν ὑμῖν ἐστιν; οὐ πλεῖστοι φόνοι;
οὐκ αἰσχροκερδεῖς; οὐ λέγοντες ἄλλα μὲν
γλώσσῃ, φρονοῦντες δ' ἄλλ' ἐφευρίσκεσθ' ἀεί;
ὄλοισθ'. ἐμοὶ μὲν θάνατος οὐχ οὕτω βαρὺς
ὥς σοὶ δέδοκται· κεῖνα γάρ μ' ἀπώλεσεν,
ὅθ' ἡ τάλαινα πόλις ἀνηλώθη Φρυγῶν
πόσις θ' ὁ κλεινός, ὅς σε πολλάκις δορὶ
ναύτην ἔθηκεν ἀντὶ χερσαίου κακόν.
νῦν δ' εἰς γυναῖκα γοργὸς ὁπλίτης φανεὶς
κτείνεις μ'. ἀπόκτειν'· ὡς ἀθώπευτόν γέ σε
γλώσσης ἀφήσω τῆς ἐμῆς καὶ παῖδα σήν.
ἐπεὶ σὺ μὲν πέφυκας ἐν Σπάρτῃ μέγας,
ἡμεῖς δὲ Τροίᾳ γ'. εἰ δ' ἐγὼ πράσσω κακῶς,
μηδὲν τόδ' αὔχει· καὶ σὺ γὰρ πράξειας ἄν.

Χο. οὐδέποτε δίδυμα λέκτρ' ἐπαινέσω βροτῶν [στρ.
οὐδ' ἀμφιμάτορας κόρους,

440 τάδ' ᾖ τότ' L P sed τότ' ex τό* corr. in L : τόδ' ᾖ τάδ' M A V B : τότ' οἴσομεν Σ 443 σοῦ (vel σου) M A P γρ. V² 444 ἀμμένει Nauck 445 ἔχθιστος M 448 πάντα πέριξ L P 450 οἱ πλεῖστοι M O P γρ. V² 453 μὲν θάνατος M : δὲ θάνατος μὲν A V : δὲ θάνατος rell. 455 ἀναλώθη codd. 456 θ'] δ' V 462 δ' ἐν Τροίᾳ M B L O. Cf. 438 πράσσω] πάσχω P. Cf. Hclid. 27 463 σύ τοι Stob. 112. 5 464 οὔποτ' ἐγὼ Nauck. Cf. v. 471 466 ἀμφιμάτερας M V B : -τρας V²

ἔριδας οἴκων δυσμενεῖς τε λύπας.
μίαν μοι στεργέτω πόσις γάμοις
ἀκοινώ-
νητον ἀνδρὸς εὐνάν.

οὐδέ γ' ἐνὶ πόλεσι δίπτυχοι τυραννίδες [ἀντ.
μιᾶς ἀμείνονες φέρειν,
ἄχθος ἐπ' ἄχθει καὶ στάσις πολίταις·
τεκόντοιν θ' ὕμνον ἐργάταιν δυοῖν
ἔριν Μοῦ-
σαι φιλοῦσι κραίνειν.

πνοαὶ δ' ὅταν φέρωσι ναυτίλους θοαί, [στρ.
κατὰ πηδαλίων δίδυμαι πραπίδων γνῶμαι,
σοφῶν τε πλῆθος ἀθρόον ἀσθενέστερον
φαυλοτέρας φρενὸς αὐτοκρατοῦς.
ἑνὸς ἁ δύνασις ἀνά τε μέλαθρα
κατά τε πόλιας, ὁπόταν εὑρεῖν θέλωσι καιρόν.

ἔδειξεν ἡ Λάκαινα τοῦ στρατηλάτα [ἀντ.
Μενέλα· διὰ γὰρ πυρὸς ἦλθ' ἑτέρῳ λέχεϊ,
κτείνει δὲ τὴν τάλαιναν Ἰλιάδα κόραν
παῖδά τε δύσφρονος ἔριδος ὕπερ.
ἄθεος ἄνομος ἄχαρις ὁ φόνος·

467 ἔριν μὲν οἰκ. Musurus (ἔριδ' P) 470 ἀνδρὸς codd. et Σ 471 γ' ἐνὶ Lenting: γὰρ ἐν codd. πόλαισι V: πόλεσσι A 472 ἄμεινον ἐσφέρειν A B O 475 ἄχθος A L V: ἄχθος τ' V² rell. Cf. v. 396. Verba suspecta 476 τεκόντοιν θ' ὕμνον ἐργάταιν Wilamowitz: τεκτόνοιν θ' ὕμνοιν ἐργάταιν fere codd. (cf. Σ M δύο ἐργάταις τεκτόσιν ὕμνων): τεκτόνων θ' ὕμνοι ἐργάταιν L (ἐργάται L²): τεκτόνοιν θ' ὕμνοις ἐργάται P (ὕμνοι P²): θ' om. B D O: ὑμνουργάταιν latere putat Headlam 479 πνοαὶ V: πνοιαὶ rell. ναυτίλοις B O (-ους Σ) 480 δίδυμαι . . . γνῶμαι M B V² O Σ: διδύμα . . . γνώμα A V L P. Punctum post γνῶμαι et post αὐτοκρατοῦς Σ et B: post ἑνός multi 481 σοφόν P 484 ἁ δύνασις] ὁ δύνασις P: ὁ δύναται Blaydes 485 εὖ ῥεῖν v. l. in Σ 486 στρατηλάτου L P: utrumque A (στρατηλάτα Choerobosc. Cann. i. 92) 487 Μενέλαε A L P 489 κτενεῖ . . . Ἰλίαν Nauck 490 ἀμφ' ἔριδος Hermann 491 ἄθεός γ' Musurus. Cf. v. 484

ἔτι σε, πότνια, μετατροπὰ
τῶνδ' ἔπεισιν ἔργων.

καὶ μὴν ἐσορῶ
τόδε σύγκρατον ζεῦγος πρὸ δόμων
ψήφῳ θανάτου [κατακεκριμένον.]
δύστηνε γύναι, τλῆμον δὲ σὺ παῖ,
μητρὸς λεχέων ὃς ὑπερθνῄσκεις
οὐδὲν μετέχων
οὐδ' αἴτιος ὢν βασιλεῦσιν.

Αν. ἅδ' ἐγὼ χέρας αἱματη- [στρ.
ρὰς βρόχοισι κεκλῃμένα
πέμπομαι κατὰ γαίας.

ΠΑΙΣ

μᾶτερ μᾶτερ, ἐγὼ δὲ σᾷ
πτέρυγι συγκαταβαίνω.

Αν. θῦμα δάιον, ὦ χθονὸς
Φθίας κράντορες. Πα. ὦ πάτερ,
μόλε φίλοις ἐπίκουρος.

Αν. κείσῃ δή, τέκνον ὦ φίλος,
μαστοῖς ματέρος ἀμφὶ σᾶς
νεκρὸς ὑπὸ χθονί, σὺν νεκρῷ ⟨τ'⟩ . . .

Πα. ὤμοι μοι, τί πάθω; τάλας
δῆτ' ἐγὼ σύ τε, μᾶτερ.

Με. ἴθ' ὑποχθόνιοι· καὶ γὰρ ἀπ' ἐχθρῶν
ἥκετε πύργων· δύο δ' ἐκ δισσαῖν
θνῄσκετ' ἀνάγκαιν· σὲ μὲν ἡμετέρα
ψῆφος ἀναιρεῖ, παῖδα δ' ἐμὴ παῖς

492 δὲ πότνια μετ. Hermann μετατροπαὶ L (τῶνδ' ἔπ. ἔρ. om. P) 495 Hemichorii notam praef. M A B σύγκροτον A L P et, ut vid. Σ M Σ B (συγκεκροτημένον) 496 κατακεκριμένον delet Hermann 497 δύστανε L P τλῆμον M A L : τλήμων rell. 503 γρ. κατὰ γαῖαν Σ B 504 ΠΑΙΣ scripsi : Μολοττός codd., hic et semper. Cf. Dram. Personas 504–509 Molosso continuant codd. : corr. Hermann 510 κεῖσ' ἤδη codd. et Σ (γρ. κεῖσο δὴ B[2]) : corr. Musgrave 512 νεκρὸς] νεκροὺς M (?) τ' add. Musurus : νεκροῖς Nauck. Cf. 534

τόνδ' Ἑρμιόνῃ· καὶ γὰρ ἀνοία
μεγάλη λείπειν ἐχθροὺς ἐχθρῶν,
ἐξὸν κτείνειν
καὶ φόβον οἴκων ἀφελέσθαι.

Αν. ὦ πόσις πόσις, εἴθε σὰν [ἀντ.
χεῖρα καὶ δόρυ σύμμαχον
κτησαίμαν, Πριάμου παῖ.
Πα. δύστανος, τί δ' ἐγὼ μόρου
παράτροπον μέλος εὕρω;
Αν. λίσσου, γούνασι δεσπότου
χρίμπτων, ὦ τέκνον. Πα. ὦ φίλος,
φίλος, ἄνες θάνατόν μοι.
Αν. λείβομαι δάκρυσιν κόρας,
στάζω λισσάδος ὡς πέτρας
λιβὰς ἀνήλιος, ἁ τάλαιν' . . .
Πα. ὤμοι μοι, τί δ' ἐγὼ κακῶν
μῆχος ἐξανύσωμαι;
Με. τί με προσπίτνεις, ἁλίαν πέτραν
ἢ κῦμα λιταῖς ὣς ἱκετεύων;
τοῖς γὰρ ἐμοῖσιν γέγον' ὠφελία,
σοὶ δ' οὐδὲν ἔχω φίλτρον, ἐπεί τοι
μέγ' ἀναλώσας ψυχῆς μόριον
Τροίαν εἷλον καὶ μητέρα σήν·
ἧς ἀπολαύων
Ἅιδην χθόνιον καταβήσῃ.

Χο. καὶ μὴν δέδορκα τόνδε Πηλέα πέλας,
σπουδῇ τιθέντα δεῦρο γηραιὸν πόδα.

519 ἄνοια omnes 520 λιπεῖν codd. (λιπεῖν μεγάλη transp. *l*) ἐχθροὺς] σκύμνους Wilamowitz ἐχθρῶν deletum in L 522 οἶκον L P: corr. *l* 528 τέλος M A V 529 λίσσου δὲ L P B: λίσσουσι (λίσσου σὺ in marg.) A 531 φίλος Matthiae: ὦ φίλος codd. 532 δακρύοισι L P B 533 στάζων L P: corr. *l* 534 ἁ om. L τάλαινα non elidunt A B L P O: de rell. dubium 535 κακῶν τί δ' ἐγὼ B L P O 537 προσπιτνεῖς M A V: προσπίπτεις rell. 538 ὣς] ἴσθ' Nauck 539 ἐμοῖς codd.: corr. Musurus ὠφελία A V: ὠφέλεια rell. V[2]

ΠΗΛΕΥΣ

ὑμᾶς ἐρωτῶ τόν τ' ἐφεστῶτα σφαγῇ,
τί ταῦτα; πῶς ταῦτ'; ἐκ τίνος λόγου νοσεῖ
δόμος; τί πράσσετ' ἄκριτα μηχανώμενοι;
Μενέλα', ἐπίσχες· μὴ τάχυν' ἄνευ δίκης. . . .
ἡγοῦ σὺ θᾶσσον, οὐ γὰρ ὡς ἔοικέ μοι
σχολῆς τόδ' ἔργον· ἀλλ' ἀνηβητηρίαν
ῥώμην μ' ἐπαινῶ λαμβάνειν, εἴπερ ποτέ. . . .
πρῶτον μὲν οὖν κατ' οὖρον ὥσπερ ἱστίοις
ἐμπνεύσομαι τῇδ'· εἰπέ, τίνι δίκῃ χέρας
βρόχοισιν ἐκδήσαντες οἵδ' ἄγουσί σε
καὶ παῖδ'; ὕπαρνος γάρ τις οἷς ἀπόλλυσαι,
ἡμῶν ἀπόντων τοῦ τε κυρίου σέθεν.

Αν. οἵδ', ὦ γεραιέ, σὺν τέκνῳ θανουμένην
ἄγουσί μ' οὕτως ὡς ὁρᾷς. τί σοι λέγω;
οὐ γὰρ μιᾶς σε κληδόνος προθυμίᾳ
μετῆλθον, ἀλλὰ μυρίων ὑπ' ἀγγέλων.
ἔριν δὲ τὴν κατ' οἶκον οἶσθά που κλύων
τῆς τοῦδε θυγατρός, ὧν τ' ἀπόλλυμαι χάριν.
καὶ νῦν με βωμοῦ Θέτιδος, ἣ τὸν εὐγενῆ
ἔτικτέ σοι παῖδ', ἣν σὺ θαυμαστὴν σέβεις,
ἄγουσ' ἀποσπάσαντες, οὔτε τῳ δίκῃ
κρίναντες οὔτε τοὺς ἀπόντας ἐκ δόμων
μείναντες, ἀλλὰ τὴν ἐμὴν ἐρημίαν
γνόντες τέκνου τε τοῦδ', ὃν οὐδὲν αἴτιον
μέλλουσι σὺν ἐμοὶ τῇ ταλαιπώρῳ κτενεῖν.
ἀλλ' ἀντιάζω σ', ὦ γέρον, τῶν σῶν πάρος

548 *πῶς ταῦτ'; ἐκ* L P : *καὶ πῶς τἐκ* M A V : *καὶ πῶς κἀκ* B O : *καὶ πῶς; ἐκ* Nauck : *πῶς τε κἀκ* Wilamowitz (*πῶς ταῦτα γέγονε καὶ τί ταῦτα* Σ M) 550 del. Wilamowitz : ante v. 547 trai. Bruhn 551 *γέροντί μοι* M[2] in loco evanido 553 suspectus : *μ'* om. L P B Σ : in parenthesi *ἐπαινῶ* (‘*benigne*’) senem dicere putat Verrall, servi auxilium abnuentem : *με καὶ νῦν* Platt 554 *οὖν* om. L P 556 *ἐνδήσαντες* Pierson 557 *οἷς* Hartung (*ὡς ὕπαρνον πρόβατον* Σ): *ὡς* codd. *ἀπόλλυται* A 566 *σέβεις*] *γρ. ἄγεις* Σ 567 *ἄγουσ'*] *γρ. ἄγειν* M 568 *οὔτε* V : *οὐδὲ* rell. 571 *κτανεῖν* codd.

πίτνουσα γονάτων—χειρὶ δ' οὐκ ἔξεστί μοι
τῆς σῆς λαβέσθαι φιλτάτης γενειάδος—
ῥῦσαί με πρὸς θεῶν· εἰ δὲ μή, θανούμεθα
αἰσχρῶς μὲν ὑμῖν, δυστυχῶς δ' ἐμοί, γέρον.
Πη. χαλᾶν κελεύω δεσμὰ πρὶν κλαίειν τινά,
καὶ τῆσδε χεῖρας διπτύχους ἀνιέναι.
Με. ἐγὼ δ' ἀπαυδῶ γ' ἄλλος οὐχ ἧσσων σέθεν
καὶ τῆσδε πολλῷ κυριώτερος γεγώς.
Πη. πῶς; ἦ τὸν ἀμὸν οἶκον οἰκήσεις μολὼν
δεῦρ'; οὐχ ἅλις σοι τῶν κατὰ Σπάρτην κρατεῖν;
Με. εἷλόν νιν αἰχμάλωτον ἐκ Τροίας ἐγώ.
Πη. οὑμὸς δέ γ' αὐτὴν ἔλαβε παῖς παιδὸς γέρας.
Με. οὔκουν ἐκείνου τἀμὰ τἀκείνου τ' ἐμά;
Πη. [ναί,]
δρᾶν εὖ, κακῶς δ' οὔ, μηδ' ἀποκτείνειν βίᾳ.
Με. ὡς τήνδ' ἀπάξεις οὔποτ' ἐξ ἐμῆς χερός.
Πη. σκήπτρῳ δὲ τῷδε σὸν καθαιμάξω κάρα;
Με. ψαῦσόν γ', ἵν' εἰδῇς, καὶ πέλας πρόσελθέ μου.
Πη. σὺ γὰρ μετ' ἀνδρῶν, ὦ κάκιστε κἀκ κακῶν;
σοὶ ποῦ μέτεστιν ὡς ἐν ἀνδράσιν λόγου;
ὅστις πρὸς ἀνδρὸς Φρυγὸς ἀπηλλάγης λέχος,
ἄκληστ' ἄδουλα δώμαθ' ἑστίας λιπών,
ὡς δὴ γυναῖκα σώφρον' ἐν δόμοις ἔχων
πασῶν κακίστην. οὐδ' ἂν εἰ βούλοιτό τις
σώφρων γένοιτο Σπαρτιατίδων κόρη,
αἳ ξὺν νέοισιν ἐξερημοῦσαι δόμους
γυμνοῖσι μηροῖς καὶ πέπλοις ἀνειμένοις
δρόμους παλαίστρας τ' οὐκ ἀνασχετοὺς ἐμοὶ
κοινὰς ἔχουσι. κᾆτα θαυμάζειν χρεὼν

577 κλάειν L P 579 ἧσσων ut vid. L : ἥττων rell. *l* 581 ἁμὸν (sic) L : ἐμὸν rell. (σὺ τὸν ἐμὸν Lenting) 586 ναί delevit Lascaris δρᾶν ⟨γ'⟩ εὖ Lenting 589 γ' A : δ' L : om. V : θ' rell. V[2] A[2] μου] μοι L 590 κἀκ om. V 592 λέχους L P 593 ἄδουλα codd. et Σ : ἄφρουρα Lenting 599 ἀνασχετὰς V : -τῶς Naber

εἰ μὴ γυναῖκας σώφρονας παιδεύετε;
Ἑλένην ἐρέσθαι χρῆν τάδ', ἥτις ἐκ δόμων
τὸν σὸν λιποῦσα Φίλιον ἐξεκώμασε
νεανίου μετ' ἀνδρὸς εἰς ἄλλην χθόνα.
κἄπειτ' ἐκείνης οὕνεχ' Ἑλλήνων ὄχλον
τοσόνδ' ἀθροίσας ἤγαγες πρὸς Ἴλιον;
ἣν χρῆν σ' ἀποπτύσαντα μὴ κινεῖν δόρυ,
κακὴν ἐφευρόντ', ἀλλ' ἐᾶν αὐτοῦ μένειν
μισθόν τε δόντα μήποτ' εἰς οἴκους λαβεῖν.
ἀλλ' οὔτι ταύτῃ σὸν φρόνημ' ἐπούρισας,
ψυχὰς δὲ πολλὰς κἀγαθὰς ἀπώλεσας,
παίδων τ' ἄπαιδας γραῦς ἔθηκας ἐν δόμοις,
πολιούς τ' ἀφείλου πατέρας εὐγενῆ τέκνα.
ὧν εἷς ἐγὼ δύστηνος· αὐθέντην δὲ σὲ
μιάστορ' ὥς τιν' εἰσδέδορκ' Ἀχιλλέως.
ὃς οὐδὲ τρωθεὶς ἦλθες ἐκ Τροίας μόνος,
κάλλιστα τεύχη δ' ἐν καλοῖσι σάγμασιν
ὅμοι' ἐκεῖσε δεῦρό τ' ἤγαγες πάλιν.
κἀγὼ μὲν ηὔδων τῷ γαμοῦντι μήτε σοὶ
κῆδος ξυνάψαι μήτε δώμασιν λαβεῖν
κακῆς γυναικὸς πῶλον· ἐκφέρουσι γὰρ
μητρῷ' ὀνείδη. τοῦτο καὶ σκοπεῖτέ μοι,
μνηστῆρες, ἐσθλῆς θυγατέρ' ἐκ μητρὸς λαβεῖν.
πρὸς τοῖσδε δ' εἰς ἀδελφὸν οἷ' ἐφύβρισας,
σφάξαι κελεύσας θυγατέρ' εὐηθέστατα;
οὕτως ἔδεισας μὴ οὐ κακὴν δάμαρτ' ἔχῃς.
ἑλὼν δὲ Τροίαν—εἶμι γὰρ κἀνταῦθά σοι—
οὐκ ἔκτανες γυναῖκα χειρίαν λαβών,
ἀλλ', ὡς ἐσεῖδες μαστόν, ἐκβαλὼν ξίφος

602 δόμον M 603 τὸ σὸν V (τὸν V^{2}): utrumque B et Σ φίλον M V^{2} 606 ἀθρήσας A et ex ἀθροίσας factum L 609 οἶκον L 619–623 damnat Wilamowitz 625 εὐηθέστατον Nauck 626 ἔχῃς L Σ: ἔχεις rell. Σ alter 629 σὺ δ' ὡς Galen. v. p. 405, Clem. Strom. ii. p. 175

φίλημ' ἐδέξω, προδότιν αἰκάλλων κύνα,
ἥσσων πεφυκὼς Κύπριδος, ὦ κάκιστε σύ.
κἄπειτ' ἐς οἴκους τῶν ἐμῶν ἐλθὼν τέκνων
πορθεῖς ἀπόντων, καὶ γυναῖκα δυστυχῆ
κτείνεις ἀτίμως παῖδά θ', ὃς κλαίοντά σε
καὶ τὴν ἐν οἴκοις σὴν καταστήσει κόρην,
κεἰ τρὶς νόθος πέφυκε. πολλάκις δέ τοι
ξηρὰ βαθεῖαν γῆν ἐνίκησε σπορᾷ,
νόθοι τε πολλοὶ γνησίων ἀμείνονες.
ἀλλ' ἐκκομίζου παῖδα. κύδιον βροτοῖς
πένητα χρηστὸν ἢ κακὸν καὶ πλούσιον
γαμβρὸν πεπᾶσθαι καὶ φίλον· σὺ δ' οὐδὲν εἶ.

Χο. σμικρᾶς ἀπ' ἀρχῆς νεῖκος ἀνθρώποις μέγα
γλῶσσ' ἐκπορίζει· τοῦτο δ' οἱ σοφοὶ βροτῶν
ἐξευλαβοῦνται, μὴ φίλοις τεύχειν ἔριν.

Με. τί δῆτ' ἂν εἴποις τοὺς γέροντας, ὡς σοφοί,
καὶ τοὺς φρονεῖν δοκοῦντας Ἕλλησίν ποτε;
ὅτ' ὢν σὺ Πηλεὺς καὶ πατρὸς κλεινοῦ γεγώς,
κῆδος συνάψας, αἰσχρὰ μὲν σαυτῷ λέγεις
ἡμῖν δ' ὀνείδη διὰ γυναῖκα βάρβαρον,
ἣν χρῆν σ' ἐλαύνειν τήνδ' ὑπὲρ Νείλου ῥοὰς
ὑπέρ τε Φᾶσιν, κἀμὲ παρακαλεῖν ἀεί,
οὖσαν μὲν ἠπειρῶτιν, οὗ πεσήματα
πλεῖσθ' Ἑλλάδος πέπτωκε δοριπετῆ νεκρῶν,
τοῦ σοῦ δὲ παιδὸς αἵματος κοινουμένην.
Πάρις γάρ, ὃς σὸν παῖδ' ἔπεφν' Ἀχιλλέα,
Ἕκτορος ἀδελφὸς ἦν, δάμαρ δ' ἥδ' Ἕκτορος.
καὶ τῇδέ γ' εἰσέρχῃ σὺ ταὐτὸν εἰς στέγος
καὶ ξυντράπεζον ἀξιοῖς ἔχειν βίον,

636 τρὶς M B v γρ. A : τις rell. 637 σπορὰ v 639 κύδιον L P et Stob. 72. 14 : κύδιστον rell. 645 τίς . . . εἴποι Porson 647 Post h. v. lacunam Jacobs : non Σ 650 τήνδ' ὑπὲρ] τῆλ' ὑπὲρ Reiske : γῆν πρὸ γῆς Wecklein. Sed cf. 710 651 ἀεί codd. et lemma Σ : ἔδει Geel 654 δὲ Brunck : τε codd. (om. A)

τίκτειν δ' ἐν οἴκοις παῖδας ἐχθίστους ἐᾷς.
ἁγὼ προνοίᾳ τῇ τε σῇ κἀμῇ, γέρον,
κτανεῖν θέλων τήνδ' ἐκ χερῶν ἁρπάζομαι.
καίτοι φέρ'· ἅψασθαι γὰρ οὐκ αἰσχρὸν λόγου·
ἢν παῖς μὲν ἡμὴ μὴ τέκῃ, ταύτης δ' ἄπο
βλάστωσι παῖδες, τῆσδε γῆς Φθιώτιδος
στήσεις τυράννους, βάρβαροι δ' ὄντες γένος
Ἕλλησιν ἄρξουσ'; εἶτ' ἐγὼ μὲν οὐ φρονῶ
μισῶν τὰ μὴ δίκαια, σοὶ δ' ἔνεστι νοῦς;
[κἀκεῖνο νῦν ἄθρησον· εἰ σὺ παῖδα σὴν
δούς τῳ πολιτῶν, εἶτ' ἔπασχε τοιάδε,
σιγῇ καθῆσ' ἄν; οὐ δοκῶ· ξένης δ' ὕπερ
τοιαῦτα λάσκεις τοὺς ἀναγκαίους φίλους;
καὶ μὴν ἴσον γ' ἀνήρ τε καὶ γυνὴ στένει
ἀδικουμένη πρὸς ἀνδρός· ὡς δ' αὔτως ἀνὴρ
γυναῖκα μωραίνουσαν ἐν δόμοις ἔχων.
καὶ τῷ μὲν ἔστιν ἐν χεροῖν μέγα σθένος,
τῇ δ' ἐν γονεῦσι καὶ φίλοις τὰ πράγματα.
οὔκουν δίκαιον τοῖς γ' ἐμοῖς ἐπωφελεῖν;]
γέρων γέρων εἶ. τὴν δ' ἐμὴν στρατηγίαν
λέγων ἔμ' ὠφελοῖς ἂν ἢ σιγῶν πλέον.
Ἑλένη δ' ἐμόχθησ' οὐχ ἑκοῦσ', ἀλλ' ἐκ θεῶν,
καὶ τοῦτο πλεῖστον ὠφέλησεν Ἑλλάδα·
ὅπλων γὰρ ὄντες καὶ μάχης ἀίστορες
ἔβησαν εἰς τἀνδρεῖον· ἡ δ' ὁμιλία
πάντων βροτοῖσι γίγνεται διδάσκαλος.
εἰ δ' εἰς πρόσοψιν τῆς ἐμῆς ἐλθὼν ἐγὼ

659 δ' om. M O 660 κἀγὼ Wilamowitz σῇ καλῆι M 661 θανεῖν A : παύειν Brunck 664 τούσδε Brunck 665 στήσει L P (corr. *p*): θήσεις γρ. B 668–677 del. Hirzel (Habet vv. 672–677 Stob. 74. 24, et v. 671 Choerob. Epim. p. 80 aliique) 672 γ' om. V L : τ' B O στένει Dobree (σ*ένει primitus M. Cf. Hec. 807) : σθένει codd. et Σ 673 αὔτως primitus L : αὕτως rell. 677 γ' ἐμοῖς γ' V ἔμ' ὠφελεῖν Stob. 74. 24 679 ὠφελεῖς M P et fortasse primitus L 682 ἀίστορες L P : ἀνίστορες rell. 684 διδάσκαλον M

γυναικὸς ἔσχον μὴ κτανεῖν, ἐσωφρόνουν.
οὐδ' ἂν σὲ Φῶκον ἤθελον κατακτανεῖν.
ταῦτ' εὖ φρονῶν σ' ἐπῆλθον, οὐκ ὀργῆς χάριν·
ἢν δ' ὀξυθυμῇς, σοὶ μὲν ἡ γλωσσαλγία
μείζων, ἐμοὶ δὲ κέρδος ἡ προμηθία.
Χο. παύσασθον ἤδη· λῷστα γὰρ μακρῷ τάδε·
λόγων ματαίων, μὴ δύο σφαλῆθ' ἅμα.
Πη. οἴμοι, καθ' Ἑλλάδ' ὡς κακῶς νομίζεται·
ὅταν τροπαῖα πολεμίων στήσῃ στρατός,
οὐ τῶν πονούντων τοὔργον ἡγοῦνται τόδε,
ἀλλ' ὁ στρατηγὸς τὴν δόκησιν ἄρνυται,
ὃς εἷς μετ' ἄλλων μυρίων πάλλων δόρυ,
οὐδὲν πλέον δρῶν ἑνὸς ἔχει πλείω λόγον.
σεμνοὶ δ' ἐν ἀρχαῖς ἥμενοι κατὰ πτόλιν
φρονοῦσι δήμου μεῖζον, ὄντες οὐδένες·
οἱ δ' εἰσὶν αὐτῶν μυρίῳ σοφώτεροι,
εἰ τόλμα προσγένοιτο βούλησίς θ' ἅμα.
ὡς καὶ σὺ σός τ' ἀδελφὸς ἐξωγκωμένοι
Τροίᾳ κάθησθε τῇ τ' ἐκεῖ στρατηγίᾳ,
μόχθοισιν ἄλλων καὶ πόνοις ἐπηρμένοι.
δείξω δ' ἐγώ σοι μὴ τὸν Ἰδαῖον Πάριν
ἥσσω νομίζειν Πηλέως ἐχθρόν ποτε,
εἰ μὴ φθερῇ τῆσδ' ὡς τάχιστ' ἀπὸ στέγης
καὶ παῖς ἄτεκνος, ἣν ὅ γ' ἐξ ἡμῶν γεγὼς
ἐλᾷ δι' οἴκων τήνδ' ἐπισπάσας κόμης·
ἣ στερρὸς οὖσα μόσχος οὐκ ἀνέξεται
τίκτοντας ἄλλους, οὐκ ἔχουσ' αὐτὴ τέκνα.

686 θανεῖν O P 688 ταῦτ' εἶ M : ταυτὶ ut vid. M[2] 689 ὀξυθυμῇ Blaydes 694 τρόπαιον Iulian. Caes. p. 331 B 698 ἔχεις P 700 οὐδενός M V[2] O (γρ. οὐδένες M) 701 μυρίων P : μυρίοι Scaliger 702 βούλευσις v. l. in Σ 707 μείζω P (ἥσσω etiam Σ) : σοῦ . . . ἥσσω νομίζων Kirchhoff : νὴ τὸν 'Ιδαῖον, Πάριν Verrall, cl. v. 603 : fortasse καὶ pro μή legendum ἐχθρόν τε ποτε M 709 ἣν ὅ γ' Ludv. Dindorf : ἣν ὅδ' codd. (σὴ ὅδ' V) (ἥ νιν οὔξ Heimsoeth) 710 τῆσδ' P : τῶνδ' Musgrave. Sed cf. 650 711 στερρὸς M B O : στεῖρος rell. (gloss. ἀττικῶς V)

ἀλλ', εἰ τὸ κείνης δυστυχεῖ παίδων πέρι,
ἄπαιδας ἡμᾶς δεῖ καταστῆναι τέκνων;
φθείρεσθε τῆσδε, δμῶες, ὡς ἂν ἐκμάθω
εἴ τίς με λύειν τῆσδε κωλύσει χέρας.
ἔπαιρε σαυτήν· ὡς ἐγὼ καίπερ τρέμων
πλεκτὰς ἱμάντων στροφίδας ἐξανήσομαι.
ὧδ', ὦ κάκιστε, τῆσδ' ἐλυμήνω χέρας;
βοῦν ἢ λέοντ' ἤλπιζες ἐντείνειν βρόχοις;
ἢ μὴ ξίφος λαβοῦσ' ἀμυνάθοιτό σε
ἔδεισας; ἕρπε δεῦρ' ὑπ' ἀγκάλας, βρέφος,
ξύλλυε μητρὸς δεσμόν· ἐν Φθίᾳ σ' ἐγὼ
θρέψω μέγαν τοῖσδ' ἐχθρόν. εἰ δ' ἀπῆν δορὸς
τοῖς Σπαρτιάταις δόξα καὶ μάχης ἀγών,
τἄλλ' ὄντες ἴστε μηδενὸς βελτίονες.

Χο. ἀνειμένον τι χρῆμα πρεσβυτῶν γένος
καὶ δυσφύλακτον ὀξυθυμίας ὕπο.

Με. ἄγαν προνωπὴς εἰς τὸ λοιδορεῖν φέρῃ·
ἐγὼ δὲ πρὸς βίαν μὲν εἰς Φθίαν μολὼν
οὔτ' οὖν τι δράσω φλαῦρον οὔτε πείσομαι.
καὶ νῦν μέν—οὐ γὰρ ἄφθονον σχολὴν ἔχω—
ἄπειμ' ἐς οἴκους· ἔστι γάρ τις οὐ πρόσω
Σπάρτης . . . πόλις τις, ἣ πρὸ τοῦ μὲν ἦν φίλη,
νῦν δ' ἐχθρὰ ποιεῖ· τήνδ' ἐπεξελθεῖν θέλω
στρατηλατήσας χὐποχείριον λαβεῖν.
ὅταν δὲ τἀκεῖ θῶ κατὰ γνώμην ἐμήν,
ἥξω· παρὼν δὲ πρὸς παρόντας ἐμφανῶς
γαμβροὺς διδάξω καὶ διδάξομαι λόγους.
κἂν μὲν κολάζῃ τήνδε καὶ τὸ λοιπὸν ᾖ
σώφρων καθ' ἡμᾶς, σώφρον' ἀντιλήψεται·

716 τήνδε L 722 ἀγκάλαις M A V[2] 723 δεσμόν scripsi: δεσμά codd.: δέσμ' ἐγώ σ' ἐν τῇ Φθίᾳ L (sic): δεσμὰ μητρός Heath 727 γένος M L P γρ. V[2] Stob. 116. 37: ἔφυ A V B O 728 ὕπερ L 731 φαῦλον οὐδὲ A 733 καὶ γὰρ ἔστιν οὐ Hartung (duplex τις habuit Σ) 735 τήνδ'] τὴν Hermann ἐπελθεῖν οὖν B O

θυμούμενος δὲ τεύξεται θυμουμένων,
ἔργοισι δ' ἔργα διάδοχ' ἀντιλήψεται.
τοὺς σοὺς δὲ μύθους ῥᾳδίως ἐγὼ φέρω·
σκιὰ γὰρ ἀντίστοιχος ὣς φωνὴν ἔχεις,
ἀδύνατος, οὐδὲν ἄλλο πλὴν λέγειν μόνον.
Πη. ἡγοῦ, τέκνον μοι, δεῦρ' ὑπ' ἀγκάλαις σταθείς,
σύ τ', ὦ τάλαινα· χείματος γὰρ ἀγρίου
τυχοῦσα λιμένας ἦλθες εἰς εὐηνέμους.
Αν. ὦ πρέσβυ, θεοί σοι δοῖεν εὖ καὶ τοῖσι σοῖς,
σῴσαντι παῖδα κἀμὲ τὴν δυσδαίμονα.
ὅρα δὲ μὴ νῷν εἰς ἐρημίαν ὁδοῦ
πτήξαντες οἵδε πρὸς βίαν ἄγωσί με,
γέροντα μὲν σ' ὁρῶντες, ἀσθενῆ δ' ἐμὲ
καὶ παῖδα τόνδε νήπιον· σκόπει τάδε,
μὴ νῦν φυγόντες εἶθ' ἁλῶμεν ὕστερον.
Πη. οὐ μὴ γυναικῶν δειλὸν εἰσοίσεις λόγον·
χώρει· τίς ὑμῶν ἅψεται; κλαίων ἄρα
ψαύσει. θεῶν γὰρ οὕνεχ' ἱππικοῦ τ' ὄχλου
πολλῶν θ' ὁπλιτῶν ἄρχομεν Φθίαν κάτα·
ἡμεῖς δ' ἔτ' ὀρθοὶ κοὐ γέροντες, ὡς δοκεῖς,
ἀλλ' εἴς γε τοιόνδ' ἄνδρ' ἀποβλέψας μόνον
τροπαῖον αὐτοῦ στήσομαι, πρέσβυς περ ὤν.
πολλῶν νέων γὰρ κἂν γέρων εὔψυχος ᾖ
κρείσσων· τί γὰρ δεῖ δειλὸν ὄντ' εὐσωματεῖν;

Χο. ἢ μὴ γενοίμαν ἢ πατέρων ἀγαθῶν [στρ.
εἴην πολυκτήτων τε δόμων μέτοχος.
εἴ τι γὰρ πάσχοι τις ἀμήχανον, ἀλκᾶς

745 σκιὰ Σ et fere codd.: σκιᾶ M σκιᾷ γ. ἀ. ὢν Reiske: σκιᾶς γὰρ ἀντίστοιχον ὣς φ. ἐ. Cramer Anecd. ii. 463, cf. Et. Magn. p. 114 (qui om. ὣς) 747 ἀγκάλης V² 752 νῦν P 757 οὐ· μὴ codd., ut vid. δειλῶν V P: corr. V¹ 759 θεοῦ L P 761 δὲ κὀρθοὶ et ὡς σὺ V (τ' ὀρθοὶ V²) 763 αὐτὸς 'sine equitibus' Wilamowitz πρεσβυτέρων M B O 764, 765 Suspecti: habuit Stob. 51. 13 764 ἔμψυχος V: γρ. εὔψυχος V² ᾖ] ὢν Kirchhoff 765 τί λύει Brunck 770 γὰρ ἂν codd.: ἂν del. Dindorf

οὐ σπάνις εὐγενέταις,
κηρυσσομένοισι δ' ἀπ' ἐσθλῶν δωμάτων
τιμὰ καὶ κλέος· οὔτοι λείψανα τῶν ἀγαθῶν
ἀνδρῶν ἀφαιρεῖται χρόνος· ἁ δ' ἀρετὰ
καὶ θανοῦσι λάμπει.

κρεῖσσον δὲ νίκαν μὴ κακόδοξον ἔχειν [ἀντ.
ἢ ξὺν φθόνῳ σφάλλειν δυνάμει τε δίκαν.
ἡδὺ μὲν γὰρ αὐτίκα τοῦτο βροτοῖσιν,
ἐν δὲ χρόνῳ τελέθει
ξηρὸν καὶ ὀνείδεσιν ἔγκειται δόμων.
ταύταν ᾔνεσα ταύταν καὶ φέρομαι βιοτάν,
μηδὲν δίκας ἔξω κράτος ἐν θαλάμοις
καὶ πόλει δύνασθαι.

ὦ γέρον Αἰακίδα, [ἐπῳδ.
πείθομαι καὶ σὺν Λαπίθαισί σε Κενταύρων ὁμιλῆσαι δορὶ
κλεινοτάτῳ· καὶ ἐπ' Ἀργῴου δορὸς ἄξενον ὑγρὰν
ἐκπερᾶσαι ποντιᾶν Ξυμπληγάδων
κλεινὰν ἐπὶ ναυστολίαν,
Ἰλιάδα τε πόλιν ὅτε πάρος
εὐδόκιμον ὁ Διὸς ἶνις ἀμφέβαλε φόνῳ,
κοινὰν τὰν εὔκλειαν ἔχοντ'
Εὐρώπαν ἀφικέσθαι.

772 κηρυσσομένοις A : κηρυσσομένων Σ rell. : corr. Hermann 778 fortasse μὴ νίκαν ἔχειν om. L 781 ἁδὺ Dindorf 784 ὀνείδεσι νείκητε M O B (εἴκειτε B): νικᾶται Wilamowitz. Super hunc versum scripsit ἀφανές V 785 ταύτην bis P 787 κράτους A L 790 πεύθομαι Headlam σε Musgrave (et fortasse Haun.) : σε καὶ fere codd. : τε καὶ B : om. A Κενταύρων L P V² : κενταύροι M, σ add. M² : κενταύροις rell. fortasse recte 793 ἄξενον L² : ἄξεινον rell. 794 ποντίαν Ξυμπληγάδα codd. (συu. L : τὴν ποντ. B O) : corr. Hermann 796 τὸ πάρος Hermann 798 εὐδόκιμος codd. : corr. Hermann (ὁ delevit Matthiae) 799 ἀμφέβαλλε V B O 801 Εὐρώπαν L V² : εὐρώταν rell.

ΤΡΟΦΟΣ

ὦ φίλταται γυναῖκες, ὡς κακὸν κακῷ
διάδοχον ἐν τῇδ' ἡμέρᾳ πορσύνεται.
δέσποινα γὰρ κατ' οἶκον, Ἑρμιόνην λέγω,
πατρός τ' ἐρημωθεῖσα συννοίᾳ θ' ἅμα,
οἷον δέδρακεν ἔργον Ἀνδρομάχην κτανεῖν
καὶ παῖδα βουλεύσασα, κατθανεῖν θέλει,
πόσιν τρέμουσα, μὴ ἀντὶ τῶν δεδραμένων
ἐκ τῶνδ' ἀτίμως δωμάτων ἀποσταλῇ,
ἢ κατθάνῃ κτείνουσα τοὺς οὐ χρὴ κτανεῖν.
μόλις δέ νιν θέλουσαν ἀρτῆσαι δέρην
εἴργουσι φύλακες δμῶες ἔκ τε δεξιᾶς
ξίφη καθαρπάζουσιν ἐξαιρούμενοι.
οὕτω μεταλγεῖ καὶ τὰ πρὶν δεδραμένα
ἔγνωκε πράξασ' οὐ καλῶς. ἐγὼ μὲν οὖν
δέσποιναν εἴργουσ' ἀγχόνης κάμνω, φίλαι·
ὑμεῖς δὲ βᾶσαι τῶνδε δωμάτων ἔσω
θανάτου νιν ἐκλύσασθε· τῶν γὰρ ἠθάδων
φίλων νέοι μολόντες εὐπιθέστεροι.

Χο. καὶ μὴν ἐν οἴκοις προσπόλων ἀκούομεν
βοὴν ἐφ' οἷσιν ἦλθες ἀγγέλλουσα σύ.
δείξειν δ' ἔοικεν ἡ τάλαιν' ὅσον στένει
πράξασα δεινά· δωμάτων γὰρ ἐκπερᾷ
φεύγουσα χεῖρας προσπόλων πόθῳ θανεῖν.

Ερ. ἰώ μοί μοι· [στρ. α
σπάραγμα κόμας ὀνύχων τε δάι' ἀ-

802–866 Τροφ.] τρ. semper B, et vv. 828, 832, 836 etiam A : θερα. semper M V L, plerumque A, vv. 802, 866 etiam P : χορ. plerumque P. Cf. ad v. 851 802 κακῶν V : κακῶς L P 810 κτείνασα L B χρῆν Elmsley θανεῖν L P V[2] et H : versum del. Cobet 812 δμῶες φύλακες L 814 μέγ' ἀλγεῖ codd. : corr. Nauck 817 ἡμεῖς L P 819 εὐπειθέστεροι codd. (εὐτυχέστεροι B O) 821 ἀγγέλουσα M V B et primitus L 822 σθένει V L P : corr. V[2] 824 κτανεῖν A 826 κόμης L P

μύγματα θήσομαι.
Τρ. ὦ παῖ, τί δράσεις; σῶμα σὸν καταικιῇ;
Ερ. αἰαῖ αἰαῖ· [ἀντ. α
ἔρρ' αἰθέριον πλοκάμων ἐμῶν ἄπο,
λεπτόμιτον φάρος.
Τρ. τέκνον, κάλυπτε στέρνα, σύνδησαι πέπλους.
Ερ. τί δέ με δεῖ στέρνα [στρ. β
καλύπτειν πέπλοις; δῆλα καὶ
ἀμφιφανῆ καὶ ἄκρυπτα δε-
δράκαμεν πόσιν.
Τρ. ἀλγεῖς, φόνον ῥάψασα συγγάμῳ σέθεν;
Ερ. κατὰ μὲν οὖν στένω [ἀντ. β
δαΐας τόλμας, ἃν ἔρεξ'·
ὦ κατάρατος ἐγὼ κατά-
ρατος ἀνθρώποις.
Τρ. συγγνώσεταί σοι τήνδ' ἁμαρτίαν πόσις.
Ερ. τί μοι ξίφος
ἐκ χερὸς ἠγρεύσω;
ἀπόδος, ὦ φίλα, 'πόδος, ἵν' ἀνταίαν
ἐρείσω πλαγάν· τί με βρόχων εἴργεις;
Τρ. ἀλλ' εἴ σ' ἀφείην μὴ φρονοῦσαν, ὡς θάνῃς;
Ερ. οἴμοι πότμου.
ποῦ μοι πυρὸς φίλα φλόξ;
ποῦ δ' εἰς πέτρας ἀερθῶ,
⟨ἢ⟩ κατὰ πόντον ἢ καθ' ὕλαν ὀρέων,
ἵνα θανοῦσα νερτέροισιν μέλω;

828 Τροφ. v. ad v. 802 829 αἰ ter M A, quater rell. 832 πέπλους Reiske : πέπλοις codd. 833 sq. δεῖ om. B : responsio iam hic dubia, post 840 incertissima : delet στέρνα et πέπλοις Bothe, etiam δεδράκαμεν πόσιν Nauck 836 μόρον L 837 δαΐας] δὲ βιαίας ut vid. B : δικαίας O (δεμίας D) 838 ὦ M B L P Σ : ἁ V : ἡ A 841 τὸ ξίφος A 842 χειρὸς codd. 843 φίλα, 'πόδος Wilamowitz : φίλ' ἀπόδος M A V B : φίλος ἀπόδος L P 844 πληγάν L 845 θάνῃς codd. et Σ : θάνοις Musurus 848 ἐκ πέτρας Usener πέρας P O 849 ἢ add. Seidler 850 μέλλω P : μένω V[2]

Τρ. τί ταῦτα μοχθεῖς; συμφοραὶ θεήλατοι
πᾶσιν βροτοῖσιν ἢ τότ' ἦλθον ἢ τότε.
Ερ. ἔλιπες ἔλιπες, ὦ πάτερ, ἐπακτίαν
[ὡσεὶ] μονάδ' ἔρημον οὖσαν ἐνάλου κώπας.
—ὀλεῖ ὀλεῖ με· τᾷδ' οὐκέτ' ἐνοικήσω
νυμφιδίῳ στέγᾳ.
τίνος ἀγαλμάτων ἱκέτις ὁρμαθῶ;
ἢ δούλα δούλας γόνασι προσπέσω;
Φθιάδος ἐκ γᾶς
κυανόπτερος ὄρνις εἴθ' εἴην,
ἢ πευκᾶεν
σκάφος, ἃ διὰ Κυανέας ἐπέρασεν ἀκτὰς
πρωτόπλοος πλάτα.

Τρ. ὦ παῖ, τὸ λίαν οὔτ' ἐκεῖν' ἐπῄνεσα,
ὅτ' εἰς γυναῖκα Τρῳάδ' ἐξημάρτανες,
οὔτ' αὖ τὸ νῦν σου δεῖμ' ὃ δειμαίνεις ἄγαν.
οὐχ ὧδε κῆδος σὸν διώσεται πόσις
φαύλοις γυναικὸς βαρβάρου πεισθεὶς λόγοις.
οὐ γάρ τί σ' αἰχμάλωτον ἐκ Τροίας ἔχει,
ἀλλ' ἀνδρὸς ἐσθλοῦ παῖδα σὺν πολλοῖς λαβὼν
ἕδνοισι, πόλεώς τ' οὐ μέσως εὐδαίμονος.
πατὴρ δέ σ' οὐχ ὧδ' ὡς σὺ δειμαίνεις, τέκνον,
προδοὺς ἐάσει δωμάτων τῶνδ' ἐκπεσεῖν.
ἀλλ' εἴσιθ' εἴσω μηδὲ φαντάζου δόμων
πάροιθε τῶνδε, μή τιν' αἰσχύνην λάβῃς,

851 Τροφ.] ἄμεινον τῆς τροφοῦ εἶναι τὸ πρόσωπον Σ: χορ. M B L P: θερα. V A 854 πάτερ *l* P (lacuna in L): πάτερ μ' rell. 855 ὡσεὶ delevit Seidler μονάδ'] μ' ὀλκάδ' Jacobs (ἐπακτρίδα με pro ἐπακτίαν Brunck) ἐνάλου L (?): ἐναλίου rell. *l* 856 ὀλεῖ μ' ὀλεῖ με δηλαδὴ πόσις codd.: μ' del. Seidler, δηλαδὴ πόσις del. *l* οὐκέτι τᾷδ' (τῶδ' B) codd.: corr. Seidler 858 στέγᾳ L P: στέγῃ rell. 859 ἄγαλμα θεῶν Jacobs 860 δούλα δούλας A V B P Σ: δούλας δούλας M: δούλα δούλοις L γούνασι L P 862 posses conicere εἴθ' εἴην: ἀερθείην Seidler (εἴην Σ) 864 ἀκτᾶς fere codd. 866 Τροφ. B: θερα. rell. Vide ad 802 τότε λίαν *l* 870 φαύλης A V P

πρόσθεν μελάθρων τῶνδ' ὁρωμένη, τέκνον.
Χο. καὶ μὴν ὅδ' ἀλλόχρως τις ἔκδημος ξένος
σπουδῇ πρὸς ἡμᾶς βημάτων πορεύεται.

ΟΡΕΣΤΗΣ

ξέναι γυναῖκες, ἦ τάδ' ἔστ' Ἀχιλλέως
παιδὸς μέλαθρα καὶ τυραννικαὶ στέγαι;
Χο. ἔγνως· ἀτὰρ δὴ τίς ⟨σὺ⟩ πυνθάνῃ τάδε;
Ορ. Ἀγαμέμνονός τε καὶ Κλυταιμήστρας τόκος,
ὄνομα δ' Ὀρέστης· ἔρχομαι δὲ πρὸς Διὸς
μαντεῖα Δωδωναῖ'. ἐπεὶ δ' ἀφικόμην
Φθίαν, δοκεῖ μοι ξυγγενοῦς μαθεῖν πέρι
γυναικός, εἰ ζῇ κεὐτυχοῦσα τυγχάνει
ἡ Σπαρτιᾶτις Ἑρμιόνη· τηλουρὰ γὰρ
ναίουσ' ἀφ' ἡμῶν πεδί' ὅμως ἐστὶν φίλη.
Ερ. ὦ ναυτίλοισι χείματος λιμὴν φανεὶς
Ἀγαμέμνονος παῖ, πρός σε τῶνδε γουνάτων,
οἴκτιρον ἡμᾶς ὧν ἐπισκοπεῖς τύχας,
πράσσοντας οὐκ εὖ. στεμμάτων δ' οὐχ ἥσσονας
σοῖς προστίθημι γόνασιν ὠλένας ἐμάς.
Ορ. ἔα·
τί χρῆμα; μῶν ἐσφάλμεθ' ἢ σαφῶς ὁρῶ
δόμων ἄνασσαν τήνδε Μενέλεω κόρην;
Ερ. ἥνπερ μόνην γε Τυνδαρὶς τίκτει γυνὴ
Ἑλένη κατ' οἴκους πατρί· μηδὲν ἀγνόει.
Ορ. ὦ Φοῖβ' ἀκέστορ, πημάτων δοίης λύσιν.
τί χρῆμα; πρὸς θεῶν ἢ βροτῶν πάσχεις κακά;
Ερ. τὰ μὲν πρὸς ἡμῶν, τὰ δὲ πρὸς ἀνδρὸς ὅς μ' ἔχει,

878 del. Nauck 880 βημάτων Brunck: δωμάτων codd. (πρὸς ἠχὼ δωμάτων Verrall, cl. Hipp. 791) 883 δὴ τίς σὺ Barnes: δὴ τίς ὢν codd. (τίς ὤν γε *l*: δὴ (πῆ ut vid. V²) πυνθάνῃ τίς ὢν V² Haun.): τίς ὢν σὺ Valckenaer 884 κλυταιμνήστρας codd. γόνος B O 892 γουνάτων B P: γονάτων rell. 894 δ' om. L 897 τῶνδε Brunck 898 Χορ. praef. M B μόνη M B O L: corr. L¹ γυνὴ] κόρη L fortasse recte 899 Ἑλένης L: corr. *l* 900 Ἀκέστωρ A B P: γρ. ἀκέστων Σ (= θεραπευτῶν μόνον θεοῖς: fortasse voluit φοιβακέστων) 901 πάσχει B O κακά L P V²: κακόν A V B Σ

τὰ δ' ἐκ θεῶν του· πανταχῇ δ' ὀλώλαμεν.
Ορ. τίς οὖν ἂν εἴη μὴ πεφυκότων γέ πω
παίδων γυναικὶ συμφορὰ πλὴν εἰς λέχος;
Ερ. τοῦτ' αὐτὸ καὶ νοσοῦμεν· εὖ μ' ὑπηγάγου.
Ορ. ἄλλην τιν' εὐνὴν ἀντὶ σοῦ στέργει πόσις;
Ερ. τὴν αἰχμάλωτον Ἕκτορος ξυνευνέτιν.
Ορ. κακόν γ' ἔλεξας, ἄνδρα δίσσ' ἔχειν λέχη.
Ερ. τοιαῦτα ταῦτα. κᾆτ' ἔγωγ' ἠμυνάμην.
Ορ. μῶν εἰς γυναῖκ' ἔρραψας οἷα δὴ γυνή;
Ερ. φόνον γ' ἐκείνῃ καὶ τέκνῳ νοθαγενεῖ.
Ορ. κἄκτεινας, ἤ τις συμφορά σ' ἀφείλετο;
Ερ. γέρων γε Πηλεύς, τοὺς κακίονας σέβων.
Ορ. σοὶ δ' ἦν τις ὅστις τοῦδ' ἐκοινώνει φόνου;
Ερ. πατήρ γ' ἐπ' αὐτὸ τοῦτ' ἀπὸ Σπάρτης μολών.
Ορ. κἄπειτα τοῦ γέροντος ἡσσήθη χερί;
Ερ. αἰδοῖ γε· καί μ' ἔρημον οἴχεται λιπών.
Ορ. συνῆκα· ταρβεῖς τοῖς δεδραμένοις πόσιν.
Ερ. ἔγνως· ὀλεῖ γάρ μ' ἐνδίκως. τί δεῖ λέγειν;
ἀλλ' ἄντομαί σε Δία καλοῦσ' ὁμόγνιον,
πέμψον με χώρας τῆσδ' ὅποι προσωτάτω
ἢ πρὸς πατρῷον μέλαθρον· ὡς δοκοῦσί γε
δόμοι τ' ἐλαύνειν φθέγμ' ἔχοντες οἵδε με,
μισεῖ τε γαῖα Φθιάς. εἰ δ' ἥξει πάρος
Φοίβου λιπὼν μαντεῖον εἰς δόμους πόσις,
κτενεῖ μ' ἐπ' αἰσχίστοισιν· ἢ δουλεύσομεν
νόθοισι λέκτροις ὧν ἐδέσποζον πρὸ τοῦ.
πῶς οὖν τάδ', ὡς εἴποι τις, ἐξημάρτανες;
κακῶν γυναικῶν εἴσοδοί μ' ἀπώλεσαν,
αἵ μοι λέγουσαι τούσδ' ἐχαύνωσαν λόγους·

906 *ἐπηγάγου* P : corr. *p* 909 *ἄνδρα* A : *ἄνδρ' ἕνα* L : *ἕν' ἄνδρα* rell. (*δισσ' ἕν' ἄνδρ' ἔχειν* Grotius) 913 *συμφορά σ'* A V² : *συμφορᾶς* rell. 920 *μ'* om. P 923 *γε*] *μοι* Musurus 924 *τ'* Matthiae : *μ'* B O : *γ'* rell. *φθέγματ'* V 929 Oresti, 930 Hermionae tribuunt codd. : corr. Lenting *πῶς οὖν ἂν εἴποι τις τάδ'* Pflugk : *ὧδ' ἐρεῖ τις* Nauck

Σὺ τὴν κακίστην αἰχμάλωτον ἐν δόμοις
δούλην ἀνέξῃ σοὶ λέχους κοινουμένην;
μὰ τὴν ἄνασσαν, οὐκ ἂν ἔν γ' ἐμοῖς δόμοις
βλέπουσ' ἂν αὐγὰς τἄμ' ἐκαρποῦτ' ἂν λέχη.
κἀγὼ κλύουσα τούσδε Σειρήνων λόγους,
[σοφῶν πανούργων ποικίλων λαλημάτων,]
ἐξηνεμώθην μωρίᾳ. τί γάρ μ' ἐχρῆν
πόσιν φυλάσσειν, ᾗ παρῆν ὅσων ἔδει;
πολὺς μὲν ὄλβος· δωμάτων δ' ἠνάσσομεν·
παῖδας δ' ἐγὼ μὲν γνησίους ἔτικτον ἄν,
ἣ δ' ἡμιδούλους τοῖς ἐμοῖς νοθαγενεῖς.
ἀλλ' οὔποτ' οὔποτ'—οὐ γὰρ εἰσάπαξ ἐρῶ—
χρὴ τούς γε νοῦν ἔχοντας, οἷς ἔστιν γυνή,
πρὸς τὴν ἐν οἴκοις ἄλοχον ἐσφοιτᾶν ἐᾶν
γυναῖκας· αὗται γὰρ διδάσκαλοι κακῶν·
ἣ μέν τι κερδαίνουσα συμφθείρει λέχος,
ἣ δ' ἀμπλακοῦσα συννοσεῖν αὑτῇ θέλει,
πολλαὶ δὲ μαργότητι . . . κἀντεῦθεν δόμοι
νοσοῦσιν ἀνδρῶν. πρὸς τάδ' εὖ φυλάσσετε
κλῄθροισι καὶ μοχλοῖσι δωμάτων πύλας·
ὑγιὲς γὰρ οὐδὲν αἱ θύραθεν εἴσοδοι
δρῶσιν γυναικῶν, ἀλλὰ πολλὰ καὶ κακά.

Χο. ἄγαν ἐφῆκας γλῶσσαν εἰς τὸ σύμφυτον.
συγγνωστὰ μέν νυν σοὶ τάδ', ἀλλ' ὅμως χρεὼν
κοσμεῖν γυναῖκας τὰς γυναικείας νόσους.

Ορ. σοφόν τι χρῆμα τοῦ διδάξαντος βροτοὺς
λόγους ἀκούειν τῶν ἐναντίων πάρα.
ἐγὼ γὰρ εἰδὼς τῶνδε σύγχυσιν δόμων
ἔριν τε τὴν σὴν καὶ γυναικὸς Ἕκτορος,

933 λέχος H 935 βλέπουσαν Σ et fere codd. (βλέπουσ' ἂν P V² B²) 937 del. Nauck 939 φυλάττειν codd. 947 συμφέρει B O 948 αὑτῇ Σ (et Haun): αὐτῇ codd. (αὐτὴν H) 953 πόλλ' ἄγαν κακὰ gnomolog. Venetum 955 μὲν οὖν codd.: corr. Canter 956 γυναικείους B O P et H νόσους] γρ. φύσεις B 957–1211 deest B 959 νόμων P: corr. p

φυλακὰς ἔχων ἔμιμνον, εἴτ' αὐτοῦ μενεῖς
εἴτ' ἐκφοβηθεῖσ' αἰχμαλωτίδος φόνῳ
γυναικὸς οἴκων τῶνδ' ἀπηλλάχθαι θέλεις.
ἦλθον δὲ σὰς μὲν οὐ σέβων ἐπιστολάς,
εἰ δ' ἐνδιδοίης, ὥσπερ ἐνδίδως, λόγον,
πέμψων σ' ἀπ' οἴκων τῶνδ'. ἐμὴ γὰρ οὖσα πρὶν
σὺν τῷδε ναίεις ἀνδρὶ σοῦ πατρὸς κάκῃ,
ὃς πρὶν τὰ Τροίας εἰσβαλεῖν ὁρίσματα
γυναῖκ' ἐμοί σε δοὺς ὑπέσχεθ' ὕστερον
τῷ νῦν σ' ἔχοντι, Τρῳάδ' εἰ πέρσοι πόλιν.
ἐπεὶ δ' Ἀχιλλέως δεῦρ' ἐνόστησεν γόνος,
σῷ μὲν συνέγνων πατρί, τὸν δ' ἐλισσόμην
γάμους ἀφεῖναι σούς, ἐμὰς λέγων τύχας
καὶ τὸν παρόντα δαίμον', ὡς φίλων μὲν ἂν
γήμαιμ' ἀπ' ἀνδρῶν, ἔκτοθεν δ' οὐ ῥᾳδίως,
φεύγων ἀπ' οἴκων ἃς ἐγὼ φεύγω φυγάς.
ὁ δ' ἦν ὑβριστὴς εἴς τ' ἐμῆς μητρὸς φόνον
τάς θ' αἱματωποὺς θεὰς ὀνειδίζων ἐμοί.
κἀγὼ ταπεινὸς ὢν τύχαις ταῖς οἴκοθεν
ἤλγουν μὲν ἤλγουν, συμφοραῖς δ' ἠνειχόμην,
σῶν δὲ στερηθεὶς ᾠχόμην ἄκων γάμων.
νῦν οὖν, ἐπειδὴ περιπετεῖς ἔχεις τύχας
καὶ ξυμφορὰν τήνδ' εἰσπεσοῦσ' ἀμηχανεῖς,
ἄξω σ' ἀπ' οἴκων καὶ πατρὸς δώσω χερί.
τὸ συγγενὲς γὰρ δεινόν, ἔν τε τοῖς κακοῖς
οὐκ ἔστιν οὐδὲν κρεῖσσον οἰκείου φίλου.

Ερ. νυμφευμάτων μὲν τῶν ἐμῶν πατὴρ ἐμὸς
μέριμναν ἕξει, κοὐκ ἐμὸν κρίνειν τόδε.

961 φύλακας V (φιλίας H) μένεις M V : corr. V² 962 φόνῳ Lenting : φόβῳ codd. et Σ 964 σὰς οὐ μένων P 965 λόγους P 966 πέμψω codd. : corr. Heath 969 σε δοὺς εἶθ' P 970 πέρσοι L : πέρσει rell. 975 γῆμαι μ' M A V² ῥᾴδιον L V² (ῥᾳδίως Σ) 980 συμφορὰς Scaliger ἐνειχόμην Dindorf 981 σοῦ et ὄγκων V : σῶν et γρ. ἄκων V² 985 Χορ. praef. Hermann γὰρ] τοι Hermann 988 ἐμοὶ . . . τάδε V : corr. V² (τάδε A)

ἀλλ' ὡς τάχιστα τῶνδέ μ' ἔκπεμψον δόμων,
μὴ φθῇ με προσβὰς δῶμα καὶ μολὼν πόσις,
ἢ πρέσβυς οἴκους μ' ἐξερημοῦσαν μαθὼν
Πηλεὺς μετέλθῃ πωλικοῖς διώγμασιν.

Ορ. θάρσει γέροντος χεῖρα· τὸν δ' Ἀχιλλέως
μηδὲν φοβηθῇς παῖδ', ὅσ' εἰς ἔμ' ὕβρισε.
τοία γὰρ αὐτῷ μηχανὴ πεπλεγμένη
βρόχοις ἀκινήτοισιν ἕστηκεν φόνου
πρὸς τῆσδε χειρός· ἣν πάρος μὲν οὐκ ἐρῶ,
τελουμένων δὲ Δελφὶς εἴσεται πέτρα.
ὁ μητροφόντης δ', ἢν δορυξένων ἐμῶν
μείνωσιν ὅρκοι Πυθικὴν ἀνὰ χθόνα,
δείξει γαμεῖν σφε μηδέν' ὧν ἐχρῆν ἐμέ.
πικρῶς δὲ πατρὸς φόνιον αἰτήσει δίκην
ἄνακτα Φοῖβον· οὐδέ νιν μετάστασις
γνώμης ὀνήσει θεῷ διδόντα νῦν δίκας,
ἀλλ' ἔκ τ' ἐκείνου διαβολαῖς τε ταῖς ἐμαῖς
κακῶς ὀλεῖται· γνώσεται δ' ἔχθραν ἐμήν.
ἐχθρῶν γὰρ ἀνδρῶν μοῖραν εἰς ἀναστροφὴν
δαίμων δίδωσι κοὐκ ἐᾷ φρονεῖν μέγα.

Χο. ὦ Φοῖβε πυργώσας τὸν ἐν Ἰλίῳ εὐτειχῆ πάγον [στρ.
καὶ πόντιε κυανέαις ἵπποις διφρεύ-
ων ἅλιον πέλαγος,
τίνος οὕνεκ' ἄτιμον ὀργᾶς
ἂν χέρα τεκτοσύνας Ἐ-

991 ἢ πρέσβυς οἴκους O D et apogr. Par. 2818 : ἢ παιδὸς οἴκους P[2] : γρ. οἴκους τε τούσδ' V[2] (unde Haun. οἴκους τε τούσδε μ') : . . . οἴκους M A V L P μαθὼν] ἐκμαθὼν M 992 μετέλθῃ primitus A : μετέλθοι rell. 993 τόν γ' P 994 φοβηθεὶς M V L O corr. L[1] V[2]) ὃς codd. : corr. Lobeck 1001 δείξω Herwerden μηδέν' V : μὴδ' ἐν M : μηδὲν V[2] rell. 1002 πικρὸς M P : πικρὰν Cobet 1006 ἐμοί A L (θεοῦ Kirchhoff) 1007 ἐχθρῶν iniuria suspectum : habuit Σ καταστροφὴν reddit unus Σ 1009 ἰὼ codd. et Σ : corr. Musurus 1011 κυανέοις V[2] Haun. 1012 ἵπποισι codd. 1014 ὀργᾶς ἂν scripsi : ὀργάναν (ὀργάνναν L) codd. et Σ 1015, 1016 χέρ' Ἐνυαλίῳ τεκτοσύνας et v. 1024 βασιλῆς Bothe, meliore metro

νυαλίῳ δοριμήστορι προσθέντες τάλαιναν τάλαι-
ναν μεθεῖτε Τροίαν;

πλείστους δ' ἐπ' ἀκταῖσιν Σιμοεντίσιν εὐίππους
ὄχους [ἀντ.
ἐζεύξατε καὶ φονίους ἀνδρῶν ἁμίλλας ἔθετ' ἀστεφάνους·
ἀπὸ δὲ φθίμενοι βεβᾶσιν
Ἰλιάδαι βασιλῆες,
οὐδ' ἔτι πῦρ ἐπιβώμιον ἐν Τροί-
ᾳ θεοῖσιν λέλαμ-
πεν καπνῷ θυώδει.

βέβακε δ' Ἀτρείδας ἀλόχου παλάμαις, [στρ.
αὐτά τ' ἐναλλάξασα φόνον θανάτῳ
πρὸς τέκνων ἀπηύρα
θεοῦ. θεοῦ νιν κέλευμ' ἐπεστράφη
μαντόσυνον, ὅτε νιν Ἁργόθεν πορευθεὶς
Ἀγαμεμνόνιος κέλωρ, ἀδύτων ἐπιβὰς
κτεάνων, ματρὸς φονεὺς . . .
ὦ δαῖμον, ὦ Φοῖβε, πῶς πείθομαι;

πολλαὶ δ' ἀν' Ἑλλάνων ἀγόρους στοναχὰς [ἀντ.
μέλποντο δυστάνων τεκέων, ἄλοχοι δ'

1016 *δορὶ μήστορι* codd. *προθέντες* codd. (etiam V P): corr. Musurus 1020 *ἐζεύξατε* om. A 1025 *οὐδ' ἔτι* M: *οὐδέ τι* rell. 1026 *λάμπει* A: *λέλαμπτε* V 1027–1046 Stropham post antistropham transp. Musgrave 1027 *Ἀτρείδαις* P V^2 1030 *πρὸς*] *πρὸ* L: corr. *l* 1031 Punctum post *θεοῦ* posui, vulgo post *ἀπηύρα* *κέλευμ'* M V: *κέλευσμ'* rell. 1032 *Ἁργόθεν* scripsi: *Ἀργόθεν* codd. (*Ἄργος* V Haun.): *Ἄργος ἐμπορευθεὶς* Lenting 1034 *ἀγαμεμνόνιος* M: *-ειος* ut vid. rell. 1035 Fortasse *κτειάνων*: *ἵκετ'* (sc. *νιν, θεὸν*) *ὢν* Wilamowitz: *ἔκτανεν* Heath: sed aposiopesis videtur esse 1037 *ἀγόρους* Barnes: *ἀγορὰς* A: *ἀχόρους* V: *ἀγορὰς ἀχόρους* M^1: *ἀγοραὶ ἀχόρους* L P V^2 Haun. et primitus M: *ἀγοραὶ ἀγόρους* O D (*ἀνὰ τὰς ἀγορὰς τῶν Ἑλλήνων* Σ) 1038 *τοκέων* A V Σ: γρ. *τευχέων* Σ (sic): *λεχέων* Wilamowitz 1039, 1040 *ἄλοχοι δ' ἐξέλειπον* scripsi: *ἄλοχοι·* (*ἄλοχον·* L) *ἐκ δ' ἔλιπον* (*ἔλειπον* M B) codd. et Σ

ἐξέλειπον οἴκους
πρὸς ἄλλον εὐνάτορ᾽. οὐχὶ σοὶ μόνᾳ
δύσφρονες ἐπέπεσον, οὐ φίλοισι, λῦπαι·
νόσον Ἑλλὰς ἔτλα, νόσον· διέβα δὲ Φρυγῶν
καὶ πρὸς εὐκάρπους γύας
σκηπτὸς σταλάσσων ⟨τὸν⟩ Ἅιδα φόνον.

Πη. Φθιώτιδες γυναῖκες, ἱστοροῦντί μοι
σημήνατ᾽· ᾐσθόμην γὰρ οὐ σαφῆ λόγον
ὡς δώματ᾽ ἐκλιποῦσα Μενέλεω κόρη
φρούδη τάδ᾽· ἥκω δ᾽ ἐκμαθεῖν σπουδὴν ἔχων
εἰ ταῦτ᾽ ἀληθῆ· τῶν γὰρ ἐκδήμων φίλων
δεῖ τοὺς κατ᾽ οἶκον ὄντας ἐκπονεῖν τύχας.
Χο. Πηλεῦ, σαφῶς ἤκουσας· οὐδ᾽ ἐμοὶ καλὸν
κρύπτειν ἐν οἷς παροῦσα τυγχάνω κακοῖς·
βασίλεια γὰρ τῶνδ᾽ οἴχεται φυγὰς δόμων.
Πη. τίνος φόβου τυχοῦσα; διαπέραινέ μοι.
Χο. πόσιν τρέμουσα, μὴ δόμων νιν ἐκβάλῃ.
Πη. μῶν ἀντὶ παιδὸς θανασίμων βουλευμάτων;
Χο. ναί, καὶ γυναικὸς αἰχμαλωτίδος φόβῳ.
Πη. σὺν πατρὶ δ᾽ οἴκους ἢ τίνος λείπει μέτα;
Χο. Ἀγαμέμνονός νιν παῖς βέβηκ᾽ ἄγων χθονός.
Πη. ποίαν περαίνων ἐλπίδ᾽; ἦ γῆμαι θέλων;
Χο. καὶ σῷ γε παιδὸς παιδὶ πορσύνων μόρον.
Πη. κρυπτὸς καταστὰς ἢ κατ᾽ ὄμμ᾽ ἐλθὼν μάχῃ;
Χο. ἁγνοῖς ἐν ἱεροῖς Λοξίου Δελφῶν μέτα.

1041 ἄλλων εὐνάτορ᾽ M : ἄλλους εὐνάστορας V² 1042 δύσφρονες] δύσφρον᾽ P ἐπέπεσον Musurus (ἐπεγένοντο Σ) : ἔ*νεπον L (ἔννεπον *l*): ἔπεσον M A V B P: ἔμπεσον Lenting 1044 Φρυγῶν καὶ] Φρυγῶν γῆν H: ὁ Φρυγῶν σφιν olim Hermann : καὶ Φρυγῶν O D 1045 γύας L et H : γυίας rell. 1046 τὸν add. Hermann (ἀεικῆ Kirchhoff) 1051 εἰ] ἦ P 1054 οἷσπερ οὖσα codd. : corr. Wecklein 1055 φυγὰς ante τῶνδ᾽ habent A V 1056 φόβῳ φυγοῦσα Herwerden 1058 μῶν ἀντίποινα Nauck 1062 ἢ codd. 1063 σῷ Lobeck : σοῦ codd. 1065 ἁγνῶς Housman (ἁγνοῖς M V P)

Πη. οἴμοι· τόδ' ἤδη δεινόν. οὐχ ὅσον τάχος
χωρήσεταί τις Πυθικὴν πρὸς ἑστίαν
καὶ τἀνθάδ' ὄντα τοῖς ἐκεῖ λέξει φίλοις,
πρὶν παῖδ' Ἀχιλλέως κατθανεῖν ἐχθρῶν ὕπο;

ΑΓΓΕΛΟΣ

ὤμοι μοι·
οἵας ὁ τλήμων ἀγγελῶν ἥκω τύχας
σοί τ', ὦ γεραιέ, καὶ φίλοισι δεσπότου.
Πη. αἰαῖ· πρόμαντις θυμὸς ὥς τι προσδοκᾷ.
Αγ. οὐκ ἔστι σοι παῖς παιδός, ὡς μάθῃς, γέρον
Πηλεῦ· τοιάσδε φασγάνων πληγὰς ἔχει
Δελφῶν ὑπ' ἀνδρῶν καὶ Μυκηναίου ξένου.
Χο. ἆ ἆ, τί δράσεις, ὦ γεραιέ; μὴ πέσῃς·
ἔπαιρε σαυτόν. Πη. οὐδέν εἰμ'· ἀπωλόμην.
φρούδη μὲν αὐδή, φροῦδα δ' ἄρθρα μου κάτω.
Αγ. ἄκουσον, εἰ καὶ σοῖς φίλοις ἀμυναθεῖν
χρῄζεις, τὸ πραχθέν, σὸν κατορθώσας δέμας.
Πη. ὦ μοῖρα, γήρως ἐσχάτοις πρὸς τέρμασιν
οἵα με τὸν δύστηνον ἀμφιβᾶσ' ἔχεις.
πῶς δ' οἴχεταί μοι παῖς μόνου παιδὸς μόνος;
σήμαιν'· ἀκοῦσαι δ' οὐκ ἀκούσθ' ὅμως θέλω.
Αγ. ἐπεὶ τὸ κλεινὸν ἤλθομεν Φοίβου πέδον,
τρεῖς μὲν φαεννὰς ἡλίου διεξόδους
θέᾳ διδόντες ὄμματ' ἐξεπίμπλαμεν.
καὶ τοῦθ' ὕποπτον ἦν ἄρ'· εἴς δὲ συστάσεις
κύκλους τ' ἐχώρει λαὸς οἰκήτωρ θεοῦ.
Ἀγαμέμνονος δὲ παῖς διαστείχων πόλιν
ἐς οὖς ἑκάστῳ δυσμενεῖς ηὔδα λόγους·

1067 *πυθικὴν ἀνὰ χθόνα* A V (corr. V[2]) 1070 *ἰώ μοι μοι* L P V[2] *ἀγγέλων* M V (corr. V[2]) : *ἀγγέλλων* A O 1073 *προσδοκῶν* P 1074 *ἔχων* A V 1075 om. M O D 1076 *αἶ αἶ* M *τί δράσῃ σ'* V 1079 *εἰ καὶ*] *εἴ τι*, ut vid., Σ *ἀμυνάθην* M 1080 *χρῄζει* A V 1081 *γῆρας* V[2] 1083 *δ'* om. L P *μου* V (corr. V[2]) et fortasse primitus M 1084 *ἀκοῦστ'* M[2] : *ἀκοῦσ'* L P O

Ὁρᾶτε τοῦτον, ὃς διαστείχει θεοῦ
χρυσοῦ γέμοντα γύαλα, θησαυροὺς βροτῶν,
τὸ δεύτερον παρόντ' ἐφ' οἷσι καὶ πάρος
δεῦρ' ἦλθε, Φοίβου ναὸν ἐκπέρσαι θέλων;
κἀκ τοῦδ' ἐχώρει ῥόθιον ἐν πόλει κακόν·
ἀρχαί τε, πληροῦντές τε βουλευτήρια,
ἰδίᾳ θ' ὅσοι θεοῦ χρημάτων ἐφέστασαν,
φρουρὰν ἐτάξαντ' ἐν περιστύλοις δόμοις.
ἡμεῖς δὲ μῆλα, φυλλάδος Παρνασίας
παιδεύματ', οὐδὲν τῶνδέ πω πεπυσμένοι,
λαβόντες ᾖμεν ἐσχάραις τ' ἐφέσταμεν
σὺν προξένοισι μάντεσίν τε Πυθικοῖς.
καί τις τόδ' εἶπεν· Ὦ νεανία, τί σοι
θεῷ κατευξώμεσθα; τίνος ἥκεις χάριν;
ὁ δ' εἶπε· Φοίβῳ τῆς πάροιθ' ἁμαρτίας
δίκας παρασχεῖν βουλόμεσθ'· ᾔτησα γὰρ
πατρός ποτ' αὐτὸν αἵματος δοῦναι δίκην.
κἀνταῦθ' Ὀρέστου μῦθος ἰσχύων μέγα
ἐφαίνεθ', ὡς ψεύδοιτο δεσπότης ἐμός,
ἥκων ἐπ' αἰσχροῖς. ἔρχεται δ' ἀνακτόρων
κρηπῖδος ἐντός, ὡς πάρος χρηστηρίων
εὔξαιτο Φοίβῳ· τυγχάνει δ' ἐν ἐμπύροις·
τῷ δὲ †ξιφήρης ἆρ'† ὑφειστήκει λόχος
δάφνῃ σκιασθείς· ὧν Κλυταιμήστρας τόκος
εἷς ἦν ἁπάντων τῶνδε μηχανορράφος.
χὣ μὲν κατ' ὄμμα στὰς προσεύχεται θεῷ·
οἱ δ' ὀξυθήκτοις φασγάνοις ὡπλισμένοι
κεντοῦσ' ἀτευχῆ παῖδ' Ἀχιλλέως λάθρᾳ.

1096 κἂν V: corr. V² 1097 sic Verrall: ἀρχαί τ' ἐπληροῦντ' εἴς τε codd.: fortasse ἀρχάς τ' 1099 ἔταξάν τ' A P *l* δρόμοις M O 1100 παρνησίας codd.: corr. Ludv. Dindorf 1102 ἧμεν codd.: corr. Heath 1105 κατευξώμεσθα M: -ώμεθα P: -όμεσθα vel -όμεθα rell. 1110 ἐφέρετ' P: ἐφαίνετ' *p* 1114 ἄρ' codd., γρ. ἀεὶ V² vel *v*: ξιφήρη σαρὸν Verrall, cl. Ion 113 (vid. Hesych. σαρός): malim ξιφήρη χεῖρ' 1115 πυκασθείς O D ὧν] ὁ δὲ Nauck κλυταιμνήστρας codd.

χωρεῖ δὲ πρύμναν· οὐ γὰρ εἰς καιρὸν τυπεὶς
ἐτύγχαν'· ἐξέλκει δὲ καὶ παραστάδος
κρεμαστὰ τεύχη πασσάλων καθαρπάσας
ἔστη 'πὶ βωμοῦ γοργὸς ὁπλίτης ἰδεῖν,
βοᾷ δὲ Δελφῶν παῖδας ἱστορῶν τάδε·
Τίνος μ' ἕκατι κτείνετ' εὐσεβεῖς ὁδοὺς
ἥκοντα; ποίας ὄλλυμαι πρὸς αἰτίας;—
τῶν δ' οὐδὲν οὐδεὶς μυρίων ὄντων πέλας
ἐφθέγξατ', ἀλλ' ἔβαλλον ἐκ χερῶν πέτροις.
πυκνῇ δὲ νιφάδι πάντοθεν σποδούμενος
προὔτεινε τεύχη κἀφυλάσσετ' ἐμβολὰς
ἐκεῖσε κἀκεῖσ' ἀσπίδ' ἐκτείνων χερί.
ἀλλ' οὐδὲν ἦνεν· ἀλλὰ πόλλ' ὁμοῦ βέλη,
οἰστοί, μεσάγκυλ' ἔκλυτοί τ' ἀμφώβολοι,
σφαγῆς ἐχώρουν βουπόροι ποδῶν πάρος.
δεινὰς δ' ἂν εἶδες πυρρίχας φρουρουμένου
βέλεμνα παιδός. ὡς δέ νιν περισταδὸν
κύκλῳ κατεῖχον οὐ διδόντες ἀμπνοάς,
βωμοῦ κενώσας δεξίμηλον ἐσχάραν,
τὸ Τρωικὸν πήδημα πηδήσας ποδοῖν
χωρεῖ πρὸς αὐτούς· οἱ δ' ὅπως πελειάδες
ἱέρακ' ἰδοῦσαι πρὸς φυγὴν ἐνώτισαν.
πολλοὶ δ' ἔπιπτον μιγάδες ἔκ τε τραυμάτων
αὐτοί θ' ὑπ' αὐτῶν στενοπόρους κατ' ἐξόδους,
κραυγὴ δ' ἐν εὐφήμοισι δύσφημος δόμοις
πέτραισιν ἀντέκλαγξ'· ἐν εὐδίᾳ δέ πως
ἔστη φαεννοῖς δεσπότης στίλβων ὅπλοις·

1120 κρούει δὲ Scaliger (ex Σ ut putat) 1121 ἐξήρκει δὲ Kirchhoff 1123 ἰδεῖν] γρ. φανεὶς V² 1128 χειρῶν codd. 1130 καὶ φυλάσσετ' codd. : corr. V² 1132 ἦνεν (M et Σ M) : γρ. ἦμεν V² : ἤνυεν rell. 1133 μεσάγκυλοι A V *l* (corr. V²) 1134 σφαγῆς ⟨τ'⟩ Hervagiana secunda 1135 δ' om. A V (add. V²) φορουμένου L (sed ορ in rasura scripsit *l*) 1136 παιδός suspectum : ποδός M L O νιν L V² : μιν rell. 1137 ἀναπνοάς L 1140 τοὶ δ' A V (οἱ suprascr. V²) 1143 ὑφ' αὐτῶν Voss γρ. στεμπόρους V² 1145 ἀντέκλαγξεν εὐδία codd. (-κλαζεν L : -κλαξεν P) : corr. Reiske (ἀντέκλαζ'· Wecklein)

πρὶν δή τις ἀδύτων ἐκ μέσων ἐφθέγξατο
δεινόν τι καὶ φρικῶδες, ὦρσε δὲ στρατὸν
στρέψας πρὸς ἀλκήν. ἔνθ' Ἀχιλλέως πίτνει
παῖς ὀξυθήκτῳ πλευρὰ φασγάνῳ τυπεὶς
Δελφοῦ πρὸς ἀνδρός, ὅσπερ αὐτὸν ὤλεσε,
πολλῶν μετ' ἄλλων· ὡς δὲ πρὸς γαῖαν πίτνει,
τίς οὐ σίδηρον προσφέρει, τίς οὐ πέτρον,
βάλλων ἀράσσων; πᾶν δ' ἀνήλωται δέμας
τὸ καλλίμορφον τραυμάτων ὕπ' ἀγρίων.
νεκρὸν δὲ δή νιν κείμενον βωμοῦ πέλας
ἐξέβαλον ἐκτὸς θυοδόκων ἀνακτόρων.
ἡμεῖς δ' ἀναρπάσαντες ὡς τάχος χεροῖν
κομίζομέν νιν σοὶ κατοιμῶξαι γόοις
κλαῦσαί τε, πρέσβυ, γῆς τε κοσμῆσαι τάφῳ.
τοιαῦθ' ὁ τοῖς ἄλλοισι θεσπίζων ἄναξ,
ὁ τῶν δικαίων πᾶσιν ἀνθρώποις κριτής,
δίκας διδόντα παῖδ' ἔδρασ' Ἀχιλλέως.
ἐμνημόνευσε δ', ὥσπερ ἄνθρωπος κακός,
παλαιὰ νείκη· πῶς ἂν οὖν εἴη σοφός;

Χο. καὶ μὴν ὅδ' ἄναξ ἤδη φοράδην
Δελφίδος ἐκ γῆς δῶμα πελάζει.
τλήμων ὁ παθών, τλήμων δέ, γέρον,
καὶ σύ· δέχῃ γὰρ τὸν Ἀχίλλειον
σκύμνον ἐς οἴκους οὐχ ὡς σὺ θέλεις·
αὐτός τε κακοῖς [πήμασι κύρσας]
εἰς ἓν μοίρας συνέκυρσας.

1147 *ἐς μέσον* A (*ἐκ μέσον* V : corr. V²) 1148 *τι* Lenting : *τε* codd. 1150–1152 om. V : add. ipse in marg. 1150 *πλευρὰ* A : *πλευρὰ** P : *πλευρᾶ* rell. 1151 *αὐτὸν* ex *τ'* corr. *v* : ante illud *τ'* spatium vacuum fuit : *ὅνπερ αὐτὸς* Hermann. Verba nondum expedita : aut *ὅσπερ—ἄλλων* aut *ὡς - ἀράσσων* delenda putat Wilamowitz : *αὐτὸν* '*ipsum Achillem*' reddit Verrall 1153 *τίς * οὐ πέτρον* L 1154 *ἀνάλωται* codd. 1159 *γόους* A : *γέρον* V Haun. : *γρ. γόοις* V² 1160 *κοιμῆσαι* V² : *κομῆσαι* M 1161 *τοῖς Ἕλλησι* Dobree 1166 *ἤδη* om. P 1171 *ἔκυρσας* M O : *πήμασι κύρσας* del. Koerner : *πήμασι Κρίσας* Verrall 1172 om. O Haun. Habuit Σ

Πη. ὤμοι ἐγώ, κακὸν οἷον ὁρῶ τόδε [στρ. α
καὶ δέχομαι χερὶ δώμασί τ' ἀμοῖς.
ἰώ μοί μοι, αἰαῖ,
ὦ πόλι Θεσσαλία, διολώλαμεν,
οἰχόμεθ'· οὐκέτι μοι γένος, οὐκέτι [μοι τέκνα]
λείπεται οἴκοις·
ὦ σχέτλιος παθέων ἐγώ· εἰς τίνα
δὴ φίλον αὐγὰς βάλλων τέρψομαι;
ὦ φίλιον στόμα καὶ γένυ καὶ χέρες,
εἴθε σ' ὑπ' Ἰλίῳ ἤναρε δαίμων
Σιμοεντίδα παρ' ἀκτάν.

Χο. οὗτός τ' ἂν ὡς ἐκ τῶνδ' ἐτιμᾶτ' ἄν, γέρον,
θανών, τὸ σὸν δ' ἦν ὧδ' ἂν εὐτυχέστερον.

Πη. ὦ γάμος, ὦ γάμος, ὃς τάδε δώματα [ἀντ. α
καὶ πόλιν ἀμὰν ὤλεσας· αἰαῖ,
†ἒ ἕ· ὦ παῖ,
μήποτε σῶν λεχέων τὸ δυσώνυμον
ὤφελ' ἐμὸν γένος εἰς τέκνα καὶ δόμον
ἀμφιβαλέσθαι
Ἑρμιόνας Ἀίδαν ἐπὶ σοί, τέκνον,†
ἀλλὰ κεραυνῷ πρόσθεν ὀλέσθαι·
μηδ' ἐπὶ τοξοσύνᾳ φονίῳ πατρὸς
†αἷμα τὸ διογενές ποτε Φοίβου
βροτὸς εἰς θεὸν ἀνάψαι.†

1173 *ἰώ μοι μοι* P 1174 *χεροῖν* L *τ'* om. L P (*θ' ἀμοῖς* plerique: *τ' ἐμοῖς* A) 1175–1177 evanidi in M, rescripsit M[2] 1176 *πόλι* Musurus: *πόλις* codd. 1177 *οἰχόμεθ'* Ludv. Dindorf: *ὀχόμεθ'* V: *ᾠχόμεθ'* rell. *μοι τέκνα* om. P O: *οὐκ ἔστι μοι τέκνα* rescr. M[2] (*γένος οὐ τέκνα* Nauck) 1178 *λείπετ' ἐν* A L P 1179 *σχέτλια παθὼν* L P B *v* 1180 *φίλον* V et suprascr. A: *φίλων* rell. *βαλὼν* codd. 1182 *γρ. ἥπαφε* V[2] 1184 *οὕτως τ'* A *ὡς* om. L *μὲν οὖν κὰκ τῶνδ'* in rasura P[1] *οὕτω τ' ἂν ὡς Ἕκτωρ* Wilamowitz 1186 *ὃς*] *ὡς* V 1187 *ἀμὰν* scripsi: *ἐμὰν* codd.: *ὤλεσας ὤλεσας ἀμάν* Hermann 1188-1192 nondum expediti 1188 Fortasse *αἰαῖ· ὦ Λήδας παῖ* 1190 *ὤφειλ'* V L P *ἐμοὶ* Musgrave (*ἐμὸν* Σ) 1192 *Ἑρμιόναν* V[2] (-*ας* Σ) *τέκον* V: corr. V[2] 1195 *Φοῖβον βροτὸς* Barnes: fortasse *Φοῖβος βροτοῦ*

Χο. ὀττοτοτοτοῖ, θανόντα δεσπόταν γόοις [στρ. β
νόμῳ τῷ
νερτέρων κατάρξω.
Πη. ὀττοτοτοτοῖ, διάδοχα δ' ὦ τάλας ἐγὼ
γέρων καὶ
δυστυχὴς δακρύω.
Χο. θεοῦ γὰρ αἶσα, θεὸς ἔκρανε συμφοράν.
Πη. ὦ φίλος,
δόμον ἔλιπες ἔρημον,
ὤμοι μοι, ταλαίπωρον ἐμὲ
γέροντ' ἄπαιδα νοσφίσας.
Χο. θανεῖν θανεῖν σε, πρέσβυ, χρῆν πάρος τέκνων.
Πη. οὐ σπαράξομαι κόμαν,
οὐκ ἐμῷ 'πιθήσομαι
κάρᾳ κτύπημα χειρὸς ὀλοόν; ὦ πόλις,
διπλῶν τέκνων
μ' ἐστέρησ' ὁ Φοῖβος.

Χο. ὦ κακὰ παθὼν ἰδών τε δυστυχὴς γέρον, [ἀντ. β
τίν' αἰῶν'
εἰς τὸ λοιπὸν ἕξεις;
Πη. ἄτεκνος ἔρημος, οὐκ ἔχων πέρας κακῶν
διαντλή-
σω πόνους ἐς Ἅιδαν.
Χο. μάτην δέ σ' ἐν γάμοισιν ὤλβισαν θεοί.
Πη. ἀμπτάμενα

1197, 1200 Sic M V: ὀττο τοτοί L: ὀτοτοῖ ὀτοτοῖ P: ὀττοτοῖ bis 1197, semel 1200 A 1198 δεσπότην L P 1199 τῷ A V: τῶν rell. κατάρξομαι A V² L P 1200 διάδοχα δ' ὦ A: διάδοχα rell. et Σ V (evanida in V): διάδοχά σοι Wilamowitz 1202 δακρύω ut vid. L 1204 ἰὼ M L 1205 ἔλειπες M L P 1208 θανεῖν θανεῖν A: θανεῖν rell. χρῆν] χρὴ L ⟨τῶν σῶν⟩ τέκνων P: ⟨Πηλεῦ⟩ τέκνων O 1210 ἐπιθήσομαι ἐμῷ codd.: traieci. *Hinc rursus incipit* B 1211 χειρὸς B: χερὸς rell. 1212 ἐστέρησ' ὁ L: ἐστέρησε rell. 1214 ἰδόν M: corr. M² δυστυχῆ Schmidt 1217 διαντλήσομαι P 1218 γάμοισιν L² P: γάμοις rell.

φροῦδα πάντα, κεῖται

. . . . . .

κόμπων μεταρσίων πρόσω.
Χο. μόνος μόνοισιν ἐν δόμοις ἀναστρέφῃ.
Πη. οὐκέτ' εἶ, πόλις, πόλις,
σκῆπτρά τ' ἐρρέτω τάδε [ἐπὶ γαῖαν,]
σύ τ', ὦ κατ' ἄντρα νύχια Νηρέως κόρη,
πανώλεθρόν
μ' ὄψεαι πίτνοντα [πρὸς γᾶν.]

Χο. ἰὼ ἰώ·
τί κεκίνηται; τίνος αἰσθάνομαι
θείου; κοῦραι, λεύσσετ' ἀθρήσατε·
δαίμων ὅδε τις λευκὴν αἰθέρα
πορθμευόμενος τῶν ἱπποβότων
Φθίας πεδίων ἐπιβαίνει.

ΘΕΤΙΣ

Πηλεῦ, χάριν σοι τῶν πάρος νυμφευμάτων
ἥκω Θέτις λιποῦσα Νηρέως δόμους.
καὶ πρῶτα μέν δὴ τοῖς παρεστῶσιν κακοῖς
μηδέν τι λίαν δυσφορεῖν παρῄνεσα·
κἀγὼ γάρ, ἣν ἄκλαυτα χρῆν τίκτειν τέκνα,
ἀπώλεσ' ἐκ σοῦ παῖδα τὸν ταχὺν πόδας
'Αχιλλέα τεκοῦσα πρῶτον Ἑλλάδος.

1219 πάντα φροῦδα P (φρ. π. Σ) κεῖται] ἀνεῖται Musgrave post 1219 supple e.g. κεῖται ⟨δ', ὤμοι μοι, πάλιν γαπετέα⟩ 1220 κόμπῳ μεταρσίῳ codd. et Σ: corr. Reiske 1221 ἀναστρέφων V: corr. V[2] 1222 οὐκέτ' εἶ scripsi: οὐκέτι μοι A P: οὔτε μοι rell. (οὐκέτ' ἐστί μοι πόλις Hermann) 1223 ἐπὶ γαῖαν del. Kirchhoff: ἐρρέτω 'πι γᾶν Hermann: fortasse τά δ' ἐπὶ γαῖαν ἐρρέτω, tum deiicit sceptra histrio 1224 βύθια suprascr. A γρ. B 1225 πρὸς γᾶν del. Seidler 1227 κοῦραι V M[2] (κούρας M): κόραι rell. (κόρα B) 1228 γρ. λευκὸν B 1231, 1232 evanidi in M: rescr. M[2] et m (ἦλθον pro ἥκω m) 1231 σοι Platt: σῶν codd. 1233 δὴ L: σοὶ rell. 1234 συμφορεῖν A ἐπῄνεσα P 1235 ἄκλαυστ' (ἄκλαυτ' M B) ἐχρῆν codd. 1236–1249 om. B

ὧν δ᾽ οὕνεκ᾽ ἦλθον σημανῶ, σὺ δ᾽ ἐνδέχου.
τὸν μὲν θανόντα τόνδ᾽ Ἀχιλλέως γόνον
θάψον πορεύσας Πυθικὴν πρὸς ἐσχάραν,
Δελφοῖς ὄνειδος, ὡς ἀπαγγέλλῃ τάφος
φόνον βίαιον τῆς Ὀρεστείας χερός·
γυναῖκα δ᾽ αἰχμάλωτον, Ἀνδρομάχην λέγω,
Μολοσσίαν γῆν χρὴ κατοικῆσαι, γέρον,
Ἑλένῳ συναλλαχθεῖσαν εὐναίοις γάμοις,
καὶ παῖδα τόνδε, τῶν ἀπ᾽ Αἰακοῦ μόνον
λελειμμένον δή. βασιλέα δ᾽ ἐκ τοῦδε χρὴ
ἄλλον δι᾽ ἄλλου διαπερᾶν Μολοσσίας
εὐδαιμονοῦντας· οὐ γὰρ ὧδ᾽ ἀνάστατον
γένος γενέσθαι δεῖ τὸ σὸν κἀμόν, γέρον,
Τροίας τε· καὶ γὰρ θεοῖσι κἀκείνης μέλει,
καίπερ πεσούσης Παλλάδος προθυμίᾳ.
σὲ δ᾽, ὡς ἂν εἰδῇς τῆς ἐμῆς εὐνῆς χάριν,
[θεὰ γεγῶσα καὶ θεοῦ πατρὸς τέκος,]
κακῶν ἀπαλλάξασα τῶν βροτησίων
ἀθάνατον ἄφθιτόν τε ποιήσω θεόν.
κἄπειτα Νηρέως ἐν δόμοις ἐμοῦ μέτα
τὸ λοιπὸν ἤδη θεὸς συνοικήσεις θεᾷ·
ἔνθεν κομίζων ξηρὸν ἐκ πόντου πόδα
τὸν φίλτατον σοὶ παῖδ᾽ ἐμοί τ᾽ Ἀχιλλέα
ὄψῃ δόμους ναίοντα νησιωτικοὺς
Λευκὴν κατ᾽ ἀκτὴν ἐντὸς Εὐξείνου πόρου.
ἀλλ᾽ ἕρπε Δελφῶν εἰς θεόδμητον πόλιν
νεκρὸν κομίζων τόνδε, καὶ κρύψας χθονὶ

1240 πρὸς] ἐπ᾽ A 1241 ἀπαγγέλλῃ A L[1]: -γέλῃ (vel -γέλει) M V[2] P O et primitus L 1244 χρὴ L A *v*: χρῆν rell. κατοικίσαι L 1246 τῶν Barnes: τὸν codd. (τῶνδ᾽ O D) 1247 βασιλείαν V: corr. V[2] δ᾽ ἐκ] κἀκ L χρὴ] δεῖ A 1248 Μολοσσίαν codd. et Σ: corr. Lenting 1251 Fortasse τ᾽· ἐπεὶ θεοῖσι (τἀκείνης Lenting) 1252 προμηθίᾳ L P suprascr. V[2] 1254 ἐν τοῖς πολλοῖς τῶν ἀντιγράφων οὐ φέρεται ὁ ἴαμβος οὗτος Σ τόκος L P 1256 τε] σε V 1257 δμοῦ M B O 1258 θεᾷ] θεῷ L

ἐλθὼν παλαιᾶς χοιράδος κοῖλον μυχὸν
Σηπιάδος ἵζου· μίμνε δ', ἔστ' ἂν ἐξ ἁλὸς
λαβοῦσα πεντήκοντα Νηρῄδων χορὸν
ἔλθω κομιστήν σου· τὸ γὰρ πεπρωμένον
δεῖ σ' ἐκκομίζειν· Ζηνὶ γὰρ δοκεῖ τάδε.
παῦσαι δὲ λύπης τῶν τεθνηκότων ὕπερ·
πᾶσιν γὰρ ἀνθρώποισιν ἥδε πρὸς θεῶν
ψῆφος κέκρανται κατθανεῖν τ' ὀφείλεται.

Πη. ὦ πότνι', ὦ γενναῖα συγκοιμήματα,
Νηρέως γένεθλον, χαῖρε· ταῦτα δ' ἀξίως
σαυτῆς τε ποιεῖς καὶ τέκνων τῶν ἐκ σέθεν.
παύω δὲ λύπην σοῦ κελευούσης, θεά,
καὶ τόνδε θάψας εἶμι Πηλίου πτυχάς,
οὗπερ σὸν εἷλον χερσὶ κάλλιστον δέμας.
κᾆτ' οὐ γαμεῖν δῆτ' ἔκ τε γενναίων χρεὼν
δοῦναί τ' ἐς ἐσθλούς, ὅστις εὖ βουλεύεται,
κακῶν δὲ λέκτρων μὴ 'πιθυμίαν ἔχειν,
μηδ' εἰ ζαπλούτους οἴσεται φερνὰς δόμοις;
[οὐ γάρ ποτ' ἂν πράξειαν ἐκ θεῶν κακῶς.]

Χο. πολλαὶ μορφαὶ τῶν δαιμονίων,
πολλὰ δ' ἀέλπτως κραίνουσι θεοί·
καὶ τὰ δοκηθέντ' οὐκ ἐτελέσθη,
τῶν δ' ἀδοκήτων πόρον ηὗρε θεός.
τοιόνδ' ἀπέβη τόδε πρᾶγμα.

1268 *κομιστήρ* V Haun. (*-την* V^2): (*-τήν* etiam Σ) 1269 Fortasse *Ζηνί τοι* 1272 *κέκραται* P O *v* *τ'* om. A L 1272–1288 om. B 1276 *παύσω* M^2 Haun. *λύπης* V 1277 *πυλίου* A V : corr. V^1 1279 *οὕτω γαμεῖν* Wilamowitz *εἰ χρὴ γαμεῖν χρὴ τὰ ἔκ τε γενναίων γαμεῖν* Stob. 72. 3 1280 *ἐς* om. V L *βούλεται* A V^1 1282 *ζαχρύσους* Stob. l. c. *εἴσεται* L *δόμους* V: corr. V^2 1283 H. v. in loco ex Antiope citato habet Stob. 70. 10 *ἐς τέλος κακῶς* legens *καλῶς* V^2. Fortasse *οἱ ἐκ θεῶν* legendum Subscriptio evanuit in M. *τέλος 'Ανδρομάχης* A ('Α. τ. V) : *Εὐριπίδου τέλος 'Ανδρομάχης* L (τ. Εὐ. 'Α. P)

COMMENTARY

Gr. Gr.	Schwyzer, E., *Griechische Grammatik*, Munich, 1939–53.
GP	Denniston, J. D., *The Greek Particles*, ed. 2, Oxford, 1954.
KB	Kühner, R., *Ausführliche Grammatik der griechischen Sprache*, Part 1, ed. 3 (revised by F. Blass), Hanover, 1890–7.
KG	id., Part 2, ed. 3 (revised by B. Gerth), Hanover, 1898–1904.
LM^2	Dale, A. M., *The Lyric Metres of Greek Drama*, ed. 2, Cambridge, 1968.

Scene

THE scene of the whole action is in Phthia, a district of Thessaly, before the house of Neoptolemus (*οἶκον τόνδε* 21, 35), which forms the back scene and has a single central door. There is also a shrine of Thetis (*Θέτιδος εἰς ἀνάκτορον . . . τόδ'* 43, *δῶμα Νηρῇδος τόδε* 161) with an altar (162, 260), and a statue of the goddess is visible (246), perhaps near the door of the house (as often) and between it and the altar. The shrine need not be a separate building with an entrance; a panel set in the back wall might serve, with an altar in front of it, perhaps with steps on which Andromache sits. (We cannot of course say, with Hyslop, 'A. is discovered sitting as a suppliant', since there was no curtain and it must have been the established convention that actors took up in view of the audience whatever positions were required for the opening scene. Other entries, e.g. that of Hecuba in *Troades*, would show still greater reliance on the power of theatrical convention.) Andromache is thus a little to one side of the central door and confronts those who emerge from the house. If at 309 Menelaus enters on the spectators' left (as usual for those coming from the country), the grouping is best if the shrine and altar are on the right of the central door. Then later, when A. and her son are brought out of the house, they will naturally be shepherded to the left away from the altar and grouped there with Menelaus and his men, who are subsequently confronted by Peleus entering from the right at 547.

PROLOGUE: 1–116

1–116 form the *πρόλογος* in the technical sense, defined by Aristotle (*Po.* 1452^b19) as all that part of the play which precedes the entrance of the Chorus. It is here divided into three parts:

(*a*) 1–55 monologue by Andromache;
(*b*) 56–90 dialogue between A. and a slave woman;
(*c*) 91–116 a further short monologue by A. ending in a lament in

elegiacs (103–16), of which there is no other example in extant Greek tragedy.

1–55. It seems that Euripides sometimes experimented with anapaestic openings; so probably in *IA* and *Andromeda*.[1] All other extant plays, however, apart from *Rhesus*, begin with a monologue in iambic trimeters, and though this does not constitute the whole *πρόλογος* in the strict sense, except in *Supplices* and *Bacchae*, it is to this characteristic opening speech that both ancient and modern critics generally refer in speaking of the Euripidean prologue.

In contrast with Sophocles, who prefers a more naturalistic dialogue opening, Euripides does not attempt to disguise the fact that the actor is explaining to the audience the situation at the time when the action begins and the events leading up to it, and sometimes predicting for their benefit the course of the action. (He is in effect doing what an actor in Comedy can openly profess, as in Ar. *Vesp.* 54 *φέρε νυν κατείπω τοῖς θεαταῖς τὸν λόγον*, and *Eq.* 36.) But though these introductory monologues are to some extent cut to pattern, there is room for considerable variety. Some are rather prosaic and matter-of-fact summaries and provide some justification for the ancient critic who described Euripides as *ἐν τοῖς προλόγοις ὀχληρός* (*Vita* 3); others are much more emotional and dramatically extremely effective, not only in exposition but also in establishing the tone and atmosphere of the play. The prologue of this play is not one of the most striking, but it is no mere factual exposition: Andromache also stirs our feelings and moves us to pity and indignation.

When the prologue begins the audience would not all be quite ignorant of what was coming. Apart from the fact that plots were based on more or less well-known legends, the subject of the play and perhaps some indication of the plot would have been publicly announced at the Proagon just before the opening of the festival (see Pickard-Cambridge, *Dramatic Festivals*, pp. 65–6).[2] Moreover some news of forthcoming productions may have spread through the actors and chorus, who must have been rehearsing for some time before the festival began. But in the absence of programmes giving the scene and 'characters in order of appearance', we naturally find that the speaker of the prologue in Greek tragedy generally identifies himself in the first few lines and then or soon afterwards indicates the scene. In this play Andromache introduces herself in vv. 4, 5, but does not indicate the scene until v. 16. The fact that her opening apostrophe does not refer, as is usual, to the present scene, but to her birthplace, presents her at the outset as one whose thoughts keep turning to the past.

---

[1] See E. Fraenkel in *Studi in Onore di U. E. Paoli*, pp. 293–304.

[2] If the play was produced at Athens; but see Intr. pp. 19–21.

1. **Ἀσιάτιδος γῆς σχῆμα**: *σχῆμα* has been taken in two ways here, though not all editors seem to be quite clear about the distinction.

(i) The scholiast (henceforward *Σ*) refers to the basic sense of *σχῆμα*, the 'form or appearance' of something, and to the extension from this to the 'characteristic or proper form' (*φαμὲν "αὕτη ἡ οἰκία σχῆμα οἰκίας οὐκ ἔχει"*). It is then assumed that by a further extension it can denote something which is a characteristic feature of a larger whole, so that to call *Θήβη Ἀσίας σχῆμα* means that Asia is not Asia without Thebes;[1] hence *σχῆμα* is in effect equivalent to words like *καλλώπισμα*, *ἀξίωμα*. Most modern editors, without comment, give a similar sense to *σχῆμα* in this passage, but it does not seem to occur elsewhere. (In E. fr. 746 *Τευθράντιον δὲ σχῆμα Μυσίας χθονός* Jebb takes the use of *σχῆμα* to be similar to that in S. *Phil.* 223 *σχῆμα Ἑλλάδος στολῆς*: 'the fashion of garb worn by the people of Teuthrania in Mysia'; but lack of context makes interpretation doubtful.) The normal word for this was probably *πρόσχημα*, as in Hdt. 5. 28 *ἡ Μίλητος τῆς Ἰωνίης ἦν πρόσχημα*, but it is possible that the existence of this meaning of *πρόσχημα* might make the extended use of *σχῆμα* a little easier, or that E. wrote *πρόσχημα*, *γῆς* having been added as a gloss.

(ii) Some of the examples cited by Paley and Wecklein in fact illustrate the quite different periphrastic use of *σχῆμα*, e.g. E. *Alc.* 911 *ὦ σχῆμα δόμων*, *Hec.* 619 *ὦ σχήματ' οἴκων*, S. *Phil.* 952 *ὦ σχῆμα πέτρας δίπυλον*. LSJ and Allen and Italie, *Concordance*, take *σχῆμα* as periphrastic here, and the fact that the other three examples of *σχῆμα* in apostrophe are all of the periphrastic use is some support for this view. In that case, however, the whole phrase is equivalent to *Ἀσιᾶτις γῆ* which would naturally mean *Ἀσία*; cf. *IT* 396 where *Ἀσιήτιδα γαῖαν* is contrasted with *Εὐρώπαν*, and S. fr. 411 *Ἀσία μὲν ἡ σύμπασα κλῄζεται, ξένε, | πόλις δὲ Μυσῶν Μυσία προσήγορος*; whereas Andromache must surely be referring throughout to her birthplace. *γῆ* is indeed sometimes used as equivalent to *πόλις* (and vice versa), e.g. *Tro.* 868 *αὐτός τε καὶ γῆ δορὶ πεσοῦσ' Ἑλληνικῷ* (Paris and Troy), and *Ph.* 245 *ἑπτάπυργος ἅδε γᾶ* (Thebes); but in such passages *γῆ* stands alone or with an epithet that indicates its equivalence to *πόλις*, whereas here *Ἀσιᾶτις* points in a different direction. However, since there is no parallel for the use of *σχῆμα* in the sense of *πρόσχημα*, perhaps it is easier to suppose that the periphrastic phrase can be used with a more limited reference, and that Andromache looks back in memory to the familiar district and then more precisely to the walled town itself: 'O Asian land, O city of Thebes.'

πόλι: the vocative form is rare. Both in Comedy and Tragedy *πόλις* is regularly used in apostrophe—nine examples in Comedy, at least

[1] Strictly speaking the name is here singular, unlike *Θῆβαι* in Boeotia.

fifteen in Euripides, and five in Sophocles. There are a few certain examples of πόλι in Comedy, but perhaps only where this form is required by metre in lyrics; see Ar. *Ach.* 971 and fr. 110; other examples are doubtful. Neil on Ar. *Eq.* 273 (followed by Rennie on *Ach.* 27 and Starkie on *Ach.* 972) asserts that the vocative form is confined to Comedy. It is, however, the reading of L in this passage and of MSS. other than L in *Phoen.* 884, and in *Andr.* 1176 (lyric dactyls) Musurus's correction of πόλις to πόλι on metrical grounds is generally accepted. In this passage there are no metrical grounds, but on the whole Murray seems to be justified in following good MS. tradition and printing πόλι, since this form has the advantage of making clear, in the absence of an interjection, that the opening line is an apostrophe, and in VP a Byzantine scholar may have 'corrected' πόλι to the more usual πόλις. If πόλι is right here it may well be right in *Ph.* 884. The form πτόλι (MAB) may be due to a scribe who took the last syllable of Θηβαία to be short.

On the structure of the first sentence see note on 7.

Θηβαία πόλι: i.e. Θήβη, a town in Mysia described by Homer (*Il.* 6. 398) as ὑποπλακίη. Athenaeus 644 a quotes Demetrius of Scepsis (third century B.C.) as saying that there was a village called Plakos six stades from Thebes; presumably it was higher up, in the foothills of Mt. Ida. See Leaf, *Strabo on the Troad*, pp. 322–3, where he identifies Thebes with the modern Edremid. This town, the birthplace of Andromache and Chryseis, was sacked by the Greeks (*Il.* 1. 366–7), though the name at any rate survived in Θήβης πεδίον, the plain of Adramyttion (Hdt. 7. 42; Xen. *Hell.* 4. 1. 41); the name is also found in the plural in *Il.* 22. 479.

In *Il.* 6. 411–30 Andromache begs Hector not to risk his life again, pleading that her father and brothers have been slain and her former home destroyed, and when Hector is dead there will be no comfort left. 'You, Hector, are father and mother and brother to me, as well as my beloved husband.' For the Athenian spectator[1] and for us the memory of this passage increases the pathos of these lines, in which Andromache, some eight years after the death of Hector, recalls the town, now in ruins, as it was when she left it as a bride. Thus here, as elsewhere, Greek Tragedy gains enormously in emotional depth by its use of traditional material already charged with passion.

2. ἕδνον (ἔεδνον) is an Epic word generally used in the plural and originally denoting gifts from the prospective bridegroom to the bride's family, a modification of or survival from the actual purchase of wives. Bridal gifts in this sense, not dowry, is the normal meaning in Homer, though the practice of providing a dowry was not unknown

---

[1] See Pl. *Ion* 535 b, where Socrates mentions among the most famous and moving scenes in the Homeric poems τὰ περὶ Ἀνδρομάχην ἐλεινά.

in the Homeric world (*Il.* 9. 146–8; *Od.* 15. 20–1). ἕδνον in the sense 'dowry' goes back at any rate to Pind. *O.* 9. 10 and this is the meaning in the present passage, as in 153 and 873. Apart from A. *Pr.* 559 ἕδνον is found in Tragedy only in this play; in *Andr.* 1282 and elsewhere E. uses the Attic φερνή. In E. *Hel.* 933 most editors accept Hermann's restoration ἑδνώσομαι in the sense 'provide with dowry'.

3. τύραννον is here adjectival: 'Priam's royal home'. So 303 below; A. *Pr.* 761 τύραννα σκῆπτρα; S. *Ant.* 1169 τύραννον σχῆμα; E. *Hipp.* 843; *Med.* 1125; *Hel.* 478; also in prose, e.g. Thuc. 1. 122, 124 τύραννος πόλις. Other words in common use either as noun or adjective are γέρων, νεανίας (604 below), παρθένος, δοῦλος. For a good discussion of types of noun in Greek and Latin which are also adjectival see Wackernagel, *Vorlesungen über Syntax*, 2. 53–61.

ἑστίαν: the accusative without preposition for motion towards is common in Tragedy; see, e.g., in this play 403, 801, 1085, 1265. The use of case endings alone where Attic prose requires a preposition belongs in general to an earlier stage of the language and is an instance of the archaizing tendency in the language of Tragedy. Apart from the touch of remoteness provided thereby, a reduction in the number of small 'empty' words adds something to the weight and dignity of a line of verse.

In recently discovered papyrus fragments of a poem, probably by Sappho, we now have a finely imagined picture of the coming of Andromache to Troy, a vivid description invested with special pathos by our foreknowledge of the fate in store for Andromache, Hector, and the child that was to be born to them: Lobel and Page, *Poetarum Lesbiorum Fragmenta*, no. 44, and Ox. Pap. 10. 1232. See Page, *Sappho and Alcaeus*, pp. 63–74 for text, translation, and discussion. I quote a few lines from his translation: 'Hector and his comrades are bringing a dark-eyed girl from Holy Thebe and the streams of Placia, dainty Andromache, in ships over the salt sea. Many golden bracelets and purple robes . . . trinkets of curious pattern, and silver cups innumerable, and ivory.' The poem ends: 'The elder women all raised a joyous shout, and all the men cried a loud lovely song, calling on Paean, the Great Archer, the Fine Harper; and they sang of Hector and Andromache like to the gods.'

4. δάμαρ: this word is inadequately treated in LSJ. It is mainly a poetic word, occurring a few times in Epic and Lyric and often in Tragedy, especially Euripides (A. 4, S. 9, E. 102). The only examples in Comedy (Ar. *Th.* 912; Eup. fr. 158) are paratragic, and it is not used by prose writers, though it apparently survived in legal terminology, since it occurs three times in laws cited in the Orators (Lys. 1. 30; Dem. 23. 53; Ps.-Dem. 46. 18), where it denotes a lawful wife as contrasted with a παλλακή. In Tragedy δάμαρ is used as a poetic equivalent for the neutral γυνή in the sense 'wife', but generally with some stress on the dignity of a lawful spouse and mistress of the house, e.g. S. *OT* 930 and *El.* 663. In S. *Tr.* 428–9 it does not mean 'wife', but there is perhaps a special point in using of Iole a word that should properly have been used only of Deianira.[1] Euripides uses the word very freely and more indiscriminately as a poetic equivalent for *γυνή*; in one passage it is used of the relationship of Andromache and Neoptolemus (*Tro.* 659). But in E. too it is more commonly used when the married state is emphasized (it is particularly frequent in *Alcestis* and *Helena*), and in the present passage it probably means, together with *παιδοποιός*, 'to be his wedded wife and the mother of his children' and stresses the contrast with Andromache's present position as slave and concubine of Neoptolemus.

παιδοποιός: cf. Dem. 69. 122 *τὰς δὲ γυναῖκας ἔχομεν* (in the sense 'wives' and contrasted with *ἑταῖραι* and *παλλακαί*) *τοῦ παιδοποιεῖσθαι γνησίως ἕνεκα*. Cf. also Men. fr. 682; *Dysc.* 842.

7. Most editors rightly reject this line. It is omitted in Ox. Pap. 3. 449 of iii A.D. (though the genuine 29 and 37 are also omitted), and Σ comments that the line was added by actors who read *νῦν δὴ τίς ἄλλη* in the previous line and took *δυστυχεστάτη* as equivalent to a comparative. Page (*Actors' Interpolations*, p. 65) observes: 'The actors either misread their copies or were pleased to improve them.' If there was a deliberate addition it may have been made to round off sense and syntax at this point and provide the sentence with a main verb; but an opening vocative left in the air is not uncommon. For a good discussion and examples of such 'hanging vocatives', originally used as a hieratic form of address and secularized by Eur., see Fraenkel, *Agamemnon*, 3. 698. Here the vocative is followed by a rel. clause depending on *ὅθεν* followed by another rel. clause depending on *ἥτις* and containing the antithesis *πόσιν μὲν . . . αὐτὴ δὲ* . . . The opening sentences of *Alc.* and *El.* have a similar vocative followed by a single rel. clause.

Hermann retained line 7, adopting in 6 *οὔτις*, the reading of V, but this involves the correction *δυστυχεστέρα*. In *Od.* 11. 483–4 *σεῖο δ', Ἀχιλλεῦ, | οὔτις ἀνὴρ προπάροιθε μακάρτατος οὔτ' ἄρ' ὀπίσσω* the superlative is used like a comparative, but this example seems to be isolated: examples cited in KG 1. 22 are different: see Schwyzer, *Gr. Gr.* 2. 185, n. 1.

8. πόσιν μέν: *μὲν . . . τε* is not rare, but in this passage *παῖδα θ'* is an extension of the *μέν* clause, which is answered by *αὐτὴ δέ* in 12, husband and child being contrasted with herself. Some MSS. read *παῖδα δ'*, a natural corruption in the circumstances; cf. *Hipp.* 1239.

ἐξ Ἀχιλλέως: it is natural enough that the agent should be thought of as the cause or origin of action, but in fact *ἐκ* with genitive in this sense is limited to Ionic prose, a few examples in early Attic, perhaps due to Ionic influence, a few in Plato and Xenophon, who admit some

---

[1] See also Kamerbeek's note ad loc.

Ionic characteristics, and to Tragedy: e.g. Hdt. 3. 62 *προδεδόσθαι ἐκ Πρηξάσπεος*; Ant. *Tetr.* 1. 1 *τῶν ἐξ ἐμοῦ πραχθέντων*; Thuc. 1. 20. 2 *ἐκ τῶν ξυνειδότων μεμηνῦσθαι*; 3. 69. 1, 6. 36. 2; S. *Ph.* 335 *ἐκ Φοίβου δαμείς*; E. *Ph.* 1602 *χρῆν γὰρ θανεῖν νιν ἐξ ἐμοῦ*; Pl. *Phaedr.* 245 b. In Lys. 16. 18 *ἐκ δὲ τῶν κινδυνεύειν ἐθελόντων . . . ἅπαντες ὠφελεῖσθε* there is special justification: 'you all derive benefit from those who are prepared to take risks.' In Isaeus 6. 57. 2 *ἐξ ἡμῶν* is a mistake for *ὑφ' ἡμῶν*, arising from *ἐξ ὧν* in the same line; see Wyse ad loc.

9. θανόντα: 'slain by Achilles'. The passive of *κτείνω* is used in Homer and Herodotus but is not found in Tragedy apart from E. *Supp.* 700 *ἔκτεινον ἐκτείνοντο*, for special effect; *θνῄσκω* is normally used instead, e.g. S. *Ph.* 336 *ὁ κτανών τε χὠ θανών* 'the slayer and the slain'.

τίκτω: the present is often used with the sense 'to be the mother of'; cf. 24 below *ἐντίκτω*, 898, and *Ion* 1560 *ἥδε τίκτει σε*.

10. In her lament over the body of Hector (*Il.* 24. 725 ff.) Andromache has a premonition of the fate in store for Astyanax: *ἤ τις Ἀχαιῶν | ῥίψει χειρὸς ἑλὼν ἀπὸ πύργου, λυγρὸν ὄλεθρον* (734–5); this is envisaged as the revenge of someone whose brother, father, or son has been slain by Hector. The *Ilias Parva* (fr. 18 Kinkel) preserves a tradition that it was Neoptolemus himself who threw Astyanax from the walls. If E. knew of this he would naturally avoid it here. In *Tro.* 721 ff. the casting from the walls is proposed by Odysseus and voted by the Greek host. See H. Kern, 'Der antike Astyanax-Mythus und seine späteren Auswuchse', *Philol.* 75 (1918), 183–201 for a discussion of traditions concerning Astyanax, including the medieval version in which it was claimed, on the authority of Dictys and Dares, that he was not killed at Troy but survived to become the ancestor of the Bourbon kings of France.

Ἀστυάνακτ': according to *Il.* 6. 402 and 22. 506 Hector called his son *Σκαμάνδριος*, *Ἀστυάναξ* being a second name or title (*ἐπίκλησις*) given him by the Trojans out of compliment to his father, *οἶος γὰρ ἐρύετο Ἴλιον Ἕκτωρ*.

11. Nauck suspected this line of being spurious and Wecklein comments that it is superfluous and trailing, but both keep it in their text. If it is not genuine, it might possibly have been added, on the model of 58, by an actor who thought it an improvement in clarity; but we should certainly be cautious about ejecting a line which is in our MSS., including the papyrus fragment referred to on v. 7 above, where there is no external evidence of interpolation and nothing positively objectionable about the line in itself or in relation to its context, merely because the sense of the passage is complete without it. Though the line is undistinguished and certainly has rather a trailing effect at the end of an already long and loosely constructed sentence, it is not without point, since, as von Arnim observed, Andromache might even be expected to refer here to the capture of Troy as the background to her personal tragedy, as she does in her elegiac lament 105–6.

Τροίας . . . πέδον: cf. 58 *τὸ Τροίας . . . πέδον*; *Or.* 522 *εἰς Τροίας πέδον*; *Hel.* 57 *τὸ κλεινὸν πέδον Σπάρτης*; S. *Phil.* 1435 *ἑλεῖν τὸ Τροίας πεδίον*. No doubt the phrase should strictly mean the town with its territory, as Jebb takes it, but it may have come to be little more than a periphrasis for the town itself.

13. οἴκων νομισθεῖσ': possessive gen. 'I, though once regarded as belonging to'; cf. E. *Hcld.* 68 *τούσδε . . . ἄξω νομίζων, οὗπέρ εἰσ', Εὐρυσθέως*; S. *Ant.* 738 *οὐ τοῦ κρατοῦντος ἡ πόλις νομίζεται;* and *OC* 38 *τοῦ θεῶν νομίζεται;*

14. The word *νησιώτης* appears to be used here and sometimes elsewhere as a term of disparagement, presumably because in general islands would be poorer in resources than mainland kingdoms. Cf. E. *Hcld.* 84 *οὐ νησιώτην, ὦ ξένοι, τρίβω βίον, | ἀλλ' ἐκ Μυκηνῶν σὴν ἀφίγμεθα χθόνα*; *Rhes.* 701 *νησιώτην σποράδα κέκτηται βίον*. For disparaging references to islanders in the Orators cf. Dem. 13. 34 *εἰ μὲν οὖν Σιφνίοις ἢ Κυθνίοις ἤ τισιν ἄλλοις τοιούτοις οὖσι συνήδειν ὑμῖν, ἔλαττον φρονεῖν συνεβούλευον ἄν· ἐπειδὴ δὲ ἔστ' Ἀθηναῖοι, τὸ τὴν δύναμιν παρασκευάσασθαι παραινῶ*; and 23. 211. Neoptolemus' mother Deidamia was a daughter of Lycomedes, king of Scyros, and he was born and brought up on that island until, after the death of Achilles, Odysseus came to take him to Troy. See 210 below and *Il.* 19. 326 *ἠὲ τὸν ὃς Σκύρῳ μοι ἔνι τρέφεται φίλος υἱός*.

Νεοπτολέμῳ: the first two syllables are scanned as one long by synizesis. So in *Tro.* 1126, S. *Phil.* 4, and 241; in *Or.* 1655 the word is scanned as five syllables. The same variation occurs with *Θεοκλύμενος*, on which see Dale on *Hel.* 9. Though N. is repeatedly mentioned in this play the name occurs only here, partly on metrical grounds, but periphrases reminding us of his lineage are sometimes dramatically effective.

δορὸς γέρας: in 155 Hermione contemptuously refers to her as *δούλη καὶ δορίκτητος γυνή*.

15. In *Tro.* 247 ff. a Greek herald announces to Hecuba the fate of the chief Trojan captives. Hecuba herself has been allotted as slave to Odysseus, Cassandra to Agamemnon, Andromache to Neoptolemus. For Andromache's feelings, as imagined by Euripides some years after the composition of the *Andromache*, see *Tro.* 657–72.

16–21. There is some doubt about the details of topography. *σύγχορτος*, lit. 'with the grass joining', was used in the sense 'bordering on' (Schol. *γείτονα, συνόρα*). In A. *Supp.* 5 *Δίαν . . . χθόνα σύγχορτον Συρίᾳ* Tucker observed that *σύγχορτος* implies the running of territories into each other without a marked natural border such as a river or mountain range; cf. E. fr. 179 *Οἰνόῃ | σύγχορτα ναίω πεδία ταῖς τ' Ἐλευθεραῖς* 'plains extending from Oenoe to Eleutherae'. In our passage the force of *σύγχορτα* is probably similar (though instead of datives we have in 16 genitives depending grammatically on *πεδία*), and here too we might expect the names of two towns. The scholiast on 16 comments *Θεσσαλίας πόλεις αὗται* and on 17 *μεταξὺ δὲ τούτων τῶν* *πόλεων ἐστὶ τὸ Θετίδειον*; but whether Phthia (later Phthiotis) was the name of a town as well as of a district seems to have been disputed in antiquity. Thus Stephanus, *Thes.* s.v.: *πόλις καὶ μοῖρα Θετταλίας· Παρμενίσκος δὲ χώραν αὐτὴν φησι καὶ οὐ πόλιν· οὐκ ὀρθῶς*. For different views see Bursian, *Geogr. v. Griech.* 1. 77; Kretschmer, *Glotta*, 4 (1913), 307; Stählin, *Das hellenische Thessalien*, p. 136.

τῇσδε implies that Phthia, whether town or district, is not far from the house of Neoptolemus in which A. is living. Perhaps N. is assumed to have taken over the house (*οἶκον ἔσχε τόνδε*) to which Peleus had brought Thetis as his bride, and this presumably forms the back scene for the play. It is apparently in a quiet country place (18 *χωρὶς ἀνθρώπων . . . φεύγουσ' ὅμιλον*).

For **Θετίδειον** LSJ gives 'temple of Thetis', citing this passage, with Strabo 9. 5. 6 and Polyb. 18. 20. 6. If this were the meaning here the words *θεᾶς χάριν νυμφευμάτων* as justification for the name would be superfluous, and in any case *αὐδᾷ* governs *νιν*, which would naturally refer to the *σύγχορτα πεδία*, evidently a locality wider than the shrine with its *τέμενος*, which in 253 (*λείψεις τόδ' ἁγνὸν τέμενος*) denotes the ground immediately about the altar; when A. leaves it she is still 'on stage' (425 ff.). The schol. on *Andr.* 17 (and on Pind. *N.* 4. 81) quotes Pherecydes as saying that *τὸ Θετίδειον* is a *πόλις Θεσσαλίας*, and it may be a place name in Polybius and Strabo, but a village rather than a town. In our passage the context suggests that originally at any rate it was merely a district, or perhaps the royal house and grounds, called *Θετίδειον* because the goddess had once been its mistress and her shrine had been set up there.

These details have dramatic relevance in that they prepare for the important part that Peleus is to play and for the appearance of Thetis as *dea ex machina* in 1231 ff., where in her first line the words *χάριν σοι . . . νυμφευμάτων* echo v. 20.

17. ἡ θαλασσία: cf. *ἁλία* (108), *ἐναλία* (253), and on Thetis as a sea goddess see Webster, *From Homer to Mycenae*, pp. 126–7.

18. Πηλεῖ ξυνῴκει: other mortals besides Peleus lay with goddesses and had children by them; for a list see Hesiod, *Theogony* 963–1020. For some, however, e.g. Aphrodite and Anchises, the union was temporary and secret, and certainly Cadmus alone seems to have shared with Peleus the special honour of a wedding ceremony in the presence of the assembled gods, with the Muses themselves to sing the marriage song (Pindar *P.* 3. 89 ff.). Some passages in Homer would naturally imply that thereafter Thetis lived with Peleus as his wife and reared their son, Achilles. Thus in *Il.* 1. 396 Achilles says: 'Often have I heard you in my father's halls declaring that once you saved the son of Cronos . . .'; in *Il.* 18. 55 ff. (= 437 ff.) Thetis laments that Achilles is doomed to perish so that she will never welcome back to the house of Peleus the child she bore and reared and sent off to Troy. On the other hand when Achilles appeals to his mother she hears him 'from the depths of the sea, sitting beside her aged father' (*Il.* 1. 358, 18. 36), and Iris finds her 'in a hollow cave with other sea goddesses about her' (*Il.* 24. 83). At any rate Homer, as the scholiast on *Il.* 18. 60 observes, seems to know nothing of the legend that Thetis in anger left the house of Peleus soon after the marriage. This legend may go back to the time of Hesiod (Kinkel, *Ep. Gr.*, p. 83), is evidently alluded to in the *Ἀχιλλέως Ἐρασταί* of Sophocles (fr. 151), and to judge by the reference in Ar. *Nub.* 1068 must have been well known in the fifth century. A tradition that Achilles was reared not by Thetis but by Philyra and her son, Cheiron the Centaur, goes back at any rate to Pindar (*Nem.* 3. 43 ff.), and is followed by E. in *IA* 708–9.

In this passage Thetis is thought of as sharing for a time the life of Peleus, though the past tense and her own words when she appears as *dea ex machina* in 1231 *χάριν σοι τῶν πάρος νυμφευμάτων ἥκω . . . λιποῦσα Νηρέως δόμους* imply that her marriage and sojourn with Peleus are things of the past. (For discussion of different traditions about the Peleus–Thetis legend see A. Lesky's article 'Thetis' in P–W, supplemented by his paper 'Peleus u. Thetis im frühen Epos', *SIFC* 27–8 (1956), 216–26, and F. Jouan, *Euripide et les légendes des chants cypriens*, pp. 55–92, with references to other literature.)

χωρὶς ἀνθρώπων . . . φεύγουσ' ὅμιλον: for similar emphasis by iteration cf. S. *Phil.* 31 *ὁρῶ κενὴν οἴκησιν ἀνθρώπων δίχα*. The emphatic expression may be meant to indicate that only in seclusion could a goddess consort with a mortal.

20. θεᾶς: scan as a single long syllable, as often in Tragedy; cf. 258, 260, 270, 311. So also *Πηλέᾱ* in 22.

22, 23. In the Heroic Age physical as well as mental vigour might be needed in the exercise of kingship, and an ageing monarch might find it necessary to abdicate in favour of his heir or might be forcibly removed. Something like this is implied in several passages in Epic and Tragedy, though it was not of course inevitable, as can be seen from the continued authority of Nestor and Priam. Thus in the *Bacchae* Pentheus, grandson of Cadmus, holds the sovereignty and protects his grandfather from wrongs or slights (*Ba.* 1320–2). In the *Odyssey* we find that Laertes, father of Odysseus, had apparently resigned the royal power to his son at some time before the Trojan Expedition, and during the long absence of Odysseus there seems to be no question of his resuming it or in any way protecting Penelope and Telemachus. In *Od.* 11. 494–7 Achilles fears that in his absence his father Peleus may be dishonoured:

> *εἰπὲ δέ μοι Πηλῆος ἀμύμονος εἴ τι πέπυσσαι,*
> *ἢ ἔτ' ἔχει τιμὴν πολέσιν μετὰ Μυρμιδόνεσσιν,*
> *ἦ μιν ἀτιμάζουσιν ἀν' Ἑλλάδα τε Φθίην τε,*
> *οὕνεκά μιν κατὰ γῆρας ἔχει χεῖράς τε πόδας τε.*

In *Andr.* 23 *οὐ θέλων* implies that Neoptolemus might have urged or driven the old Peleus to resign the sceptre, but in fact he allowed him to reign in Pharsalus, while he himself withdrew to Phthia, perhaps to rule over that district. In the *Alcestis*, Admetus is king in Pherae though his father, Pheres, is living.*

24. ἄρσεν' ἐντίκτω: Barnes conjectured *ἄρσεν' ἕνα τίκτω* on the strength of the scholiast's comment that Euripides alone assigns one child to Andromache by Neoptolemus, whereas others speak of three boys and a girl. But this is not an adequate reason for emending the text; there is no reason why in this context Andromache should stress the fact that it is an only child. She does so in 47 below, where it is dramatically effective to draw attention to this point. For the compound cf. E. *Hipp.* 642 *τὸ γὰρ κακοῦργον . . . ἐντίκτει Κύπρις* | *ἐν ταῖς σοφαῖσιν*, Thuc. 3. 104 *προεῖπον μήτε ἐναποθνῄσκειν ἐν τῇ νήσῳ μήτε ἐντίκτειν.* Barnes's conjecture is also doubtful on metrical grounds, since resolution here is always part of a word of three or more syllables; see Snell, *Gr. Met.*, p. 10.

25. πλαθεῖσ': cf. A. *Pr.* 897 *μηδὲ πλαθείην γαμέτᾳ τινὶ τῶν ἐξ οὐρανοῦ*; E. *Tro.* 203 *λέκτροις πλαθεῖσ' Ἑλλήνων*; Bacchyl. 16. 35 *πλαθεῖσα . . . Ποσειδᾶνι.* This form of the aor. pass. is also found in *Hec.* 890 and three times in *Rhesus*, always with the variant *ἐπλάσθην.*

δεσπότῃ γ' ἐμῷ: see apparatus criticus. Murray accepts Brunck's correction and Denniston (*GP*, p. 139) includes this passage as an example of 'epexegetic *γε*' without mentioning the MS. reading *τε* or Elmsley's *δέ*. Confusion of *γε* and *τε* is of course extremely easy and common, but it should be noted that in almost all the examples of this use of *γε* cited by Denniston we have a pronoun or rather colourless noun amplified and explained by a longer and more expressive phrase, e.g. S. *OC* 1278 *ὡς μή μ' ἄτιμον τοῦ θεοῦ γε προστάτην* | *οὕτως ἀφῇς* 'me, the suppliant of the god'. There is a similar epexegetic use of *τε*, e.g. A. *Ag.* 10 *φάτιν ἁλώσιμόν τε βάξιν.* (Denniston observes that *γε* gives force and urgency to an addition or supplement; perhaps a greater urgency distinguishes *γε* from *τε* in this idiom.) There is, however, a different and fairly common idiom in which two attributes connected by *δέ* or *τε* are used to denote the same person, both being of similar length and importance (though emphasis will naturally tend to fall a little more strongly on the one placed second), and generally but not invariably *eiusdem generis*; thus A. *Pers.* 150 *μήτηρ βασιλέως, βασίλεια δ' ἐμή*, E. *Hec.* 534 *παῖ Πηλέως, πατὴρ δ' ἐμός*, E. *Med.* 970 *πατρὸς νέαν γυναῖκα δεσπότιν τ' ἐμήν* 'she who is your father's new wife and my mistress', *IA* 1454 *πατέρα τὸν ἀμὸν μὴ στύγει πόσιν τε σόν.* Cf. *GP*, pp. 163–4. So here for Andromache it is significant both that Neoptolemus is son of Achilles and so her enemy, and that he is her master, to whom she must submit.

As between *δέ* and *τε*, Elmsley (on *Med.* 940 = O.C.T. 970), Hermann,

Fraenkel (on A. *Ag.* 1585), and others seem to be right in maintaining that δέ is usual, and it may be that the relatively few examples of τε should be corrected; those known to me are A. *Ag.* 1585, E. *Med.* 970, *Andr.* 25, *IA* 1153, 1454. There is, however, no intrinsic objection to τε in this sense; it is merely a matter of usage and some variation may have been possible. Here, then, I should prefer either to keep the MS. reading or accept Elmsley's δέ, the balance of probability being perhaps slightly in favour of the latter.

27. **προσῆγε**: there may be no example of προσάγω with infinitive, but προσάγομαι is so used with personal subjects in the sense 'urge' or 'induce' in E. *Ion* 659 χρόνῳ δὲ καιρὸν λαμβάνων προσάξομαι | δάμαρτ' ἐᾶν σε σκῆπτρα τἄμ' ἔχειν χθονός and S. *OT* 131 ἡ . . . Σφίγξ ἡμᾶς προσήγετο σκοπεῖν τὰ πρὸς ποσί; cf. also Hdt. 2. 172 προσηγάγετο τοὺς Αἰγυπτίους ὥστε δικαιοῦν δουλεύειν. With the impersonal subject ἐλπίς the active verb may be possible, and 'hope urged me to find' would be a slightly compressed form of 'hope led me to think that I should find'. So Wecklein 'spes me adduxit ad credendum'. Bornmann compares Cicero, *De Div.* 1. 35 'adducor hanc esse patriam tuam'. Méridier translates 'l'espoir m'attirait de trouver . . . une défense', but in his note prefers 'm'attirait à lui (sc. Neoptolemus)'. This is a well-attested sense of προσάγω, but seems less in keeping with Andromache's train of thought in this passage. For another less probable interpretation see Verrall, *Four Plays of Euripides*, App. I. 24 ff. Lack of exact parallel for the construction in the text has led to emendations, of which Reiske's προῆγε is the easiest and may be right; it is used with infin. in Thuc. 3. 45 and Dem. 18. 206, and it may be accidental that it is not found elsewhere in Tragedy.

σωθέντος: the papyrus reading τεχθέντος is unlikely since the aor. pass. of τίκτειν is not found in the classical period.

τέκνου: Andromache's son is called Μολοττός in the list of dramatis personae given in MSS. and by the scholiast on 309 and 709, but the name does not appear in the text and is certainly a later addition. As A. M. Dale observes on *Alc.* 393, children are usually anonymous in Greek Tragedy, except where the name has a special significance, as with Eurysaces and Astyanax. Here the name Μολοσσός could have had a genealogical significance, but if E. himself had assigned this name to the child he would surely have mentioned it in 1243 ff., where Thetis predicts that Andromache and her child will dwell in the γῆ Μολοσσία, just as he indicates the connection in *Ion* 1587 τοῦδε δ' ὀνόματος χάριν | Ἴωνες ὀνομασθέντες ἕξουσιν κλέος. Cf. E. Hiller, *Hermes*, 8 (1874), 444 ff. As Miss Dale notes (loc. cit.) the form Μολοττός betrays itself. The earliest recorded reference to the name is in fact ascribed to Eratosthenes (Schol. *Od.* 3. 188; *FHG* 2. 1020) and it was perhaps invented for genealogical reasons by him or some other historian.

28. There is a close resemblance between this line and S. *OT* 218 *ἀλκὴν λάβοις ἂν κἀνακούφισιν κακῶν*. We do not know which play was composed first, but in any case *ἐπικούρησις* is quite appropriate here and there is no need to emend, with Elmsley, to *κἀπικούφισιν*.

29. Λάκαιναν: in the first reference to Hermione we are reminded that she is a Spartan.

30. παρώσας: cf. E. *El.* 1037 *ὅταν δ' . . . ἁμαρτάνῃ πόσις τἄνδον παρώσας λέκτρα*.

δεσπότης δοῦλον: note the effective juxtaposition. The adjectival use of *δοῦλος* is not actually found before Sophocles, but thereafter is common.

31. κακοῖς: *λέγει γάρ* in the following line suggests that the meaning is 'reproaches' rather than 'ill treatment'; cf. *Alc.* 675–6 *ὦ παῖ, τίν' αὐχεῖς . . . κακοῖς ἐλαύνειν;*

32. φαρμάκοις κεκρυμμένοις: *φάρμακον* and cognate words are used rather like our 'drug' for specific potions and ointments both beneficial and harmful; cf. *Od.* 4. 230 *φάρμακα, πολλὰ μὲν ἐσθλὰ μεμιγμένα πολλὰ δὲ λυγρά*. They are also used more vaguely for imaginary enchanted potions and philtres such as the *φάρμακον οὐλόμενον* by which Circe changed men into swine (*Od.* 4. 394) and the antidote (4. 302), and for the love philtre of which the Nurse speaks in the *Hippolytus* and Phaedra asks *πότερα δὲ χριστὸν ἢ ποτὸν τὸ φάρμακον;* (*Hipp.* 516). Here the 'secret drugs' belong to the sphere of magic rather than to Greek pharmacopoeia. For a similar magic potion having the opposite effect and perhaps for use on a male compare Medea's promise to Aegeus *παύσω δέ σ' ὄντ' ἄπαιδα . . . τοιάδ' οἶδα φάρμακα* (*Med.* 718). Later in the play we hear Hermione making this accusation (157 ff.) and Andromache denying it (205, 355 ff.).

33. πόσει: the dative of the agent is the normal construction with the verbal adjective and is fairly common with the perfect and pluperfect passive, but rare with other tenses. It belongs essentially to the same category as the dative of the person concerned in the action, and in some passages it can be taken in this way rather than as an exact equivalent of *ὑπό* with the genitive. So Thuc. 1. 51 *αἱ Ἀθηναίων νῆες τοῖς Κερκυραίοις οὐχ ἑωρῶντο* 'the ships were unobserved as far as the Corcyreans were concerned'. In Homer this use is particularly common with the passive of *δάμνημι*, and the sense may be 'subdued to' 'in the interest of' rather than 'by'; thus *Ἀχιλῆι δαμασθείς* (*Il.* 22. 55) is the passive equivalent of *μιν . . . Ἀχιλῆι δαμάσσομεν ἐσθλὸν ἐόντα*. Similarly in the present passage, 'hateful in the eyes of her lord'; cf. 157 *στυγοῦμαι δ' ἀνδρί*.

34. αὐτὴ . . . αὐτῆς: the repetition with reference to different persons perhaps jars a little, but there is no ambiguity; *αὐτὴ δὲ . . . θέλω* is contrasted with *νιν τίθημι . . .* A suggestion by T. B. L. Webster that *αὐτή* means in effect 'as mistress' gives more point to the line, and it is possible that *αὐτή* could be so used, as *αὐτός* certainly is, though in more colloquial contexts.

ναίειν often suggests the notion of permanence: 'to make this my home instead of hers'. Cf. Electra's indignant denunciation of Aegisthus: *φρονεῖ μέγ'· ἐν γὰρ τοῖς ἐμοῖς ναίει δόμοις* (*El.* 1120). The verb is similarly used, though in a causal sense, in *Od.* 4. 174 *καί κέ οἱ Ἄργεϊ νάσσα πόλιν* 'I would have given him a town in Argos for his home'.

35. λέκτρα τἀκείνης: 'her bridal couch', standing for Hermione as a wife. Elsewhere *λέκτρα* alone stands for a person, as in 928 *νόθοισι λέκτροις* (Andromache) and in 123 and 465, where the Chorus speak of *δίδυμα λέκτρα* with reference to two women present as rivals in the house of Neoptolemus. In 36 the relative *ἅ* refers to *λέκτρα*, by which Andromache now seems to mean not the whole status of wife, but the physical union with Neoptolemus.

βία sometimes denotes not physical force or violence but some other form of constraint. In 730 when Menelaus says *πρὸς βίαν . . . μολών* he means presumably constrained by entreaties or warnings of Hermione, and in *Alc.* 1116 *βιάζῃ μ' οὐ θέλοντα δρᾶν τάδε* Admetus stresses the compelling urgency of Heracles' request. In this passage *βία* refers mainly to the constraint of magic arts, and perhaps also suggests the general idea of violent disturbance of domestic peace.

36. οὐχ ἑκοῦσ': cf. 390–1.

37. εἰδείη: the optative of wish here replaces the imperative which is usual in such phrases, e.g. *IT* 1077 *ὡς ἔκ γ' ἐμοῦ σοι πάντα σιγηθήσεται—ἴστω μέγας Ζεύς—ὧν ἐπισκήπτεις πέρι*: *IA* 1413, S. *Tr.* 349. In these passages the reference is to future intention. For reference to the past, as in our passage, cf. [Dem.] *Ep.* 2. 16 *οὔτε γὰρ ἠδίκηχ' ὑμᾶς οὐδέν, ὡς ἴστωσαν οἱ θεοὶ καὶ ἥρωες.*

38. Wecklein, following Nauck and supported by Méridier, ejects this line as an interpolation, on the ground that it repeats the sense of 36, and that the appeal to Zeus in 37 must be meant to underline the essential fact that she no longer shares the bed of Neoptolemus and is therefore no longer a rival of Hermione, whereas if 38 is kept *τάδε* looks forward to the following *ὡς* clause. It is true that Andromache's argument is logically complete at *ἐκλέλοιπα*, but it is natural to infer from passages in this play, esp. 22 ff., 403, as well as from the established picture of A. in the *Iliad* as the devoted wife of Hector, that she feels her union with Neoptolemus as a betrayal of the memory of Hector, and she may well seek to comfort herself by insistence on the involuntary nature of that union. (For a similar repetition, logically unnecessary but dramatically appropriate, see S. *Tr.* 684, with Jebb's note.) The repetition of this protestation, perhaps on a rising note of passion, prepared for by the invocation of Zeus and followed by a drop in tone to the mournful *ἀλλ' οὔ σφε πείθω*, would no doubt give scope for histrionic ability and it is conceivable that some actor interpolated the line for that reason; but it has also emotional and dramatic justification and I see no sufficient reason to doubt its authenticity. It may perhaps be said that there is no place for all this feeling in the unemotional and prosaic Euripidean prologue, but some critics are apt to exaggerate the uniformity of Euripidean prologues in these respects, and a generalization (especially if it is negative) needs to be very clearly established before it can supply compelling arguments against the MS. tradition.

43. **Θέτιδος ἀνάκτορον**: any shrine, altar, or sacred precinct might be regarded as affording a refuge, in the sense that to use force against a fugitive who is in the precinct or touching an altar would be to commit sacrilege; naturally the greater the reverence inspired by a shrine the more potent its protection (45–6), but the pursuer might of course take the risk of sacrilege. In *Ion* 1255 ff. the Chorus urge Creusa to take refuge at the altar; her pursuers may slay her, but if so they will incur pollution: *τοῖς ἀποκτείνασί σε | προστρόπαιον αἷμα θήσεις*. In 1275 Ion exclaims in his fury that neither the altar nor the temple of Apollo will save her, but, eventually, when she refuses to leave the altar he seems to admit that while she is there she cannot be touched (1312 ff.). This form of divine protection could be claimed even by a slave, as Andromache has now become; cf. E. *Supp.* 267 *ἔχει γὰρ καταφυγὴν θὴρ μὲν πέτραν, | δοῦλος δὲ βωμοὺς θεῶν*, and Thuc. 1. 128. The protection afforded could, however, hardly be more than temporary; the suppliant could generally be brought by promises, threats, or starvation to leave sanctuary.

In the fifth century the notion that violation of sanctuary involved pollution seems to have been still sufficiently established in popular feeling to make it worth while for the Athenians and Spartans to bring public charges and counter-charges against each other for such offences (Thuc. 1. 126–35), and the fact that at Corcyra men were dragged from sanctuaries or put to death in them is noted by Thucydides as an example of the extreme savagery of civil strife in that island in the early years of the Peloponnesian War (Thuc. 3. 81).

Suppliants taking refuge at an altar is a common scene in Euripides and occurs in six of the extant plays. In the *Heracleidae* and *Supplices* it is characteristic of the more secular atmosphere of Euripidean tragedy, as contrasted with that of the *Supplices* of Aeschylus, that it is the power of Athens to protect fugitives rather than that of the gods to which the appeal is primarily directed. In *Andromache*, *Heracles*, and *Ion* the dramatist seems to find the altar scene a convenient device to give otherwise helpless victims a breathing-space in which to state their case, arouse pity, and prolong suspense, before rescue eventually comes. Cf. H. Strohm, *Euripides*, 1. 1, 'Agon und Altarmotiv'.

44. **ἤν . . . κωλύσῃ**: *ἤν* with subj. or *εἰ* with opt., generally with the

addition of πως or που, 'in the hope that', is closely akin to a purpose clause but often carries the implication that the speaker has doubts, real or ironically assumed, about the likelihood of the purpose being fulfilled. In *Od.* 9. 228 ἐγὼ οὐ πιθόμην . . . ὄφρ' αὐτόν τε ἴδοιμι καὶ εἴ μοι ξείνια δοίη, there seems to be a distinction between the immediate purpose and a more remote possibility. In E. *HF* 847 παραινέσαι δὲ . . . Ἥρᾳ θέλω σοι τ', ἢν πίθησθ' ἐμοῖς λόγοις it is unlikely that the goddess will relent; in *Hel.* 1049 Helen speaks ironically ἄκουσον ἤν τι καὶ γυνὴ λέξῃ σοφόν. In some passages the context indicates that the possibility of fulfilment is thought of as still more remote, e.g. Thuc. 3. 45. 3 διεξεληλύθασί γε διὰ πασῶν τῶν ζημιῶν οἱ ἄνθρωποι . . . εἴ πως ἧσσον ἀδικοῖντο ὑπὸ τῶν κακούργων 'in the vain hope of suffering less wrong'. In this passage Andromache is aware of the insecurity of her refuge, even without the warning of the Chorus (134–5) τὸ κρατοῦν δέ σ' ἔπεισι. τί μόχθον | οὐδὲν οὖσα μοχθεῖς; See also 54 below.

45. ἔκγονοι: strictly speaking Neoptolemus seems to be at this time the only relevant ἔκγονος, so that the plural is loosely used; possibly E. is including, by anachronism, the descendants of N.

46. ἑρμήνευμα: the scholiast gives as equivalents ὑπόμνησιν, ἄγγελον, σημεῖον, μνημόσυνον, τεκμήριον; so LSJ, for this passage only, 'symbol' 'monument'. Something like this is certainly the sense required, but there seems to be no other example of this meaning for the word or its cognates, which generally involve the notion of explanation or interpretation. In Xen. *Mem.* 4. 3. 12 ἑρμηνεία means the expression of thought in words; so perhaps ἑρμηνεύειν in Thuc. 2. 60. 3 γνῶναί τε τὰ δέοντα καὶ ἑρμηνεῦσαι ταῦτα. Here perhaps it may be said that the shrine expresses in stone their pride in the connection by marriage with a Nereid, and this is put in condensed form by calling it ἑρμήνευμα γάμων. Wecklein takes ἑρμήνευμα as accusative in apposition not to νιν but to the sentence Πηλεύς . . . σέβουσιν, a common construction in Euripides. But his sense 'a thing which is explained or accounted for by the marriage with the Nereid' does not seem likely for ἑρμήνευμα.

47. μόνος: the limitation to a single child is dramatically effective, and may be an innovation of Euripides. See on 24 above.

According to Verrall (*Studies in Greek and Latin Scholarship*, pp. 179 ff.) a pause in sense between the third and fourth foot of an iambic trimeter, dividing the line into two equal parts, is rarely found in earlier plays of Euripides except for special effect. Here it may certainly have a rhetorical significance in adding emphasis to μόνος.

ὑπεκπέμπω: the same verb is similarly used in *Hec.* 6 and 14. In *Andr.* 69 and 310 we have ὑπεξέθου, which in prose seems to be the *vox propria* for evacuating to a place of safety, as in Thuc. 1. 89 ὑπεξέθεντο παῖδας καὶ γυναῖκας, Lys. 2. 34 ὑπεκθέμενοι παῖδας ἐς Σαλαμῖνα, Hdt. 8. 4.

49–50. οὔτ' ἐμοὶ . . . παιδί τ' οὐδέν: *οὔτε . . . τ' οὐ* is rare but not unparalleled. Denniston, *GP*, p. 508, cites E. *Tr.* 487 *κοὔτ' ἐξ ἐκείνων ἐλπὶς ὡς ὀφθήσομαι, | αὐτή τ' ἐκείνας οὐκέτ' ὄψομαί ποτε* and two other examples from Tragedy (to which the present passage may be added), two examples from Thuc., and one from Plato.

50. οὐδέν ἐστ': 'is of no account, no use'. Cf. 134, 641 *σὺ δ' οὐδὲν εἶ*, 700 *ὄντες οὐδένες*, 1077. *Ant.* fr. 187 *ἀργὸς μὲν οἴκοις καὶ πόλει γενήσεται φίλοισι δ' οὐδείς*. To the spectator who knows that by tradition Neoptolemus was killed at Delphi this phrase may, as Kamerbeek observes, have a touch of dramatic irony, well brought out by Paley's 'as good as dead'.

51. αἶαν: an epic form of *γαῖα*, found rarely in Sophocles but about sixteen times each in Aeschylus and Euripides. It is generally said to be used in Tragedy *metri gratia*, but E. Harrison points out in *Proc. Camb. Phil. Soc.* 178 (1941), 7 that in many passages the modification needed to accommodate *γαῖα* was so slight that the choice of *αἶα* cannot have been wholly due to metrical reasons.

51–5. The general sense of this passage is clear: that Neoptolemus first visited Delphi to claim satisfaction from Apollo for his share in the death of Achilles (for the first reference to this see *Il.* 19. 417, 22. 359), and then made a second visit to offer amends to the god for his presumption. These visits are again referred to in 1002–4 and 1106–8. In *Or.* 1656–7 Apollo speaks only of the claim against himself *δίκας Ἀχιλλέως πατρὸς ἐξαιτοῦντά με*. Essentially the same version of the first visit was given in the *Hermione* of Sophocles, according to Eustath. *Od.* p. 1479, 10 *ὅτε τὸν Ἀπόλλωνα τινύμενος τὸν τοῦ πατρὸς ἐξεδίκει φόνον* (sc. *Νεοπτόλεμος*). For the legend as presented here and other versions found elsewhere see Intr., pp. 1 ff.

There are, however, two points of uncertainty about the text.

52. Reiske's *ᾗ*, which with the iota adscript could easily become *ἥν*, gives a satisfactory construction: 'the madness in which (or by reason of which) he demanded satisfaction . . .' An acc. of respect would be possible, as in Pl. *Phdr.* 249 d (if *ἥν* is sound), but in our passage it is more difficult. Hyslop and Kamerbeek keep *ἥν* and take it as referring back to *δίκην* in 51, but this is surely ruled out by the occurrence of *δίκην* in 53.

53. If with Murray we keep the reading of most MSS. *κτείνει*, *οὗ* is the relative attracted to the case of its antecedent *πατρός*: 'he demanded satisfaction from Phoebus for his father whom he (Phoebus) slew.' The present *κτείνει* is probably not historic, but emphasizes the continuing guilt: 'he is the slayer'; see on *τίκτειν* (9), and cf. S. *Ant.* 1174 *καὶ τίς φονεύει; τίς δ' ὁ κείμενος;* 'Who is the murderer, and who lies dead?' This may be the true reading, but the MS. variants *τίνει*, *'κτίνει* are better accounted for by Hermann's correction *'κτίνειν*: 'he called upon Phoebus to give satisfaction in full for his (N.'s) father.' οὗ is then the possessive adj. (= suus), which is common in Homer and found in a few passages in Tragedy, e.g. E. *Med.* 955 ἐκγόνοισιν οἷς, S. *Aj.* 442, *Tr.* 266, but is not used in Attic prose and is sufficiently rare and unfamiliar to cause corruption. The MS. readings would then be due to the assumption that οὗ was the relative and required a finite verb. For ἐκτίνειν δίκην cf. E. *El.* 260, and for αἰτεῖν with infin. cf. *Andr.* 1107 ᾔτησα γὰρ | πατρός ποτ' αὐτὸν αἵματος δοῦναι δίκην.

54–5. εἴ πως . . . παράσχοιτ': see on 44 above. There is a disquieting sound about this which may be intended to prepare for the news that eventually comes from Delphi (1070 ff.).

56–90. The second 'scene' of the πρόλογος is a dialogue between Andromache and a female slave, whose entry at 56 is, as usual with such characters in Euripides, not prepared. In Tragedy, as distinguished from Comedy, slaves, messengers, sentries, and the like are always anonymous. In addition to any distinguishing marks in their appearance (in *El.* 107–8 Electra is taken for a slave on account of her close-cropped hair) slaves often indicate their status at once by the use of words like ἄναξ or δέσποινα, as here and in *Hipp.* 88. In this passage there is a pathetic loyalty in this address from a slave to a former mistress, now a fellow slave.

56. δέσποιν'—ἐγώ τοι . . .: cf. 64 and *Hel.* 1193. Imitations by Aristophanes in *Thesm.* 582 and *Vesp.* 1297 suggest that he may have seen in this form of opening a characteristic Euripidean or tragic idiom; see Dale on *Hel.* 1193 and Starkie on *Vesp.* 1297.

57. καλεῖν: for φεύγειν with infin. in the sense 'shrink from doing something' cf. E. *HF* 1072 τὸ φάος ἐκλιπεῖν μὲν . . . οὐ φεύγω, *Tro.* 891, Hdt. 4. 76. 1.

ἐπείπερ καί: καί cannot here be intensificatory: it would be absurd to say: 'I called you mistress even in your own home.' Here καί really belongs to the main clause: 'since I called you mistress then, now also I address you thus.' For examples of this inversion whereby καί is placed in a causal or relative clause when logically it belongs to the main clause, see *GP*, pp. 295. iii and 296. (2).

ἠξίουν: sc. καλεῖν σε τόδε.

58. τὸν σόν: the reading τὸ σόν could be regarded as equivalent to σε, and ἠξίουν would then mean 'I respected you'; but τὸν σὸν οἶκον, stressing the contrast with her present position, is more pointed.

59. εὔνους: slaves in Greek Tragedy are almost by definition loyal.

καί cannot of course be taken with the following τε in the same sense as τε . . . καί; moreover the main point here is to link her loyalty in the past with the loyalty she now shows in risking punishment by bringing news to Andromache. This sense is given if, with Kamerbeek, we take καί as correlative with καί in the next line, but the position of καί is against this, and the juxtaposition of δὲ καί (where καί cannot be intensificatory) is awkward. If we are to emend, Hartung's δ' ἀεί provides the better correlative with *καί νῦν*, but Badham's δ' ἐκεῖ is closer to the MSS. and may be justified by the local reference in 58. According to LSJ, indeed, ἐκεῖ is used, though rarely, of time. This, however, seems to be doubtful; in S. *Ph.* 395 ἐκεῖ may well have its usual sense; in Dem. 22. 38 ἐκεῖ can hardly mean 'there', but if that passage is isolated Richards's correction ἐπεί is probably right.

ἦ: ἦ, contracted from ἦα, is the older Attic form; see Rutherford, *New Phrynichus*, p. 242 and E. Harrison, *CR* 56 (1942), 6–9. ἦν is found sometimes in MSS. of Sophocles but is never required by the metre (unless *OT* 1525 is genuine and spoken by Oedipus) and is perhaps rightly corrected to ἦ. In this passage and regularly in E. the MS. reading is ἦν (or παρῆν). In six places (*Alc.* 655, *Hipp.* 1012, *HF* 1416, *Ion* 280, *Hel.* 992, *IA* 944) ἦν is required by the metre; cf. Harrison, loc. cit., for discussion. Most editors correct ἦν to ἦ in all except these six passages, apparently on the assumption that copyists invariably substituted the later form in MSS. of E. though not always in Aeschylus, Sophocles, Aristophanes, and Plato; some also emend the six passages cited. In Aristophanes there is good authority for ἦ in five passages (three in lyric metre); in nine ἦν is the MS. reading (the Budé editor prints ἦν throughout except in *Lys.* 644, 645). It is rather striking that of these nine examples the only ones certified by metre are in the last play (*Pl.* 29, 695, 822), but at any rate if ἦν is to be accepted for Aristophanes in the other six passages there seems little justification for removing it from E., who in some other respects is nearer than A. or S. to Aristophanes and the spoken language of his day.

59–60. The sense and sequence of thought are clear, though there is a slight anacoluthon in construction. ἐγώ τοι . . . πέδον is a parenthetic justification of the word δέσποινα, and δέ is strictly superfluous but may be justified on the ground that the main sentence continues the train of thought in the parenthesis: 'I called you mistress and was faithful.'

60. νέους: here, as very often, νέος referring to news or events is used euphemistically with sinister connotation; cf. *Med.* 37 δέδοικα δ' αὐτὴν μή τι βουλεύσῃ νέον, *Supp.* 91, 99.

61. φόβῳ εἰ: an indirect question clause depending on a word of fearing may be in effect equivalent to *vereor ut*, as in *Med.* 184 φόβος εἰ πείσω δέσποιναν ἐμήν, *Hcld.* 791, or to *vereor ne*, as in this passage and S. *Tr.* 666 ἀθυμῶ δ' εἰ φανήσομαι τάχα | κακὸν μέγ' ἐκπράξασα. Strictly speaking this construction should presumably stress the element of doubt that is involved in fear; so here we might translate 'anxiously wondering whether . . .'; but we cannot be sure that the distinction between it and the more usual μή clause was always clearly felt.

62. οἴκτῳ τῷ σῷ: 'out of pity for you'; causal dative.

64. σύνδουλε: cf. *Hec.* 60 ἄγετ' ὀρθοῦσαι τὴν ὁμόδουλον, . . . πρόσθε δ' ἄνασσαν.

65. τῇδε: referring to the speaker, as often in Tragedy.

70. πέπυσται: who? Menelaus or Hermione? Pflugk, followed by Hermann and Paley, would make Hermione the subject on two grounds: that she is most prominent in the mind of Andromache and that if Menelaus had been the subject the slave would not have mentioned his name in 73. Wecklein merely asserts that Hermione is supplied by the context and Hyslop remarks without comment '*sc.* Hermione'. Bassi thinks the subject could be either H. or M. but prefers the former 'la quale aveva ordito tutta la trama', much the same argument as Pflugk's; so too Kamerbeek and Méridier: 'Hermione, l'âme de toute la machination'. But neither of the two reasons given is convincing. Verses 40 ff. suggest that it is the arrival of Menelaus to help his daughter that makes Andromache realize that her danger has become acute, and in 63 Menelaus is mentioned first with *παῖς* added as an afterthought; there is no evidence that H. had 'devised the whole plot'. On Pflugk's second point, even if M. is the subject of *πέπυσται*, the intervening *ἐκείνων* in 72 makes it natural to use his name in 73. I agree with Bassi that the subject could be H. or M., but I am not so clear that the former is more likely. If we must choose, *Σ*, who in contrast with all modern editors who accept the MS. reading takes the subject to be M., is as likely to be right. If then after the four plurals in 66–8 the singular leaves us guessing, we have an example of careless writing, a possibility that can hardly be ruled out.

To remove the difficulty L. Dindorf conjectured *πέπυσθε*, which W. Dindorf accepted and Pflugk described as *elegans et ingeniosa* but did not accept, and Nauck *πέπυσθον*. The corruption to *πέπυσται* is easy enough (*ε* and *αι* often confused and for *στ* replacing *σθ* see Schwyzer, *Gr. Gr.*, pp. 204–5, and Jackson, *Marginalia Scaenica*, p. 63), but the sudden apostrophe to the absent Menelaus and Hermione is abrupt and unusual. There is therefore something to be said for Radermacher's transposition whereby 73 follows 69. The subject of *πέπυσται* would then obviously be Menelaus, and the sequence of thought would also be slightly improved. Andromache's cry of despair in 70 would more naturally follow the revelation not merely that her enemies are intending to kill her child, which she already suspects (48), but that Menelaus has actually gone to fetch him, with the implication that the secret refuge has been discovered. If 73 was omitted in copying and added in the margin a subsequent copyist might have inserted it in its present position in order to preserve the uniformity of two-line dialogue at this point. See L. Radermacher, *Observationes in Euripidem Miscellae*, Bonn, 1891, pp. 9–10; but his argument based on the symmetrical structure of this scene does not seem to me to be cogent.

71. ὦ δύστηνος: contrast *ὦ δύστηνε σύ* (68). This exclamatory use of the nom. occurs fairly often from Homer onwards; cf. *Il.* 1. 231 *δημοβόρος* βασιλεύς, ἐπεὶ οὐτιδανοῖσιν ἀνάσσεις; E. *Hel.* 862 ὦ δύστηνος ὡς ἀπωλόμην; *Med.* 61 ὦ μῶρος, εἰ χρὴ δεσπότας εἰπεῖν τάδε; Pl. *Phaedr.* 227 c ὦ γενναῖος. Here we have in effect a predicate without subject or verb; in other passages a subject is expressed, e.g. E. *Hipp.* 1378 ὦ πατρὸς ἐμοῦ δύστηνος ἀρά; *Med.* 96 ἰώ, δύστανος ἐγώ.

72. ἐκείνων: presumably other slaves in the house.

75. γῦπες: we are familiar with metaphorical vultures, but I know no other example in Greek. In Ar. *Av.* 891 ἁλιαιέτους καὶ γῦπας are mentioned as among the more rapacious birds.

κεκλημένος: the paternity of Neoptolemus is not being questioned; the contrast here is between being (rightly) called father and behaving like a father, i.e. protecting his child. Contrast. *Alc.* 637 οὐδ' ἡ τεκεῖν φάσκουσα καὶ κεκλημένη | μήτηρ μ' ἔτικτε; and Dale's note.

77. οὐκ ἂν . . . ἄν: ἄν fairly often occurs twice and occasionally three times with a single verb, sometimes mainly anticipatory, when the main sentence is broken by a subordinate clause, e.g. Thuc. 2. 94 ὅπερ ἄν, εἰ ἐβουλήθησαν μὴ κατοκνῆσαι, ῥᾳδίως ἂν ἐγένετο, and sometimes for rhetorical effect, to emphasize the preceding word, e.g. E. *Med.* 250 τρὶς ἂν παρ' ἀσπίδα | στῆναι θέλοιμ' ἂν μᾶλλον ἢ τεκεῖν ἅπαξ. This repeated ἄν is particularly common to emphasize a negative, as in this passage and in 934–5, or an interrogative, and may even have come to be so used a trifle mechanically, with slight rhetorical justification, as in S. fr. 739 πῶς ἂν οὐκ ἂν ἐν δίκῃ | θάνοιμ' ἄν; See KG 1. 246–8.

78. νῦν δ': here, as often, not primarily temporal, but used to contrast reality with something that might have been: 'but as it is . . .'.

80. γέρων . . . ὥστε: most modern editors (Wecklein, Kamerbeek, Bassi) take the meaning to be 'too old to help', i.e. as equivalent to γεραίτερος ἢ ὥστε; but if the ability of Peleus to give any help is thus ruled out it is odd that there is no further reference to this point and the dialogue proceeds on the assumption that the main difficulty is to convey the appeal for help. The sense required is rather that old age will be a handicap but not necessarily a fatal handicap, and Méridier rightly translates 'Il est bien vieux pour te venir en aide.'

It seems to be the established view that a positive adjective denoting weakness or deficiency, e.g. γέρων or νέος, followed by ὥστε with infin. has the same force as the comparative followed by ἢ ὥστε; see KG 1. 503, Anm. 2, Goodwin, *MT*, § 588, Schwyzer, *Gr. Gr.* 2. 678. 3, LSJ, s.v. ὥστε B I 2. It can however be argued that, as in the present passage, the use of a positive adjective of this type with infinitive does not altogether deny the possibility of the action but indicates an obstacle not necessarily fatal. For discussion of relevant passages, including Pl. *Prt.* 314 b, Xen. *Mem.* 3. 13. 3, Ant. 5. 79, *Il.* 24. 369, see *CR* N.S. 11 (1961), 102–3.

82. μῶν οὖν: this collocation, which also occurs in A. *Ch.* 177, Ar. *Pl.* 845, and several times in Plato, shows that the origin of *μῶν* from *μὴ οὖν* has been forgotten; cf. also *μῶν μή*, Pl. *R.* 505 c, *Lys.* 208 c.

83. πόθεν; 'of course not!' Andromache must have had some hope of success when she tried to send messages, but the pessimistic words of the slave woman in 82 are a sharp reminder that she cannot now command the services of others, and she exclaims in bitter realization.

For *πόθεν* in this sense cf. E. *Alc.* 780 *οἶμαι μὲν οὔ· πόθεν γάρ; El.* 656–7 *ἥξει κλύουσα λόχιά μου νοσήματα. | Πρ. πόθεν; τί δ' αὐτῇ σοῦ μέλειν δοκεῖς τέκνον; Hec.* 613; *Ph.* 1620. This seems to be a colloquial idiom and is common in Comedy and Plato, e.g. Ar. *Ra.* 1455–6 *τίσι χρῆται; πότερα τοῖς χρηστοῖς; Δι. πόθεν; | μισεῖ κάκιστα; V.* 1144; *Eq.* 389, 976; Pl. *Smp.* 172 c, *Grg.* 471 d; Dem. 18. 47 *ἀλλ' οὐκ ἔστι ταῦτα· πόθεν; πολλοῦ γε καὶ δεῖ*; ibid. 140; Aeschin. 1. 109.

85. Perhaps a modification of some proverbial expression. The scholiast harshly comments *ἐν οὐ δέοντι γνωμολογεῖ τοσούτων αὐτὴν περιεστώτων κακῶν*, but the sentence is brief and relevant enough. For other passages where women admit or boast of less harmless *μηχαναί* cf. *Med.* 407 *πεφύκαμεν | γυναῖκες, ἐς μὲν ἔσθλ' ἀμηχανώταται | κακῶν δὲ πάντων τέκτονες σοφώταται; Hipp.* 480 *ἦ τἄρ' ἂν ὀψέ γ' ἄνδρες ἐξεύροιεν ἄν, | εἰ μὴ γυναῖκες μηχανὰς εὑρήσομεν.* See also *Andr.* 272; *Med.* 265; fr. 323; and for similar comments by men cf. *Andr.* 911; *IT* 1032 *δειναὶ γὰρ αἱ γυναῖκες εὑρίσκειν τέχνας*; *Ion* 843–5; fr. 276. In the plays of E. it is in fact generally the women who devise the plots, whether the murderous plots of Medea, Hecuba, Creusa (*Ion* 1029 ff.), Electra (*El.* 610 ff. *Or.* 1191 ff.) or the more defensive deceptions of Helen (*Hel.* 1049 ff.) and Iphigeneia (*IT* 1029 ff.). It has often been noted that, whatever the position of women in Athenian society, on the Attic stage, especially in Euripides, they are often represented as equal and indeed superior to men, whether more noble and self-sacrificing or more resourceful and more ruthless.

86. οὐ σμικρὸν φύλαξ: most MSS. give *σμικρὰ φύλαξ*, but the Ambrosian has *σμικρὸν φίλον*, hence Kirchhoff's *σμικρὸν φύλαξ*. If *σμικρόν*, the *lectio difficilior*, is right it is probably predicative: 'as a *φύλαξ* H. is no small thing'; for the neuter cf. 209 *ἡ Λάκαινα μὲν πόλις μέγ' ἐστί; Or.* 784. It is less likely to be used adverbially, as in *Hcld.* 792 *μέγιστον εὐκλεεῖς*, with *φύλαξ* as an adjective: 'very watchful'.

87. ὁρᾷς; 'you see?', 'there you are'. For this use of *ὁρᾷς* pointing (often reproachfully) at a proof or illustration of something that the speaker has been saying or thinking, cf. E. *El.* 1121 *ὁρᾷς; ἀν' αὖ σὺ ζωπυρεῖς νείκη νέα*; S. *El.* 628 *ὁρᾷς; πρὸς ὀργὴν ἐκφέρει.* This use is also frequent in Comedy and may be another colloquialism; cf. Ar. *Ra.* 1234 *ὁρᾷς, προσῆψεν αὖθις αὖ τὴν λήκυθον*; *Av.* 1616; *Nu.* 691; *Eq.* 1164; Men. *Sam.* 250; id. fr. 835; Pl. *Prt.* 336 b.

89. ἐπεί τοι: in Eur. and Plato this combination is almost invariably followed by *καί*, and the two particles merely add emphasis and liveliness to the causal clause; see *GP* 545. iii (1). *Σ* refers to another reading *καί* for *κοὐ*, and comments *ὥστε ἐν εἰρωνείᾳ τοὐναντίον λέγεσθαι.* D. L. Page suggests the possibility that the change was made by an actor that he might utter the sentence with bitter sarcasm in his voice (*Actors' Interpolations*, p. 65). *οὐ περίβλεπτος* 'not admired by all' 'not enviable' is a good example of understatement.

91. χώρει νυν: exit the slave woman. Andromache is alone again, and her next lines are a prelude to her elegiac lament in 103–16.

92. θρήνοισι: the nouns in this line are attracted into the case of the relative *οἷσπερ* by so-called 'inverse attraction'. Cf. S. *OC* 56 *ὃν δ' ἐπιστείβεις τόπον | χθονὸς καλεῖται τῆσδε χαλκόπους ὁδός*: Pl. *Lys.* 221 b *οἷόν τε οὖν ἐστι . . . τούτου οὗ ἐπιθυμεῖ καὶ ἐρᾷ μὴ φιλεῖν;*

93. πρὸς αἰθέρ': there are many passages in Greek drama where the speaker, alone on the stage, addresses himself ostensibly to the air and sky. Where a doubtful or evil dream is so recounted there is the special reason that the sunlight will dispel the terrors of the night. Thus on S. *El.* 424–5 (Clytemnestra's dream) *τοιαῦτά του παρόντος, ἡνίχ' Ἡλίῳ | δείκνυσι τοὔναρ, ἔκλυον . . . Σ* comments *τοῖς γὰρ παλαιοῖς ἔθος ἦν ἀποτροπιαζομένους τῷ Ἡλίῳ διηγεῖσθαι τὰ ὀνείρατα.* See Jebb ad loc., and cf. E. *IT* 42–3 *ἃ καινὰ δ' ἥκει νὺξ φέρουσα φάσματα | λέξω πρὸς αἰθέρ', εἴ τι δὴ τόδ' ἔστ' ἄκος.* It is also of course dramatically necessary that these dreams should be communicated to other actors and/or the audience.

In *Med.* 50 ff. Euripides, characteristically, draws attention to the fact that the Nurse has been talking all by herself, and makes her explain (56) *ἐγὼ γὰρ ἐς τοῦτ' ἐκβέβηκ' ἀλγηδόνος, | ὥσθ' ἵμερός μ' ὑπῆλθε γῇ τε κοὐρανῷ | λέξαι μολούσῃ δεῦρο δεσποίνης τύχας.* Elsewhere it is taken as an accepted convention, as in this passage and e.g. S. *El.* 86 *ὦ φάος ἁγνὸν καὶ . . . ἀήρ, ὥς μοι πολλὰς μὲν θρήνων ᾠδάς . . . ᾔσθου.* As we should expect, this sort of thing attracted parodies in Comedy, e.g. Philem. fr. 79 *ὡς ἵμερός μοὐπῆλθε γῇ τε κοὐρανῷ λέξαι μολόντι τοὔψον ὡς ἐσκεύασα.* See further Page on E. *Med.* 57–8, and Schadewaldt, *Monolog und Selbstgespräch*, p. 13.

In Tragedy the effect of course depends on the context. In A. *Pr.* 88 ff. we are certainly far away from mere convention: to whom but the elements should the lonely Titan cry out when he breaks silence with *ὦ δῖος αἰθὴρ καὶ ταχύπτεροι πνοαί . . .*?

94. κακῶν: objective gen. depending on *τέρψις*; *ἔχειν* in the next line is an explanatory infin. Cf. S. *Aj.* 1200 *οὔτε βαθειᾶν κυλίκων νεῖμεν ἐμοὶ τέρψιν ὁμιλεῖν*; *El.* 542 *τῶν ἐμῶν Ἅιδης τιν' ἵμερον τέκνων . . . ἔσχε δαίσασθαι*; E. *Med.* 1399; *Hipp.* 1375; Pl. *Crit.* 52 b *οὐδ' ἐπιθυμία σε ἄλλης πόλεως . . . ἔλαβεν εἰδέναι.*

τέρψις: for the pleasure in giving expression to grief rather than enduring in silence cf. the Homeric *τεταρπώμεσθα γόοιο* (not specially characteristic of women) and e.g. Eur. *El.* 125–6, *Tro.* 608–9. Plato deplored such pleasures as vicariously enjoyed by spectators *ὅταν ἅμα χαίροντες κλάωσι* (*Phil.* 48 a, *R.* 605 d). See J. de Romilly, *L'Évolution du pathétique d'Eschyle à Euripide*, p. 88.

96. οὐχ ἓν ἀλλὰ πολλά: emphasis by denial of the opposite, in the form 'not A but B' or 'B and not A', is a common idiom in Hdt. and in the dialogue of Attic Tragedy, and sometimes, especially in Euripides, seems to become a mannerism which to us, not necessarily to an Athenian, gives an effect of flatness; e.g. *Hcld.* 531 *ἑκοῦσα κοὐκ ἄκουσα*; *Tro.* 1157 *λυπρὸν θέαμα κοὐ φίλον*; fr. 635 *δυστυχὲς κοὐκ εὐτυχές*; Hdt. 2. 43 *οὐχ ἥκιστα ἀλλὰ μάλιστα*; cf. also 357 below. Here a single conception is presented from the positive and negative aspects. The same antithesis 'not A but B' has a quite different effect when both rejection and affirmation have their separate significance: 'I bring not peace but a sword'; *οὔτοι συνεχθεῖν ἀλλὰ συμφιλεῖν ἔφυν.*

97–9. These lines point forward to the following elegiac lament; they also recall and sum up the first fifteen lines of the prologue, except that Astyanax is not mentioned here.

98. στερρόν here gains emphasis from its position; cf. E. fr. 273 *πτηνὰς διώκεις, ὦ τέκνον, τὰς ἐλπίδας*. The word is a collateral form of *στερεός* and to be distinguished from *στερρός* 'barren'. Cf. E. *Hec.* 1295 *στερρὰ γὰρ ἀνάγκη*.

τὸν ἐμὸν δαίμον': it is not always possible to distinguish clearly between *δαίμων* as (1) a personified form of the destiny of an individual (or of a family), his good or evil genius whereby he is *εὐδαίμων* or *κακοδαίμων*, and (2) a more impersonal fate or lot, virtually equivalent to *πότμος* or *τύχη*. The former sense is apparently found in Phocylides, fr. 15 *ἀλλ' ἄρα δαίμονές εἰσιν ἐπ' ἀνδράσιν ἄλλοτε ἄλλοι*, where the plural implies that each has his own particular *δαίμων*, and perhaps in Hesiod, *WD* 314 *δαίμονι δ' οἷος ἔησθα* and Theognis 161 *πολλοί τοι χρῶνται δειλαῖς φρεσί, δαίμονι δ' ἐσθλῷ*, though in the last two passages the impersonal sense is not excluded. It may well be that a protest against this notion is to be seen in Heracleitus *ἦθος ἀνθρώπῳ δαίμων* and Epicharmus *ὁ τρόπος ἀνθρώποισι δαίμων ἀγαθός, οἷς δὲ καὶ κακός* (fr. 258 Kaibel). *δαίμων* is clearly so used in Aeschylus, *Ag.* 1569 *δαίμονι τῷ Πλεισθενιδῶν*, and probably in Sophocles, *OT* 1311 *ἰὼ δαῖμον, ἵν' ἐξήλου* and Euripides, *Supp.* 591 *δαίμονος τοὐμοῦ μέτα στρατηλατήσω*; in the last passage the *δαίμων* of Theseus, which he contrasts with the *τύχη* of Adrastus, should itself perhaps be regarded as anticipating the later personification of *Τύχη* and *Fortuna*. In the fourth century this sense of *δαίμων* finds frequent expression, e.g. in Menander, fr. 167 K. *ἅπαντι δαίμων ἀνδρὶ συμπαρίσταται | εὐθὺς γενομένῳ*, Anaxandrides, fr. 1 *τὸν γὰρ οἴακα στρέφει δαίμων ἑκάστῳ*, and, with deeper philosophic meaning, in Plato, e.g. *Phaedo* 107 d, *R.* 617 d–e. See Dodds, *The Greeks and the Irrational*, p. 42, from whom some of these examples are taken.

The impersonal sense may go back to Homer, *Il.* 8. 166, where the phrase πάρος τοι δαίμονα δώσω in our MSS. seems to be equivalent to πότμον ἐφήσω (which Zenodotus read in this passage); so also Pindar, *I.* 7. 43 θνᾴσκομεν γὰρ ὁμῶς ἅπαντες, δαίμων δ' ἄϊσος. In the fifth century the general tendency is for δαίμων to be used in this more impersonal and abstract sense, not clearly distinguished from μοῖρα, τύχη, and similar words. This is clear in, e.g., S. fr. 653 μὴ σπεῖρε πολλοῖς τὸν παρόντα δαίμονα; E. *Or.* 504 νῦν δ' ἐς τὸν αὐτὸν δαίμον' ἦλθε μητέρι; *IA* 1136 ὦ πότνια μοῖρα καὶ τύχη δαίμων τ' ἐμός; *An.* 973 ἐμὰς λέγων τύχας | καὶ τὸν παρόντα δαίμονα. If pressed to distinguish, Euripides would probably have agreed with E. R. Dodds (op. cit., pp. 58, 80) that δαίμων is the religious interpretation, τύχη (or συμφορά) the profane or non-committal view; but when, for instance, in *Alc.* 551 the Chorus refer to the death of Alcestis in the words τοιαύτης συμφορᾶς προκειμένης and in 561 ask, in relation to the same situation, πῶς οὖν ἔκρυπτες τὸν παρόντα δαίμονα; it seems unlikely that there is any appreciable difference in the point of view.

Thus in the present passage, and several others in the tragic dramatists, there may be some ambiguity between these two coexistent senses of the word δαίμων, but in view of the general tendency at this period it should be taken here as impersonal 'my hard lot'. For this use of δαίμων in prose cf. Antiph. Soph. B 59 (cited by Fraenkel on *Ag.* 1342) αὕτη ἡ ἡμέρα, αὕτη ἡ νὺξ καινοῦ δαίμονος ἄρχει, καινοῦ πότμου.

συνεζύγην: a common metaphor in this context: E. *Hel.* 255 τίνι πότμῳ συνεζύγην; *Hipp.* 1389 οἵᾳ συμφορᾷ συνεζύγης; S. *Aj.* 123 ἄτῃ συγκατέζευκται κακῇ; cf. also ζύγον ἀνάγκης in E. *Or.* 1330, fr. 475, *IA* 443.

99. δούλειον ἦμαρ: a Homeric echo, recurring in *Hec.* 56; for ἦμαρ in the sense 'condition' or 'state' cf. *Il.* 6. 455 ἐλεύθερον ἦμαρ and 463 δούλιον ἦμαρ, both referring to Andromache. LSJ cite only Homer for this use of ἦμαρ, but refer to a similar use of ἡμέρα in S. *Tr.* 654 and E. *Hec.* 364.

101. θανόντος: gen. abs., sc. αὐτοῦ.

The commonplace 'call no man happy before death' is first recorded in Greek literature in A. *Ag.* 928, but it is described in S. *Tr.* 1 as an ἀρχαῖος λόγος and according to a tradition accepted by Aristotle (*EN* 1100a10) goes back to Solon; see Hdt. 1. 30–3. It occurs frequently in Tragedy, as might be expected, and sometimes in phraseology similar to the present passage, as in S. fr. 646 and *OT* 1528–30. See further Jebb on S. *OT* 1528 and Fraenkel on A. *Ag.* 928 (but in S. fr. 662 Pearson is probably right that τελευτήσαντα is neut. pl. and has nothing to do with death or this commonplace).

The effect of this sentiment naturally depends on the context. Here it is not a warning, as in Herodotus, or a mere caveat, as in the *Agamemnon*, but a pathetic reminder that for Andromache too there was a time when the future looked bright enough.

103–16. See D. L. Page's paper 'The Elegiacs in Euripides' *Andromache*' in *Greek Poetry and Life*, pp. 206–30, to which this commentary is indebted for several points. Page argues persuasively that this elegiac lament, unique in extant Greek Tragedy, is an imitation of a kind of poetry that flourished in the Northern Peloponnese in the seventh and early sixth centuries and was associated in ancient tradition with the names of Echembrotos and Sakadas; but no actual examples have survived and it remains a hypothesis. It would account for the fact that the Doric α for η is used here, whereas in early Greek elegy in general we find mainly Ionic forms.

103. αἰπεινᾷ: a Homeric epithet for *Ἴλιος*; see Bowra, 'Homeric Epithets for Troy', *JHS* 80 (1960), 18, where he gives five examples and notes the aptness of this adj. for a town that rises steeply from the plain. The fem. *Ἴλιος* is also Homeric, *Ἴλιον* being the usual form in Tragedy. Other Homeric echoes are *θῖνα θαλάσσας* (109), *ἐν κονίαις* (112), *περὶ χεῖρε βαλοῦσα* (115).

103–4. If *γάμον* and *ἄταν* are in apposition to *Ἑλέναν*, *γάμος* must have the sense 'bride', as in S. *Tr.* 1139 *ὡς προσεῖδε τοὺς ἔνδον γάμους* and probably E. *Ino*, fr. 409; but though *γάμος* can refer to a person, it does not follow that it could be used in apposition to her name. It is better to take *γάμον* as in apposition to the sentence *ἠγάγετ'* . . . *Ἑλέναν*. This construction is particularly common in Eur. (KG 1. 284. 6) and, as Barrett has shown (on *Hipp.* 752–7), it may either be added to a sentence already complete without it, as in *Or.* 1105 *Ἑλένην κτάνωμεν, Μενέλεῳ λύπην πικράν*, in which case it naturally follows the main sentence, or it may be integral with the sentence, as in *Hel.* 77 and in this passage, in which case it may precede or follow the main verb. It is, as Barrett says, a special form of the internal acc., the force of which is here 'he brought Helen home, not marriage-wise but disastrously'.

For the thought cf. also A. *Ag.* 406 *ἄγουσά τ' ἀντίφερνον Ἰλίῳ φθοράν*, and *Hec.* 848–9.

105. δηιάλωτον: proleptic; this adjective is found only here and in A. *Th.* 72.

106. χιλιόναυς: the Catalogue in the *Iliad* gives a total of 1,186 ships and Thucydides calls it 1,200 (1. 10. 4). The round number 1,000, first recorded in A. *Ag.* 45 and common in Eur., became traditional in poetry, e.g. Virg. *Aen.* 2. 198; Marlowe, *Faustus*, 1328.

106. ὠκὺς Ἄρης: the epithet *ὠκύτατον* is attached to Ares as an individual in *Od.* 8. 331 and points the contrast with the slow limping Hephaestus: where Ares stands for 'war' the epithet is *ὀξύς*, e.g. *Il.* 2. 330 *ἐγείρομεν ὀξὺν Ἄρηα*, hence Schaefer's *ὀξύς* in this passage. Here, however, the context shows that Ares stands for the warriors of Hellas; cf. *Ph.* 1081 *ὁ Καδμείων Ἄρης κρείσσων κατέστη τοῦ Μυκηναίου δορός*. *ὠκύς* and *θοός* as laudatory epithets are more appropriate for individual fighters (*Il.* 16. 494, 1. 364), but may perhaps be used of the host in general.

107. τὸν ἐμὸν μελέας: cf. S. *Phil.* 1126 τὰν ἐμὰν μελέου τροφάν; E. *El.* 366 πόσις ἐμὸς τῆς ἀθλίας.

τόν: used as relative, as often in Homer and more rarely in Tragedy. Page's suggestion τρίς (corrupted to τοῖς, which was then 'corrected' to τόν) certainly improves the run of the sentence and preserves the completeness of each couplet in the first ten lines, but the rejection of the MS. reading is hardly justified.

περὶ τείχη: in Homer Achilles dragged Hector towards the Greek ships (*Il.* 22. 465) and later round the tomb of Patroclus (*Il.* 24. 16). Virgil (*Aen.* 1. 483) gives the same account as Euripides, who may be following a different tradition, or may merely have forgotten the Homeric version. See W. R. Paton, *CR* 27 (1913), 45–7.

110. ἀμφιβαλοῦσα: the middle would be more usual, but cf. *Il.* 17. 742 κράτερον μένος ἀμφιβαλόντες.

111. κατέβα: this verb nearly always has a personal subject, but cf. *Il.* 14. 19 καταβήμεναι ἐκ Διὸς οὖρον and Pl. *Crit.* 118 d καταβαίνοντα ῥεύματα.

χροός: for χρώς in the sense 'face' or 'cheek' cf. *Hel.* 1419 μή νυν ἄγαν σὸν δάκρυσιν ἐκτήξῃς χρόα.

112. ἐν κονίαις: the plural is Homeric, as in the formula ἐν κονίῃσι πεσών; it refers only to πόσιν, and even so is not literally true, at any rate according to *Iliad* 24, where Achilles restores the body of Hector to Priam.

113. ὤμοι: the second syllable is shortened before a vowel (correption), as usual in hexameters and elegiacs; so also the third syllable of τάκομαι in 116, and cf. 284, 1173.

115. πρὸς τόδ' ἄγαλμα: ἱκετεύω (from ἱκνέομαι) can mean 'approach as a suppliant', e.g. *Il.* 16. 574 ἐς Πηλῆ' ἱκέτευσε. So here the idea of motion towards is implied in ἱκέτις.

περὶ . . . βαλοῦσα: tmesis, as often in Epic: cf. *Od.* 11. 211 περὶ χεῖρε βαλόντε. According to E. Hasse, *Der Dualis im Attischen*, p. 47, this is the only example in Tragedy of the dual χεῖρε; in A. *Ag.* 1559 MSS. have περὶ χεῖρα βαλοῦσα emended to χεῖρε by Porson, and in E. *Ba.* 615 Nauck, followed by most editors, emended χεῖρα to χεῖρε. In our passage, and perhaps in *Ag.* 1559, the influence of epic usage might be expected. (In *Med.* 973 ἐς χεῖρ' ἐκείνης Page assumes that χεῖρ' = χεῖρε, but this passage cannot be used as evidence.)

116. 'I dissolve in tears like a gushing stream flowing down a rock.' Elsewhere in literature πέτρινος means 'made of rock', but cf. πέτρινος ῥόος in a Dorian inscription from Argos (Schwyzer, *Dial. Graec. ex. epigr.* 89. 5). The general comparison of fast-flowing tears to a spring in a rock-face goes back to Hom. *Il.* 16. 3; cf. E. *Supp.* 79–82 and 532–4 below. Here the epithet πιδακόεσσα would recall the familiar πολυπίδακος Ἴδης; as Stinton says, Andromache, sick for home, thinks naturally of her native mountains. The image may also recall the legend of Niobe turned into a rock streaming with tears for her children: see S. *Ant.* 828 ff. with Jebb's notes.

PARODOS: 117–146

The Chorus is composed of women of Phthiotis (119), perhaps members of the household of Hermione (142 δεσποτῶν ἐμῶν, though this might merely refer to the authority of the ruling house). They are sympathetic to Andromache but a little condescending to a foreigner (119, 128), and their advice to her to leave sanctuary and submit to her masters stresses her weakness and isolation.

Metre. The rhythm is mainly dactylic and trochaic, thus following naturally upon the preceding elegiacs.

Metrical Scheme:

Strophe and antistrophe (*a*): 117–25 = 126–34

117 (= 126)	1.	– ∪ ∪ – ∪ ∪ – ∪ ∪ – ∪ ∪ – ∪ ∪ – –	dactylic hexameter
	2.	– ∪ – ∪ – –	ithyphallic
	3.	– ∪ ∪ – ∪ ∪ – ∪ ∪ – ∪ ∪ – ∪ ∪ – –	dactylic hexameter
120 (= 129)	4.	– ∪ – ∪ – –	ithyphallic
	5.	∪ – – – ∪ – ∪ – ∪ –	bacchiac + cretic + iambic metron
	6.	– ∪ ∪ – ∪ ∪ – ∪ ∪ – ∪ ∪ – ∪ ∪ – –	dactylic hexameter
	7.	– ∪ – ∪ – –	ithyphallic
	8.	∪ ∪ – ∪ ∪ – ∪ ∪ – ∪	paroemiac
125 (= 134)	9.	– ∪ – ∪ – –	ithyphallic

Note:

5 may be taken as a syncopated iambic trimeter; cf. 4 in strophe (*b*).

Strophe and antistrophe (*b*): 135–40 = 141–6

135 (= 141)	1.	– ∪ ∪ – ∪ ∪ – ∪ ∪ – ∪ ∪ – ∪ ∪ – –	dactylic hexameter
	2.	– ∪ – ∪ – ∪ –	lekythion
	3.	– ∪ ∪ – ∪ ∪ –	hemiepes
	4.	∪ ∪∪ – – ∪ – ∪ – ∪ –	bacchiac + cretic + iambic metron (= syn. iambic trimeter)

	5.	– – – ∪ – ∪ –	molossus + iambic metron
140 (= 146)	6.[1]	– – ∪ – ∪ – –	iambic dimeter cat.

117. δάπεδον καὶ ἀνάκτορα: i.e. 'the floor of the shrine'; cf. *Ion* 121 *δάπεδον θεοῦ*. For *θάσσειν* governing an acc. cf. *IT* 277; *Ion* 91.

118. δαρόν: 'for a long time', used, as often, adverbially and with the connotation 'too long'; cf. A. *PV* 648 *τί παρθενεύῃ δαρόν, ἐξόν σοι γάμου | τυχεῖν;*

119. Ἀσιήτιδα γένναν: 'your Asian stock' for 'you who are of Asian stock'. Murray has doubts about *γένναν* and suggests *Ἀσιάτιδ' ἰωάν*, but *ἰωή* generally means a loud cry or shout, and is not very appropriate for A.'s elegiac lament.

120. εἰ δυναίμαν: see on 44 and 54–5.

121. ἄκος . . . τεμεῖν: 'to contrive a remedy'. In A. *Ag.* 17 *ὕπνου τόδ' ἀντίμολπον ἐντέμνων ἄκος* Page translates 'incising a cure', i.e. 'curing by means of an incision', but the surgical metaphor, always used elsewhere of a drastic remedy and ruthless action (A. *Cho.* 539 *ἄκος τομαῖον*; *Ag.* 849; S. *Ai.* 582) is inappropriate for humming a tune to keep oneself awake. Here[2] and in our present passage the metaphor is perhaps derived from the different use of *τέμνειν* in *Alc.* 971 *ὅσα Φοῖβος Ἀσκληπιάδαις ἔδωκε | φάρμακα πολυπόνοις ἀντιτεμὼν βροτοῖσι*, where the reference is to the cutting of herbs or roots for medicinal purposes: cf. also the use of *ῥιζοτόμος* in medical writings.

122–5. If the MS. readings are accepted, *τλάμον'* and *ἐοῦσαν* must refer either to Andromache or to Hermione. *λέκτρον* means 'marriage-bed', or possibly here 'spouse'; cf. 928 *δουλεύσομεν νόθοισι λέκτροις* i.e. to Andromache, and the similar use of *λέχος*, e.g. Sappho, fr. 121 *λέχος νεώτερον* and E. *Hipp.* 835. The exact sense of *ἐπίκοινον* is not certain (see below), but in any case it must refer to Neoptolemus. The construction will thus be *τλάμον' ἐοῦσαν ἀμφὶ ἐπίκοινον διδύμων λέκτρων* 'unhappy over one who is shared by (or has a share in) two couches (or two women) ⟨that is⟩ over the son of Achilles'.

There are several difficulties here. If *τλάμον'* refers to Andromache it is odd that the Chorus should commiserate with her for having to share N. with his lawful wife, and this has certainly not been the burden of her own lament; yet it is equally unlikely that the Chorus would now transfer their interest wholly to Hermione. Linguistically the repetition of *ἀμφί* is unsatisfactory, and in this sense it generally

---

[1] The text as printed cannot be right: either 140 or 146 must be emended to provide metrical correspondence. The metrical scheme above assumes a correction of 140 which adds a long syllable; see notes ad loc.

[2] For the compound *ἐντέμνειν* in the sense 'cut up' cf. Ar. *Lys.* 192.

depends on a verb, e.g. μάχεσθαι ἀμφί, or a verbal noun. Moreover, ἐοῦσαν adds little to the sense, and the form is not found elsewhere in Eur. or in Greek Tragedy, except that in A. *Pers.* 782 many editors accept ἐών. Thus Murray was right to obelize and comment *locus nondum emendatus*.

The general sense of the strophe seems clear enough. The Chorus begin by pitying Andromache and go on to express sympathy for her and Hermione, both caught in the net of rivalry for the affection of Neoptolemus. That in the last lines the Chorus are thinking of both together is strongly suggested by 122 and confirmed by 465 ff. Without emendation τλάμον' can stand for the dual τλάμονε, but ἐοῦσαν will not do, and we are left with the double ἀμφί. Krause's ἐούσα (dual) is, like ἐοῦσαν, without parallel in Tragedy, and involves hiatus. ἀμφὶ παῖδ' Ἀχίλλεως rounding off the strophe looks right, and probably the first ἀμφί should go. Two ingenious emendations have been proposed by J. Jackson, *Marginalia Scaenica*, p. 29. For ἀμφὶ λέκτρων he suggests ἀμφιλέκτωι in agreement with ἔριδι, comparing E. *Ph.* 500 ἀμφίλεκτος ἔρις and *Med.* 637 ff.; the comma is then of course placed after ἀμφιλέκτῳ, not συνέκλῃσαν. We then need a noun with διδύμων, which Jackson supplies by proposing εὐνᾶν for ἐοῦσαν. εὐνή without any qualification often means 'marriage-bed' and is sometimes virtually equivalent to 'bedfellow', as in *An.* 907 ἄλλην τιν' εὐνὴν ἀντὶ σοῦ στέργει πόσις; The sense of 122 ff. is then: 'They have involved you and Hermione, poor women, in hateful contentious strife over the son of Achilles, who shares in two beds.' For ἀμφί c. acc. instead of the more usual gen. cf. S. *Tr.* ἀμφί νιν γοώμενος. εὐνᾶν however involves a metrical change, giving an enoplian colon instead of a paroemiac in 124, and it is a serious objection that this means emending in the antistrophe the reading of all MSS., which is in itself blameless; see note on 133.

ἐπίκοινον is taken by Jackson and LSJ to mean 'sharing in'; so also Radermacher (*Charisteria A. Rzach*, pp. 152–3), who cites only a passage from the astrological writings of Vettius Valens (ii A.D.). It is true that Ionic and poetic words often reappear in the Koine, from which the language of Tragedy can sometimes be illustrated, but since ἐπίκοινος in the classical period occurs only in Hdt., where it always means 'common' 'shared', it is more likely that, however the text is emended, ἐπίκοινον will have the passive sense, N. being shared by the two women.

126. γνῶθι τύχαν: cf. *Hec.* 227 γίγνωσκε δ' ἀλκὴν καὶ παρουσίαν κακῶν | τῶν σῶν.

λόγισαι: rather a prosaic word for lyrics; not in Aesch. and found only in iambics in Soph. (4 times) and in Eur. (12 times).

τὸ παρὸν κακόν: the sense is repeated in εἰς ὅπερ ἥκεις, hence Wecklein's τ' ἄπορον κακόν, but the tautology is not impossible.

128. ἐγγενέτῃσιν: only here in Eur. On this form of the dative see Barrett on *Hipp.* 101. In inscriptions the early Attic dat. pl. seems to have been -ῃσι or -ᾳσι (according to whether the dat. sing. is ῃ or ᾳ); later from *c.* 420 B.C. only -αις; see Meisterhans, p. 94; Schwyzer, *Gr. Gr.* 559; Wade-Gery, *JHS* 51 (1931), 78–82. We should not expect to find -ῃσι in choral lyric, where case endings in η are avoided, and in fact MSS. usually have -αισ(ι), and in the five or six passages in Euripidean lyric where -ῃσι appears as a variant it may be an intrusive Homericism, as Barrett thinks. Here then we should print ἐγγενέταισιν, the reading of MSS. other than LBO, with Hermann, Nauck, Wecklein, and Méridier.

129. δεξίμηλον: only in Eur.; see 1138 and *Ph.* 632, and cf. Pind. *P.* 3. 27 μηλοδόκῳ Πυθῶνι.

130. ποντίας: ποντίου L is possible, but this is generally a three-termination adj.

θεοῦ: 'goddess', as in 253 ἐναλίας θεοῦ and often. θεᾶς, the original reading of LP, is equally common.

131. καιρός: Σ explains ἀντὶ τοῦ ὠφέλεια. The sense 'opportunity or right time' easily passes over into 'profit or advantage'. So here 'In what respect is it the moment to waste away . . .?', i.e. 'What avails it . . .?' See Jebb on S. *Phil.* 151 and Page on *Med.* 128.

αἰκέλιον: proleptic. 'What use in your distress to mar your face with weeping?'

132. ἀνάγκαις: probably causal dative: 'because of the harsh constraint of your masters'. Some editors take it as instrumental with ἀτυζομένᾳ, but this verb is generally used absolutely, except *Il.* 8. 183 ἀτυζομένους ὑπὸ καπνοῦ.

133. τὸ κρατοῦν: for this use of the neuter participle, equivalent to κράτος cf. S. *Ph.* 674 τὸ νοσοῦν = νόσος; Xen. *Mem.* 1. 2. 42 τὸ κρατοῦν τῆς πόλεως. See KG 1. 267 γ for numerous examples in Thuc.

δέ σ' ἔπεισι: Hermann's correction of the unmetrical MS. reading δέ σε πείσει, based on the explanation of Σ οἱ δεσπόται κατὰ σοῦ ἐλεύσονται.

τί . . . μοχθεῖς: Jackson's εὐνᾶν in 124 would involve excision of τί; it could conceivably have been inserted to obtain correspondence with a corrupt strophe, but the rhetorical question is more effective and follows naturally after the previous τί σοι καιρός . . .

136. ἐπὶ ξένας: sc. γᾶς; cf. S. *OC* 184 ξεῖνος ἐπὶ ξένης; *Ph.* 135.

137. δμωίς here has its original sense of slave woman taken in war; it is also used more widely for any female slave.

ἐπ' ἀλλοτρίας πόλεος: ἀλλότριος is a stronger word than ξένος, which merely means 'foreign', whereas ἀλλότριος can have the connotation 'strange' or even 'hostile'. Hermann's correction of the MS. πόλεως is to obtain metrical correspondence. For this form see Jebb on S. *Ant.* 162, and cf. E. *El.* 412, where πόλεως, the reading of

LP, must be corrected to *πόλεος* on metrical grounds. *πόλις* here means 'country', but its use may help to suggest that An. is subject to an alien jurisdiction. The rhetorical effect would be weakened by altering *ἐπ'* to *ἀπ'*.

140. The corresponding line 146 as printed in OCT has an extra long syllable. Here L² has *ὦ παντάλαινα*, but this looks rather like a fill-up, and Wilamowitz's *πασᾶν, τάλαινα* is tempting. See also note on 146.

141. οἴκους: for the acc. see on *ἑστίαν* in 3 above.

143. ἡσυχίαν ἄγομεν: a prosaic expression.

144. τὸ σόν: 'your plight'.

οἴκτῳ φέρουσα: for the modal dative with *φέρειν* cf. *Supp.* 556 *ἀδικουμένους μέτρια μὴ θυμῷ φέρειν*; Thuc. 1. 31 *ὀργῇ φέροντες τὸν πόλεμον*; though this verb seems more suitable for expressing endurance of something than pity for another's suffering. Badham's *σκότῳ* is not necessary and is unmetrical. The point of *οἴκτῳ* has indeed already been made by *οἰκτροτάτα* (141), but such repetition is characteristic of the whole parodos, in which the Chorus keep saying in slightly different phrasing 'you must realize your present position as a helpless slave in a foreign land'.

145. Διὸς κόρας: i.e. Helen, daughter of Zeus and Leda.

μὴ . . . εἰδῇ depends on *φόβῳ* in 142, 144 being parenthetical.

146. To obtain correspondence with 140 Hartung and Wecklein excise *σοί*, but though the pronoun is not indispensable, its presence makes the sense clearer and it is better to emend 140.

After 146 Murray and others follow Musgrave in assuming a lacuna in which the coryphaeus announces in iambics or anapaests the entrance of Hermione, and presumably either makes some allusion to her splendid appearance or urges her to deal gently with Andromache: the reference to her in 145–6 would naturally lead into the common formula *καὶ μὴν ὁρῶ* . . . or the like. So in *Alc.* 136–40, where after the parodos the Chorus leader has five lines of iambics announcing the entrance of a slave girl, who hears and answers the last three lines. The chief reason for this assumption is that in 154 Hermione refers to the previous lines as her reply, and *ὑμᾶς* would naturally mean the Chorus.

Some editors take it that H. is reacting to the sympathy expressed for Andromache by the Chorus in the last lines of the Parodos, but characters do not normally allude to what is said in choral odes (S. *OT* 216 is exceptional), and in any case the connection between 141–6 and the lines given to H. is too slight and vague to justify *ἀνταμείβομαι* in 154. Matthiae suggested that *ὑμᾶς* might refer to H.'s attendants, to whose plea or comment she replies as she comes from the house, but there is no real parallel for this, even in Comedy. In some passages in Euripides it is possible that two characters when they enter continue a conversation already begun; see *Alexandros*, fr. 23 (Snell), Page, *Lit. Pap.* (Loeb), p. 58. 13 ff.; *Supp.* 381, 837 (but the text is doubtful); *IA* 303 ff. In Ar. *Nub.* 1214 the creditor's first words suggest that he enters in the midst of grumbling to the witness he brings with him. There are several passages in New Comedy, e.g. Men. *Dysc.* 206, 456 ff.; *Perik.* 61, where a character comes from a house and calls out something to those inside; but he does not make a speech, and it is always immediately obvious from the text what is happening.

The remaining possibility is to delete 154, which Hunger (*Rh. M.* 95 (1952), 369 ff.) takes to be an interpolation by an actor, perhaps thinking to provide a pretext for Hermione's boasting. Without this line there is no great difficulty. Hermione enters worked up into a state of indignation, and in her first seven lines is probably addressing the Chorus but talking *at* Andromache, to whom she turns at 155. It is a slight objection that Hermione's entrance is then unheralded, since when this occurs elsewhere the name of the new arrival is given, generally within a few lines, as in 309 ff. (Menelaus) and *Med.* 446 ff. (Jason), whereas Hermione is not named at all; she is however identified by *Μενέλαος πατήρ* in 152.

I think the choice is between lacuna and interpolation, and on the whole the latter seems to me the easier assumption.

First Epeisodion: 147–273

The quarrel scene between Hermione and Andromache, beginning with set speeches followed by a passage of stichomythia.

147. κόσμον . . . χρυσέας χλιδῆς: a golden diadem. The reminiscence of *πολυχρύσῳ χλιδῇ* in 2 may well be deliberate.

μέν: probably *μέν solitarium*. Denniston, *GP* 382, notes a tendency for speeches in early oratory and in drama to open with *μέν* where there is no antithesis to come. It is less likely that *μέν* is resumed by *μὲν οὖν* in 154 and then answered by *δέ* in 155.

148. χρωτός: objective gen. with *στολμόν*.

πέπλων: gen. of material; cf. *Alc.* 216 *μέλανα στολμὸν πέπλων*.

151. Λακαίνης: Eur. keeps reminding us of the Spartan nationality of Hermione and Menelaus.

152. δωρεῖται: the tense indicates present relationship: M. is the donor; cf. S. *Ant.* 1174 *καὶ τίς φονεύει;* 'and who is the slayer?'

153. ἕδνοις: 'dowry'; see on 2 above.

ἐλευθεροστομεῖν: sc. *ἐμέ*. H. claims that wealth gives her the right to say what she likes.

156–8. These are precisely the accusations mentioned by Andromache in 32–5.

157. ἀνδρί: see on *πόσει* in 33.

159–60. ἠπειρῶτις . . . ψυχὴ γυναικῶν: hypallage for *ψ.ἠπειρωτιδῶν γυναικῶν*; cf. *Tro.* 1110 *πατρῷον θαλάμον ἑστίας*. The periphrasis with *ψυχή* is unusual and has caused suspicion. Since planning and contriving are involved Nauck suggested *τέχνη* and Schenkel the all-embracing term *φύσις*. But Dodds perhaps exaggerates a little in saying (*The Greeks and the Irrational*, p. 139) that before Plato *ψυχή* is seldom if ever spoken of as the seat of reason. *ψυχή* is a mind that conceives or apprehends plans in Hdt. 7. 16a. 2 *διδάσκειν τὴν ψυχὴν πλέον τι δίζησθαι ἀεὶ ἔχειν τοῦ παρεόντος* and probably S. *Ph.* 1014 *ἡ κακὴ σὴ ψυχή* 'your evil intelligence' and *Tro.* 1171 *γνούς . . . σῇ ψυχῇ*. See T. B. L. Webster, *JHS* 77 (1957), 150.*

ἠπειρῶτις: here and in 652 'Asiatic'. Elsewhere this adj. and the noun *ἠπειρωτής* are used only in the sense 'dwelling on the mainland' in contrast with *νησιωτής*; but *ἤπειρος* often means 'continent', e.g. S. *Tr.* 101 *δισσαὶ ἄπειροι*, and particularly the continent of Asia, e.g. A. *Pers.* 718. The most famous example of a sorceress from the East was of course Medea, Pindar's *παμφάρμακος ξείνα*.

163. δ' οὖν: Denniston, *GP* 465 'the speaker hypothetically grants a supposition which he denies, doubts or reprobates'; cf. *Hcld.* 714 *ἢν δ' οὖν, ὃ μὴ γένοιτο, χρήσωνται τύχῃ* and 338 below. In the following lines Hermione dwells with satisfaction on the humiliation she can inflict on Andromache, and Verrall and Norwood (*Gk. Trag.*, p. 226) take it that this and not death is the vengeance she really wants; but the deadly intention in 161–2 is confirmed in 245; see also 806–7.

164. ὀλβίων φρονημάτων: the combination well illustrates the connection of material resources and independence of spirit.

165. πτῆξαι: cf. Xen. *Cyr.* 3. 1. 26 *τοῦ αὐτοῦ ἀνδρὸς εἶναι καὶ εὐτυχοῦντα ἐξυβρίσαι καὶ πταίσαντα ταχὺ πτῆξαι*.

166. σαίρειν: cf. *Hyps.* fr. 1. ii. 15–18 (Bond) *πότερα δώματος εἰσόδους σαίρεις ἢ δρόσον ἐπὶ πέδῳ βάλλεις οἷά τε δούλα; Hec.* 363.

167. τευχέων is scanned as a disyllable by synizesis, as in *El.* 496.

'Αχελῴου: not of course the real river A. (the modern Aspropotamo), which rises to the West of Phthiotis and flows into the Ionian Sea. Achelous is often used by metonymy for water; cf. *Hyps.* fr. 753 (where the scene is in Nemea) *δείξω μὲν Ἀργείοισιν Ἀχελῴου ῥόον*. See Bond's note ad loc. and Dodds on *Ba.* 625–6, and for the rather lofty expressions for housework cf. *Phaethon*, fr. 773. 12–14.

168. γνῶναί θ' ἵν' εἶ γῆς: Norwood's suggestion (*Gk. Tr.*, p. 277) that 'the very sound and fall of the words, with the two long monosyllables, can only be described as a verbal box on the ears' is rather fanciful, though it is not disproved by the fact that exactly the same metrical effect occurs, e.g in vv. 62 and 342, where it can have no significance. Hermione is in effect echoing the advice of the Chorus in 136 ff.

τάδε means in effect 'here'. In this idiomatic use it always follows a negative and often, as here, has a sarcastic or contemptuous connotation; cf. Hom. *Od.* 1. 226 *οὐκ ἔρανος τάδε γ' ἐστίν*; Thuc. 6. 77 *οὐκ Ἴωνες τάδε εἰσὶν . . . ἀλλὰ Δωριῆς ἐλεύθεροι*; *Cyc.* 204; also more generally, e.g. *Tro.* 99 *οὐκέτι Τροία τάδε*; *Hyps.* fr. 1. ii. 9.

169. χρυσός, interrupting the series of proper names, has been suspected, but perhaps needlessly. It goes closely with *Πρίαμος*, 'Priam and his gold'; cf. *Tro.* 994 *τὴν Φρυγῶν πόλιν | χρυσῷ ῥέουσαν.*

170. ἀμαθίας: for the sense 'lack of finer feeling' see Denniston on *El.* 294–5 and Verrall on *Med.* 223.

172. αὐθέντου: as Hermione has just said, it is actually the father of Neoptolemus who is *αὐθέντης* in relation to Hector. J. Helland conjectured *αὐθεντῶν*, a generalizing plural as in *Tro.* 660 *Ἀχιλλέως με παῖς ἐβουλήθη λαβεῖν | δάμαρτα· δουλεύσω δ' ἐν αὐθέντων δόμοις.* This may be right; cf. 403 below *φονεῦσιν Ἕκτορος νυμφεύομαι.*

173–6. In reply to Hermione's assertion that among *βάρβαροι* incest between parents and children and between brother and sister is sanctioned by *νόμος*, Andromache cannot unfortunately quote Hdt. 1. 135, where, speaking of Persians, he observes *ἀπ' Ἑλλήνων μαθόντες παισὶ μίσγονται.* In 3. 31 he refers to the union of Cambyses and his sister but speaks of it as being without precedent among the Persians. The audience would no doubt think of their own times, and apart from Herodotus there are other fifth-century references, though perhaps later than this play, to the current practice of incest in foreign countries. See, with reference to the Magi, Xanthus of Lydia[1] (*FHG* iiic, 765 F 31) *Ξάνθος δὲ ἐν τοῖς ἐπιγραφομένοις Μαγικοῖς "μίγνυνται δὲ" φησὶν "οἱ μάγοι μητράσι".* (It is uncertain whether the following words *καὶ θυγατράσι καὶ ἀδελφαῖς μίγνυσθαι θεμιτὸν εἶναι* are to be attributed to the same author.) See also *Δισσοὶ Λόγοι* (end of fifth cent.) *τοὶ δὲ Πέρσαι . . . καλὸν νομίζοντι καὶ τᾷ θυγατρὶ καὶ τᾷ ματρὶ καὶ τᾷ ἀδελφᾷ συνίμεν* (D–K ii. 408).

175–6. οἱ φίλτατοι: the reference is, as often, to those bound by ties of kinship.

διὰ φόνου χωροῦσι: oriental families could not provide better examples than the House of Atreus.

181. The periphrasis with *χρῆμα* is equivalent to *θήλεια φρήν*, 'a woman's heart is a jealous thing'. All the MSS. here give *ἐπίφθονόν τι χρῆμα θηλειῶν ἔφυ* and this was the reading used by the excerptor in the *Gnomologium Vatopedianum* (*CQ* N.S. 9 (1959), p. 139). It is in itself satisfactory and is printed by Hermann and Méridier; similar examples, where the MS. reading is not questioned, are *Ph.* 198 *φιλόψογον δὲ χρῆμα θηλειῶν ἔφυ*; *Andr.* 957 *σοφόν τι χρῆμα τοῦ διδάξαντος*

---

[1] His date is disputed and may be after 425. See also Simon Pembroke (to whom I am indebted for the reference to Xanthus) in *Journal of Warburg and Courtauld Institutes*, 30 (1967), 9 and 17.

. . .; Pl. *Theaet.* 209 e ἡδὺ χρῆμ' ἂν εἴη τοῦ καλλίστου . . . λόγου. In this passage however *Σ* has for one note the lemma θηλείας φρενός, and this reading is implied in explanations given in other notes; also Stobaeus quotes the line in that form. There appear to be alternative traditions and there is little to choose between them. In any case it is not necessary to emend τι to τοι (Dobree) or to τό (Valckenaer).

We should probably distinguish between three common types of expression illustrating the pleonastic or periphrastic use of χρῆμα: 1. σκαιόν τι χρῆμα πλοῦτος (E. fr. 96, and see 727 below); 2. συὸς μέγιστον χρῆμα (S. fr. 401); 3. σμικρὸν τὸ χρῆμα τοῦ βίου (*Supp.* 953). The present example, whichever reading is adopted, is a mixture of 1 and 3, and is a compressed form of ἐπίφθονόν τι χρῆμα ⟨ἐστι⟩ τὸ χρῆμα θηλείας φρενός. These idiomatic uses of χρῆμα are practically confined to Euripides in Tragedy, and are common in Comedy and in other colloquial contexts. For further discussion see L. Bergson in *Eranos*, 65 (1967), 79–115.

184 ff. It is natural that in the last decades of the fifth century the rhetorical techniques which must have become familiar to educated Athenians should be employed, sometimes perhaps instinctively, in the verbal contests in the theatre. This speech of Andromache, like so many law-court speeches, opens with a προοίμιον (184–91) in which the speaker stresses the special disadvantages under which she labours. In 192–204 she employs the argument ἐκ τῶν εἰκότων in a series of rhetorical questions involving *reductio ad absurdum* and designed to demonstrate that the idea of her being able to supplant Hermione is so absurd that the accusation lacks all probability.

This sort of approach is not strictly appropriate to a discussion between two persons or likely to prove persuasive in those circumstances. Andromache would have been more likely to win over Hermione by talking to her with tact and sympathy than by preaching at her and scoring debating points; but in fact nobody is ever won over in a Euripidean agon of this type, the purpose of which is to enable each character to state his or her case, as much for the benefit of the audience as of anybody else. Perhaps the presence of the Chorus, who listen and comment, though they are not a jury and are generally powerless to intervene, may make the forensic rhetoric seem more plausible. This is different from the quasi-judicial type of agon, where opponents argue before a 'judge', who then delivers his verdict, as in *Hec.* 1129 ff. (Polymestor *v.* Hecuba before Agamemnon) and *Tro.* 895 ff. (Helen *v.* Hecuba before Menelaus).

184. κακὸν . . . τὸ νέον: *Σ* explains διὰ τὴν προπετείαν. The folly and rashness of youth is a commonplace in Tragedy, e.g. *Hipp.* 118, *IA* 489, *Ion* 545.

185. A ὅστις clause is often found in apposition to an abstract noun, e.g. *Hel.* 271 τοῦτο μεῖζον . . . κακόν, | ὅστις τὰ μὴ προσόντα κέκτηται κακά. Here, however, the infin. which it replaces (τὸ μὴ δίκαιον εἶναι) would be parallel to τὸ νέον. Andromache again stresses the youth of Hermione in 192, 238, and esp. 326, where she describes her as ἀντίπαις.

186. τὸ δουλεύειν: an Athenian might think of the παρρησία which a citizen could claim but a slave could not; cf. *Ph.* 392 δούλου τόδ' εἶπας, μὴ λέγειν ἃ τις φρονεῖ and *Ion* 674–5; but in the present context Andromache's apprehension seems rather unreal.

188. κρατήσω: 'if I win', almost as though they were arguing in a court of law.

ὄφλω: here in the general sense to incur or bring upon oneself, but the use of this word, which in its technical sense meant to be the loser in a lawsuit, brings out the irony of the situation in which to 'win her case' will do her harm.

189. πνέοντες μαγέλα: cf. 327 and *Ba.* 640 κἂν πνέων ἔλθῃ μέγα.

κρείσσους: 'the winning arguments', looks back to κρατήσω.

190. ὕπο can be explained as due to the idea of being worsted implied in κρείσσους, but Hermann's correction ἄπο 'coming from' would be more natural and may be right.

191. ἁλώσομαι: the regular legal term for being convicted and condemned: 'I shall not let my case go by default'; cf. S. *OT* 576.

192–204. Rearrangements of these lines to produce a more logical argument, such as those of Bothe and Dobree, are not justified.

192. ἐχεγγύῳ: another legal term. As Jebb notes on *OC* 284 (though there the sense is different), it generally means 'having a good security (ἐγγύη) to give', and so 'trustworthy'; cf. *Med.* 387. In *Ph.* 759 it is connected with ἐγγύησις, formal betrothal.

194. τῶν Φρυγῶν: brachylogy for τῆς τῶν Φ. πόλεως; cf. ἀρσένων in 220. Scaliger's τῆς Φρυγῶν is not necessary.

Trojans and Phrygians are distinguished in Homer (*Il.* 3. 184–9) but regularly synonymous in Tragedy; cf. 204, 291, 363, *et saep.*

195. The MS. reading printed in OCT apparently goes back to Σ, who explains τῇ εὐδαιμονίᾳ ὑπερβάλλει ἡ Φρυγῶν πόλις τὴν Λάκαιναν; but this involves a very abrupt and awkward change of subject, made rather worse by the brachylogy in 194. There is also some lack of balance in the sentence, since the comparison of cities has been made in 194 and 195 should deal with comparison of persons.

Dindorf, followed by Hyslop, removes the difficulty by emending 194 to ὡς τῆς Λακαίνης ἡ Φρυγῶν μείζων πόλις, but this is much too drastic a change. Hermann and Paley print τύχη, the reading of B, and supply ἡ ἐμή, an extremely harsh ellipse; σε must also be supplied. Wecklein and Méridier print Lenting's correction τύχῃ θ' ὑπερθεῖ τἄμ' ἐλευθέραν θ' ὁρᾷς. τἄμ' for κἄμ' is an easy correction and με can be supplied (from τἀμά), and σε as object of ὑπερθεῖ. The smallest possible change to avoid the main difficulties is however, as Murray suggests, to take ὑπερθεῖ as 2nd pers. sing. passive, perhaps reading ὑπερθέῃ, but the passive is rather odd here and does not lead naturally to the second half of the line. Possibly *ἐλευθέρου*, the reading of B, conceals *ἐλευθέρων*, and if we accept Lenting's *τἄμ'* and make the small correction of *ὕπερθεν* for *ὑπερθεῖ*, we have *τύχῃ θ' ὕπερθεν τἄμ' ἐλευθέρων ὁρᾷς;* Andromache then asks in bitter irony, 'Is Sparta less than Troy, and do you regard me, a slave, as superior in fortune to those that are free (i.e. yourself)?' Once *τἄμ'* had become *κἄμ'* the other changes might easily follow. For *τἀμά* equivalent to *ἐμέ* cf. 235.

197 πόλεως: many editors accept Brunck's *πλούτου*, but there is no variant reading, and perhaps *μεγέθει* goes better with *πόλεως*.

199–202. The *reductio ad absurdum* is rather less convincing here, since the birth of other male children to Andromache by Neoptolemus would tend to strengthen her position, and *δούλους* is a rhetorical exaggeration: the children of Neoptolemus by a concubine would not actually have been slaves in Homeric society (or in the Athens of Euripides). In 942 Hermione describes the children of Andromache as *ἡμιδούλους* and *νοθαγενεῖς*. As *νόθοι* their status would normally be inferior to *γνήσιοι*, but for exceptions see *Od.* 14. 202; *Il.* 8. 284 and 2. 727. In 1246 it is implied that Andromache's son will become a king and founder of a royal line.

200. ἐφολκίδα: the same metaphor is used twice in *HF* 631, 1424.

201. τις here as often means something like 'public opinion'.

203–4. All editors except Murray and Méridier follow *Σ* in taking these lines as ironical statements, but it is better to regard them as continuing the series of rhetorical questions from 195 onwards.

204. *ἀμαυρός* in Tragedy means 'dim, obscure' or 'weak' or perhaps sometimes both; here the first sense predominates; cf. Wilamowitz on *HF* 124.

ἦ: it is probably better to keep the MS. reading *ἦν*; see on 59.

206. The regular use of *εἰ* instead of *ὅτι* after verbs expressing emotion does not give a hypothetical flavour to the following clause. Andromache gives specific instances in 209–12.

207. φίλτρον: Bornmann compares Menander, fr. 571 K. *ἓν ἔστ' ἀληθὲς φίλτρον, εὐγνώμων τρόπος, | τούτῳ κατακρατεῖν ἀνδρὸς εἴωθεν γυνή.* See also on 540.

τόδε: i.e. wifely virtue rather than beauty; cf. fr. 909 *οὐδεμίαν ὤνησε κάλλος εἰς πόσιν ξυνάορον | ἀρετὴ δ' ὤνησε πολλάς.*

208. ἀρεταί: the proper qualities in a wife. *Σ* explains *ἀρετὴ δὲ γυναικὸς ἡ πρὸς τὸν ἄνδρα ὁμόνοια.* Cf. 213–14 and *El.* 1052 *γυναῖκα γὰρ χρὴ πάντα συγχωρεῖν πόσει.*

209. κνισθῇς: cf. *Med.* 568 *εἴ σε μὴ κνίζοι λέχος.*

209–12. From *ἡ Λάκαινα* to *Ἀχιλλέως* (212) A. is describing the line of argument which she believes H. to adopt when irritated by her husband.

210. Σκῦρον: see on *νησιώτῃ* in 14 above.

οὐδαμοῦ: cf. S. *Ant.* 183 *τοῦτον οὐδαμοῦ λέγω*; E. *HF* 841; *IA* 954; Xen. *Mem.* 1. 2. 52 *μηδαμοῦ τοὺς ἄλλους εἶναι πρὸς ἑαυτόν.*

211. οὐ πλουτοῦσι: virtually a compound, equivalent to *πένησι*. The negative would in any case be *οὐ* since the reference is to specific persons, i.e. Neoptolemus and his family.

σοι: 'in your eyes'.

212. ταῦτα: adverbial 'for this reason'; cf. *Hec.* 13–14 *ὅ καί με γῆς | ὑπεξέπεμψεν*; Ar. *Nub.* 320 *ταῦτ' ἄρ' . . . ἡ ψυχή μου πεπότηται*: 'So that's why . . .'

215. χιόνι: Thrace conventionally suggested snow; cf. *Hec.* 81 *χιονώδη Θρῄκην*; *Alc.* 67; Hor. *Carm.* 3. 25. 11 'nive candidam Thracen'.

220–1. Difficulties in these lines are hardly sufficient to justify their deletion.

220. αἰσχρόν γε: this is certainly abrupt, and must presumably refer not to the hypothetical situation in the previous sentence (which would require an ellipse of *ἂν ἦν*) but rather to the whole behaviour of Hermione implied in the previous lines.

καίτοι: Murray's *ἐπεὶ κεἰ* is presumably intended to give a more logical connection of thought, but no change is needed. *καίτοι* is used in self-correction and also, as *Σ* observes, in anticipation of objections by Hermione, and the sequence of thought is: 'disgraceful indeed; though admittedly women are more afflicted in this way than men—but this is no excuse for Hermione, for women do or should conceal their passion.' For other examples where a modification introduced by *καίτοι* is then countered by the stronger adversative *ἀλλά* see *GP* 557–8.

221. προύστημεν: gnomic aorist. *Σ* rightly paraphrases *καλῶς περιστέλλομεν αὐτὰ καὶ οὐ φανεραὶ γιγνόμεθα*. 'We stand in front of, we conceal our weakness'; cf. 955 *χρεὼν | κοσμεῖν γυναῖκας τὰς γυναικείας νόσους*. For the sense of *προστῆναι* see Jebb on S. *El.* 980. Hermann corrected to *προσταῖμεν*, a wish, on the ground that as a statement it is false; but the reproach against Hermione is that women in general are assumed to do this, whereas she does not. Wecklein compares Nonnus, *Dionys.* 42. 209 *πᾶσα γυνὴ ποθέει πλέον ἀνέρος αἰδομένη δὲ | κεύθει κέντρον ἔρωτος*. Teiresias put it differently when, giving Zeus and Hera the benefit of his unique experience as man and woman, he pronounced that women have nine times as much pleasure as men from sexual intercourse (Pfeiffer on Call. fr. 576; I owe the ref. to H. Lloyd-Jones).

223. ξυνήρων: not quite, with Paley, 'I loved those whom you loved', but 'I helped you in these affairs'; so Méridier 'j'allais jusqu'à m'associer à tes amours'. This slightly extended sense of *ξυνερᾶν* seems possible, and Reiske's *ξυνῆρον* is not necessary.

224–5. μαστὸν . . . ἐπέσχον: perhaps suggested by *Il.* 5. 70 where Theano is said to have reared a bastard son of her husband Antenor *χαριζομένη πόσεϊ ᾧ*. Extant early Epic has no mention of *νόθοι* of Hector, but the existence of *'Εκτορίδαι* is referred to by Hellanicus of Lesbos

(Jacoby, fr. 31 = D. Hal. *AR* 1. 47) and may therefore have been known to Euripides.

225. ἐνδοίην: 'show, betray' suits the context better than 'cause'; cf. *Hel.* 508 ἤν δ' ἐνδίδῳ τι μαλθακόν 'betray any weakness'; Ar. *Pl.* 988; Hdt. 7. 52. σοι is then dat. of person concerned and πικρόν has the sense 'bitterness', 'anger', for which see S. *Ant.* 423 with Jebb's note.

227. A striking example of hyperbole.

229. φιλανδρία: LSJ give 'love for a husband', or, in this passage, 'wifely jealousy' as the only meaning in the classical period, the bad sense 'love of male sex' being only found in late Greek. The former sense is appropriate for Hermione in this context, but not for her mother, Helen. Probably both meanings were possible at this period, and Andromache is taking advantage of an ambiguity inherent in the word. Certainly φίλανδρος, which has the sense 'loving one's husband' in Luc. *Halc.* 8 and often in epitaphs, can also have a bad sense, as in Pl. *Smp.* 191 e γυναῖκες φίλανδροί τε καὶ μοιχεύτριαι.

230. γάρ, long by position, violates Porson's canon that in the tragic trimeter the final long syllable of a word may not fall in the anceps of the third metron, i.e. before the final cretic. This rule does not apply to a monosyllable unless, like γάρ, it is a postpositive and thus for metrical purposes counts as part of the preceding word. Violations of this canon are so rare, especially after discounting certain apparent exceptions for which there is special justification, that where they occur it is natural to suspect corruption. Hence Elmsley's δέ, which may be right, since δέ where γάρ might be expected is not rare in verse. See *GP* 169, and for the replacement of δέ by γάρ in MSS. cf. S. fr. 951 with Pearson's note. It is however just possible that in τῶν . . . μητέρων, where the words run together to form a single phrase, the violation was felt to be less objectionable.

231. τέκν' οἷς (τέκνα οἷς MBO), the MS. reading, is unmetrical and most editors print τέκν' ὅσοις, the reading of the second hand of L. It has, however, been pointed out by Jackson, *Marginalia Scaenica*, p. 46, that rearrangement of the words without change will give νοῦς οἷς ἔνεστι χρὴ τρόπους φεύγειν τέκνα.

232–3. These lines, conciliatory but favouring Andromache, balance 181–2.

προσίσταται is printed by most editors except Hermann, but the sense required seems to be 'as far as an easy opportunity offers' so far as she can go without 'losing face'; so Σ ὅσον ἐνδέχεται. For this sense παρίσταται, the reading of P, is better. In Thuc. 4. 133 the MS. reading παρεστηκός (= πάρον) 'opportunity having been given' should probably be kept, rather than Krüger's παρεσχηκότος.

233. τῇδε: Wecklein's τῇσδε would give a more usual construction, but it is possible for συμβῆναι to govern both τῇδε and λόγοις.

234. σεμνομυθεῖν occurs only here and *Hipp.* 490 τί σεμνομυθεῖς; οὐ λόγων εὐσχημόνων | δεῖ σ' ἀλλὰ τἀνδρός. In both passages the sense is 'indulge in lofty moralizing'.

235. ὡς δή: ironical, as usual. Each woman accuses the other of lack of σωφροσύνη—Hermione because Andromache lies with Neoptolemus, son of her husband's slayer, Andromache because Hermione has no reticence in matters of sex, including her jealousy of Andromache.[1]

τἀμά: for τὰ ἐμά = ἐγώ (or ἐμέ) cf. 195; *Or.* 296 ὅταν δὲ τἄμ' ἀθυμήσαντ' ἴδῃς; *Hel.* 1194; *Ion* 615; *Ph.* 775; A. fr. 138.

236. λόγοις: presumably her arguments in 170–80.

237. νοῦς picks up the words of Andromache in 231.

ξυνοικοίη: for the metaphor cf. E. *Hipp.* 162; Xen. *Smp.* 8. 24 ὁ σύνοικος ἐμοὶ ἔρως, and (with the person as subject) E. *Hcld.* 996 μὴ συνοικοίην φόβῳ.

239. δρᾷς: H. still maintains her accusations of witchcraft against Andromache.

δύνῃ: the normal Attic form is the uncontracted δύνασαι. The contracted form δύνᾳ is the MS. reading in S. *Phil.* 849 (lyr.) and Theocr. 10. 2. In this passage and in *Hec.* 253 and S. *Phil.* 798 all MSS. give δύνῃ, but some editors accept Porson's δύνᾳ in all three passages, assuming that this Ionicism is due to copyists. There are, however, other Ionicisms in Eur. in form and vocabulary, and it is not certain that correction is necessary. An exactly parallel form ἐπίστῃ is found in Theogn. 1085, but ἐπίστᾳ in Pind. and Aesch. See KB ii. 68 Anm. 4; Schwyzer, 1. 2. 668; Rutherford, *New Phryn.* 463–5; Björck, *Das Alpha Impurum*, p. 150 (but δύνῃ in Ar. *Eq.* 491 is subj.).

240. οὐκ αὖ σιωπῇ . . .; αὖ is used elliptically, as Hermann pointed out: 'you're at it again! keep quiet, can't you?' Cf. Pl. *Euthyd.* 296 a οὐκ αὖ, ἔφη, παύσῃ παραφθεγγόμενος;

241. τί δ'; 'What!', expressing astonishment; for this common elliptic use see *GP* 175 iv (*a*).

πρῶτα: Hermione means first in importance and therefore a natural subject for discussion, but Andromache in her reply takes it to mean the greatest good.

242. [ναί]: here ναί is found in MSS. other than P and in 586 it is the reading of all MSS.; editors are not justified in omitting or bracketing it. For *ναί extra metrum* cf. S. *Tr.* 425; *IT* 742; *Hel.* 99; *Cyc.* 147. The sense is certainly complete without it, but redundant ναί is similarly used in assent followed by qualification in S. *Tr.* 425 ναί, κλύειν γ' ἔφασκον. ταὐτὸ δ' οὐχὶ γίγνεται . . ., and this is a common use in Platonic

---

[1] See P. Boulter, 'Sophia and Sophrosyne in *Andromache*', *Phoenix*, 20 (1966), 51 ff., for a discussion of the use of these terms in different senses by opposing characters; but I cannot accept her thesis that the whole plot is constructed to provide examination of these concepts and derives its unity from this.

dialogue, e.g. *R.* 415 e *Ναί, ἦν δ' ἐγώ, στρατιωτικάς γε, ἀλλ' οὐ χρηματιστικάς*. For redundant *ναί* see also *Alc.* 1119 and Hdt. 1. 159. 4.

243. Hermione harks back to her line of thought in 173 ff., but may also be alluding to 242, in the sense that it is not for *βάρβαροι* to lay down the law about what is or is not *καλόν*.

245. σοφὴ σοφή: cf. *Ba.* 655 *σοφὸς σοφὸς σύ*. In each passage it is the retort of someone who is worsted in argument: 'very clever, but . . .'

248. A combination of 'Helen, not I' and 'not I, but your mother'.

249. ἦ . . . γάρ: introduces a surprised question, as in S. *Ant.* 44 *ἦ γὰρ νοεῖς θάπτειν σφε;* *καί* intensifies *πρόσω*.

250. ἰδού (with this accent)[1] is the regular conversational idiom to indicate compliance with a request made or (as here) implied; cf. 411. There are 43 examples in Aristophanes, 20 in Euripides and 3 in Sophocles. *καὶ δή* with the same sense, found in Aeschylus and Sophocles and more rarely in Euripides, was perhaps felt to be less colloquial.

251. ἐκεῖνο must refer forward to the question in 253. It can hardly, as Paley supposes, refer to a question *τί με ἀπωθεῖς γνησίων νυμφευμάτων*, which he infers from 193. On that topic Hermione launched a series of threats and accusations but asked no questions.

ἐστάλην: AV give the variant *ἱκάνω*, with some other changes. There is little reason for a gloss on *ἐστάλην*, and it is odd that in *Med.* 668 LP give the same variant (*ἱκάνεις* for *ἐστάλης*), though in that passage the sense requires a past tense.

εἵνεκ': I should prefer (with Méridier) to accept *οὕνεκ'*, the reading of most MSS. (see app. crit.). *ἕνεκα* and the Attic by-form *οὕνεκα* coexist in the fifth century; *οὕνεκα* is, mainly for metrical reasons, the dominant form in MSS. of dramatists, but disappears before the end of the fourth century, only *ἕνεκα* being found in New Comedy. The metrically equivalent Epic–Ionic *εἵνεκα* also occurs in MSS. of dramatists as a variant of *οὕνεκα* or more rarely instead of it; but compared with *οὕνεκα* it is rare and likely to be a corruption, since *οὕνεκα* soon disappeared whereas *εἵνεκα* was known in late Greek and might easily replace the true form in some passages. See Di Benedetto on *Or.* 611, Barrett on *Hipp.* 456, Platnauer on Ar. *Pax* 203 (where he notes that in the Laurentian MS. of Sophocles *οὕνεκα* alone is found, never *εἵνεκα*). See also Wackernagel, *KZ* 28 (1887), 109 ff. (= *Kl. Schr.* 591 ff.).

252. Not a reply to 251, but to preserve the flow of stichomythia *λέγω* mockingly picks up *λέξον* and introduces a line of general invective. For the sense cf. *Hipp.* 105 *νοῦν ἔχων ὅσον σε δεῖ*; perhaps this had

[1] It is generally so distinguished from the ordinary imperative *ἰδοῦ* (Schwyzer, 799²), though in some passages the distinction is not clear; see Bond, *Hyps.*, p. 57 (on fr. 764. 1) and Wilamowitz on *HF* 1131.

become a stereotyped expression. *οἷον*, conjectured by Nauck here and by Wakefield in *Hipp.* 105, is shown to be wrong in Barrett's note ad loc.

254. εἰ μὴ θανοῦμαι: 'if I am not to die', i.e. 'provided that I have assurance of safety'. It appears from 256 that the assurance she has in mind is the return of Neoptolemus, whom she seems to trust.

εἰ δὲ μή: 'otherwise', often used after a negative.

255. ὡς τοῦτ' ἄραρε: the same phrase occurs in a somewhat similar context in *Med.* 322. For the elliptical use of *ὡς* 'be sure that' cf. 587, 923; *Hec.* 346, 400, *et al.* It is not found in Aesch., rarely in Soph. but fairly often in Eur. and Comedy, and may be colloquial.

256. ἀλλ' οὐδ' . . . μήν: 'nor will I surrender . . .' The same particles are used to introduce a counter-resolve in *Hec.* 401; cf. *GP* 345 (ii).

ἐκδώσω: *ἐκδίδωμι* is the *vox propria* for surrender to a superior right or to overmastering force; cf. *Hcld.* 97, 319, 442; Dem. 21. 30.

με for *ἐμαυτόν*, as often; cf. 553; *Hel.* 842 *σε κτανὼν ἐμὲ κτενῶ*; *Hipp.* 1409; *IA* 677.

257–60. Suppliants could eventually, without sacrilege, be forced by starvation to leave sanctuary; a threat of burning would produce quicker results, as it does in *HF* 240–4, but if carried out might presumably incur divine displeasure; certainly to kill or wound a suppliant at the altar would be gross sacrilege. Thus in 258 Andromache only says that the gods will take note of the threat of burning, but in 260 warns Hermione that if she sheds blood the goddess will punish her. There is in fact no need for either of these threats, since H. knows (264) that she has other means of causing A. to leave sanctuary. Perhaps we should take it that throughout the stichomythia Andromache, in spite of all, maintains an attitude of calm contempt (cf. 238, 248, 252) which goads Hermione to almost hysterical fury. Contrast 163–5, where H. seems less sure that A. must die.

257. τὸ σὸν προσκέψομαι: it is not necessary to assume, with Murray, that the sense is incomplete: the phrase may well be complete in itself with the sense 'I will show no consideration for you'; cf. *Med.* 460 *τὸ σὸν . . . προσκοπούμενος*.

258. δ' οὖν: 'burn away then'. For this 'permissive' use see *GP* 466 (4).

259. ἀλγηδόνας is governed by *προσοίσω* in 257.

261. θρέμμα is not in itself abusive: in S. *Ph.* 243 and *OT* 1143 it means foster child (*τρέφω*); but it is often used with an abusive epithet, e.g. S. *El.* 622 *ὦ θρέμμ' ἀναιδές* 'shameless creature'; A. *Sept.* 181.

θράσος: abstract for concrete. This is the only example of *θράσος* so used, but cf. *ὦ μῖσος Med.* 1323; *IT* 525; *Hcld.* 52, 941. In general this use of abstract nouns is common in Eur., e.g. *Or.* 477 *κήδευμα*, 480 *στύγημα*; *Tro.* 1104 *λάτρευμα*; *Ph.* 1492 *ἁγεμόνευμα*; see 446 and 1273 below.

262. ἐγκαρτερεῖς: this verb governs an accusative only here and in the same phrase in *HF* 1351, the sense being 'face death with resolution'. Hermione, infuriated by failure to break Andromache's spirit, boasts that she will first be removed from sanctuary and so deprived of the consolation that her death will bring divine anger upon the slayers.

263. ἕκουσαν: i.e. without using physical force.

264. ἀλλὰ γάρ: used in breaking off a train of thought; see *GP* 103. 2 (ii).

λόγους κρύψω: rather an odd phrase for 'I will say no more.'

265. τό δ' . . . σημανεῖ: 'the facts will speak for themselves', 'you'll soon see'. Cf. *Ph.* 623 *αὐτὸ σημανεῖ*; *Ba.* 976 *τἄλλα δ' αὐτὸ σημανεῖ*; S. fr. 388 *τάχ' αὐτὸ δείξει τοὔργον* (*Hel.* 151 *πλοῦς αὐτὸς σημανεῖ* is rather different). These phrases, probably colloquial in tone, are variants on the regular expression *αὐτὸ δείξει*, as in Ar. *Lys.* 375; Pl. *Hipp. Mai.* 288 b, where the scholiast comments: *παροιμία ἐπὶ τῶν ἀπιστούντων τι μὴ γενέσθαι.*

266. ἔχοι: many editors print the MS. reading *ἔχει*, but the optative is normal in a hypothesis of this kind, and Murray rightly prints Bruhn's correction (already tentatively suggested by Hermann).

267. τηκτὸς μόλυβδος: the expression was probably suggested to Eur. by the use of melted lead to fix a statue to its base. Cf. Ar. *Ec.* 1109 *εἶτα τὼ πόδε μολυβδοχοήσαντες κύκλῳ περὶ τὰ σφυρὰ ἄνω 'πιθεῖναι.*

268. With this threat Hermione goes back into the house. This has been disputed. Garzya in *Dioniso*, xv (1952), 136 thinks it possible that Hermione is present during the first stasimon and the following scene (309–463), but this is unlikely. Andromache naturally does not leave her sanctuary, and in other plays there are examples of a silent figure in the background while the Chorus sing an ode (e.g. Creon in S. *Ant.* 582 ff. and perhaps 781 ff.); but the presence of Hermione in addition has no special justification. In the following scene she does not speak and is never addressed, but is ten times referred to in the third person and discussed in 344–8. The only passage in the text that could be construed as evidence on the other side is 459–60, and this does not necessarily imply the presence of Hermione.

269. δεινὸν δ' . . .: the form of the sentence recalls a type familiar in Attic oratory—*πῶς οὐ δεινὸν εἰ . . .* followed by *μέν* and *δέ* clauses.

270. θεῶν τινα: the chief patron deity of the art of healing was Apollo.

271. ὅ: the MS. reading *ἅ* is not impossible; for a similar plural where the singular might be expected cf. *Ion.* 731 *ἃ μὴ γένοιτο δ', εἴ τι τυγχάνοι κακόν . . .*, where Stephanus would emend to *ὅ*. See A. Braunlich in *AJP* 83 (1962), 395, though some other examples there adduced do not seem to me to be strictly parallel. (Garzya would keep *ἅ* as nom. sing. fem., but this form is unlikely in iambic dialogue.)

ἐχίδνης καὶ πυρός: elsewhere *ἔχιδνα*, like viper and snake, is generally used of domestic treachery, as in A. *Cho.* 249, 992 (Clytemnestra); S. *Ant.* 531 (Creon on Ismene); *Ion* 1262 (Ion on Creusa). Here the reference is rather to the venomous nature of Hermione; cf. *Alc.* 310 μητρυιὰ . . . ἐχίδνης οὐδὲν ἠπιωτέρα. For πυρός cf. fr. 429 ἀντὶ πυρὸς γὰρ ἄλλο πῦρ | μεῖζον ἐβλάστομεν γυναῖκες πολὺ δυσμαχώτερον.

For similar judgements on the female sex see 353; *Med.* 265; *Ion* 843; fr. 276. It was no doubt such passages as these that helped to establish the notion of Eur. as a misogynist.

273. The comment in Σ on 272 implies that 273 was not in his MS. It is certainly weak and otiose, and Cobet, Wilamowitz, and Page ('probably an expansive interpolation') may well be right to reject it.

First Stasimon: 274–308

This song has no direct relevance to the dramatic situation, but, as often in plays dealing with some aspect of the Trojan legends, the Chorus or actors go back to the ἀρχὴ κακῶν in the Judgement of Paris, as in the first strophe, or even further back to his birth, as in the second strophe. So *Hel.* 23 ff.; *Tro.* 919 ff. (where Helen is defending herself against Hecuba) ἀρχὰς ἔτεκεν ἥδε τῶν κακῶν | Πάριν τεκοῦσα; *Hec.* 629 ff.; *IA* 1283 ff. For full discussions of this theme see T. C. W. Stinton, *Euripides and the Judgement of Paris*, and F. Jouan, *Euripide et les légendes des Chants Cypriens*, pp. 95–142, to whom I am indebted for several points in the following commentary. In the final antistrophe (301 ff.) the Chorus sing still of the bitter consequences of the Judgement, though now with more immediate reference to their own lives and that of Andromache, whom they directly address in 301. Thus the last lines of the ode lead back into the play. So also in the second, third, and fourth choral odes, which all consist mainly of generalizations or go back into the past, and all end with a reference to the current situation and/or a direct address to a character in this play. For other choral odes in this form cf. S. *OT* 863 ff. and *Ant.* 332 ff., and see Kranz, *Stasimon*, pp. 197 ff.; cf. also Pindar, *Ol.* 12.

Metrical Scheme:

Strophe + antistrophe (*a*): 274–83 = 284–93

	1.	– ∪ ∪ – ∪ ∪ – ∪ ∪ – ∪ ∪ – – –	4 dactyls + molossus (prosodiac)
275 = 285	2.	– ∪ – – ∪ –	2 cretics
	3.	– ∪ – ∪ – ∪ –	lekythion
	4.	∪ – ∪ – ∪ – ∪ –	iambic dimeter
	5.	∪ – ∪ – – ∪ – ‖	iambic dimeter syncopated

	6.	∪∪–∪∪–∪∪–∪∪––∪–	anapaestic dimeter + cretic
280 = 290	7.	––∪∪––‖	reizianum
	8.	∪⏓∪–∪⏖∪–∪–∪–	iambic trimeter
	9.	∪–– }	bacchiac
	10.	–∪–∪–– }	ithyphallic

Notes:

1. See Dale, *LM*² 168 ad fin. In the corresponding line of the antistrophe the second syllable of ἐπεί is shortened by correption, as often in lyric dactyls.
2. Perhaps a syncopated iambic dimeter.
6. In the ant. (289) the MS. reading λόγοις δολίοις gives a concluding anapaest, which does not correspond with the strophe (there is no reason to suspect εὐμορφίας). λόγοισι would give the ending ⏖∪– i.e. a resolved cretic, but resolution in this context seems to have no exact parallel and most editors accept Murray's correction.

9, 10. These should be regarded as a single colon, probably an iambic trimeter with syncopation.

Strophe + antistrophe (*b*): 293–300 = 301–8

293 = 301	1.	–⏓∪–∪∪–∪∪–∪∪	dactylic tetrameter
	2.	–∪–∪–∪–	lekythion (iambic dim. syn.)
	3.	∪–– }	bacchiac
295 = 303	4.	–∪–∪–∪– }	lekythion
	5.	∪∪–∪∪–∪∪–––	anapaestic dimeter
297 = 305	6.	⏓–∪–⏓–∪–	iambic dimeter
	7.	∪∪–∪∪–∪∪–––	anapaestic dimeter
	8.	∪–∪–∪–∪–∪–∪–	iambic trimeter
	9.	–∪∪–	choriambus
	10.	–∪–∪––	ithyphallic

Notes:

1. In 293 ἀλλ' εἴθ' should probably be emended to εἰ γάρ, which would give correspondence with 301; see note ad loc.

3, 4. These should be counted as a single colon, an iambic trimeter with syncopation.

5, 7. It is possible that these cola should be regarded as enoplia: see *LM*² 168–9.

6. In the antistrophe 305 the text is unmetrical; for the reading assumed in this scheme see note ad loc.

274. ἀχέων . . . ὑπῆρξεν: if *ὁ . . . Διὸς τόκος* (Hermes) is subject of *ὑπῆρξεν*, which, as Stinton notes, usually stresses the initiative of the agent, Hermes may seem to be given undue prominence here. Possibly Eur. was influenced by vase paintings of the Judgement, in which he is generally a conspicuous or even a dominant figure, although his role is in a sense subordinate; cf. Stinton, op. cit., p. 15 and Clairmont, *Das Parisurteil in der antiken Kunst*, p. 106. Bornmann takes *ὑπῆρξεν* as impersonal: 'It began the sorrows when . . .', but cites no parallel.

277. τρίπωλον ἅρμα δαιμόνων: lit. 'a three-horse team of deities', i.e. Hera, Athena, and Aphrodite. *ἅρμα*, as A. M. Dale notes on *Alc.* 66, can mean chariot, chariot and team, or team alone. Cf. S. fr. 511 *τριολύμπιον ἅρμα*, E. *Hel.* 357 *τριζύγοις θεαῖσι*, both referring to the Judgement of Paris, and E. fr. 357 *ζεῦγος τριπάρθενον*, the three daughters of Erectheus.

Some have taken *ἅρμα* literally, supposing that Hermes escorts the goddesses in a three-horse chariot, but it would be odd to specify the number of horses and not, as usual, of goddesses, and in most representations of the scene the goddesses are on foot. There are a few exceptions, e.g. an Attic pyxis in Copenhagen (*CVA* Copenhagen, Fasc. iv, Pl. 163. 1) where the three goddesses are shown each in her own chariot; but in any case this could hardly be the meaning of *τρίπωλον ἅρμα*, as Wecklein supposed. So too in *Tro.* 924 *ἔκρινε τρισσὸν ζεῦγος ὅδε τριῶν θεῶν* can only mean 'he judged the triple team consisting of three goddesses'.

278. καλλιζυγές: the main emphasis is on the first half of the compound, but the second carries on the metaphor in *ἅρμα*.

279. ἔριδι στυγερᾷ . . . εὐμορφίας: the beauty contest is 'hateful' partly because in Homer and later *ἔρις* and *πόλεμος* traditionally have some such epithet (cf. 122 above), but also because of its dire consequences; cf. *IA* 1308 *κρίσιν ἐπὶ στυγνὰν ἔριν τε καλλονᾶς*; ibid. 184 *ἔριν μορφᾶς*. The frequent use of *ἔρις* in this context may recall the part played by *Ἔρις*, personification of strife, in the account given in the *Cypria* of events leading up to the Judgement.

κεκορυθμένον: lit. 'helmeted' and so more generally 'equipped'; its use here is in keeping with the rather ornate 'decorated' style of the passage; see Webster, *Gk. Art and Lit.*, pp. 137–8.

280. βούτα: Doric gen. of *βούτας*. This or a cognate word is the regular description of Paris in this context; so in the next line and S. fr. 90 *βοτήρ*; *Hec.* 646 *ἀνὴρ βουτάς*; *IA* 180, 574, 1291 *βουκόλος*.

281. ἀμφί with a verb of motion is strictly 'to the neighbourhood of'; cf. A. *Pr.* 830 *ἦλθες . . . ἀμφὶ Δωδώνην*.

μονότροπον properly denotes a way of life, as it does in the comedy of Phrynichus with that title, but here it may not be more than a variant on *ἔρημον*: 'to the solitary young herdsman and his lonely hearth and home'. As Pearson observes on S. fr. 511, Eur. was attracted by the contrast between the splendour of the divinities and the rustic seclusion of Paris, whose association with Oenone is ignored by Eur. See, e.g., *Hel.* 357; *IA* 180, 1291; *Hec.* 646; and on the early life of Paris see below on 293 ff.

νεανίαν: here adjectival; see on *τύραννον* in 3 above.

284–6. For the toilet of the three goddesses before the contest cf. *Hel.* 676 *λουτρῶν καὶ κρηνῶν ἵνα θεαὶ μορφὰν ἐφαίδρυναν, ἔνθεν ἔμολεν κρίσις*. The scene is well illustrated on a contemporary *κρατήρ* dated in the last quarter of the fifth cent. (Trendall, *The Red-Figured Vases of Lucania, Campania, and Sicily*, p. 102, no. 532), where Athena has laid aside her shield and washes her hands in running water; Hera looks in a mirror and arranges her hair; Aphrodite surrenders to the ministrations of Eros. See also C. Dugas, *Ant. Class.* 6 (1937), 12–13.

284. ταί: an epic form used as relative or demonstrative, and in Doric as def. article. It occurs only once in iambics (A. *Pers.* 424) and is rare in lyrics; see Jebb on S. *Aj.* 1404.

285. πιδάκων: only here in Tragedy; cf. *πιδακόεις* in 116 above. *πολυπῖδαξ* (-*πίδακος*) 'many-fountained' was the fixed epithet of Mt. Ida in Epic, e.g. *Il.* 8. 47, 14. 157, 283; *Cypr.* fr. 5; *H. Ven.* 54.

νίψαν: Hermann's correction of *νίψαντο* LP, which does not correspond metrically with 275. The active is common in this sense in Homer, but thereafter the middle is usual. The omission of the syllabic augment, fairly common in dramatic lyric, as also in Pindar, and found occasionally in messenger speeches, is a survival from Epic.

αἰγλᾶντα: *αἰγλαεντα* (codd.) is Homeric; the contracted Doric form (proposed by Musgrave) gives correspondence with 276.

287. Πριαμίδαν: the acc. without prep. for goal of motion is common of places and often extends to groups of persons as occupying places; see Dodds on *Ba.* 847–8. It is more rarely used of a single person; cf. *Supp.* 835–6 *σε . . . ἦλθε*; *Hipp.* 1371.

287–8. ὑπερβολαῖς . . . παραβαλλόμεναι: *ὑπερβολαῖς λόγων* must surely refer to the extravagant offers traditionally made to Paris by the contestants, and *παραβαλλόμεναι* is probably a middle used absolutely in the sense 'vying with each other'; there may be no precise parallel, but the middle is used transitively in this sense in *IT* 1904 *σοι παραβάλλομαι θρήνους* 'I set my songs against you (i.e. yours)', and the passive is used similarly in S. *OC* 231 *ἀπάτα δ' ἀπάταις παραβαλλομένα*. *δυσφρόνων* presumably refers to the ill will of the contestants towards each other; it cannot be related to Paris, as in a paraphrase in *Σ* *ἐπαγγελίαις λόγων βλαπτόντων αὐτόν*, since though *βλαπτόντων* might be justified as describing the outcome, *δύσφρων* indicates intention and could not be applied to any of the offers in relation to Paris. Hermann printed a stop after *Πριαμίδαν* and conjectured *λόγων δ' εὐφρόνων* (in which case no δ' is needed in 289). This gives good sense: 'They came to Priam's son. And as they vied with each other in the excessive graciousness of their promises, the Cyprian won . . .'; it leaves παραβαλλόμεναι as strictly speaking a *nom. pendens*, though this is easier where one of a group is in apposition to the whole group (KG II p. 288, Anm. 11). Murray's tentative ὑπερβολαῖς πόθων δυσφόρων (the last word is the reading in P) is a considerable change and stresses too much the anxiety of the goddesses; moreover the repetition λόγων . . . λόγοις has point, since, as Stinton observes, it was by words that the contest was fought and won. On the whole it is best to accept the MS. reading.

A less likely interpretation is implied in another paraphrase in Σ and adopted by some editors, i.e. that the goddesses are represented as disputing among themselves and disparaging each other's charms before the contest. The fact that on some vases representing the three goddesses on their way to Paris the second is shown turning to speak to the third is perhaps consistent with this interpretation but hardly a confirmation; cf. Clairmont, op. cit., K63, K70, K94.

289. δολίοις . . . λόγοις: Murray's correction of the MS. reading Κύπρις εἷλε λόγοις δολίοις, which is metrically doubtful (see Metrical Scheme, n. on 6) and involves an awkward asyndeton. Musgrave suggested that δολίοις might have been a gloss on αἰόλοις or αἱμύλοις, but the asyndeton remains and in any case neither adjective is specially associated with Aphrodite, as are δόλιος and cognate words, e.g. δολοπλόκος (Sapph. 1. 2), δολόμητις (Simon. 43), δόλιος (*Hel.* 238), δολιόφρων (*IA* 1300). These epithets are used of the traditional wiles of Aphrodite and do not necessarily imply treachery; she certainly kept her promise to Paris, and may not have known that the result would prove disastrous.

ἕλε: for this epic form, not found elsewhere in Eur. or in Soph., cf. A. *Sept.* 83. The verb is probably used absolutely: 'Κύπρις won the day', though this is a legal use and without precise parallel in Tragedy; cf. Pl. *Leg.* 762 b ἐὰν δ' ἕλῃ 'If he wins his case'; Dem. 26. 11 τῶν ἑλόντων 'the successful litigants'. A. *Ag.* 340 is different, since ἑλόντες picks up γῆς ἁλούσης in 339. It is possible but less likely that ἕλε governs Πριαμίδαν; cf. *Hec.* 1269.

291. σύγχυσιν: acc. in apposition to the sentence δολίοις . . . λόγοις. The structure of the sentence is irregular, since πικρὰν σύγχυσιν is linked by the use of μέν and δέ to the adjective τερπνοῖς in agreement with λόγοις. Murray's τέρψιν for τερπνοῖς is presumably intended to restore some parallelism, but could not be taken as a noun in apposition to the preceding sentence since the *victory* of Aphrodite could not be called 'a delight'. Σ explains σύγχυσιν as object of ἔχουσι understood, with λόγοι supplied from λόγοις as subject, but the ellipse is too harsh. Jackson, *Marg. Scaen.* 102, suggests that ἔχουσι dropped out before the similar σύγχυσιν, Φρυγῶν being subsequently added to make up the iambic trimeter. Perhaps, however, in spite of some formal irregularity the text can stand. *σύγχυσις*, no doubt a worn metaphor, occurs again in 959 and elsewhere in Eur.; otherwise it is confined to prose, but *συγχέω* is used twice by Sophocles.

293 ff. Eur. is alluding to the legend, no doubt familiar to most of his audience, that before Paris was born Hecuba dreamed that she gave birth to a firebrand which set fire to the citadel of Troy. This was interpreted to mean that her child would bring about the destruction of the city. Of what followed there were different versions. In one the infant was exposed on Mt. Ida, i.e. left to die, but was saved by a shepherd; in another, adopted by Eur. in *Tro.* 919–22, it seems that an old retainer was instructed to kill the child, but did not do so. Here it is implied that it was Cassandra who interpreted the dream, and that Hecuba (or Priam) refused to put the infant to death, and when Cassandra tried to persuade the Trojan elders to intervene, the curse of Apollo ensured that they would not believe her.

293. ἀλλ' εἴθ', printed in the OCT, does not correspond with 301. The necessary – ∪ can be provided by *εἴθε δ'*, the reading of *l*, or by Murray's *εἴθ' ἄρ'*; elsewhere however *εἴθε* is used without a connective. Jackson's *εἰ γάρ* (*Marg. Scaen.* 102–3) had already been suggested by Paley and may be right. Denniston, *GP* 92, n. 1 observes that *εἰ γάρ* is in drama almost confined to answers; but cf. A. *Cho.* 345; E. *Supp.* 369. Wilamowitz (*Griechische Verskunst*, p. 550) suggested *εἰ τόθ'*, making the whole strophe the protasis of a conditional sentence, with the antistrophe as the apodosis; but the unfulfilled wish is more poignant in this context.

ὑπὲρ κεφαλὰν ἔβαλεν: it seems clear that *εἴθε* must introduce a wish that Hecuba had in fact obeyed the warning of Cassandra and killed the child, and *κτανεῖν* (297) and still more *φονεύειν* (300) suggest a violent death rather than exposure. On the other hand *ὑπὲρ κεφαλὰν ἔβαλε* can hardly mean 'struck on the head' as Paley apparently thought. He cites *HF* 992 *ὑπὲρ κάρα βαλὼν | ξύλον καθῆκε παιδὸς ἐς ξανθὸν κάρα*, but here Wilamowitz rightly interprets 'schwingt er die Keule hoch über sein Haupt'. The only parallel is *Or.* 497, but the MS. reading *πληγεὶς θυγατρὸς τῆς ἐμῆς ὑπὲρ κάρα* is probably corrupt. Most editors, keeping to the normal sense of *ὑπὲρ κεφαλάν*, take the phrase to allude to the practice of getting rid of a *κάθαρμα*, a polluted object, by casting it behind one's back; cf. A. *Cho.* 98–9. Perhaps this disastrous infant could be similarly regarded as something unclean; cf. *πόλεως λώβαν* in 298. The phrase then stands for the general notion of casting out the new-born child to die. No actual support for the expression *ὑπὲρ κεφαλάν* in this context is given, apart from the Virgilian parallel *transque caput iace* (*Ec.* 8. 101).

294. Πάριν (which should be obelized in the text), if it is genuine, must be the subject of *κατοικίσαι*, but the proper name seems intrusive and it may well have been a marginal gloss on *νιν*; cf. *Κύπρις* in *Hipp.*

1403 and examples collected by Barrett ad loc. Hermann's substitution of *μόρον* was based on the paraphrase in *Σ εἴθε ὑπὲρ κεφαλῆς Πάριδος ἔβαλεν θάνατον ἡ τεκοῦσα τὸν Πάριν*. In this sentence *Πάριδος* seems improbable, and Jackson (*Marg. Scaen.* 102) emends to *πατρίδος* which he takes with *θάνατον*: the birth of Paris is the death of Troy. There does not, however, seem to be any example of *θάνατος* or *μόρος* used of a person; *ὄλεθρος* and *φθόρος* are so used but only as colloquial terms of abuse. Murray's *μύσος* would certainly fit the context of banishing a pollution; but *κακὸν μόρον* may well be right if taken, not as object of *ἔβαλεν*, but as acc. in apposition to the sentence *ὑπὲρ . . . ἔβαλεν . . . νιν*. For the hyperbaton cf. *Hel.* 77 and see Stinton, op. cit., pp. 73–4, and for a detailed discussion of the range and variety of this usage see Barrett on *Hipp.* 752–7.

295. λέπας: LSJ give 'bare rock' as the only meaning, but here, as in *Ba.* 677, 751, 1045 and *Rh.* 287, it must include upland pasture as well as rock and forest, as Dodds points out on *Ba.* 677–8.

296. παρὰ θεσπεσίῳ δάφνᾳ: editors compare Virg. *Aen.* 2. 513 (referring to the court-yard of Priam's palace) 'ingens ara fuit iuxtaque veterrima laurus, | incumbens arae'. Here, however, the reference may be to a precinct of Apollo; cf. E. *Alexandros*, fr. (a) (Page, Loeb *Lit. Pap.* 9, p. 54), where there is almost certainly a reference to a shrine of Apollo; *Tro.* 329 (Cassandra speaking) *κατὰ σὸν ἐν δάφναις ἀνάκτορον*. In any case *θεσπέσιος* 'divine', 'oracular' is appropriate, since the bay-tree was regularly associated with Apollo and prophecy; *Δαφνηφορία* was the name of a Boeotian festival in his honour and *Δαφνηφόρος* is a cult title (Paus. 9. 10. 4).

297. κτανεῖν depends on *βόασε*, which is equivalent to a verb of commanding; cf. S. *OT* 1287 *βοᾷ διοίγειν κλῇθρα*. For *βοᾶν* and similar words for the loud cries of prophecy cf. A. *Cho.* *ἀμβόαμα* and ibid. 271 *ἐξορθιάζων*.

299. τίν' οὐκ . . . ποῖον οὐκ: for this rhetorical question Kamerbeek compares S. *OT* 420–1, *Aj.* 1012, Theocr. 2. 90. In E. *Ph.* 878 *τί ⟨οὐ⟩ δρῶν, ποῖα δ' οὐ λέγων ἔπη* there is doubt about the text, but anyhow *ποῖος* seems to be used, as here, as a mere variant of *τίς*; cf. 388–90 below. The variation becomes a mannerism in Call. *H.* 3. 183 *τίς δὲ νύ τοι νήσων, ποῖον δ' ὄρος . . ., τίς δὲ λιμὴν ποίη δὲ πόλις ;**

δαμογερόντων: cf. *Il.* 3. 149 ff., where the *δημογέροντες* are also called *Τρώων ἡγήτορες*.

301 ff. In this antistrophe, as in the fourth stasimon of this play and often elsewhere, Eur. stresses the anguish and suffering that war brings to Greek and Trojan alike. With 301–2 cf. *Tro.* 599–600 *ζυγὰ δ' ἤνυσε δούλια Τροίᾳ*.

301. Unless Wilamowitz's *εἰ τόθ'* in 293 is accepted, the protasis must be supplied from the context: 'for then [i.e. if Cassandra had not failed to win belief] the yoke of slavery would not have come . . .'

This sort of ellipse is generally introduced by γάρ, e.g. E. *IA* 1256 φιλῶ τ' ἐμαυτοῦ τέκνα· μαινοίμην γὰρ ἄν. See *GP* 62 (3).

ἤλυθε: Denniston on *El.* 168 notes that this epic form is used by Euripides, mainly in lyrics, but not by Aeschylus or Sophocles.

304. παρέλυσε: the sense seems to be 'cut loose the toils from Hellas' i.e. prevent them from happening; cf. Is. 4. 10 τὴν τοῦ παιδίου ἀμφισβήτησιν παρέλυσε 'abandoned, cancelled'. An impersonal subject for παρέλυσε can be supplied from the context: 'and it (i.e. the early elimination of Paris) would have prevented . . .' If the subject is personal it could be Cassandra (Wecklein) but is perhaps more likely to be ἁ τεκοῦσα, since though these words are far removed from παρέλυσε it is the idea of Hecuba's responsibility that dominates the strophe.

305. The MS. reading does not correspond with 297 and must be corrupt. The simplest change is, as Murray suggests, οὓς ἀμφὶ Τρωΐαν πόνους, a modification of Headlam's proposal. In meaning, there is nothing to choose between πόνους (*Pl* and perhaps *Σ*) and μόχθους; and the phrases τὸν μακρῶν ἀλάταν πόνων (S. *Aj.* 888) and ἀλατείαις πόνων (A. *Pr.* 900) suggest the possibility of ἀλᾶσθαι πόνους (cogn. acc.). For the Doric form Τρωΐαν cf. A. *Cho.* 363 Τρωΐας. In E. *El.* 440 LP give Τροίας but most editors print Seidler's Τρωΐας.

306. ἀλάληντο: another epic form, found only here in Tragedy. ἀλᾶσθαι often has the special sense 'to be outcast, banished', e.g. S. *OC* 444; Thuc. 2. 102, and so may suggest here that military service at Troy is a kind of exile. Stinton (op. cit., p. 22) takes this verb to emphasize the distress and lack of direction of the Greek warriors: 'the brilliant heroic exploits of the Trojan War shrink in the end, like Stendhal's Waterloo, to the aimless toing and froing of bewildered patrols; the word thus deflates the pomp of martial manœuvres.' An interesting suggestion and a characteristic Euripidean point, though it is a good deal to read into the verb.

λόγχαις: 'in arms'; dative of accompaniment (instrumental).

307. Cf. 1039–41 and A. *Pers.* 133–4.

308. τεκέων: gen. of separation depending on ὀρφανοί.

Second Epeisodion: 309–463

Andromache is still at the altar of Thetis. Enter Menelaus and attendants with Andromache's child.

The scene can be considered as an agon between Andromache and Menelaus, though there is a striking lack of balance in that M. has thirty-eight lines and A. ninety-eight. Pleading, argument, and invective have no effect on M. and the main purpose of the scene is to demonstrate his unscrupulous and ruthless brutality. In *Orestes* 1610 ff. Menelaus is himself the victim of similar blackmail when Orestes threatens to kill Hermione unless M. will save him from execution, and perhaps in the *Telephus* the life of the infant Orestes was similarly threatened (cf. Handley and Rea, *The Telephus of Euripides*, pp. 27, 37). For other examples in Eur. of the refinement of cruelty which strikes at parents through their children see J. de Romilly, *L'Évolution du pathétique*, pp. 32–4.

311. ηὔχεις: this is often a verb of thinking rather than saying; so here 'you confidently expected'. Cf. *Hcld.* 832 *πόσον τιν' αὐχεῖς πάταγον ἀσπίδων βρέμειν;* where, as Fraenkel rightly notes on *A. Ag.* 1497, *πόσον αὐχεῖς* is a poetic equivalent for the colloquial *πόσον δοκεῖς;* see also *Hcld.* 931; *Tro.* 770.

σῴσειν: Dobree's correction of *σῶσαι*, the reading of all MSS., is not inevitable. It is true that there is no certain example of *αὐχεῖν* with a plain aor. infin. referring to the future; in *Hel.* 1619 *οὐκ ἂν ηὔχουν . . . λαθεῖν* it is possible to take *ἂν λαθεῖν* together; in S. *Phil.* 869 *οὐ . . . τοῦτ' ἂν ἐξηύχησ' ἐγώ, τλῆναι . . .*, *ἄν* should be taken with *ἐξηύχησα*, but here *τλῆναι* may be explanatory of *τοῦτο*, as Pearson (on *Hel.* 1619) suggests. However, in view of the frequent use of an aor. infin. after other verbs of hoping and expecting (Goodwin, *MT*, § 136; KG 2. 1. 195, Anm. 7), I should prefer, with Paley and others, to keep *σῶσαι*.

313. ἧσσον φρονοῦσα: 'less astute'.

τοῦδε Μενέλεω: *ὅδε* is regularly used in Tragedy by a speaker referring to himself. As usual, a new character not previously announced identifies himself in the first few lines.

314. πέδον: this word is regularly used of a sacred precinct; e.g. *Φοίβου πέδον* in 1085 and in *IT* 972 is the precinct of Apollo at Delphi, and in Ar. *Pl.* 772 *Παλλάδος κλεινὸν πέδον* is the Acropolis. Here it denotes a very small space immediately round the altar, referred to in 253 as *ἁγνὸν τέμενος*.

315. τοῦ σοῦ σώματος: for the periphrasis cf. *Alc.* 636 *οὐκ ἦσθ' ἄρ' ὀρθῶς τοῦδε σώματος πατήρ*, and *Andr.* 1278 *σὸν δέμας*.

σφαγήσεται: a brutal word: 'he will be butchered.' *σφάζειν* in Homer is always used of cutting the throat of sacrificial victims; later it is more widely used, but generally of killing those who are defenceless, e.g. *Andr.* 260, 412; *Or.* 1107; Thuc. 7. 84. Perhaps Men. or an attendant holds a sword at the child's throat.

319–23. Here, as fairly often, the speaker begins with a short quasi-soliloquy in general terms, speaking not *to* but *at* her opponent; cf. 693–702 below and *Hipp.* 936–42. In *Hipp.* 616–50 for special reasons, admirably discussed by Barrett ad loc., almost the whole speech takes this form. Cf. also S. *OT* 380–9 and *Aj.* 1093–6. Apart from special reasons, the denunciation of an individual was presumably more convincing if it followed an allusion to some recognized type of which he is yet another instance or to some well-known aspect of human nature which he exemplifies. See also Schadewaldt, *Monolog und Selbstgespräch*, p. 122.

320. οὐδὲν γεγῶσι does not of course refer to humble birth, which would not be relevant to Menelaus, but means 'of no importance as born', i.e. by their innate capacity; *πεφυκόσι* would be more usual in this sense.

βίοτον here equivalent to *βίον. μέγαν* is proleptic.

321 ff. The main point here is the prevalence of false or inflated reputations, but whenever there is a contrast between true and false both halves of the antithesis are usually made explicit. The contrast between appearance and reality, here used as a debating point, is in one form or another a frequently recurring motif in the dramatists; it is the source of tragic irony, and sometimes lies at the heart of tragedy. The application of Andromache's generalization to Menelaus is that in view of his present conduct it is incredible that he should have taken Troy at the head of his troops (there is some stress on *στρατηγῶν λογάσιν*), so that his military reputation must be spurious.

321. ἀληθείας ὕπο: a reputation 'truly earned'. Cf. *El.* 845 *ἀνδρείας ὕπο* 'bravely'; Hdt. 6. 107; see also Pearson on *Hel.* 816.*

322. τοὺς δ': sc. *εὔκλειαν ἔχοντας*, as though the first half of the antithesis had been *τοὺς μὲν εὔκλειαν ὑπ' ἀληθείας ἔχοντας*.

ἔχειν: sc. *αὐτήν*, i.e. *εὔκλειαν*.

323. ἀξιώσω: if there is stress on the future some addition such as 'henceforward' might be expected; otherwise the present would be more natural, and a small change would give *οὐκ ἀξιῶ 'γώ*;[1] in uncials Γ and are easily confused.

πλὴν τύχῃ φρονεῖν δοκεῖν: lit. 'except by chance or luck to seem to be wise'; as we might say 'though they may seem . . .'; for the form of expression cf. *Ph.* 501 *οὔθ' ὅμοιον οὐδὲν . . . πλὴν ὀνομάσαι* 'though we may use the term'. *φρονεῖν* has been thought intrusive on the ground that in this context one would expect *εὔκλεια* to mean primarily warlike glory. Hence, e.g., Nauck's *πλὴν ὅσον δοκεῖν μόνον* 'save only the semblance'. However, good counsel is an aspect of leadership, as in Hom. *Il.* 6. 78, where Hector and Aeneas are *ἄριστοι . . . μάχεσθαί τε φρονέειν τε*; also *φρονεῖν* may be brought in here with reference to M.'s sneering *ἧσσον φρονοῦσα* in 313. The paraphrase in *Σ τῆς τύχης τούτοις χαρισαμένης ἀκρίτως φρονεῖν μέγα ἐπὶ εὐτυχίᾳ* suggests that his text had *φρονεῖν*, which was regarded as equivalent to *φρονεῖν μέγα*, as it sometimes is in post-classical writers.

325. φαῦλος: Andromache's values are in the heroic tradition, in which one aspect of the *φαῦλος* is that he has no high ambition: his aims are petty and ignoble. On this aspect of the antithesis *φαῦλος – σπουδαῖος*

---

[1] The suggestion had already been made by Hirzel.

see Else, *Aristotle's Poetics*, pp. 71–8, So here the charge is not so much depravity as the pettiness of outlook that leads Menelaus to deploy his resources against a slave woman.

326. ἀντίπαιδος: on the analogy of ἀντίθεος, 'godlike', ἀντίδουλος and similar words ἀντίπαις would mean 'like a child'; cf. A. *Eu.* 38 δείσασα γὰρ γραῦς οὐδέν, ἀντίπαις μὲν οὖν. It is less likely that the word has its technical sense denoting the age just below that of ἔφηβος, i.e. a little under eighteen. See Pearson on S. fr. 564.

328. The punctuation after ἀγων' should be a colon.

329. The sense is 'I consider you not good enough to be conqueror of Troy and Troy too good to be conquered by you.' For the shift in the meaning of οὐκ ἀξιῶ cf. 'You don't deserve this', which can mean either you are not good enough or you are too good. See *El.* 186–9, where Denniston comments: 'A victor who demeans himself demeans also the vanquished, who are regarded as having yielded to an unworthy foe.' In the *Helena* the same notion is expressed from a different point of view by a very different Menelaus, ridiculous rather than odious, struggling to maintain in trying circumstances the reputation of Troy's conqueror; see *Hel.* 808 ἄνανδρά γ' εἶπας Ἰλίου τ' οὐκ ἄξια, and ibid. 948 Τροίαν γὰρ ἂν | δειλοὶ γενόμενοι πλεῖστον αἰσχύνοιμεν ἄν; cf. also *Cyc.* 198–200. Here, however, A. scorns M. without admitting a consequential depreciation of Troy.

330–2. It is odd that Eur. should insert here another generalization on the same lines as 319–23; moreover Stobaeus 104. 14 cites 330 and 331 (with the substitution of εὐτυχεῖν for εὖ φρονεῖν) as from Menander: see Koerte–Thierfelder, *Men. Rel.* ii, fr. 627. Menander *could* have taken these two (or three) lines from Eur., but it is more likely that they were written in the margin of a MS. as a parallel to 319 ff. and later incorporated in the text. If so, the corruption goes back at any rate to Didymus (i B.C.) who according to Σ censured these lines as σεμνότεροι ἢ κατὰ βάρβαρον γυναῖκα καὶ δυστυχοῦσαν. On 332 see below.

330–1. ἔξωθεν and **ἔνδον** must here mean 'outwardly' and 'inwardly': cf. *Or.* 1514 δειλίᾳ γλώσσῃ χαρίζῃ, τἄνδον οὐχ οὕτω φρονῶν.

332. πλὴν εἴ τι πλούτῳ: sc. διαφέρουσι. On the ground that this line follows strangely after 331, since wealth can hardly be counted among τὰ ἔνδον in the present sense, some have regarded this line as a later addition to 330–1 and Koerte does not include it in Men. fr. 627. A double interpolation is, however, difficult and it is possible that this line reverts to the point made in 330: 'it's only in wealth (which is external) that they differ.'

333. The appeal to Menelaus by name is rather abrupt and the number of resolutions is unparalleled for a play of this period; also φέρε δή, mainly colloquial in the fifth century, is not found elsewhere in Tragedy, though this would not in itself carry much weight.

Wilamowitz was probably right to eject the line, which might well have been added to join up the previous interpolated lines to the text, and perhaps also to substitute *εἶεν*, which can certainly stand alone *extra metrum* (*Med.* 386; *Ion* 275; *IT* 467) and is often used before passing on to a new phase of the argument.

334. τέθνηκα τῇ σῇ θυγατρί: 'suppose I have died at your daughter's hand . . .' I know of no other example of a bare verb indicating imaginary realization, which is normally expressed by *καὶ δή* (*GP* 252. v); possibly *δή* alone could be so used,[1] so that Reiske's *δή* for *τῇ* would be an improvement.

θυγατρί: dat. of agent with *τέθνηκα* used as equivalent to a passive.

336. ἐν τοῖς πολλοῖς: at the bar of public opinion. For the forensic *ἐν* denoting the tribunal cf. S. *Ant.* 459; *OT* 677; Pl. *Grg.* 464 d, and see note on 591.

ἀγωνίῃ: 'you will fight a charge of murder.' *ἀγωνίζεσθαι* in this sense is a legal term; cf. *ἀγῶνα* (or *δίκην*) *ἀγωνίζεσθαι* Lys. 7. 39, 3. 20. Here we have a compressed form of expression for *ἀγῶνα φόνου ἀγωνίῃ*.

337. τὸ συνδρῶν χρέος: an unusual expression (Bornmann's comparison with *Or.* 406 *συνδρῶν αἷμα* is not to the point, since *συνδρῶν* there is masc.). LSJ s.v. *χρέος* V put *χρέος* in this passage in a category by itself and translate 'the circumstance of being an accomplice'. *τὸ συνδρῶν* by itself could mean this, so that *χρέος* is redundant, and is equivalent to *χρῆμα*; cf. LSJ s.v. II. 2. Perhaps, however, it should be related to the common sense 'obligation'; the obligation arising from your co-operation will compel you to take responsibility.

338. δ' οὖν: see on 163.

ἐγὼ μέν: as though the sentence were to continue *τὸν δὲ παῖδα κτανῆτε*, but the second half of the protasis is replaced by an indignant question. Wecklein's *τὸ μή* is not necessary. For *μή* with an epexegetic infin. (not with *ὑπεκδράμω*) cf. *Hcld.* 506 *φευξόμεσθα μὴ θανεῖν*.

341. Andromache sounds almost proud of Neoptolemus. It must of course be remembered that a Greek dramatist in composing speeches for his characters is often more concerned with effective argument than with characterization.[2] Thus Eur. makes Andromache refer to the

---

[1] One might expect the main weight in *καὶ δή* to rest on *δή*, and as most examples of this idiom, but not the present passage, occur in the course of argument and refer to something already mentioned, perhaps *καὶ δή* was at first equivalent to '*and* suppose . . .' e.g. E. *Hel.* 1058 *θάψαι . . . αἰτήσομαι. Με. καὶ δὴ παρεῖκεν· εἶτα πῶς . . .;* 'And suppose he agrees; what then?' Some instances of *καὶ δή* where this does not work, e.g. Ar. *V.* 1224, might be explained by analogy; but if *δή* alone could mean 'suppose . . .' we should expect to find more than one example.

[2] This point is admirably brought out by A. M. Dale, *Alcestis*, Intr., pp. xxvii–xxviii.

prowess displayed by N. in the Trojan War chiefly because this is rhetorically effective in support of her argument that Menelaus and Hermione had better beware of his anger. Still, in considering what impression, if any, we are expected to derive from the play of the relationship between Andromache and her master, we must take some account of this passage.

καλεῖ: the tense indicates that Andromache goes back in thought to the time when Troy still existed.

342. εἶσιν οἷ χρή: 'he will take the necessary steps.' *γάρ* amplifies the previous statement and Murray's suggested emendations are not needed.

344. ἐκδιδούς: 'offering in marriage'.

346. ἀλλὰ πεύσεται: the MS. reading is *ἀλλὰ ψεύσεται* and this is the lemma in Σ. Porson regarded this as a violation of his canon (see on 250) and emended to *ἀλλ' ἐψεύσεται*, but *ἀλλά* may be regarded as prepositive, i.e. metrically attached to the following word. However with the MS. reading the verb must be passive in force (KG i. 114) and the sense is poor: '⟨your words⟩ will be falsely said' is a weak retort; so is Porson's *ἐψεύσεται* 'he will have been cheated'; this would not worry Menelaus. Kiehl's *πεύσεται* 'he will learn ⟨the truth⟩' is open to the same objection, and I should prefer Pflugk's *ἀλλ' οὐ πείσεται* (metrically a single unit) 'but he will not listen'. This may indeed have been in the MS. tradition, since Σ has *τινες οὕτως· ψευδῆ σε νομίσει ὁ ἀκούων καὶ οὐ πεισθήσεται*, which does not seem a possible paraphrase of our MS. reading.

348. χήραν . . . πολιόν: proleptic: 'will you have her on your hands till she becomes grey-haired in her widowhood?'

καθέξεις: Menelaus will resume paternal authority, but *κατέχειν*, generally meaning 'restrain' 'hold down', is rather surprising.

τλήμων ἀνήρ: some MSS. have the unmetrical *τλῆμον* and all have *ἄνερ. τλήμων*, the reading of LP, is clearly right, and most editors print Dindorf's correction *ἀνήρ*. The nom. instead of voc. is fairly common in poetry from Homer onwards, e.g. E. *Hel.* 1399 *ὦ καινὸς ἡμῖν πόσις*; for other examples see KG i. 47–8 and for discussion Wackernagel, *Vorlesungen über Syntax*, i. 306–7. The vocative here might have been substituted in ignorance of this usage, with *τλῆμον* as a consequence. A combination of nom. and voc. is not however unsupported; see S. *Ai.* 923 *ὦ δύσμορ' Αἴας* and ibid. 903, where LA give *ὦ ταλαίφρων γύναι*, though here *ταλαῖφρον* (rec.) is metrically equivalent and is printed by Pearson. There may be ambiguity in the tradition since Sophocles would in any case have written 'O'. The same difficulty applied in S. *Ant.* *ὦ φίλταθ' Αἷμον* (*αἷμον* A rec.: *αἵμων* L). Thus *ὦ τλήμων ἄνερ*, which is accepted by Kühner and Méridier, is not impossible here. See also West on Hes. *Theog.* 964.

350. εὐνάς: acc. of respect with *ἠδικημένην*; for *εὐνή* used of a person cf.

907 and *IA* 1355 *τὴν ἐμὴν μέλλουσαν εὐνήν* 'my bride to be'. A.'s argument seems to be that if M. carries out his threats the consequences for him and his daughter will be such (as indicated in 335–45) that it would be better not merely to put up with A. as Neoptolemus' concubine but with many others in the same position.

352–4. An appeal to M. to remain detached from feminine jealousies; cf. 366, 387. For A.'s strictures on her own sex cf. 272–3.

355. ἡμεῖς . . . ἑκόντες: the masculine adj. is normal where a woman speaks of herself in the plural. The combination of plural verbs and the singular *ὀφείλω* (360) in the same sentence is also fairly common, and the juxtaposition is more striking in other examples, e.g. *Tro.* 904 *οὐ δικαίως ἢν θάνω θανούμεθα* and *HF* 858 *μαρτυρόμεσθα δρῶσ' ἃ δρᾶν οὐ βούλομαι.*

357. ἑκόντες οὐκ ἄκοντες: see on 96.

358. αὐτοί: 'of my own accord'. Kirchhoff's *αὐτῇ* would presumably refer to Hermione, but no change is needed.

359. γαμβροῖς: for pl. used of a single person cf. 378, 391, 539, 568. *γαμβρός* (like *πενθερός*) can denote various relationships by marriage. Here it means son-in-law, i.e. Neoptolemus; in 641 it means father-in-law.

360. βλάβην ὀφείλω: a legal expression for incurring a penalty; cf. Lys. 1. 32 *διπλῆν τὴν βλάβην ὀφείλειν.*

361. ἡμεῖς . . . τοιοίδε: this picks up *ἡμεῖς* in 355 and sums up 355–60: 'that is my case.'

τῆς . . . φρενός: a gen. of respect: 'as for *your* disposition'; see KG i. 363, Anm. 11, and Fraenkel on *Ag.* 950. The dash after *φρενός* is not needed. Garzya explains as gen. of exclamation, but this is normally preceded by an interjection, e.g. *φεῦ, τῆς ἀνοίας*, and used with words more significant than *φρενός*.

362. σου: partitive gen. 'one thing I fear in you.' The repetition of *σῆς* and *σου* is for emphasis and no change is needed.

διὰ γυναικείαν ἔριν: what A. fears is not stated but implied, i.e. that as Menelaus was ruthless on account of Helen, so he will be now on behalf of Hermione. The common factor is a woman, but not strictly speaking *γυναικεία ἔρις* 'strife over a woman'; hence emendations such as *διὰ γυναῖκα γὰρ τὸ πρίν* (Schmidt), but the MS. reading, though not strictly logical, can perhaps be accepted. It is now supported by Ox. Pap. 31 (1966), 2543 (ii A.D.) *δια [γ]υν[αικ]ειαν ερι[ν].*

364–5. The general sense of these lines is clear: the Chorus leader is reproaching Andromache with talking too much and too boldly for a woman speaking before men. There are, however, difficulties in 365, and no completely satisfactory interpretation has been given of the text as it stands.

The only other example of *ἐκτοξεύειν* used metaphorically is Ar. *Pl.* 34 *νομίζων ἐκτετοξεῦσθαι βίον*, where the sense is 'thinking that

I have shot my bolt, i.e. used up my life'; the simple verb is similarly used in A. *Eu.* 676 πᾶν τετόξευται βέλος. LSJ take this to be the sense here: τὸ σῶφρον 'has shot away all its arrows, i.e. has no resource left'. If so, an object to the verb has to be supplied, and in any case using up all one's modesty is not a possible way of describing an immodest speech. Seager's ἐξετόξευσας, with τὸ σῶφρον as its object, avoids the first objection but does not touch the second.

If the text is accepted, it seems best, with Kamerbeek, to take ἐξετόξευσεν as intransitive and φρενός as gen. of separation: 'restraint has fled from your spirit.' I know no exact parallel for this use of ἐκτοξεύειν, but it seems possible on the analogy of ἐξακοντίζειν 'dart away' in Aristotle, and the intransitive use of ἀκοντίζειν in *Or.* 1241. On the other hand the simple verb τοξεύειν and the compounds ἀποτοξεύειν and ἐξακοντίζειν are certainly used metaphorically of loosing off verbal shafts in an unrestrained manner; e.g. A. *Sup.* 446 γλῶσσα τοξεύσασα μὴ τὰ καίρια; *Hec.* 603 καὶ ταῦτα μὲν δὴ νοῦς ἐτόξευσεν μάτην; Men. fr. 1091 (Kock, trag. adesp. 529 Koerte) γλώσσῃ ματαίους ἐξακοντίζειν λόγους; Pl. *Theaet.* 180 a. If the object of ἐξετόξευσεν were some word standing for the speech which Andromache has made, this sense of the verb would suit the context very well, but then the text must be corrupt. The general sense expected could be represented by something like οὐ γὰρ (or οὔ τοι) τὸ σῶφρον ἐξετόξευσεν τάδε 'for it is no womanly modesty that has let fly such words as these'; but this is rewriting rather than emendation.

366–7. Menelaus partially admits the truth of Andromache's words in 324–9.

368–9. These lines are a variation on the proverbial saying that the best thing of all is to get what you want; cf. the concluding words of the elegiac couplet inscribed on the προπύλαιον of the temple of Leto at Delos (Arist. *EN* 1099ᵃ25) ἥδιστον δὲ πέφυχ' οὗ τις ἐρᾷ τὸ τυχεῖν, repeated with some variations in Theognis 255–6 and S. fr. 356.

372. δεύτερα: 'of secondary importance'. For the thought cf. *Med.* 569 ὀρθουμένης | εὐνῆς γυναῖκες πάντ' ἔχειν νομίζετε, | ἢν δ' αὖ γένηται ξυμφορά τις ἐς λέχος, | τὰ λῷστα καὶ κάλλιστα πολεμιώτατα, | τίθεσθε.

375. τοὺς ἐμούς: 'members of my family'; the masc. is used in this general sense, but M. is of course thinking of Hermione.*

376–7. An amplified and thereby much weakened form of the proverbial κοινὰ τὰ φίλων. For this use of ὀρθῶς cf. *IT* 610 ὡς . . . πέφυκας τοῖς φίλοις τ' ὀρθῶς φίλος; S. *Ant.* 99; *IA* 560 τὸ δ' ὀρθῶς ἐσθλὸν σαφὲς αἰεί. For this usage as reflecting philosophical discussions on ὀρθότης ὀνομάτων see Wilamowitz on *HF* 56.

378. τοὺς ἀπόντας: i.e. Neoptolemus; for the pl. cf. 359 γαμβροῖς and 391 δεσπόταισι.

379. φαῦλος . . . κοὐ σοφός: contemporary interest in arguments based on shifts in the connotation of value terms such as φαῦλος, σοφός, *σώφρων*, and many others is reflected in Euripides and Thucydides, and to a lesser extent in Sophocles. For Thuc. see especially 3. 82 with Gomme's notes; in Eur. compare the different senses of *σώφρων* and cognates in *Hipp.* and in this play (see note on 235), and of *σοφός* and cognates in *Ba.* and elsewhere. In this play, to Andromache Menelaus is *φαῦλος* 'ignoble' in his conduct to her; to Menelaus failure in any enterprise would make him *φαῦλος* 'ineffectual' 'a poor thing', whereas to be *σοφός* is to be resourceful in gaining his ends, whatever they may be. See Adkins, *Merit and Responsibility*, pp. 244–9, for the use of *φρόνιμος* in the late fifth century of 'the intelligent handling of one's own interests'.*

381. ἐκφεύγει: the present stresses the certainty of the result; cf. Thuc. 6. 91 *εἰ αὕτη ἡ πόλις ληφθήσεται, ἔχεται ἡ πᾶσα Σικελία* 'once this city is captured, all Sicily is ours'. Menelaus' emphatic promise aggravates the subsequent deception.

382. οὐ θελούσης: a participle representing the protasis of a conditional sentence normally requires *μή*, but *οὐ θέλειν* is treated as a single word 'refuse'; so also with *οὐ φάναι* 'deny', e.g. Pl. *Ap.* 25 b *ἐάν τε . . . οὐ φῆτε ἐάν τε φῆτε.*

384. κλήρωσιν αἵρεσίν τε: *κλήρωσις* (only here in verse) and cognates are elsewhere used only with reference to the operation of the lot. The proper distinction between *κλήρωσις* and *αἵρεσις* is seen in Pl. *Phaedr.* 249 b *ἐπὶ κλήρωσίν τε καὶ αἵρεσιν τοῦ δευτέρου βίου*, where the order of choice is decided by lot but the choice is free; cf. *R.* 617 e *πρῶτος δ' ὁ λαχὼν πρῶτος αἱρείσθω βίον.* Méridier accepts this sense for *κλήρωσις* and explains it as indicating that the choice is so cruel that Andromache can only leave the decision to chance. This is highly improbable: Andromache is surely assuming that she has a free choice, although in spite of apparent hesitation at this point there may be little real doubt what she will choose; certainly Menelaus and Hermione have taken it for granted that she will leave sanctuary to save her child (262–4, 311 ff.). It seems, therefore, that *κλήρωσις* must be used loosely, as we can speak of a 'chance of survival' without necessarily implying that it is a matter of luck. Meredith translates 'Ah, what bitter chance and choice of life you offer.'

385. λαχοῦσα: sc. *τὸ ζῆν. λαγχάνω*, properly 'obtain by lot', is often used of what is imposed from above, e.g. *IT* 913 *τίνα ποτ' Ἠλέκτρα πότμον | εἴληχε βιότου.* Neither sense is strictly compatible with *αἵρεσις*, but the second is more appropriate to the helplessness of Andromache before the dilemma imposed upon her.

ἄθλιος is often hardly distinguishable in meaning from *δυστυχής*, but it can have the further connotation of moral degradation, which would be relevant here; cf. 410.

386. καθίσταμαι: we might, as Wecklein says, have expected *φανήσομαι.* It closely follows *καθίστης*, but such repetition is fairly common in

Eur., e.g. *Hec.* 655–6; *El.* 44–5, and presumably was not regarded as a blemish.

387. μεγάλα πράσσων . . .: cf. 352, where she makes the same point, and Menelaus' admission in 366–7.

388. πιθοῦ: a regular formula of appeal; when it stands alone it is elsewhere in Eur. used with reference to a request already made (*Alc.* 1101, 1109; *Hec.* 842; *IA* 739, 1209; *Or.* 1101); in phrases like *ἀλλ' ἐμοὶ πιθοῦ* (*Hec.* 402; *Hel.* 323) it leads up to some petition. Here there is no specific appeal, but something of the sort may be regarded as implicit in 388–93.

ποίαν . . . τίνα . . . ποῖον: there is no distinction in meaning; see note on 299.

390. βίᾳ: 'constraint' rather than physical force; see note on 35 and cf. 38 *οὐχ ἑκοῦσα τῷδ' ἐκοινώθην λέχει.*

391. δεσπόταισι and **κεῖνον** both refer to Neoptolemus.

κᾆτ': Denniston, *GP* 311. ii (a), notes that *κᾆτα* and *κἄπειτα* are particularly common in Euripides and Aristophanes in surprised, indignant (as here), or sarcastic questions.

394 ff. After this appeal to Menelaus, the failure of which may be indicated by some movement or gesture, the following lines down to 410 are virtually a soliloquy in which Andromache looks into the past and sees nothing but miseries since the death of Hector, and for the future no hope except in her son.

394. κακῶν: causal genitive, as usual with *οἴμοι* and similar exclamations.

397 ff. 397–8 offer difficulties of interpretation in themselves and in relation to the following lines. Most editors accept Porson's correction *ταῦτα δύρομαι*, which provides a normal caesura, but almost everything else has been disputed. On the assumption that *τὰ ἐν ποσὶν κακά* must refer to the immediate peril and that this is contrasted with *ταῦτα*, the latter might possibly refer to Andromache's regret in the previous lines that she had given birth, but would more naturally refer to the former sorrows to which she constantly reverts in this play. In any case, after blaming herself for dwelling on the past she would hardly devote the next four lines to lamenting over Hector and Troy. If these two lines are genuine but out of place, the simplest change giving a satisfactory sequence of thought is, with Musgrave, to transpose 397–8 and 404–5. This brings together a series of rhetorical questions, and *παρελθούσας τύχας* leads to the reference to the past in 399 ff. A. then breaks off with *ἀτὰρ τί ταῦτα* . . . and *τὰ ἐν ποσὶν κακά* leads naturally to 406–7.

In 398 the chief difficulty is *ἐξικμάζω*, a scientific and medical term meaning to extract the moisture from something. Here it must be used metaphorically, but the sense can only be conjectured, and explanations in *Σ* are of little value. We might expect a sense roughly similar to that of *λογίζομαι*. In 316 Menelaus used the same word (*ταῦτ' οὖν λογίζου*) in bidding A. consider whether to die herself or allow her child to perish. This is exactly what she does in 406–10 (which by the suggested re-arrangement follow immediately) and *λογίζομαι* again denotes calm consideration; cf. also 126 *λόγισαι τὸ παρὸν κακόν*. Kamerbeek and Bornmann may then be right in regarding *ἐξικμάζω* as similar to *ἰσχναίνω*, which also means literally 'make dry', and is used as a medical term in the sense 'reduce a swelling' and hence metaphorically of reducing or calming passion. Thus *ἐξικμάζω* would mean something like 'view dispassionately' 'reduce to proper proportions'.

H. Lloyd-Jones suggests that the meaning is 'squeeze out to the last drop' i.e. 'dwell upon'. This is in itself attractive as being very easily derived from the literal meaning, and as the text stands it fits the context, since A. goes on to enumerate her sorrows in the past; but if the passage is rearranged as suggested it does not fit so well, since in 406 ff. A. does not dwell on her present troubles, but briefly considers the alternatives and gives a reason for her decision.

Murray follows Hartung in bracketing 397–8. It is true that the passage makes good sense without them, but there seems to be no special reason why they should have been a later insertion. Emendations have of course been suggested, especially for *ἐξικμάζω*, e.g. *ἐξιχνεύω* or similar glossed by *ἐξετάζω* (Dindorf), *ἐξιθμάζω* (Baynes), *ἐξιχμάζω* (Rutherford), but apart from the fact that the existence of the last two forms is conjectural, their sense would be similar to *ἐξιχνεύω*, and 'tracking down' seems inappropriate for *τὰ ἐν ποσί*. For discussions of the passage and other views (to me unconvincing) see R. Ellis, *J. Phil.* 1 (1891), 182; Parmentier, *Bull. Ac. R. de Belgique* (1920), 366; Kamerbeek, *Mnem.* s. 3, 11 (1943), 59.

399. σφαγὰς τροχηλάτους: according to Homer (*Il.* 22. 395 ff.) Hector was dead when bound to the chariot of Achilles, and in Andromache's elegiac lament 105–8 the implication seems to be that Hector was killed by the spear. 'Wheel-drawn slaughter' might possibly be a condensed expression for the slaughter of Hector (afterwards) dragged behind the wheels, but it would more naturally mean death by being dragged. This version of the death of Hector is given in S. *Ai.* 1030–1 in words that are allusive (thereby implying an established tradition) but unambiguous, and Eur. is probably following this account, even if there is some inconsistency with 105–8.

402. ἐπισπασθεῖσ': *ἀποσπασθεῖσ'* LP is not impossible, but elsewhere it is always used with specific reference to being dragged away from something, nearly always with a gen. of separation, and the compound with *ἐπί* is certainly more appropriate; cf. 710 below; *Hel.* 116; *Tro.* 882.

403. φονεῦσιν: i.e. Neoptolemus; not merely pl. for sing. but a generalizing pl. denoting here the son of the actual *φονεύς* (Achilles); cf. *Tro.* 660 (Andr. speaking) *δουλεύσω δ' ἐν αὐθεντῶν δόμοις*.

404. ἐμοί: Radermacher, *Obs. in Eur. Misc.* 11, observes that emphasis is not on the pronoun and that in similar expressions the unemphatic form is normal, e.g. *HF* 1301 τί δῆτά με ζῆν δεῖ; *Hec.* 349; *Alc.* 960; *Med.* 798; S. *Aj.* 393; he would therefore read τί δῆτά μοι. The case would be strengthened by Musgrave's transposition, since with 404 where it is some emphasis on the pronoun is possible.

406. εἷς, which gains emphasis from its position, goes with both παῖς and ὀφθαλμός: he is her only child and her only hope. ὀφθαλμός is often used metaphorically of anything precious; so in A. *Cho.* 934 Orestes is ὀφθαλμὸς οἴκων; cf. A. *Pers.* 168 ἀμφὶ δ' ὀφθαλμῷ φόβος. | ὄμμα γὰρ δόμων νομίζω δεσπότου παρουσίαν; Pi. *O.* 6. 16; S. *OT* 987.

408. εἵνεκ': most MSS. have οὕνεκ'; for the form see note on 251. The sense is probably 'not if my poor life can prevent it', i.e. by being offered in exchange.

409. ἐν τῷδε . . . ἐλπίς: the phrase could mean 'my hope rests in him', i.e. Andromache's hope can only be that the child at least will live, and perhaps honour her memory; cf. 414–18. But the contrasting μὲν . . . δέ show that she means that for him there is hope, if he lives, but for her only shame if she lives on at the cost of his life.

411. ἰδού: see on 250.

χειρία: equivalent to the prose form ὑποχείριος 'under someone's hand or control'.

412. σφάζειν: see on 315.

δεῖν after σφάζειν φονεύειν seems something of an anticlimax, and Bornmann is perhaps over-subtle in suggesting that the illogical order is deliberately intended to mark Andromache's indifference to what may happen to her.

ἀπαρτῆσαι δέρην: ἀπαρτᾶν can mean either 'separate' or 'hang up'; thus with δέρην it could mean 'behead' (Hesychius explains as χωρίσαι, διαστῆσαι); but Σ is probably right to explain as equivalent to κρεμάσαι, πνῖξαι 'hang, strangle'. So in 811 below ἀρτῆσαι δέρην refers to suicide by hanging; cf. Ap. Rh. 3. 789 λαιμὸν ἀναρτήσασα μελάθρῳ.

414. ἢν δ' ὑπεκδράμῃς: this may refer to future hazards, and does not necessarily imply suspicion of Menelaus. The audience may have doubts about his good faith, but it is dramatically more appropriate that for the moment Andromache should not.

415 ff. Everyone would like his self-sacrifice to receive proper recognition, and characters in Greek Tragedy (and perhaps real Greeks) never hesitated to state their own claims; cf. *Alc.* 323–5; *Hcld.* 579–80, 588–90; *IA* 1383–4.

416. διὰ φιλημάτων ἰών: equivalent to φιλήματα δίδους; cf. *Tro.* 916 διὰ λόγων ἰόντα. These lines suggest that though her union with N. was by constraint (35–8) at any rate she has no hatred for him.

419. ψυχὴ τέκνα: cf. Hes. *Op.* 686 χρήματα γὰρ ψυχή. For a different point of view about children see *Med.* 1090–3; fr. 575.

420. δυστυχῶν εὐδαιμονεῖ: a straightforward oxymoron, with no reference to the distinction sometimes observed between *εὐτυχής* and *εὐδαίμων*, as indicated in e.g. *Med.* 1228–30. The emphasis is, as often, on the participle, as the actor's delivery would presumably make clear.

421. ᾤκτιρ': the so-called 'momentary' or 'instantaneous' aorist referring to the immediate past and in English represented by a present; cf. 919 *συνῆκα*. For the sentiment cf. *El.* 290–1.

423. The variants given in the app. crit. from APBO are rather awkward devices for supplying the missing syllable in the reading of MVL, which Kirchhoff achieved by a simple transposition. The quarrel is essentially between Hermione and Andromache, and Menelaus is being asked to reconcile them. This attempt, characteristic of a chorus leader (cf. 232–3), is here an almost absurdly forlorn hope and is of course ignored by Menelaus.

425. ἀμφελίξαντες χέρας: a stronger variant of *χεῖρας ἀμφιβάλλειν* 'seize'.

427. ἐγώ σ': Murray and Bassi alone print this, the reading of all MSS. Lobeck's *ἔγωγ'* (anticipated by the corrector of Vaticanus) is accepted by Wecklein, Méridier, and Hyslop, and Hermann's *ἐγὼ δ'* by Paley, Kamerbeek, and Bornmann. Some stress on the personal pronoun suits the egotism of Menelaus (cf. 312–13) but *ἔγωγε* gives too much, and both this and *ἐγὼ δ'* sound like attempts to correct hiatus. Neither Murray's tentative *εἰδώς* nor Kirchhoff's *ἑλών σ'* is very convincing, and among emendations proposed Jackson's *ἔχω σ'*· (*Marg. Scaen.* 180) is the most plausible;[1] he compares *Or.* 1617 *ἔχεις με* 'you have me in your toils', spoken by Menelaus caught in a similar trap.

I am not, however, certain that the MS. reading is impossible. The general sense of the sentence is 'I have tricked you into leaving sanctuary', and Eur. might have begun with *σε* even though the main verb *προὔτεινα* governs *θάνατον* and would strictly require a dative of the person threatened. It would be essentially the same explanation to say that *σε* (427) anticipates the *σε* before *ὑπήγαγον*. Eur. might also have been influenced by the idiom whereby a phrase treated as a periphrasis for a transitive verb governs an accusative, e.g. *Or.* 860 *τὸ μέλλον ἐξετηκόμην γόοις* (= *ἐγόων*); *Ba.* 1288; though this passage is not strictly parallel, since *προὔτεινα . . . θάνατον* is not a mere periphrasis for *ἠπάτησα*.

428. προὔτεινα . . . θάνατον: *προτείνειν* when used metaphorically generally means 'put forward as a pretext' (so, rather strangely, LSJ for this passage) or 'offer as an inducement'. *θάνατος* is certainly not a pretext, and not strictly an inducement, unless this term includes threats. There seems, however, to be no reason why *προτείνειν* should not be used of making a threat, and editors rightly reject Wecklein's *βίοτον*.

---

[1] Garzya now accepts this conjecture.

433. ἀλλ' ἕρπ' ἐς οἴκους: the same phrase recurs in *Hec.* 1019 and *Phaethon* fr. 773. 10; cf. also *Hel.* 477 ἀλλ' ἕρπ' ἀπ' οἴκων.*

437. Εὐρώτᾳ: the famous river of Sparta, often standing for the country, e.g. *Tro.* 133, where Helen is called τῷ Εὐρώτᾳ δυσκλείαν.*

σοφά: 'shrewdness', 'worldly wisdom': 'Is this your Spartan statecraft?' See on 379. For ἐν 'in the judgement of' cf. *Hipp.* 988 οἱ ἐν σοφοῖς φαῦλοι; *Or.* 488.

438. Τροίᾳ: local dative, as in 462; prose would require ἐν. Menelaus implies that retaliation is universally accepted as a valid principle, and justifies any means; cf. *Hcld.* 881–2 παρ' ἡμῖν μὲν γὰρ οὐ σοφὸν τόδε, | ἐχθροὺς λαβόντα μὴ ἀποτείσασθαι δίκην. This was the accepted principle. Adam on Pl. *R.* 331 e collects many illustrations from Hesiod onwards, and observes that Plato was the first Greek who protested systematically against it.

439. τὰ θεῖα δ' οὐ θεῖ' . . .: 'Is God not God? Does he not judge the world?' (Meredith).

ἔχειν δίκην: in addition to the common meaning 'to be punished', this phrase can also mean 'to have satisfaction' (Hdt. 1. 45); 'to have justice on one's side' (*Alc.* 38, 39); in Pl. *R.* 520 b δίκην ἔχει = δίκαιόν ἐστι. None of these quite confirms the sense we should expect here, which is 'to maintain justice'. Perhaps, however, in view of the common possessive gen. in θεῶν or δαιμόνων δίκη, ἔχειν δίκην may, in this context, mean 'to be in charge of', as (with the concrete sense of δίκη), in Dem. 47. 45 διαιτητῶν ἐχόντων τὰς δίκας.*

For the notion that the gods prove their own existence by punishing wickedness cf. *H.F.* 841–2 θεοὶ μὲν οὐδαμοῦ . . . μὴ δόντος δίκην; fr. 577 εὖτ' ἂν τοὺς κακοὺς ὁρῶ βροτῶν | πίπτοντας, εἶναί φημι δαιμόνων γένος; *El.* 583–4. An appeal to divine justice is the only card left for Andromache to play; her words do not necessarily imply belief on her part, still less of course on the part of Euripides.

440. Perhaps an echo of the Homeric κῆρα δ' ἐγὼ τότε δέξομαι, ὁππότε κεν δὴ | Ζεὺς ἐθέλῃ τελέσαι.

ὅταν τάδ' ᾖ: i.e. punishment from the gods, implied in 439; but we should expect ἔλθῃ or γένηται.*

441. νεοσσόν: 'nestling'; the context here stresses the live metaphor, as in *Tro.* 751 νεοσσὸς ὡσεὶ πτέρυγας ἐσπίτνων ἐμάς, and *HF* 71–2.

443. τί οὐ καταστένω: τί οὐ is often used to introduce a phrase formally interrogative but equivalent to a command or exhortation: 'Oh, let me mourn for thee, my child.' A more common form of the idiom is τί οὐ with the second person used to express an impatient command, generally with the aorist but occasionally with the present, e.g. Ar. *Ach.* 359 τί οὖν οὐ λέγεις; where Coulon rightly translates 'Mais parle donc.' See also Barrett on *Hipp.* 1060–1.

444. ἀναμένει: resolutions in the third metron are not found anywhere else in plays earlier than *HF* (or *El.*), so that Nauck's ἀμμένει should be accepted here. Cf. *Hec.* 1281, where ἀναμένει is the MS. reading but Murray rightly prints ἀμμένει, Triclinius' correction in L, and *Andr.* 1137 ἀμπνοάς.

445–53. In view of the brutality and treachery of Menelaus and Hermione this famous tirade is dramatically relevant, though in some respects it goes beyond what the situation requires, and was influenced by patriotic sentiment. The accusations of treachery and double-dealing, of cruelty and avarice frequently recur in Athenian writers during the Peloponnesian War and afterwards. So E. *Supp.* 187 Σπάρτη μὲν ὠμὴ καὶ πεποίκιλται τρόπους; Ar. *Ach.* 308 οἷσιν [Spartans] οὔτε βωμὸς οὔτε πίστις οὔθ' ὅρκος μένει; *Lys.* 629, 1269–70; Thuc. 2. 39. 1 (where Pericles implies Spartan reliance on ἀπάται), 5. 105; Ar. *Pax* 622 [Spartans] ἅτ' ὄντες αἰσχροκερδεῖς; Arist. fr. 544 (*ap.* Schol. Ar. *Ach.* 308) cites a prophecy ἁ φιλοχρηματία Σπάρταν ὀλεῖ ἄλλο δέ γ' οὐδέν; cf. also Hdt. 9. 54 ἐπιστώμενοι τὰ Λακεδαιμονίων φρονήματα ὡς ἄλλα φρονεόντων καὶ ἄλλα λεγόντων, where H. seems to reflect Athenian prejudice. Such charges are often brought against enemies and rivals; cf. *Punica fides* and *perfide Albion.* Here the objective narrative of Thucydides indicates some basis of fact for Athenian accusations, e.g. the treacherous slaughter of two thousand helots in 424 (Thuc. 4. 80); the massacre of the Plataean prisoners in 427 (Thuc. 3. 68. 1); the betrayal of Scione (Thuc. 5. 18. 7); see Gomme's notes on the last two passages, where it is suggested that though Athenians might be guilty of brutality, unscrupulous dishonesty was in fact more characteristic of Spartans than of Athenians.

For the bearing of this passage on the date of production of the *Andromache* see Intr., p. 15.

446. βουλευτήρια: cf. A. *Sept.* 575 κακῶν τ' Ἀδράστῳ τῶνδε βουλευτήριον 'counsellor of evil'; as used of the Spartans the sense of the word is perhaps rather 'cunning plotters'. Some editors compare E. *Or.* 590 εὐνατήριον 'wife', but here the word may have its normal meaning 'bed-chamber'.

447. ψευδῶν ἄνακτες: for the metaphorical use of ἄναξ cf. A. *Pers.* 378 κώπης ἄναξ; E. *IA* 1260 ὅπλων ἄνακτες; *Alc.* 498 πέλτης ἄναξ; fr. 700 κώπης ἀνάσσειν. In all these examples it means master of some tool or weapon; here the phrase is contemptuous, suggesting that lies are the Spartan weapons.

μηχανορράφοι κακῶν: cf. *Ba.* 573 τᾶς εὐδαιμονίας . . . ὀλβοδόταν.

448. ἑλικτά: tortuous, not straightforward; cf. 'a twister'. The metaphor is continued in πᾶν πέριξ. I know no other example of ἑλικτός and cognates or of πέριξ in precisely this metaphorical sense; in *Or.* 892 καλοῖς κακοὺς λόγους ἑλίσσων the sense is 'mingling praise and blame'. Compare the metaphorical use of σκολιός and πλάγιος, e.g. Pind. *I.* 3. 5 πλάγιαι φρένες 'crooked souls'; Pl. *Theaet.* 173 a. In *IA* 332 πλάγια φρονεῖν means 'erratic' rather than 'crooked'.

οὐδὲν ὑγιές: used metaphorically in the sense 'unsound', 'rotten'. This expression, which recurs in 952, is probably colloquial, since apart from nine examples in Eur. it is found only once in Tragedy (S. *Ph.* 1006) but is common in Aristophanes, e.g. *Thesm.* 394 *τὰς οὐδὲν ὑγιές*, in Plato, and occasionally in the Orators, e.g. Lys. 9. 4 *ἐπὶ μηδενὶ ὑγιεῖ κατειλέχθαι*; it also occurs once in Thucydides 3. 75.

450. φόνοι: the audience might think of the Plataean prisoners or of the 2,000 helots (see on 445–53), but there need not be any specific reference.

451–2. Cf. Hdt. 9. 54 cited above on 445–53.

453–4. ἐμοὶ μέν: if the reading of M is accepted, this may be added to the numerous examples of *μέν solitarium* with personal and demonstrative pronouns given in *GP* 381 (ii). The implicit contrast is here perhaps with other victims of Spartan cruelty. Some editors print *ἐμοὶ δέ*, the reading of most other MSS.

ὡς σοὶ δέδοκται: the equivalents in *Σ*, *νενόμισται* and *δεδοκίμασται*, do not mean, as Hyslop thought, 'as has been supposed by you' but denote something sanctioned or enacted. The sense must be 'as you have resolved', and the phrase refers back to *θάνατος*: 'for me death, in accordance with your decree, is not as grievous ⟨as you think⟩.' For *οὕτω* with a correlative clause understood cf. *El.* 1105 *οὐχ οὕτως ἄγαν χαίρω* 'not so much ⟨as you may think⟩'; but this ellipse is a bit awkward when *οὕτω* is actually followed by a *ὡς* clause that is not the correlative. Eur. may have relied on the actor's delivery to make all clear, in which case we should print a comma after *βαρύς*. Alternatively Lenting's *ὅς* for *ὡς*, accepted by Hermann, involves only slight change. A. Y. Campbell would also replace *οὕτω* by *οὗτος*, which then brings out the contrast with *κεῖνα*: 'this coming death which you have decreed does not weigh so heavy upon me; it was then that I died, when Troy perished and Hector'—ingenious and effective, but *οὕτω* remains blameless in itself.

456–7. πολλάκις . . . ναύτην ἔθηκεν: this hardly squares with the Homeric account, in which Hector and the Trojans only once reached the ships (*Il.* 15. 653 ff.), and their purpose, foiled by Patroclus, was to burn the ships, not to force the Achaeans to sail away. Andromache's essential point, however, that in battle Menelaus was inferior to Hector is in accordance with Homeric tradition; see especially *Il.* 7. 104–5. But though not equal to the greatest of the Achaeans or Trojans, he is in the *Iliad* no mean warrior and very different from the Menelaus described here and in 616–18, and sometimes elsewhere in Attic Tragedy, e.g. *Or.* 754 *οὐ γὰρ αἰχμητὴς πέφυκεν ἐν γυναιξὶ δ' ἄλκιμος*. He is indeed once called *μαλθακὸς αἰχμητής* (*Il.* 17. 588), but this is isolated special pleading and contradicted by his prowess on several occasions, especially in the fighting over the body of Patroclus; compare too his epithet *δουρικλειτός* in *Il.* 5. 55 and Hes. fr. 99.

458. γοργὸς ὁπλίτης: exactly the same phrase is used in 1123 of Neoptolemus facing his enemies; here it is sarcastic: Menelaus can be a grim warrior when his opponent is a woman.

459–62. Grube (p. 205 n. 1) cites these lines as 'an example of sigmatism to express a hissing contempt'. We may note that the Greek for 'my tongue' in the gen. must in any case produce five sigmas, and Page on *Med.* 476 cites three examples of sigmatism not specially effective and presumably accidental: S. *OT* 1507 (8), *OT* 425 (10), and *Ion* 386 (8), though in the last two it may in fact be held to reinforce the expression of anger or contempt. Add *Or.* 450 (8), where the tone is one of pleading and sigmatism has no point. But where it *is* effective, as in *Med.* 476 and in this passage, Page rightly observes that it is perverse to regard it as accidental. Similarly the repeated *τ* is effective and intended in S. *OT* 371 but not in *Aj.* 687–8.

459. κτείνεις μ'. ἀπόκτειν': there is no difference in meaning; the variation is probably for metrical convenience. In prose the compound is far more commonly used, in verse the simple verb, and it is characteristic of the more prosaic flavour of Euripides' diction that *ἀποκτείνω* is found thirty-eight times in him, once in Aeschylus and never in Sophocles. *κτείνεις* is the conative present: 'you seek to slay me.'

460. γλώσσης: a genitive of separation depending on *ἀθώπευτον*. So often with adjectives compounded with privative alpha, e.g. 612 *παιδῶν ἄπαιδας*; 714 *ἄπαιδας τέκνων*; *El.* 1130 *ἀγείτων φίλων*; S. *Ant.* 847 *φίλων ἄκλαυτος*; Dem. 18. 270 *ἀθῷος τῆς Φιλίππου δυναστείας*; Isaeus 3. 1. See KG 412, Anm. 7.

καὶ παῖδα σήν: perhaps added as an afterthought; it need not imply that Hermione is present.

462. δὲ . . . γ': this combination is generally found in dialogue or where there is 'a sense of imaginary dialogue' (*GP* 155 (4) (i)); so here *σὺ μὲν* . . . represents what Menelaus is presumed to be thinking and *ἡμεῖς δέ* . . . *γε* is Andromache's retort.

463. μηδέν: adverbial acc.

πράξειας ἄν: sc. *κακῶς*.

SECOND STASIMON: 464–493

The Chorus begin with a general statement deploring the quarrels and distress that arise when two women in a house are rivals for the affection of one man; in the second and third stanzas they give three more examples of disastrous rivalry in other spheres, leading up to a general rule that in private and public life success depends on entrusting control to a single person. Thus down to 485 we have an extended example of the form described as *comparatio paratactica*, i.e. a general statement illustrated and supported by one or more analogous or contrasting observations from other spheres; for a very brief example see below 636–8. For discussion and examples of this traditional form in Greek and other poetry, and of the Priamel, which is a particular variety of it, see Dornseiff, *Pindars Stil*, pp. 97 ff.; van Otterlo, *Mnem.* 8 (1940), 145 ff.; H. Friis Johansen, *General Reflection in Tragic Rhesis*, pp. 16–49 and 160–70, and other literature cited there. The ode concludes with a reference to previous events in the play which illustrate the general statement at the beginning, and ἔδειξεν in 486 is justified only on the assumption that it refers back to that statement; for in spite of some obscurities of detail in the middle stanzas, it is clear that their contents have only a superficial resemblance to the initial generalization and little relevance to the dramatic situation. Kranz may be right in suggesting (*Stasimon*, p. 218) that E.'s choice of illustrations was influenced by topics familiar in current sophistic discussions.

The first stanza is dramatically relevant, but may also have a topical reference. There is some evidence for a decree at Athens, probably soon after the plague, permitting citizens to have two legitimate wives or (by another account) legitimate children by a concubine. See Diog. L. 2. 5. 26; Ath. 13. 556; Harrison, *The Law of Athens*, p. 17; Mathieu, *REG* 40 (1927), 98. The opening and closing stanzas, then, are directly relevant to this play, though, as K. Aldrich has pointed out (*Andromache of Euripides*, p. 92), they would be more appropriate immediately after the quarrel scene between Andromache and Hermione, i.e. in the place now occupied by the first stasimon. Thus 177–9 would suggest the opening words of this ode, and the reference in the last stanza to the fiery rage of Hermione and her intention to kill Andromache and the child would naturally follow her threats in 259 and 261 ff., whereas in its present position the ode follows an epeisodion in which Hermione is not present and it is Menelaus (barely mentioned in this ode) who does all the threatening. Aldrich also urges (with less cogency, I think) that the first stasimon is out of place and would be much more relevant after the second epeisodion. It would certainly fit in here, but chiefly because it is concerned with the Judgement of Paris, the ἀρχὴ κακῶν behind the whole play, and has no special relevance to any one part of the action. I do not think that the degree of irrelevance of this second stasimon to its immediate context is in itself sufficient to make a transposition of stasima a tenable hypothesis.

Metre. The rhythm is mainly iambic.

Metrical Scheme:

Strophe + antistrophe (*a*): 464–70 = 471–8

464 = 471	1.	– ⏖ ⏑ ⏖ ⏑ – ⏑ – ⏑ – ⏑ –	iambic trimeter with resolutions
	2.	⏒ – ⏑ – ⏑ – ⏑ –	iambic dimeter

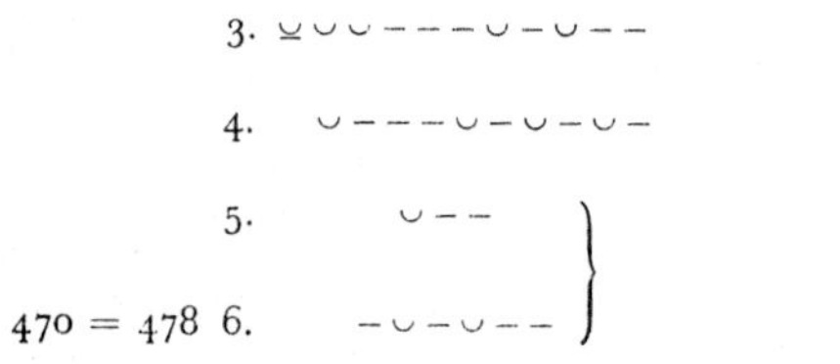

	3.	choriambus + iambic dim. catalectic
	4.	iambic trimeter syncopated
	5.	bacchiac + ithyphallic = iambic trimeter syncopated
470 = 478	6.	

Notes:

3. The short first syllable in 467 is anomalous and ἔριδας may be corrupt; see note ad loc.

Strophe + antistrophe (*b*): 479–85 = 486–93

	1.	⏑ – ⏑ – ⏑ – ⏑ – ⏑ – ⏑ –	iambic trimeter
480 = 487	2.	⏑ ⏑ – ⏑ ⏑ – ⏑ ⏑ – ⏑ ⏑ – ⏓ –	enoplian, with dragged close in strophe
	3.	⏓ – ⏑ – ⏑ ⏖ ⏑ – ⏑ ⏖ ⏑ –	iambic trimeter
	4.	– ⏑ ⏑ – ⏑ ⏑ – ⏑ ⏑ –	dactylic tetrameter catalectic
	5.	⏑⏖⏑ ⏑⏖⏑ ⏑⏖⏑ ⏑⏖⏑	iambic dimeter with total resolution
	6.	⏑⏖⏑ ⏑⏖⏑ ⏑⏖⏑ –	iambic dimeter catalectic
485 = 493	7.	– ⏑ – ⏑ – –	ithyphallic

Notes:

2. In the antistrophe (487) the last word should be printed λέχει. For an enoplian ending ⏑ – in response to – – see *LM*² 168.

4. Assuming that αὐτοκρατοῦς in 482 is sound, in 490 we must emend ἔριδος ὕπερ or accept a resolved dactyl, which virtually never occurs (see *LM*² 25 n. 1). Hermann's ἀμφ' ἔριδος may be right. T. C. W. Stinton suggests (*CR* 15 (1965), 142) that this may be another instance of the sequence 2 dactyls + iambic metron found at E. *Hipp.* 1108; but in that passage the change occurs with an iambus, which is easier.

5. In 483 the MS. reading ἑνὸς ἁ is metrically unacceptable, since initial ⏑ ⏑ – does not occur elsewhere in lyric iambics. The scheme assumes some correction such as ἐνὶ δέ; see note ad loc.

5–7. A. M. Dale suggested the following revised colometry:

ἔνῐ δἔ δῠνᾰσῐς ᾰνᾰ τἔ μἔλᾰθρᾰ κᾰτᾰ τἔ πŏλῐᾰς	resolved iambic trim.
ŏπŏτᾰν εῠρεῖν θἔλωσῐ καῑρŏν	syn. iambic trim. cat.

on the ground that this keeps a sequence of long cola, and that a resolved bacchiac such as ὁπόταν εὗ rarely if ever occurs at the end of a colon, only at the beginning.

465. λέκτρ': for the sense 'bedfellow' see notes on 35 (*λέκτρα*) and 350 (*εὐνάς*).

βροτῶν: possessive genitive depending on *λέκτρα*. The word sometimes appears to be otiose, as in 643 *οἱ σοφοὶ βροτῶν*, but here the Chorus are piously limiting their criticism to mortals.

466. ἀμφιμάτορας κόρους: sons of the same father by different mothers, i.e. half-brothers. It is of course not the *κόροι* but the whole situation of which the Chorus disapprove, a situation which does not exist in the household of Neoptolemus, where there is only one child.

467. ἔριδας . . . λύπας: accusative not strictly in apposition to the sentence *οὐδέποτε . . . ἐπαινέσω*, but to the situation implied in 465–6. *ἔριδας* is probably corrupt, since the first syllable should be long to correspond with 475. Schroeder, *Eur. Cantica* (1928), p. 215 suggested *δήριας*, Ionic accusative of *δῆρις*, 'contest', found in Epic only in the accusative *δῆριν*. There is no parallel for *δήριας*, but the genitive *δήριος* appears in A. *Ag.* 942; cf. also the Ionic accusative *πόλιας* in 484. The less familiar word might have been glossed by *ἔριδας*.

δυσμενεῖς: rarely used of things, perhaps only where there is a personal hostile agent in the background; see A. M. Dale on *Alc.* 617.

468. γάμοις: a locative dative 'in wedlock'.

469–70. ἀνδρὸς εὐνάν: the two words are taken together by most editors in the sense 'marriage bed'. Examples cited are not really parallel, since in Hom. *Il.* 18. 433 *ἔτλην ἀνέρος εὐνήν* it is natural for a woman to use this phrase, as also in E. *Supp.* 822, but it is less appropriate here, where the subject of *στεργέτω* is a man. On the other hand the speakers are women, and the phrase may have become stereotyped. On this view the sense is 'Let my lord be content with one marriage bed unshared', which in this context would naturally mean not shared with another woman.

Σ however, followed by Wecklein and Méridier, takes *ἀνδρός* as gen. of separation with *ἀκοινώνητον*. This gives a different sense, 'May my lord be content with one bed not shared ⟨by me⟩ with ⟨another⟩ man', and introduces a fresh point. But the sense of *μίαν μοι στεργέτω πόσις εὐνάν* is clear enough, and *ἀκοινώνητον* is more likely to be used to reinforce this than to bring in a new point so briefly and ambiguously.

It is *ἀνδρός* that causes the difficulty; among emendations suggested are *ἁμός* (Herwerden) and *ἁγνός* (Nauck).

471. οὐδέ γ' ἐνί: Lenting's correction provides correspondence with 465, and since *οὐδέ γε*, the negative counterpart of *δέ γε*, is more appropriate here than *οὐδὲ γάρ*, which is either causal or used in retorts (*GP* 111, 156), this is better than Nauck's solution of keeping the MS. reading *οὐδὲ γὰρ ἐν* (which is anyhow metrically inferior) and reading *οὔποτε δή* (not *οὔποτ' ἐγώ*) in 465.

δίπτυχοι τυραννίδες: as often with 'twofold', the second part of the compound has lost its original force. The word is a favourite of Eur., who uses it about eighteen times, as compared with one doubtful example in Soph. and none in Aesch. Cf. *Ph.* 1354 διπτύχων παίδων.

Some have thought that there is an allusion here to the dual kingship at Sparta, others to domestic rivalries in Athens, between Nicias and either Cleon or Alcibiades. Such speculation is not very profitable, and we cannot be sure that there is any specific historical reference.

476. The MS. readings are metrically impossible and it is unlikely that the synonyms τέκτονες and ἐργάται (in the plural or dual) are both right. τέκτονες is a natural metaphor for poets and well attested, e.g. Ar. *Eq.* 532 τέκτονες εὐπαλάμων ὕμνων; Pi. *Pyth.* 3. 13; *Nem.* 3. 4; there seems to be no other example of ἐργάτης in the sense poet or musician, though ἐργάζεσθαι is used of composition, as in Pi. *Isth.* 2. 46 (ὕμνους . . . εἰργασάμαν. Perhaps it should be kept as being the less familiar word. Wilamowitz's correction, printed in the OCT and accepted by most modern editors, certainly gives metrical correspondence with 468, and this metaphorical sense of τίκτειν is fairly common, e.g. *HF* 767 ἔτεκον ἀοιδάς; *Supp.* 180; Cratin. fr. 199; Ar. *Ra.* 1059; but it is not free from difficulties. It is not clear what form the rivalry between poets is supposed to take. *Σ* and some editors refer to Hesiod's καὶ πτωχὸς πτωχῷ φθονέει καὶ ἀοιδὸς ἀοιδῷ, but in that passage (*WD* 11–26) Hesiod is speaking of the good kind of ἔρις, 'emulation'. Similarly it is sometimes assumed that Eur. has in mind two poets composing poems on the same theme, as when Aeschylus and Simonides were said to have composed rival epitaphs on those who died at Marathon (*Vit. Aesch.* 8); but this is normal professional rivalry, whereas in the present series we have two women quarrelling over a man, two rulers quarrelling over a state, and perhaps two steersmen quarrelling over the tiller, all with disastrous results, and we ought to have two poets quarrelling over a poem which they are presumably composing in collaboration. Pohlenz (*Erl.* S. 84) suggested that Eur. might be thinking of Aristophanes and Eupolis collaborating over the *Knights*. This, however, unlike the other instances, would be a voluntary partnership; and in that case, as Kamerbeek points out, we ought to have a present participle. Moreover, if this is the sense required, whatever the precise text may be, it is odd that such collaboration should be common enough to provide an obvious instance of divided authority and to justify the frequency implied by φιλοῦσι.

479–82. It makes sense and suits the context of this ode to say that when a ship is sailing swiftly before the wind, divided counsels at the helm will be dangerous, but it is not clear how this generally accepted meaning is derived from the text. *Σ* (1) takes 480 as by itself constituting the apodosis to 479, the predicate being κατὰ πηδαλίων ⟨εἰσί⟩, and explains δύο κυβερνῆται ἐν μιᾷ νηὶ διχοστατοῦντες κατὰ τῶν πηδαλίων γίγνονται, οὐχ ὑπὲρ τῶν πηδαλίων; but to say that two steersmen are 'against the rudder' is an odd expression and puts too much weight on the prepositional phrase. Σ (2) would supply as predicate ἐπιβλαβεῖς εἰσι, but such an ellipse is hardly possible. If the text is sound we seem driven to take 480 more closely with the following lines, perhaps omitting the comma at γνῶμαι, and supply some form of ἀσθενής from 481. On this view it might be better to accept the variant διδύμα . . . γνώμα (AVLP), which could be qualified by a neuter singular adjective. The whole sentence down to αὐτοκρατοῦς would then refer to the ship, and the danger of two steersmen with different views merges into the disadvantage of a number of experts as compared with a single captain. It is doubtful whether κατὰ πηδαλίων can mean 'at the tiller' (as Bornmann thinks); we should expect ἐπί with dative as in *Alc.* 439 ἐπὶ κώπᾳ πηδαλίῳ τε . . . ἵζει. It may, however, mean more vaguely 'in respect of', as in Pl. *Phd.* 70 d μὴ κατ' ἀνθρώπων σκόπει μόνον τοῦτο; id. *Smp.* 193 c. πηδαλίων is used in the plural since a Greek ship was normally steered by two paddles, one on each quarter of the stern, fastened together by ropes. One further point is that unless this is meant as a hypothetical situation, it may be asked why two steersmen should be in action at the same time. Paley suggested that the reference is to the κυβερνήτης and his subordinate the πρῳρεύς who must work in harmony if the ship is to go safely. For this subordination see Arist. *Pol.* 1253ᵇ28–9; Xen. *Oec.* 8. 14. It would not, however, be very accurate to speak of both as being κατὰ πηδαλίων.

483–5. The MS. reading ἑνὸς ἁ (the MSS. actually vary between ἁ and ὁ), retained by Murray, does not correspond metrically with 491, where the text seems to be sound; Musurus's ἄθεός γ' can be ruled out since γε is not elsewhere used in such phrases. To keep the same sense and mend the metre Wilamowitz (*Gr. Versk.*, p. 427) proposed ἑνὶ δὲ δύνασις: 'power goes to one person in palaces and cities, whenever . . .' The two situations in which singleness of direction is particularly needed are when there is grave danger of destruction or when it is necessary to seize opportunities. Some think the former is relevant here; thus Méridier 'quand on veut trouver le salut'; but though the sense of καιρός can pass from 'opportunity, right time' to 'profit, advantage' (see on 131 above) it is doubtful whether it could mean 'salvation'. For the latter situation καιρός is of course the natural word to use, but in that case εὑρεῖν is less appropriate and λαβεῖν or χρήσασθαι would be more normal. Good sense without much alteration would be provided by ὁπότε τηρεῖν θέλωσι καιρόν, but perhaps the objection to εὑρεῖν is not strong enough to justify emendation.

Some editors put a stop at ἑνός instead of αὐτοκρατοῦς and read ὅ or ἃ δύνασις. This has the advantage of making explicit the antithesis of one and two, as in previous examples, and the antecedent of the relative is then the situation implied by the preceding words: 'authority in the hands of one person, a thing which means effectiveness . . .' So Méridier: 'Voilà ce qui fait la force . . .' But with this text the sense of δύναμις is doubtful. Its natural meaning in this context, 'political power', would make the statement purely tautologous, and I know no exact parallel for the sense 'force, effectiveness'; moreover on this view the limitation indicated by the ὁπόταν clause seems less relevant.

484. πόλιας: this Ionic form should also be read in *Hel.* 223; cf. Zuntz, *Inquiry into the Transmission*, p. 44.

486. ἔδειξεν: this must refer back to the first stanza: what H. has demonstrated is the consequences of δίδυμα λέκτρα.

στρατηλάτα: Doric gen.

487. διὰ πυρὸς ἦλθ': 'she raged like fire against her rival'; the whole phrase governs a dative on the analogy of verbs of attacking, e.g. ἐπιτίθεσθαι. Cf. 416 διὰ φιλημάτων ἰών; *El.* 1183 διὰ πυρὸς ἔμολον . . . ματρὶ τᾷδε; and such phrases as διὰ φιλίας, δι' ἔχθρας ἰέναι or γίγνεσθαι 'to be on terms of friendship or enmity'.

ἑτέρῳ λέχεϊ: 'the other woman'. For this use of λέχος cf. *Hipp.* 835 ὤλεσας κεδνὸν λέχος; *IA* 389; Sappho, 121 λέχος ἄρνυσο νεώτερον; and see notes on λέκτρα (35) and εὐνάς (350). The trisyllabic form λέχεϊ is not needed; see note on metre.

489. κτείνει: conative present, as in 459, 'she seeks to slay'; there is no need for Nauck's κτενεῖ.

490. ἔριδος ὕπερ: Hermann's ἀμφ' ἔριδος restores correspondence with 482 and may well be right.

491. ἄθεος ἄνομος ἄχαρις: with this example of the common privative τρίκωλον cf. *Il.* 9. 63 ἀφρήτωρ ἀθέμιστος ἀνέστιος; E. *IT* 220 ἄγαμος ἄτεκνος ἄπολις ἄφιλος (the only fourfold example); A. *Cho.* 53 ἄμαχον ἀδάματον ἀπόλεμον; S. *Ant.* 876. It is more common in Eur., e.g. *Hel.* 1148 ἄπιστος ἄδικος ἄθεος; *Ba.* 995 ἄθεον ἄνομον ἄδικον; *Or.* 310; *Hec.* 669; *HF* 434. So also in rhetorical prose, e.g. Gorg. *Pal.* 36 ἄθεον ἄδικον ἄνομον; Dem. 9. 40. For the same effect in English cf. Milton, *PL* 5. 895 'Unmoved, unshaken, unseduced, unterrified', and see Fraenkel's discussion in *Agamemnon*, 2. 217. ἄθεος was sometimes a generic term for wicked, as in S. *Tr.* 1038, and its strict sense need not be assumed in a series such as this, where it is often used in conjunction with ἄνομος and ἄδικος. ἄχαρις is rather surprising. Kamerbeek observes that it is an example of litotes, and the word is certainly so used in conversational style in Aristophanes and Herodotus, e.g. *Av.* 156 οὐκ ἄχαρις ἐς τὴν τριβήν 'not unpleasant'; but we should not expect this series to end with understatement. It is noticeable that elsewhere in Tragedy ἄχαρις and ἀχάριτος are always used in the oxymoron χάρις ἄχαρις; so *IT* 566 κακῆς γυναικὸς χάριν ἄχαριν ἀπώλετο; *Ph.* 1757; A. *Ag.* 1545; *Cho.* 42; *Pr.* 545 χάρις ἄχαρις (codd.). Perhaps therefore the word would by itself suggest that the killing of Andromache to gratify Hermione will prove no boon but a χάρις ἄχαρις. In the next line the Chorus speak of retribution or change of fortune overtaking H.

492. ἔτι: as usual in threats or warnings: 'a time will come when . . .'

πότνια: the Chorus, after referring to Hermione in the third person in 486–90, now address her directly, though she is in the house. For similar apostrophe to one not present cf. *IT* 1123 καὶ σὲ μέν, πότνι', Ἀργεία | πεντηκόντορος οἶκον ἄξει, where the Chorus address the absent Iphigenia; *Hipp.* 141 ff.; and A. *Ag.* 83 ff., with Fraenkel's note; but the parodos of S. *Ajax* is not strictly comparable, since there the whole ode is addressed by a group of sailors to their commander.

Hermann read δέ for σε and took πότνια as nominative and an epithet of μετατροπά; but σε is desirable as object of ἔπεισι and with σε a vocative is needed. There is no objection to the use of πότνια referring to Hermione; cf. *El.* 487 and *Ion* 1053, and see Bond on *Hyps.* fr. 60. 5, where he notes that Eur. uses the vocative 11 times of human beings, 25 times of gods and abstractions.

μετατροπά: Σ explains as μεταμέλεια, μετάνοια; so also Méridier 'le regret te viendra'; but though this meaning can be derived from the basic sense of μετατρέπειν, the use of cognate words suggests that the sense is 'retribution' (LSJ) or more likely 'reversal', both of which suit ἔπεισι, generally used of hostile approach. In Hes. *Th.* 89 μετάτροπα ἔργα τελεῦσιν refers to reversing actions; in Pind. *P.* 10. 21 μετατροπίαι are reversals of fortune, and in A. *Pers.* 943 δαίμων μετάτροπος has a similar sense. In *El.* 1147 μετάτροποι πνέουσιν αὖραι δόμων and Ar. *Pax* 495 πολέμου μετάτροπος αὖρα the veering wind stands for a change of fortune. The essential meaning of μετατροπά and cognates is probably reversal of fortune, though no doubt in many contexts, as here and in *El.* 1147, the reversal does in fact bring retribution. Certainly it is reversal of fortune that in due course Hermione comes to dread: that she instead of Andromache will perish, or that she, the mistress, will become the slave; see 856, 860, 927–8.

Third Epeisodion: 494–765

The scene opens with introductory anapaests by the Chorus, followed by a passage (501–44), mainly in lyric metre, in which Andromache and her child lament their fate and plead with Menelaus. The rest of the scene is in iambics and presents the rescue of Andromache by Peleus. The central part (577–746) consists of an agon between Peleus and Menelaus, beginning with a short passage in stichomythia (577–89) and continuing with set speeches separated by conventional comments by the Chorus. Peleus had already appeared as the protector of persecuted innocence in the *Phoenix* of Euripides; see Webster, *The Tragedies of Euripides*, pp. 84–6.

Metre

The lyric portion 501–544 is in the form of a μέλος ἀπὸ σκηνῆς (not a κομμός, since after the anapaests the Chorus take no further part in the scene). It is divided into a strophe and an antistrophe, which consist of dialogue between Andromache and her child (*ἀμοιβαῖον*), and after each Menelaus speaks seven lines of anapaests followed by a paroemiac clausula. The strophe and antistrophe consist entirely of glyconics and pherecrateans (the catalectic form of glyconic).

Metrical Scheme:

Strophe + antistrophe: 501–14 = 523–36

501 = 523	1.	– ∪ – ∪ ∪ – ∪ –	glyconic
	2.	– ∪ – ∪ ∪ – ∪ –	glyconic
	3.	– ⊻ – ∪ ∪ – –	pherecratean
	4.	– – – ∪ ∪ – ∪ –	glyconic
505 = 527	5.	∪͡∪ ∪ – ∪ ∪ – –	pherecratean
	6.	– ⊻ – ∪ ∪ – ∪ –	glyconic
	7.	– – – ∪ ∪ – ∪ –	glyconic
	8.	∪͡∪ ∪ – ∪ ∪ – –	pherecratean
510 = 532	9.	– ∪̄ – ∪ ∪ – ∪ –	glyconic
	10.	– – – ∪ ∪ – ∪ –	glyconic
512 = 534	11.	∪͡∪ ∪ – ∪ ∪ – ∪ –	glyconic
	12.	– – – ∪ ∪ – ∪ –	glyconic
	13.	– ∪ – ∪ ∪ – –	pherecratean

Note

11. In 512 Musurus's *τ'* avoids hiatus, though this might be acceptable before the interjection *ὤμοι*.

494. καὶ μήν, generally, as here, followed by some part of *ὅδε*, is the regular formula for introducing a new actor, either on first appearance, e.g. 545 (Peleus) and 879 (Orestes), or on return to the stage, e.g. here and 1166 (Peleus). See *GP* 356 (6) and Addenda, p. 586.

495. σύγκρατον: lit. 'mixed together' i.e. closely united. The word is only found here in the classical period, but cf. *σύγκρασις* in Eur. and Thuc. and *συγκεράννυσθαι*, e.g. Xen. *Cyr.* 1. 4. 1 *τοῖς ἡλικιώταις συνεκέκρατο* 'he was closely united with his comrades'. ALP have *σύγκροτον*, which is also implied by the comment in *Σ συγκεκροτημένον*. *σύγκροτον* is not otherwise attested for any period, and though *συγκροτεῖν* is fairly common in the sense 'to weld together' and metaphorically 'to organize', the second sense is inappropriate here and the former would be misleading with its suggestion that the two captives were fettered together, which they evidently were not (529–30, 722).
ζεῦγος: for the metaphor see on *ἅρμα* (277), and cf. *HF* 454 *ὦ τέκν', ἀγόμεθα ζεῦγος οὐ καλόν*.

496. ψήφῳ: from the sense 'vote' the word came to be used for any resolve or decree; cf. 518, 1272, and S. *Ant.* 60 *ψῆφος τυράννων*; *OT* 607.

κατακεκριμένον: Murray brackets and notes '*del.* Hermann'; but H. in his text does not bracket the word and only raises the possibility of interpolation; without it *ψήφῳ* is dative of instrument with *σύγκρατον* taken as equivalent to a passive. But *σύγκρατον* can stand alone, and there is no real objection to *κατακεκριμένον*; it is otherwise found only in prose writers, but Euripides tends to use prosaic words, and it is better not to interrupt the series of anapaestic dimeters.

497. δύστηνε γύναι, τλῆμον δὲ σὺ παῖ: other single instances of two cola or half-cola in precise metrical correspondence, reinforced by repetition, rhyme, and assonance, are found scattered through Tragedy, especially but not always in scenes of lamentation, and there is a series of such cola in A. *Sept.* 967 ff. They may perhaps reflect a stylistic feature of earlier poetry composed for ritual lamentation and thanksgiving. Cf. 1168 below; *Ph.* 1292 *δι' ἀσπίδων, δι' αἱμάτων*; ibid. 1033 *ἰάλεμοι δὲ ματέρων, ἰάλεμοι δὲ παρθένων*; *Phaeth.* fr. 775. 50 (in a joyful hymn) *θεὸς ἔδωκε θεὸς ἔκρανε*; S. *El.* 1233. For further examples in Aeschylus see J. Diggle in *CR* 18 (1968), 3; see also Kranz, *Stasimon*, pp. 127 ff.*

τλῆμον: most MSS. have *τλήμων*, which may be right; see note on 348 above.

500. βασιλεῦσιν: dative of the person judging. The reference is to Menelaus and Hermione; even they cannot impute any guilt to the child; cf. 570. In 519 ff. Menelaus gives the reason more bluntly.

501. χέρας: acc. of respect. *χείρ* can mean 'arm' as well as hand'; here we may translate 'wrists'. She has been so harshly fettered as to draw blood; cf. 719–20.

504 ff. Murray rightly prints *ΠΑΙΣ* instead of the name *Μολοττός* which appears in all MSS. See note on *τέκνου* in 27 above.

In extant Attic Tragedy speaking parts are assigned to children only in four plays of Euripides: this passage, *Alc.* 393 ff., *Supp.* 1123 ff., and *Med.* 1271 ff. (where the voices of children are heard within). This in itself may be regarded as an example of the introduction of *οἰκεῖα πράγματα* by Eur.; but there is no attempt to make them talk like children, except that in *Alc.* 393 *μαῖα* may be a nursery equivalent for *μᾶτερ*. As A. M. Dale observes (*Alcestis*, p. 85) 'the child sings the sentiments its elders feel for it. Macduff cries "all my pretty chickens", but Alcestis' child calls himself "I, your chick", and Andromache's says to her *ἐγὼ δὲ σᾷ πτέρυγι συγκαταβαίνω*.' However, to blame Euripides, as Grube does (*Drama of Euripides*, p. 136), because 'the boy is far too much a miniature adult', and to censure him as 'not very happy in his presentation of children' is to underestimate the conventions of Attic Tragedy within which he worked.

The boy is still present when Peleus enters at 547, so that we have an extra speaking part; cf. *Supp.* 1123–64. Apparently one or more children could be brought in as extras, with small speaking (singing) parts.

506. θῦμα: nominative in apposition to ἐγώ in 501, the child being included with herself. The word means strictly 'sacrificial victim', animal or human, but is used here metaphorically of non-sacrificial killing, perhaps suggesting the helplessness of the victim; so also in *HF* 995, where the same word is used of the killing by Heracles of one of his own children.

δάϊον (trisyllabic) generally means 'hostile' 'destructive'; in Tragedy it is sometimes doubtful whether it means this or 'wretched', as it certainly does here and in S. *Aj.* 784 ὦ δαΐα Τέκμησσα.

507. κράντορες: this word, found only here and *AP* 6. 116, properly means rulers (κραίνειν) and Hyslop takes it as referring to Peleus and Neoptolemus. It is more likely that Andromache is invoking the leading men of the country, as in S. *OT* 629 Oedipus appeals to the πόλις. In *OT* 911 Iocasta refers to the Theban elders as χώρας ἄνακτες; cf. also S. *Ant.* 940 λεύσσετε Θήβης οἱ κοιρανίδαι; *Ion* 13, where γῆς ἄνακτες seems to mean 'the inhabitants'.

510. ὦ φίλος: the nominative is often used in address from Homer onwards; cf. 530, 1204, 1211. For the masculine adj. with τέκνον (*constructio ad sensum*) cf. *Tro.* 740 ὦ περισσὰ τιμηθεὶς τέκνον.

According to Denniston, *GP* 276 (3), δῆτα in affirmative sentences almost always echoes a word or words of the previous speaker. He notes *Andr.* 514 as one of the very rare exceptions. Jackson, however, (*Marg. Scaen.* 87, n. 1) suggested that in 510 Eur. wrote ὦ τάλας echoed by τάλας δῆτ', and that φίλος was substituted owing to φίλοις in 509.

512. σὺν νεκρῷ ⟨τ'⟩: the added τ' to avoid hiatus is printed by Murray and Méridier, but in view of the change of speaker and the following interjection hiatus is perhaps admissible.

513. τί πάθω; πάσχειν has here its proper passive sense and this is a question about the future rather than deliberation about a course of action: 'What will become of me?' The subjunctive is not deliberative but a survival of the future sense common in Homer; cf. Hom. *Od.* 5. 465 ὤ μοι ἐγώ, τί πάθω; τί νύ μοι μήκιστα γένηται; A. *Sept.* 297 τί γένωμαι;

516. δύο δ' ἐκ δισσαῖν: emphasis on numerical coincidence (or contrast) occurs elsewhere in Tragedy, most notably in S. *Ant.* 13 δυοῖν ἀδελφοῖν ἐστερήθημεν δύο | μιᾷ θανόντοιν ἡμέρᾳ διπλῇ χερί. In Eur. the best example is *HF* 328 ἡμῖν ἵν' ἀμφοῖν εἷς ὑπουργήσῃς διπλᾶ; less striking examples are S. *Ant.* 55, 141; E. *Hipp.* 258; *Ph.* 423. I know no close equivalent in Aeschylus, though the contrast between one and many is certainly emphasized in all three dramatists and in fifth-century *Kunstprosa*. Fraenkel on A. *Ag.* 1455 has collected examples, to which others could be added.

519 ff. For this sentiment cf. *Cypria*, fr. 25 Allen (22 Kinkel) νήπιος ὃς πατέρα κτείνας παῖδας καταλείπει, which probably became proverbial;

see Hdt. 1. 155. 1; E. *Hcld.* 1005–7; *HF* 168–9; Arist. *Rhet.* 1376a6. It was in accordance with this maxim that Astyanax was thrown from the walls of Troy.

520. ἐχθροὺς ἐχθρῶν: 'foes descended from foes' (gen. of origin); *σκύμνους* (Wilam.) is not needed.

521. ἐξόν: the impersonal accusative absolute is mainly a prose idiom, fairly common in Euripides but not elsewhere in Tragedy, except possibly S. fr. 193. The acc. abs. in personal construction with *ὡς* occurs in S. *OT* 101 and *OC* 381.

523. πόσις: this form, like *πόλις*, is regularly used in apostrophe. To Andromache Hector is still her husband.

526. δύστανος: see on 71 above.

μόρου: objective genitive; cf. *Ion* 1230 *οὐκ ἔστιν θανάτου παρατροπά μοι*; *Ph.* 586 *θεοὶ . . . τῶνδ' ἀπότροποι κακῶν*.

530. ὦ φίλος: one who had proved himself *ἐχθρός* could nevertheless be described as *φίλος* in the sense of being bound by close ties, generally of kinship; cf. A. *Cho.* 233 *τοὺς φιλτάτους γὰρ οἶδα νῷν ὄντας πικρούς.** Here, however, Andromache and the child cannot claim that *φιλία* in this sense exists with Menelaus, and the adjective is presumably euphemistic and propitiatory. See note on 540.

532. λείβομαι: lit. 'I am poured forth in tears.' *δάκρυσιν* is instrumental dative and *κόρας* accusative of respect: 'my eyes are wet with tears.'

534. Here, as in 116, the image of the smooth rock streaming with water may be meant to recall the legend of Niobe.

537. πέτραν ἢ κῦμα: rocks and sea were regularly used as symbols of the pitiless and implacable. So *Med.* 28 *ὡς δὲ πέτρος ἢ θαλάσσιος | κλύδων ἀκούει νουθετουμένη φίλων*; *Hipp.* 304 *πρὸς τάδ' αὐθαδεστέρα | γίγνου θαλάσσης*. Cf. also *Il.* 16. 34 *γλαυκὴ δέ σε τίκτε θάλασσα | πέτραι τ' ἠλίβατοι, ὅτι τοι νόος ἐστὶν ἀπηνής*.

540. φίλτρον: this word, more common in Eur. (14) than in Aesch. (1) and Soph. (2), presumably meant originally 'love-charm', and hence more generally 'charm', 'spell'. In Xen. *Mem.* 2. 3. 14 *τὰ ἐν ἀνθρώποις φίλτρα* are 'means of persuasion'. In Eur. it is used several times of anything that inspires love, e.g. *HF* 1407, where it is the sight of his children that will act as a *φίλτρον* upon Heracles, and *Tro.* 52, where *αἱ συγγενεῖς ὁμιλίαι* are said to be *φίλτρον οὐ σμικρόν*. Cf. also 207 above and fr. 103 *δεινόν τι τέκνων φίλτρον ἔθηκεν | θεὸς ἀνθρώποις*. So here the sense is probably 'I have no incitement to love you', though we might rather have expected 'You have no means of inspiring love in me.' In any case it is a direct rejection of the claim made in 530–1.

LSJ give as a third meaning for *φίλτρον* (but only in pl. for the classical period) 'love, affection', which would give good sense here, but the examples cited are doubtful: in *El.* 1309 *τῶν σῶν φίλτρων* may, as Keene says, mean rather 'thy endearments', and *Tro.* 859 *τὰ θεῶν δὲ φίλτρα φροῦδα Τροίᾳ* ends a song about Trojans who had won the love of gods, and Parmentier translates 'Troie n'a plus le charme qui séduisait les dieux'; thus in both passages *φίλτρον* may have its normal sense.

541. μέγα . . . ψυχῆς μόριον: some editors take this to refer to the long time spent on the siege, but I know no other example of *ψυχή* used like *βίος* to denote life as a period of time. A more likely sense in this context is 'vital force'; so Wecklein 'Lebensmark'. *Σ*, taking *ψυχή* in a collective sense, explains as *πολλὰς ψυχὰς ἀπολέσας*, but this is an improbable rendering for the Greek phrase, and it is more in keeping with the egotism of Menelaus to speak of the cost to himself of the victory for which he now claims all the credit, as in *Hel.* 393–6, 401–2.

543. ἀπολαύων: a prosaic verb found four times in Eur. but not elsewhere in Tragedy, or in verse apart from Comedy. It is here used ironically, as in *IT* 526 and *Ph.* 1205: 'you will have her to thank for your descent to Hades.'

545. καὶ μήν: see on 494.

Πηλέα πέλας: this sort of jingle, when it has no significance, seems to us displeasing, but perhaps did not jar on a Greek ear; cf. *Ba.* 189 *γέροντες ὄντες*; *Or.* 238 *ἕως ἐῶσι* and other examples cited by Denniston on *El.* 606; but in some of these the jingle disappears if they are pronounced with pitch accent. See B. A. Ramsden, 'Euripidean Assonance', *CR* 18 (1968), 260–1.

546. τιθέντα γηραιὸν πόδα: for the periphrasis cf. *IT* 32; *Supp.* 171. The age of Peleus is constantly emphasized; cf. 80, 645, 678, 759 ff., and especially 551.

547. Enter Peleus with an attendant (551), perhaps the slave woman sent by Andr. (91) and now returning as a *κωφὸν πρόσωπον*. We might expect him to have several attendants, and it would perhaps seem appropriate, as Meredith observes (op. cit. 132), that Menelaus and Peleus should have approximately equal escorts, so that, though the victory of Peleus is essentially a moral victory, the withdrawal of Menelaus may not appear quite incredible. Nevertheless the implication of 752 ff. is that Peleus has at present no bodyguard, though he is in his own country and claims that he can command an army if need be.

ὑμᾶς: Peleus is probably addressing not the Chorus (as some think) but the attendants of Menelaus, as he certainly does in 549.

τὸν ἐφεστῶτα: 'the man in charge'; cf. *IT* 726 *τοῖς ἐφεστῶσι σφαγῇ*: *Hel.* 1582. The reference is presumably to Menelaus himself; the impersonal description followed by *Μενέλα', ἐπίσχες* in 550 is justified if we suppose that Peleus begins speaking as soon as he is in sight; he is very old and in rather a state, and at first takes in only the general picture of imminent execution; in 550 he recognizes and addresses Menelaus.

548. τί ταῦτα; πῶς ταῦτ'; 'what's this? what's all this about?' the reading of LP seems satisfactory in this context; cf. *Or.* 732 *τί τάδε; πῶς ἔχεις; τί πράσσεις;*

ἐκ τίνος λόγου: 'for what reason?' Cf. A. *Cho.* 513 *ἐκ τίνος λόγου | μεθύστερον τιμῶσ' ἀνήκεστον πάθος;* So *ἐκ τίνος* E. *Hel.* 93, 1270.

νοσεῖ: for the metaphorical use, common in verse and prose, cf. 950; *Tro.* 27; S. *El.* 1070; Dem. 2. 14.

549. ἄκριτα μηχανώμενοι: LSJ translate 'engaged in rash attempts'. 'Acts performed without discrimination' is a sense of *ἄκριτα* related to the basic meaning of the verb, but no examples from classical Greek are cited, only *κατ' ἄκριτον* and *ἀκρίτως* 'rashly' in Philodemus and Polybius. The most common sense of the word that is relevant here is 'without trial' in phrases such as *ἀκρίτους ἀποκτεῖναι*; so also *Hipp.* 1056 *ἄκριτον ἐκβαλεῖς με γῆς*. Most editors take *ἄκριτα* in this sense, and this is supported by the subsequent references to summary execution in 550, 555, and 567. *μηχανᾶσθαι* in itself suggests a plot, not a legal process, so that the two words give emphasis by repetition, and the sense is something like 'What execution are you plotting without trial?'

550. ἐπίσχες: the usual word in Eur. for sudden arrest of action; cf. *El.* 962; *Ion* 1320; *Or.* 1069; *Ph.* 92, 452; *Hyps.* 60. 22. Menelaus is perhaps menacing Andromache with drawn sword; he is surely not already 'endeavouring to sneak off' as Paley puts it: this is too much even for Menelaus. Wilamowitz originally deleted this line, and Bruhn would place it before 547, but see note on 547. Wilamowitz later changed his mind: 'Ich muss mich schämen den Vers 550 angezweifelt zu haben' (*Hermes*, 60 (1925), 284 ff.).

551. ἡγοῦ: the implication that Peleus cannot move about unaided shows that Eur. represents him as very old and physically feeble, in spite of his bold words in 588.

ὡς ἔοικέ μοι: I know no other example where *ὡς ἔοικε* in the impersonal sense is followed by a dative of the personal pronoun, and here we should probably divide and punctuate, with Wilamowitz, *οὐ γάρ, ὡς ἔοικ', ἐμοί* . . . 'for my task, it seems, brooks no delay.'

552 ff. Peleus resembles in some respects another ageing hero, Iolaus in *Heracleidae*; cf. esp. 740 ff. Aristophanes may be parodying both passages in *Lys.* 669.

553. ἐπαινῶ: if the text is right the verb is used like *παραινῶ* in the sense 'advise, recommend'. For other examples of this sense see S. *Aj.* 1360; *El.* 1322; *OC* 665; but the only example with an accusative is A. *Supp.* 996 *ὑμᾶς δ' ἐπαινῶ μὴ καταισχύνειν ἐμέ.* *με* must stand for *ἐμαυτόν*, as in 256 and elsewhere. Meaning and construction are thus unusual but not unparalleled; it is however odd to say 'I advise myself to recover my youth', and the text has come under suspicion. We might have expected a wish or prayer for the recovery of youth, as in *Hcld.*

740; hence Platt's *με καὶ νῦν λαμβάνειν*. It is doubtful whether in prayers as distinct from decrees this acc. and infin. construction is used except after an invocation, as in A. *Sept.* 253 *θεοὶ πολῖται, μή με δουλείας τυχεῖν*; see KG 2. 22–3; but the infin. could perhaps depend on *ἔργον*, in that case followed by a comma. This suggestion also provides *νῦν* as a correlative to *εἴπερ ποτέ*, though this is not essential. *μενοινῶ* (Herwerden) gives good sense, but the smallest alteration is Hermann's *ἐπαιτῶ*, omitting *μ'*, which is not found in some MSS.; but there is no example with a dependent infinitive. On the whole, in the absence of a convincing restoration, it is best to keep the MS. reading. Verrall does not emend but offers a quite different interpretation of *ἐπαινῶ* (see app. crit.), which seems to me improbable: *ἐπαινῶ* is certainly used to denote polite rejection of a specific offer, but here no offer is made or implied in the text, and it is risky to base an interpretation on purely speculative stage business.

554. πρῶτον μέν: 'the first thing' or 'the main thing', sometimes used where the speaker apparently has no specific second thing in mind. At any rate Peleus breaks off to ask a question and listen to the reply. See *GP* 382 (iv).

554–5. *Σ* is probably right to suppose that the image is of a ship in distress (Andromache) saved by a favouring wind (Peleus). Bornmann thinks that the point lies in the metaphorical sense of *ἐμπνεύσομαι, κατ' οὖρον* . . . being added merely to amplify the metaphor; but it is not clear just what metaphorical sense he would give to *ἐμπνεύσομαι*. It can of course mean 'inspire hope or strength', but then requires an object such as *θράσος* or *μένος*. In this passage it can only mean 'fill the sails', which suggests a picture such as *Σ* assumes.

556. ἐκδήσαντες: this compound normally means 'fasten something to or on something else', hence Pierson's *ἐνδήσαντες*, which is used elsewhere to mean simply 'bind'. In combination with other verbs, however, *ἐκ* can denote completeness or thoroughness and this possibility cannot be ruled out for *ἐκδέω*. (In S. *Ant.* 578 Pearson prints Bruhn's conjecture *ἐκδέτους* 'fast bound'; elsewhere the word appears only in *AP* 9. 97, used of Hector bound to the chariot.)

557. οἷς: Hartung's correction of the MS. reading is palaeographically plausible but not certain, since *ὕπαρνος* might by itself indicate a ewe with its lamb.

558. τοῦ κυρίου: i.e. Neoptolemus. The primary sense of the word here is 'master of the household', so that it is for him, not Menelaus, to deal with Andromache; but *κύριος* was also the term used in Athens for a legal guardian or trustee, and may here have the secondary connotation of guardianship and protection. In 580 Menelaus picks up the word and claims that his authority over A. is superior to that of Peleus.

561. κληδόνος προθυμίᾳ: 'not with one eager summons'; cf. *Ion* 1109 *τίς* προθυμία | ποδῶν ἔχει σε; In *Ph.* 1430 σὺν παρθένῳ τε καὶ προθυμίᾳ ποδός the whole line has been suspected. κληδών in the sense 'cry, appeal' is distinctively poetic and rare (Fraenkel on *Ag.* 228 has missed this passage).

562. ὑπ' ἀγγέλων: cf. S. *Tr.* 391 οὐκ ἐμῶν ὑπ' ἀγγέλων . . . πορεύεται. μυρίων must be a rather wild exaggeration, and A. here assumes that some of her messages reached Peleus. She speaks differently in 81–3.

565 ff. Andromache naturally stresses the special interest of Peleus in the shrine of Thetis. Although ἀποσπάσαντες (567) is not literally true and strictly speaking Menelaus has not violated the shrine but has 'persuaded' Andromache to leave sanctuary before seizing her, the charges against him are in essence justified.

568. οὔτε: only in V and perhaps a 'correction'; most MSS. have οὐδέ, and there are other examples of οὔτε . . . οὐδέ, giving the effect of climax in the second limb: 'neither . . . nor yet . . .' See *GP* 193 (i).

τοὺς ἀπόντας: i.e. Neoptolemus.

570. τέκνου . . . ὄν: see on 510.

571. κτενεῖν: all MSS. have κτανεῖν, which most editors rightly accept, since μέλλω + aor. infin. is established for Eur., e.g. *Ion* 760, *Med.* 393 θανεῖν; *Hcld.* 709 λιπεῖν.

573. πίτνουσα: Andromache remains kneeling before Peleus until 717 ἔπαιρε σαυτήν.

χειρί: a pathetic touch; Andromache holds up her fettered wrists to show that she cannot perform the usual act of supplication. It is much less likely that, as some editors suppose, her status as a slave forbids her to touch Peleus.

576. αἰσχρῶς ὑμῖν: Andromache, even considered as a mere slave, is part of the household of Neoptolemus, and failure to protect her from outside interference would damage the prestige of the House of Aeacus.

577. κλαίειν: in threats κλαίειν, 'someone will smart for this', is very common in Aristophanes and is probably a colloquial idiom. Apart from this passage it occurs six times in Eur. (see 634 and 758 below), once in Aesch., and three times in Soph. In the tragedians there are several poetic modifications, e.g. S. *Ant.* 931 (lyr.) τοῖσιν ἄγουσιν κλαύμαθ' ὑπάρξει βραδυτῆτος ὕπερ. For the menacing τις referring to the person addressed cf. S. *Ai.* 1138 τοῦτ' εἰς ἀνίαν τοὔπος ἔρχεταί τινί 'pain for someone I know'.

578. διπτύχους: here the second part of the compound is not irrelevant but gives the picture of two hands placed together and bound.

579. δὲ . . . γε: 'yes, and . . .' or 'yes, but . . .', as often in retorts.

ἄλλος: 'I on my side'; cf. *nous autres* and *noialtri*.

581. ἀμόν: ἁμόν, the reading of L, may well be right. The form ἁμός and the by-form ἀμός are both found in Homer as equivalent to ἡμέτερος, and like ἡμέτερος can be used with reference to one person.

Both forms survive in Tragedy and there seems to be no distinction in meaning. LSJ cite only Aesch. and Soph., but in Eur. apart from this passage there are three examples in lyrics and at least two in dialogue: *El.* 555 *τὸν ἁμὸν πατέρ'*; *Hel.* 531 *πόσιν τὸν ἁμόν*. In *IA* 1454 Scaliger's *πατέρα τὸν ἁμόν* should probably be accepted. On these forms see KB 1. 602; Schwyzer, 2. 202 (a) 1, 4; Bjorck, *Das Alpha Impurum*, pp. 125, 244.

οἶκον οἰκήσεις: perhaps a popular expression for managing one's own affairs; cf. *IA* 331 *οὐχὶ δεινά; τὸν ἐμὸν οἰκεῖν οἶκον οὐκ ἐάσομαι;* *Ph.* 602 *οὐκ ἀπαιτούμεσθ'· ἐγὼ γὰρ τὸν ἐμὸν οἰκήσω δόμον*; fr. 144 *μὴ τὸν ἐμὸν οἴκει νοῦν· ἐγὼ γὰρ ἀρκέσω*, parodied in Ar. *Ra.* 105 *μὴ τὸν ἐμὸν οἴκει νοῦν· ἔχεις γὰρ οἰκίαν.*

583. ἐγώ is emphatic by position. In the *Iliad* Menelaus is quite overshadowed by Agamemnon; here, as in 540, he thinks of himself as conqueror of Troy and apparently asserts a sort of overriding claim on all captives. In 585, however, he shifts his ground and falls back on the proverbial maxim *κοινὰ τὰ φίλων*; cf. 374–8.

586. [ναί]: see on 242. Lenting's *δρᾶν γ' εὖ* may be right.

βίᾳ, apparently superfluous with *ἀποκτείνειν*, may be meant to suggest illegality as well as violence.

587. ὡς . . . ἀπάξεις: see on 255.

588. In *IA* 311 in answer to the stubborn *οὐδ' ἔγωγ' ἀφήσομαι* it is natural to retort *σκήπτρῳ τάχ' ἆρα σὸν καθαιμάξω κάρα* 'then I will give you a bloody head'; but in answer to 'You shall not take her away . . .' it is odd to reply 'But I will give you . . .', and it does not help to take 588 as a question, as only Murray does. Hence the suggestion *σκήπτρῳ γε τῷδε σὸν καθαιμάξας κάρα*: 'You shall not take her . . .' 'Yes, I will, after giving you . . .' See Zieliński in *Eos*, 31 (1928), 27, but this proposal had in fact been anticipated by Pflugk. The text implies that Menelaus makes a threatening gesture, to which Peleus replies with an explicit threat.

589. ψαῦσον . . . καὶ πρόσελθε: an example of *ὕστερον πρότερον*: the action on which more stress is laid comes first, without regard to order in time; cf. *Hcld.* 307–8 *δεξίαν δότε . . . καὶ προσέλθετε*; Hom. *Od.* 5. 264 *εἵματά τ' ἀμφιέσασα θυώδεα καὶ λούσασα*; ibid. 12. 134 *θρέψασα τεκοῦσά τε.*

590 ff. Leaving aside for the moment the immediate point at issue, Peleus embarks on a general tirade against Menelaus; first he was a weakling to lose his wife; then when he found her a wanton he should not have called Greece to arms to recover her; finally when she was recovered, instead of executing justice upon her he weakly succumbed to her charms. With this is thrown in for good measure an attack on the immodesty of Spartan girls, though the reference here is to customs that were not supposed to go back earlier than Lycurgus. On the ground that 591 virtually repeats 590, that the sense of 592 is given again in 603–4, and that the question in 602 would be more pointed if it followed 590, F. W. Schmidt, with some support from Wecklein, regarded 591–601 as an interpolation. The first point however is doubtful, and though the speech as a whole might well be thought more effective without these anachronistic and largely irrelevant lines, this does not justify us in deleting them.

590. μετ' ἀνδρῶν: 'are you to be counted among real men?'

κάκιστε κἀκ κακῶν: phrases of this type are fairly common and it is not always clear whether the speaker has in mind any specific ancestor or ancestors in general. It is clear that in S. *OT* 1397 *κακός τ' ὢν κἀκ κακῶν* Oedipus is thinking of himself and of Iocasta, and in S. *El.* 589 *εὐσεβεῖς κἀξ εὐσεβῶν* the reference is specific; but in Ar. *Ra.* 731 *πονηρὸς κἀκ πονηρῶν* and Dem. 22. 68 *δούλους ἐκ δούλων καλῶν αὑτοῦ βελτίους καὶ ἐκ βελτιόνων* the reference is more vague and may have become little more than a conventional amplification of *πονηρός* etc. So also Lys. 13. 64; 10. 23. In Pl. *Phaedr.* 246 a Hackforth is right to take *ἀγαθοὺς καὶ ἐξ ἀγαθῶν* in its literal sense 'good and of good stock', but, as he observes, the same expression when used in 274 a applies to the gods and means simply 'most excellent'. The expression is most likely to be conventional when the superlative is used in abusive attacks. Thus in S. *Ph.* 384 *τοῦ κακίστου κἀκ κακῶν* it is doubtful whether, as Jebb thinks, there is a reference to Odysseus as the reputed son of Sisyphus, and in the present passage it is unlikely that Peleus is actually thinking of earlier crimes of the House of Atreus.

591. ποῦ: in some passages *ποῦ* clearly cannot have a local sense, but is used in indignant or ironical questions, probably, as A. S. Owen says, expressing greater incredulity than *πῶς;* e.g. *Ion* 528 *ποῦ δέ μοι πατὴρ σύ;* 'how can you be my father?' S. *Ai.* 1100 *ποῦ σὺ στρατηγεῖς τοῦδε;* So here, though in this context the local sense ('in what country' Paley) is not actually impossible; cf. *Hcld.* 369; S. *OT* 390.

ὡς ἐν ἀνδράσιν: editors mostly supply *ὄντι* in agreement with *σοί* and take the sense of the line to be 'In what respect have you any share in consideration as being among men?' i.e. 'what right have you to be reckoned as a man?' Cf. *Or.* 1528; *IA* 945. In that case P. is repeating the sense of *σὺ γὰρ μετ' ἀνδρῶν* in 590. It is, however, possible that *ἐν* means 'in the eyes of', as in S. *Ant.* 925 *τάδ' ἐστὶν ἐν θεοῖς καλά* (essentially the forensic *ἐν* denoting the tribunal, as Jebb observes) and that *ὡς* is limitative, as in *Ba.* 454 *ὡς ἐς γυναῖκας* 'to a woman's taste, at least'. The sense is then 'What claim have you to esteem, at any rate in the eyes of men?' and the line does not merely repeat 590: P. says, in effect: 'You cannot be counted as a man or be esteemed by men.' Cf. fr. adesp. 304 *δοῦλος πέφυκας, οὐ μέτεστί σοι λόγου.*

592. ἀνδρὸς Φρυγός: in the epic tradition the Trojans were formidable enemies, but in the fifth century the fact that many slaves in Athens were Phrygians and Lydians (cf. Ar. *Vesp*. 433, 1309) led by anachronism to such slighting allusions as *Alc*. 675 *τίν' αὐχεῖς πότερα Λυδὸν ἢ Φρύγα | κακοῖς ἐλαύνειν ἀργυρώνητον σέθεν;* and perhaps influenced the contemptuous treatment of the Phrygian eunuch in *Or*. 1506 ff., with the unjustified taunt in 1518 *ὧδε κἂν Τροίᾳ σίδηρος πᾶσι Φρυξὶν ἦν φόβος;* cf. ibid. 1351 *ἄνδρας, οὐ Φρύγας κακούς*. So here Peleus probably speaks in a tone of contempt, though *Φρύγες* is of course regularly used in Tragedy for Trojans with no such connotation.

ἀπηλλάγης λέχος: after *πρὸς ἀνδρός* we might expect some word for losing or being deprived of (Nauck actually conjectured *ἀπώλεσας*); instead Peleus substitutes *ἀπαλλάσσεσθαι*, the regular Attic for divorcing a wife or breaking off less formal engagements; cf. Isae. 6. 24. 5 *ἀπηλλάγη γυναικός* 'he got rid of the woman'; Dem. 31. 13; Isoc. 19. 7; Pl. *Leg*. 868 d. Possibly the suggestion is that M. took so little care of his wife that one would have thought he wanted to get rid of her. Elsewhere *ἀπαλλάσσεσθαι* always takes a gen. and here we should probably read *λέχους* (LP); if *λέχος* (MBAV) is right the verb must be treated as equivalent to a *verbum privandi*, which may take a retained acc., as in 661 below and *Hel*. 938. For *λέχος* 'bedfellow' see on 488.

593. ἄκληστ' ἄδουλα . . . λιπών: we need not take these words literally to mean that no slaves were left in the house: the whole phrase expresses in exaggerated form the charge that M. had taken no precautions to see that Helen was suitably guarded and watched over. The text can stand.

In *Tro*. 943–4 Eur. follows the account in *Cypria* (acc. to Proclus), where Menelaus is said to have sailed away to Crete leaving Helen to entertain Paris and his companions. This version would be appropriate in the present context, where the folly of trusting Helen is stressed; but the wording would rather suggest that M. had gone before P. arrived, as is clearly indicated in *IA* 76 *ἔκδημον λαβὼν Μενέλαον*. *Il*. 13. 626–7 leaves this point open.

δώμαθ' ἑστίας: an unusual expression; *ἑστία*, the centre of the house, naturally stands for the house as a whole and *δῶμα* is perhaps used like *δωμάτιον* to mean 'room'; cf. the similar use of *δόμος* in *Med*. 1137, where *νυμφικοὺς δόμους* probably means bridal apartments. The most similar phrase is *Tro*. 1111 *θάλαμον ἑστίας* 'Helen's chamber in her home'.

594. ὡς δή: with a participle *ὡς δή* is 'almost always ironical, sceptical or indignant in tone' (*GP* 230). Here it expresses incredulity that Menelaus could really have thought Helen to be *σώφρων*.

595. πασῶν κακίστην: 'when in fact she was the most wanton of women'. The ellipse of the participle in this context is unusual, and since in MS. *ουδαν* and *ουσαν* might look almost identical we should not rule out the possibility that Eur. may have written something like

πασῶν κακίστην οὖσαν· οὐ γὰρ οἶσθ' ὅτι
οὐκ ἄν ποτ' οὐκέτ', οὐδ' ἂν εἰ βούλοιτό τις, . . .

and that two half lines were then omitted.

κακίστην: so often of Helen, cf. *Or.* 741 *τὴν κακίστην*; *IT* 566; *IA* 488; *Andr.* 608.

598. γυμνοῖσι μηροῖς: so Ibycus (fr. 61) called them *φαινομηρίδες*. They wore a single garment (cf. *Hec.* 933 *μονόπεπλος . . . Δωρὶς ὡς κόρα*) open at the sides in such a way as to show their thighs when they moved about.

599. δρόμους παλαίστρας τ': cf. Xen. *Lac.* 1. 4 *δρόμου καὶ ἰσχύος ὥσπερ καὶ τοῖς ἀνδράσιν οὕτω καὶ ταῖς θηλείαις ἀγῶνας ἐποίησε* (Lycurgus); Plut. *Lyc.* 14. In Theoc. 18. 22 *αἷς δρόμος ωὑτός | χρισαμέναις ἀνδριστὶ παρ' Εὐρώταο λοετροῖς* the Lycurgan institutions are, as in Eur., transferred to the Heroic Age.

οὐκ ἀνασχέτους ἐμοί: there is no justification for supposing, with Kamerbeek and Bornmann, that *ἐμοί* is in effect Eur. himself. As Paley observes, this tirade against the alleged immodesty of Spartan girls is in character for Peleus, famous for *σωφροσύνη*; cf. Ar. *Nub.* 1067 *τὴν Θέτιν γ' ἔγημε διὰ τὸ σωφρονεῖν ὁ Πηλεύς.*

601. Cf. S. *OC* 919 *καίτοι σε Θῆβαί γ' οὐκ ἐπαίδευσαν κακόν.*

603. τὸν σὸν Φίλιον: sc. *Δία*. For *Ζεὺς Φίλιος*, patron god of friendship and family affections cf. Pl. *Phaedr.* 234 e *εἰπὲ πρὸς Διὸς Φιλίου* 'as one friend to another'; *Grg.* 500 b *πρὸς Φιλίου* 'in friendship's holy name' (Dodds); *Alc.* 109 e *Σκώπτεις, ὦ Σώκρατες. Οὐ μὰ τὸν Φίλιον τὸν ἐμόν τε καὶ σόν*; Ar. *Ach.* 730; Pherecr. fr. 172. This use of *Φίλιος* alone seems to be confined to Comedy and Plato, except for this passage, and is perhaps colloquial. The effect here is to stress the ties, religious and natural, which Helen had broken. For *φιλία* of the relationship between husband and wife cf. E. *Alc.* 279 *σὴν γὰρ φιλίαν σεβόμεσθα* and 930 *ἔθανε δάμαρ, ἔλιπε φιλίαν.* For the possessive adj. cf. *Hec.* 345 *πέφευγας τὸν ἐμὸν ἱκέσιον Δία.*

Nilsson (*Gesch. der gr. Rel.* 1. 765) thinks that Zeus Philios here appears as the patron god of the symposium and that *τὸν σὸν . . . ἐξεκώμασε* means that Helen abandoned the party to roam about the streets. *κῶμος* and *κωμάζω* certainly can refer to the sequel to a symposium when drinkers sally out to serenade a mistress, e.g. Theoc. 3. 1 *κωμάσδω ποτὶ τὰν Ἀμαρυλλίδα*; but here the circumstances are different and I should take *ἐξεκώμασε* as a colloquial exaggeration describing the spirit of her departure: she rioted off to another country. For other compounds used metaphorically cf. Ar. *Ach.* 982 *ἐπικωμάσας* 'breaking in like a reveller'; *Vesp.* 1025 *παλαίστρας περικωμάζειν.*

Radermacher (*Mythos u. Sage*, p. 321) prefers to read *τὸ σὸν φίλιον*, with some MSS. and apparently *Σ*, and takes the reference to be to love tokens exchanged between spouses, but the evidence for this seems doubtful.

Broadhead (*Tragica*, p. 113) doubts the text on the ground that even in Comedy and Plato *Φίλιος* is so used only in adjurations, where the reference to Zeus (or some god) is unmistakable, and suggests *τῶν σῶν λιποῦσά σ' ἄφιλον*; but his objection does not seem to me fatal.

604. νεανίου; for the adjectival use see on *τύραννον* in 3 above. Paris would certainly be younger than Menelaus.

605. ἐκείνης οὕνεχ': in *Tro.* 864 Menelaus is represented as sensitive to this reproach: *ἦλθον δὲ Τροίαν οὐχ ὅσον δοκοῦσί με | γυναικὸς οὕνεκ', ἀλλ' ἐπ' ἄνδρ' ὃς ἐξ ἐμῶν | δόμων δάμαρτα ξεναπάτης ἐλῄσατο.*

606. ἤγαγες: it suits Peleus to treat Menelaus as chiefly responsible, as he himself claimed to be in 583.

607–8. Cf. Hdt. 1. 4, 2.

609. μισθὸν δόντα: almost a touch of comedy. The emphasis is, as often, on the participial phrase: 'you should have paid Paris to keep her in Troy'; cf. *IA* 389 *σὺ μᾶλλον (μαίνει), ὅστις ἀπολέσας κακὸν λέχος | ἀναλαβεῖν θέλεις*; *Or.* 501. The exaggeration is characteristic of Peleus in this speech.

611. ψυχὰς πολλάς: a Homeric reminiscence; cf. *Il.* 1. 3 *πολλὰς δ' ἰφθίμους ψυχὰς Ἄϊδι προΐαψεν*. That one woman caused the deaths of many is a stock antithesis in Tragedy, e.g. A. *Ag.* 1455 *μία τὰς πολλάς . . . ψυχὰς ὀλέσασ' ὑπὸ Τροίᾳ*; *Tro.* 368; *Cyc.* 283–4.

612. παίδων ἄπαιδας: for the gen. of separation with a cognate privative adj. cf. *Hel.* 524 *ἄφιλος φίλων*; *Supp.* 35 *πολιὰς ἄπαιδας . . . μητέρας τέκνων*; *Ba.* 1305; *Andr.* 714. For similar wording cf. *Cyc.* 306–7 *ἀλόχους τ' ἀνάνδρους γραῦς τ' ἄπαιδας ὤλεσεν | πολιούς τε πατέρας.*

613. This line repeats the general sense of 612, but also leads into the personal reference that follows.

614. *αὐθέντης* in Attic means 'murderer' and is also used adjectivally, as in A. *Ag.* 1572. *μιάστωρ* 'one who defiles' is applied to Clytemnestra (A. *Cho.* 944) and Oedipus (S. *OT* 353) and to Helen (*Or.* 1584), described as *τὴν Ἑλλάδος μιάστορα*. Aegisthus is described as *αὐθέντης* and *μιάστωρ* by Electra in S. *El.* 272–5. Here the gen. *Ἀχιλλέως* must depend on *αὐθέντην*, to which *μιάστορα* is in apposition. To call M. the actual slayer of Achilles is rather wild, and *μιάστορα*, though modified by *τινα*, makes the exaggeration worse. For similar hyperbole cf. *Hel.* 280 (Helen speaking) *μήτηρ δ' ὄλωλε, καὶ φονεὺς αὐτῆς ἐγώ*, and for M.'s retort see 655–6.

616–18. οὐδὲ τρωθείς: some editors follow *Σ* in seeking to reconcile this with the wounding of M. by Pandaros (*Il.* 4. 139–40), on the ground that he was only struck by an arrow (*βληθείς*) whereas *τρωθείς* means stabbed, the accusation then being that M. was never wounded in hand-to-hand conflict. The distinction is doubtful: e.g. in Antiphon *βάλλειν* and *τιτρώσκειν* are both used with reference to a javelin. The fact is surely that Peleus is being unfair, as can be seen from the next two lines, where he makes the absurd accusation that M.'s weapons were never used in battle.

618. ὅμοι': i.e. they looked the same as when he set out for Troy, because they were never used.

619–23. Wilamowitz changed his mind about rejecting these lines (see app. crit.) 'in face of deeper insight into the vices of Euripidean rhetoric'; see *Hermes*, 60 (1925), 290 ff.

619. κἀγὼ μέν: when the contrasted idea is not expressed *μέν* is in effect a particle of emphasis and is naturally common with personal pronouns: this is what *I* said (though others may differ); cf. *GP*, p. 381 (ii).

τῷ γαμοῦντι: i.e. Neoptolemus; the participle could be either future or conative present.

621. κακῆς γυναικός: i.e. Helen.

πῶλον: lit. 'colt' or 'filly'. *πῶλον* is occasionally used of a youth (*Ph.* 947) and often of a young girl, e.g. Anacr. 84; *Hipp.* 546; *Hec.* 142; cf. the similar use of *μόσχος* in 711 below.

621–2. ἐκφέρουσι . . . μητρῷ' ὀνείδη: *ὀνείδη* stands for the qualities that brought disgrace on the mothers, and these, as we might say, 'come out' in the daughters, *ἐκφέρειν* being the transitive equivalent: the bad qualities planted like a seed are brought to fruition. For the literal use of *ἐκφέρειν* in this sense Kamerbeek compares Hdt. 1. 193 *χώρη ἀρίστη καρπὸν ἐκφέρειν*, and for the metaphorical use A. fr. 99 *ἄρουραν οὐκ ἐμέμψατο | τοῦ μὴ ἐξενεγκεῖν σπέρμα γενναίου πατρός*, and perhaps Plut. *Mor.* 552 b *οὐδὲν γὰρ αἱ μεγάλαι φύσεις μικρὸν ἐκφέρουσιν. ἐκφέρειν* could also mean 'exhibit, display', but this sense is less pointed and emphatic here. It is not necessary, with LSJ, to assume, for this passage only, a special sense 'betray, show signs of'. Méridier's note that *ἐκφέρειν* means literally 'bring as a dowry' seems to be unsupported; this sense might be possible for *εἰσφέρουσι*, *EK* for *EIC* being a common corruption, but elsewhere the middle is used for this meaning.

622–3. σκοπεῖτέ μοι, μνηστῆρες: for this parainetic imperative, used to point the moral of the dramatic situation and addressed to a purely imaginary audience, cf. 950 below; *Or.* 804 *τοῦτ' ἐκεῖνο, κτᾶσθ' ἑταίρους*; fr. 609 (*Peliades*) *ἀλλὰ τὰς ὁμιλίας | ἐσθλὰς διώκειν, ὦ νέοι σπουδάζετε*; fr. 464. The comment in *Σ* on 622 *διαλέγεται πρὸς τὸ θέατρον* is mistaken here, though it may be true of *Or.* 128. See further Schadewaldt, *Monolog u. Selbstgespräch*, pp. 10 and 129 and, for a somewhat different point of view, Fraenkel, *Zu den Phoenissen des Eur.*, p. 111 (but in S. *Aj.* 1028 there is no reason why Teucer should not be addressing the Chorus).

623. λαβεῖν: the infin. used to express command is common in Epic and occasionally found in Tragedy, the historians, and Plato, e.g. S. *OT* 452; Thuc. 5. 9; Pl. *R.* 473 a.

624. οἵ': this is the exclamatory use; it cannot be a direct interrogative and the question mark at the end of 625 is wrong.

625. κελεύσας: here and in *IA* Eur. represents Menelaus as urging the sacrifice of Iphigenia for selfish reasons, whereas in Aeschylus there is no suggestion that M. attempts to influence Agamemnon's decision; see *Ag.* 205–17.

εὐηθέστατα: with *σφάξαι; εὐήθης* is regularly used of good-natured folly, and here Ag. is represented as weakly giving in to Menelaus. Nauck's *εὐηθέστατον*, agreeing with *ἀδελφόν*, is not necessary.

626. Spoken in scornful irony: Menelaus was afraid he would not recover his wife, though he must have realized that she was not worth it. I should however prefer (with Bornmann and Garzya) to take this line as a question.

627. κἀνταῦθα: Peleus is ready to go back in thought to Menelaus' great achievement; for even in that hour of triumph he showed himself weak and shameless in his treatment of Helen.

629–30. According to *Σ* here and on Ar. *Lys.* 155 the tradition that Menelaus was disarmed at the sight of Helen's beauty goes back to the *Ilias Parva* and Ibycus. In *Or.* 1287 Electra fears that Orestes' plan to kill Helen has miscarried for the same reason: *ἆρ' ἐς τὸ κάλλος ἐκκεκώφηται ξίφη;*

630. προδότιν αἰκάλλων κύνα: *αἰκάλλειν* is only found here in Tragedy, but according to *Σ* on Ar. *Eq.* 211 and Ath. 3. 99 e it is properly used, like the more common *σαίνειν*, of a dog fawning upon someone, but is also used of persons e.g. Ar. *Eq.* 48. There is thus some awkwardness in making it govern *κύνα* in the metaphorical sense of a shameless woman, as used by Helen herself in self-reproach (*Il.* 6. 344, 356). At any rate Peleus achieves a double insult: Helen is a *κύων* but Menelaus fawns upon her like a dog.

632. τέκνων: i.e. Neoptolemus.

633. ἀπόντων: sc. *ἐκείνων*, referring to *τέκνων*.

634. κτείνεις: conative present.

κλαίοντα: see on 577 above.

636. τρὶς νόθος: lit. 'a third-generation bastard', like *τρίδουλος* 'third-generation slave' in S. *OT* 1062, but the literal sense is too obviously inappropriate for the child of a princess and *τρίς* is loosely used to intensify the idea of *νόθος*, as in *τρισμακάριος, τρισκακοδαίμων*, and the like.

637. *ξηρὰ γῆ*, generally dry land as opposed to water, here evidently means poor soil. *βαθύς* often has the connotation rich, abundant, e.g. Hom. *Il.* 2. 147 *βαθὺ λήϊον* 'a deep cornfield'; here it suggests deep, rich soil contrasted with dry, stony, shallow soil; cf. Hdt. 4. 23 *μέχρι μὲν τῆς τούτων . . . πᾶσα πεδιάς τε γῆ καὶ βαθύγαιος, τὸ δ' ἀπὸ τούτου λιθώδης . . .**

ἐνίκησε: gnomic aorist. The point seems to be that as poor ground if well tilled may yield better results than rich soil neglected, so bastards may turn out better than true born. The comparison is curiously inapt, since there is no necessary connection between bastardy and inferior stock, and in this instance both parents are royal.

Numerous references to the general question of the stigma of bastardy suggest that it may have interested Eur. himself in relation to the *νόμος – φύσις* antithesis; compare fr. 168 *ὀνόματι μεμπτὸν τὸ νόθον, ἡ φύσις δ' ἴση* with fr. 141 *τῶν γνησίων γὰρ οὐδὲν ὄντες ἐνδεεῖς* (sc. *νόθοι*) *νόμῳ νοσοῦσιν*; cf. also *Hipp.* 309 *νόθον φρονοῦντα γνήσια*; fr. 377.

639. **ἐκκομίζου παῖδα**: Peleus apparently bids Menelaus take his daughter, now in the house, back to Sparta. He repeats this in 708–9, but Menelaus in fact abandons her with a vague promise to return later (737–8); hence the complications that follow in the next epeisodion.

κύδιον: the superlative *κύδιστος* 'most honoured' is fairly common as an epithet of gods and kings, and the neuter occurs in A. *Supp.* 13; the comparative is rare, but it is the MS. reading in *Alc.* 960 (where Murray prints Purgold's *κέρδιον*) and is more appropriate here than the superlative, which is the reading of MSS. other than LP. See Tucker on A. *Supp.* 13 and Dale on *Alc.* 960.

640. Denniston on *El.* 253 notes that the use of two adjectives more or less contrasted in sense but without an adversative particle between them is characteristic of Eur., and that when, as in this passage and often, there is a comparison between two composite phrases, in the second the correlatives are usually linked by *καί*.

643. **γλῶσσα** naturally stands for eloquence, the power of words; cf. *Hec.* 1187–8 *οὐκ ἐχρῆν ποτε τῶν πραγμάτων τὴν γλῶσσαν ἰσχύειν πλέον*. So in Ar. *Ra.* 892 *γλώττης στρόφιγξ* 'the pivot of the tongue' is one of the private deities to whom Eur. prays.

644. **τεύχειν ἔριν**: cf. A. *Pers.* 190 *τεύχειν στάσιν*.

645. **γέροντας**: for the acc. where *περί* with gen. would be normal cf. S. *El.* 520 *με . . . ἐξεῖπας ὡς θρασεῖα καὶ πέρα δίκης ἄρχω*; Xen. *Cyr.* 7. 3. 5 *γυναῖκα λέγουσιν ὡς κάθηται χαμαί*.

σοφοί picks up the words of the Chorus leader in 643.

646. **τοὺς φρονεῖν δοκοῦντας** can hardly refer to the Seven Sages, as Paley supposes: it must, like *γέροντας* in 645, refer to a class to which Peleus belongs. The line is not superfluous with its indication that P. is not merely old but famous.

647. **ὅτε . . . λέγεις**: 'at a time when' followed by a present tense naturally shades off into 'since', whereas *ὅτε* in the purely temporal sense more often refers to past or future.

πατρὸς κλεινοῦ: i.e. Aeacus, son of Zeus, who in his lifetime was said to have acted as arbitrator in disputes among the gods (Pind. *Isth.* 8. 26) and was traditionally one of the judges in the underworld, together with Minos, Rhadamanthos, and (sometimes) Triptolemos (Pl. *Ap.* 41 a; *Grg.* 523 e).

648. κῆδος συνάψας: if the text is sound *ἡμῖν* or *ἐμοί* must be supplied; M. then picks up P.'s words in 620 and retorts in effect that the connection by marriage as well as P.'s renown and ancestry should have restrained him from the insults he has uttered. The ellipse is difficult, though the reference back to 620 is some help, and the point not very satisfactory; but perhaps the text can stand. Some editors have thought that the reference is to P.'s marriage with Thetis; thus Musgrave conjectured *θεῷ* for *γεγώς*, and Wecklein and others mark a lacuna after 647. Jackmann, *Nachr. Gött. Ges.*, 1936, pp. 206 ff. regards *καὶ πατρὸς . . . συνάψας* together with 646 as an interpolation, and reads *πολιός* instead of *Πηλεύς*.

649. διὰ γυναῖκα βάρβαρον: M. naturally begins with his strongest point, an appeal to Hellenic sentiment with the reminder that Andromache was 'one of the enemy', widow of the most dangerous of them all and sister-in-law of the man who killed Achilles. He thus prepares the way for his assumption in 659, in itself unjustified, that Andromache's children by Neoptolemus are also to be considered as enemies.

650. ἣν . . . τήνδ': this use of a pleonastic demonstrative referring back to a previous relative also occurs in 710 and perhaps in 1116. I know no other clear and exact parallel. The nearest is Hypereides, *Euxen.* 3 *ὧν οὐδεμία δήπου τῶν αἰτιῶν τούτων οὐδὲν κοινωνεῖ τῷ εἰσαγγελτικῷ νόμῳ*. In other examples of similar pleonasm there are special reasons. Thus the idiom is more natural where many words intervene between the relative and the demonstrative that picks it up. In Xen. *Lac.* 10. 4 *ὃς ἐπειδὴ κατέμαθεν . . . ἐκεῖνος . . .* sixteen words intervene before the demonstrative; so also E. *Ph.* 1597 *ὃν καὶ πρὶν ἐς φῶς μητρὸς ἐκ γονῆς μολεῖν | ἄγονον Ἀπόλλων Λαΐῳ μ' ἐθέσπισε*. (There is generally a similar gap before a pleonastic *αὐτόν* or *νιν* e.g. S. *OT* 248; Aeschin. 3. 128; Xen. *An.* 3. 3. 16.) In Hdt. 4. 44 *ποταμὸν ὃς κροκοδείλους δεύτερος οὗτος . . . παρέχεται* the numeral makes a difference. In other passages different interpretations are possible: in S. *Tr.* 136 *ἃ καί σε . . . ἐλπίσιν λέγω τάδ' αἰὲν ἴσχειν*, *ἃ* may be adverbial 'wherefore' so that *τάδε* is not pleonastic; in S. *Phil.* 315–16 *οἷς 'Ολύμπιοι θεοὶ | δοῖέν ποτ' αὐτοῖς ἀντίποιν' ἐμοῦ παθεῖν* (where Jebb regards Porson's *οἵ'* for *οἷς* as certain) *αὐτοῖς* could in any case be emphatic. Though there may be no exact parallel these examples seem to me sufficiently comparable to lend some support to the MS. reading here and in 710 and 1116. Among emendations Jackson's transposition (*Marg. Scaen.* 47) *τήνδ', ἣν ἐλαύνειν χρῆν σ' . . .* is perhaps the most attractive and preferable to Reiske's *τῆλ'* for *τήνδ'* (elsewhere in Tragedy only in A. *Pers.* 232) or Dindorf's *τήν* (sc. *ὁδόν*).

650–1. ὑπὲρ Νείλου ῥοὰς ὑπέρ τε Φᾶσιν: Phasis in Colchis flowing into the Euxine to the East and the Nile to the South were traditional for distant parts; cf. Pind. *Isth.* 2. 41–2; Hdt. 4. 45 *οὐρίσματα αὐτῇ (γῇ) Νεῖλός τε . . . καὶ Φᾶσις*. For exile in different directions cf. *Hipp.*

1053, where Theseus would banish Hippolytus *πέραν γε πόντου* (the Euxine) *καὶ τόπων Ἀτλαντικῶν*. Barrett points out that the Greek notion of exile was essentially not relegation to a place but exclusion from a place or area.

651. κἀμὲ παρακαλεῖν ἀεί: i.e. you and I should have been allies against Andromache; but Peleus would hardly need assistance and *ἀεί* has little point; neither have proposed emendations, e.g. *ἅμα* (Schenkel) and *ἔδει* (Geel).

652–3. οὗ . . . νεκρῶν: 'where so many sons of Hellas fell and died by the spear'. The antecedent to *οὗ* is *ἤπειρος*, easily supplied from *ἠπειρῶτιν*; cf. *Hec.* 711 *Θρήκιος ἱππότας, ἵν'* (i.e. in Thrace) *ὁ . . . πατὴρ ἔθετό νιν*. With *πεσήματα νεκρῶν* editors compare *HF* 1131 *τέκνων πεσήματα*, but the periphrasis with *νεκρών* is more striking and the twofold emphasis with *πέπτωκε* seems too elaborate here. For *Ἕλλας* standing for *Ἕλληνες* cf. *Or.* 648 *ἀδίκως ἀθροίσας Ἑλλάδ' ἦλθ' ὑπ' Ἴλιον*.

654. δέ: Brunck's correction of the MS. reading *τε* is not necessary, since *μὲν . . . τε* is not rare in verse, especially when, as here, there is no contrast between the two clauses; see *GP* 374–6.

655–6. Nauck, with approval from Paley and Hyslop, regarded these lines as an interpolation. They sound rather like an explanatory gloss and the explanation is a bit laboured; on the other hand some justification of the previous line might be expected. 656 is also metrically unsatisfactory. The opening single-word dactyl is not found elsewhere before *Troades*, where however there are three examples (415, 510, 653); the pause after *ἦν* dividing the line into equal parts is normally avoided unless there is rhetorical justification, as, e.g., in 47 and 973; the elided trochaic word before the final cretic belongs mainly to E.'s later style. Verrall in *CR* 20 (1906), 241 makes too much of these irregularities individually, but their cumulative effect is certainly a very halting rhythm and strengthens the case for interpolation, for which the arguments are strong but not conclusive.

659. παῖδας ἐχθίστους: see on 649; in fact Andromache's child by Neoptolemus is in a sense acknowledged by Peleus in 723–4 and described by Thetis in 1246 as *τῶν ἀπ' Αἰακοῦ μόνον λελειμμένον*.

660. ἁγώ: the text is probably sound, as in *Ph.* 878, *ἅ* being used adverbially in the sense 'wherefore'. The singular *ὅ* is so used several times, e.g. *Hec.* 13 *νεώτατος δ' ἦ Πριαμιδῶν, ὃ καί με γῆς | ὑπεξέπεμψεν*; *Ph.* 155, 263; cf. *ταῦτα* 'for that reason' in 212 and Pl. *Prt.* 310 e *ἀλλ' αὐτὰ ταῦτα καὶ νῦν ἥκω*. Thus *κἀγώ* (Wilamowitz) or *παύειν* for *κτανεῖν* (Brunck) are not needed.

προνοίᾳ τῇ σῇ: 'care for you'; cf. S. *OC* 332 *σῇ, πάτερ, προμηθίᾳ*; Thuc. 1. 33 *φόβῳ τῷ ὑμετέρῳ πολεμησείοντες* 'through fear of you'.

661. τήνδε is direct object of *κτανεῖν* and retained acc. with the passive *ἁρπάζομαι*.

662. καίτοι: 'There is usually a certain combative tone in *καίτοι*' (*GP*

556). This particle does not appear in Aeschylus, except four times in *Pr*, but is fairly common in Sophocles and Euripides in rhetorical, argumentative passages. In this passage Denniston considers that '*καίτοι φέρ'* is almost equivalent to *ἀτάρ* and marks something of a new departure'. It has, however, its normal adversative sense in relation to 661: 'you thwart my attempts to destroy Andromache; and yet if she lives and has children, see what will happen.'

φέρ' . . . ἢν: cf. *Ph.* 571 *φέρ', ἢν ἕλῃς γῆν τήνδε . . .*; *Hel.* 832, 1043. *ἅψασθαι . . . λόγου* is of course parenthetical, the point of *οὐκ αἰσχρὸν* being, as Bornmann observes, that M. is justifying in these circumstances an allusion to the sterility of Hermione. *ἅπτεσθαι λόγου* is a prosaic expression at home in philosophic contexts, e.g. Pl. *R.* 461 a, 538 c.

663. The *μέν* clause is hypothetical and the *δέ* clause keeps the conditional form, though Andromache has in fact had one child.

665–6. βάρβαροι . . . γένος: M. ignores the fact that they may be fathered by Neoptolemus. When he claims that the rule of *βάρβαροι* over *Ἕλληνες* is an example of *τὸ μὴ δίκαιον* (667) the significance of *δίκαιος* is not so much legal or moral but related to *δίκη* in the sense 'the right way', 'the order of nature': it is 'unnatural'. This line of thought belongs more to the fifth century than to the Heroic Age and is a particular aspect of the relationship between Greek and foreign so often alluded to in Eur. See on 173 above and cf. especially *IA* 1400–1 *βαρβάρων δ' Ἕλληνας ἄρχειν εἰκός, ἀλλ' οὐ βαρβάρους, | μῆτερ, Ἑλλήνων τὸ μὲν γὰρ δοῦλον οἱ δ' ἐλεύθεροι* (Arist. *Pol.* 1252b8 cites the first five words with the introduction *φασιν οἱ ποιηταί*, but he may only mean Eur.); fr. 717; *Hel.* 276.

667. ἔνεστι νοῦς: a Euripidean phrase; cf. fr. 212; 231 *ὅσοις ἔνεστι νοῦς*; Ar. *Lys.* 1124 *ἐγὼ γυνὴ μέν εἰμι, νοῦς δ' ἔνεστί μοι* is said by *Σ* to be taken from E. *Melanipp. Soph.* For the same antithesis as here cf. fr. 25 *νοῦς δ' οὐκ ἔνεστιν οἰόμεσθα δ' εὖ φρονεῖν* and *Hipp.* 920.

668–677. These lines, weak in argument and confused in expression, are bracketed by Murray and other editors, following Hirzel, and are pronounced by Page (*Actors' Interpolations*, p. 65) to be 'an expansive interpolation, probably histrionic, specially written for this passage'; he notes that it is not as well composed as such passages usually are. 678 certainly follows quite naturally after 667. The whole passage must be earlier than the fifth century A.D. since 671 is quoted by Choeroboscus and 672–7 by Stobaeus.

668–9. εἰ σὺ . . . δούς: *nom. pendens*, but not a harsh instance; instead of continuing 'you had seen her treated thus' M. substitutes the more direct 'she had been treated thus'.

τοιάδε: he means presumably the presence of Andromache and her child by Neoptolemus.

670–1. ξένης δ' ὕπερ . . .: if the reference is to Andromache this is a rather weak repetition of the reproach in 649. We might have expected the argument to be 'you would not allow such things to happen to your own daughter: do not blame me for defending mine.' Parmentier (*Extr. des Bull. de la classe des lettres etc. de l'Académie de Belgique*, 1920, p. 21) tried to extract some such sense from the text, taking *ξένης* to refer to Hermione: 'when we are concerned with one who is a stranger to you why do you shout at her own kin ⟨when they seek to defend her⟩'; but I agree with Méridier (to whom I owe the reference) that this sense can hardly be extracted from the Greek.

672–6. If we accept Dobree's **στένει** in 672 the sense seems to be 'a husband and wife lament equally, the wife if she is wronged by her husband and in the same way a husband if he has a wanton wife [does M. here think of his own?]. And [we might have expected 'but'] the husband has great physical strength [and so can chastise his wife], whereas the wife's affairs depend upon parents and friends.' *στένει* is rather odd, since we should expect a word for feeling distress rather than for its outward expression. The MS. reading *σθένει*, the only reading known to *Σ*, may well be right, the sense being 'husband and wife are of equal account'. Bornmann compares fr. 360. 20 *οὑνὸς οἶκος οὐ πλέον σθένει | πταίσας ἁπάσης πόλεος* 'the fall of one house is not of more account than that of a whole city'. But whatever the reading here, the clumsiness of expression in these lines must tell against their genuineness.

674. μωραίνουσαν: for *μῶρος* and cognates used of sexual intemperance, a sense apparently confined to Eur., see *Hipp.* 644, 966; *Ion* 545; *Tro.* 1059; *El.* 1035; *Hel.* 1018; fr. 331. *μῶρος* is less strong than *μαργός* 'lewd', but Denniston (on *El.* 1035) is wrong in saying that it 'half condones a moral failing by representing it as an intellectual one'. On the other hand it is too sweeping to regard it as always 'strongly condemnatory' (Barrett on *Hipp.* 644): in *Ion* 545 Xuthus is not condemning his youthful escapade. In fact the word covers a wide range, just as *ἀμαθία* ranges from mere 'tactlessness' (*Ion* 374) to savagery (*Ph.* 763).

676. ἐν γονεῦσι: cf. 409 and S. *OT* 314.

678. τὴν ἐμὴν στρατηγίαν: Peleus takes up this challenge in 693 ff.

680. ἐμόχθησ': here euphemistic, like our 'trouble'.

ἐκ θεῶν: a brief allusion to the notion of Helen as a mere instrument of Aphrodite, or of the gods in general, a defence elaborated elsewhere in Eur., e.g. *Tro.* 948–50; cf. also Gorg. *Hel.* § 6.

681–4. A sophistic paradox. I know no other extant example of this particular argument, but it may not have been invented by Eur., since the working out of arguments in defence of Helen was probably a regular rhetorical exercise, the *Helena* of Gorgias being the only surviving example.

682. ὅπλων . . . ἀίστορες: a rather gross exaggeration. The expedition was, however, according to Thuc. 1. 3, the first common enterprise of Hellas.

683. ὁμιλία: the relations between men, i.e. experience, here presumably with special reference to experience in battle; cf. *ὁμιλεῖν* in the sense 'join battle'. This *sententia* recalls by contrast the proverbial warnings about *κακαὶ ὁμιλίαι*; see Theognis 31; A. *Pers.* 752; Hdt. 7. 16a.

686. ἔσχον μὴ κτανεῖν: for the intrans. use of *ἔσχον* cf. *Hipp.* 658 *οὐκ ἄν ποτ' ἔσχον μὴ οὐ τάδ' ἐξειπεῖν πατρί.*

686–7. ἐσωφρόνουν 'I showed restraint' marks the contrast between himself and Peleus, who, together with his brother Telamon, killed Phocus, a son of Aeacus by the nymph Psamathe. Pind. *Nem.* 5. 14–18 makes a discreetly veiled allusion to this story, which goes back to Epic (Alcmaeon, fr. 1 Kinkel). There is an ironic suavity in the form of expression: 'I would rather you had not murdered Phocus.'

688. ταῦτ': an extension of the cognate acc. with *ἐπῆλθον*: 'I have made this attack on you'; cf. *IA* 349 *ταῦτα μέν σε πρῶτ' ἐπῆλθον.*

εὖ φρονῶν: again ironical in the circumstances.

689. ὀξυθυμῆς . . . γλωσσαλγία: both Euripidean words not found elsewhere in Tragedy; *ὀξυθυμεῖν* and cognates also belong to the medical vocabulary.

690. προμηθία: Norwood observes that Menelaus ends with a word that sums up his attitude: 'forethought', of course for his own welfare. He would have agreed with the Theban herald in *Supp.* 510 *καὶ τοῦτ' ἐμοὶ τἀνδρεῖον, ἡ προμηθία*; cf. S. fr. 302.

691–2. The Chorus leader's attempt at peace-making is regular, conventional, and, as usual, ignored by both contestants.

693–702. These democratic sentiments are ostensibly provoked by boasts of Menelaus (see 703–5), but in fact in the speech to which Peleus is replying M. hardly boasts at all, and these lines, not particularly appropriate to the context or the speaker, may well have some contemporary reference.[1] To judge from allusions in the Orators to contrasts between the early fifth century, when the glories of Marathon and Salamis were ascribed to the Athenians, and their own day, when credit for military successes was claimed by an Iphicrates or a Chabrias, it looks as though there was a growing tendency for generals to take more credit to themselves. See, e.g., Dem. 23. 198; Aeschin. 3. 183, 185, 243. If the play was completed after 425, it is just possible that Eur. had Cleon in mind; cf. Ar. *Eq.* 392 *κᾆτ' ἀνὴρ ἔδοξεν εἶναι τἀλλότριον ἀμῶν θέρος.*

According to some accounts it was the quotation of 693–8 by Kleitos at the climax of his quarrel with Alexander that roused the latter to

[1] Compare repeated claims in Eur. that Agamemnon was a duly elected general, e.g. *Or.* 1168, *ἦρξ' ἀξιωθεὶς . . . οὐ τύραννος*; *IA* 85 *κἀμὲ στρατηγὸν . . . εἵλοντο*; *El.* 1082; *IA* 337 ff. (canvassing for votes).

such fury that he killed his friend; see Plutarch, *Alex.* 51; Arrian, *Anab.* 4. 8. 1–5; see also A. Aymard in *Mélanges Henri Grégoire*, 1. 43–74.

693. *οἴμοι* sometimes, as here, denotes indignation or impatience, rather than lamentation; cf. S. *Ant.* 82 *οἴμοι, καταύδα* 'Oh, denounce it!'

νομίζεται: impersonal: 'how wrong the practice is'.

694. τροπαῖα πολεμίων στήσῃ: for the genitive (on the analogy of verbs of mastering) cf. S. *Tr.* 1102 *οὐδεὶς τροπαῖ' ἔστησε τῶν ἐμῶν χερῶν* 'no man has triumphed over my prowess'; Andoc. 1. 147 *πολλὰ τροπαῖα τῶν πολεμίων ἀπέδειξαν*. This phrase came to mean 'triumph over' and is often purely metaphorical, as in 763 below. In this passage too the main point is the victory, though here the literal sense is also appropriate.

695. πονούντων: *πόνος* is common in Homer and later of the toil of war, e.g. *Il.* 6. 77 *ἐπεὶ πόνος ὔμμι μάλιστα . . . ἐγκέκλιται*; *Od.* 12. 117 *πολεμήϊα ἔργα . . . καὶ πόνος*; in the fifth century it denotes particularly the service of the common soldier. Cf. 705; S. *Ai.* 1112 *οἱ πόνου πολλοῦ πλέῳ*, with Jebb's note; *Hcld.* 932.

696. δόκησιν: 'reputation', for which *δόξα* is usual. Cf. *El.* 381 *δοκήσει ὠγκωμένος*; Thuc. 4. 18 *ἀκίνδυνον δόκησιν ἰσχύος . . . καταλιπεῖν*. Nouns in *-σις*, mainly abstract, were probably fashionable in intellectual circles in the late fifth century and are characteristic of Eur. See G. R. Vowles, 'Studies in Greek Noun Formation: Words in *-σις*', *CPh* 23 (1928), 38–59; E. W. Handley, '*-σις* nouns in Aristophanes', *Eranos*, 51 (1953), 129–42; W. Breitenbach, *Untersuchungen zur Sprache der Euripideischen Lyrik*, p. 29, 14.

697–8. An oddly prejudiced and limited view of a general's function, which may have gone down well with some private soldiers in the audience but comes rather surprisingly from Peleus. It is likely that Athenian independence and initiative would sometimes overflow into military operations; for an occasion when the common soldiers seem to have taken matters into their own hands see Thuc. 4. 4.

698. λόγον: 'esteem', 'consideration'.

699–702. The absence of any noun or pronoun to indicate a change of subject suggests that the plural *σεμνοί* is used as though *στρατηγός* had been plural. The change is awkward; moreover the wording of the sentence suggests the political, not the military scene, and the new complaint in 700–2 breaks the continuity of thought between 693–8 and 703–5. These points, and perhaps the disproportionate length of the opening generalization as it stands, raise the possibility of interpolation, but are not conclusive. On the other hand the words *σεμνοὶ ἐν ἀρχαῖς ἥμενοι* in 699 are picked up by *ἐξωγκωμένοι κάθησθε στρατηγίᾳ* in 703–4. If these lines are genuine and in their right place we must suppose that the accusation against generals leads to a complaint about other unworthy holders of positions of authority, and that Peleus thinks of Menelaus and Agamemnon as really no better than jacks in office. P. is not convincing, but perhaps a certain wildness and inconsequence is in keeping with his great age and waning powers, as indicated or suggested elsewhere; see 80, 547, 551, 713–14, 717 ff. and notes ad locc.

σεμνοί: here 'arrogant'; cf. A. *Cho.* 975 (Orestes is speaking of Aegisthus and Clytemnestra) *σεμνοὶ μὲν ἦσαν ἐν θρόνοις τόθ' ἥμενοι*; *Hipp.* 94 *τίς δ' οὐ σεμνὸς ἀχθεινὸς βροτῶν*; *Alc.* 773; *Med.* 216.

700. 'They look down upon the people, though they themselves are nobodies.' For this sense of *οὐδένες* cf. *IA* 371 *τοὺς οὐδένας*; S. *Aj.* 1114 *τοὺς μηδένας*; Hdt. 9. 58 *οὐδένες ἄρ' ἐόντες*. For the similar use of *οὐδέν* cf. *HF* 635 *οἵ τ' οὐδὲν ὄντες*. See A. C. Moorhouse, *CQ* 15 (1965), 31–40.

701. οἱ δ': members of the *δῆμος*.

μυρίῳ: this adverbial use of the dative is elsewhere found only in Plato, e.g. *R.* 520 C *μυρίῳ βέλτιον* 'infinitely better'.

702. Editors explain this sentence as a mixed condition, as in 770–1 below and elsewhere, e.g. S. *Ant.* 666, 1032. This accounts for the change of mood from *εἰσί* to *προσγένοιτο*, but the difficulty here is the lack of logical connection between protasis and apodosis: the existence of *σοφία* cannot depend on the addition of *τόλμα* or *βούλησις*. It is presumably for this reason that *Σ* in one version substitutes *βελτίονες* for *σοφώτεροι* and Paley seems to think that *σοφώτεροι* can be translated 'better men'. If the text is right it looks as though the true apodosis is suppressed and the sense must be something like 'they are far wiser ⟨and, e.g., might become rulers⟩ if only they had also boldness and a common purpose'.

βούλησις seems to mean 'common will' or 'purpose'; see on *δόκησις* in 696. *βούλησις* appears first in this passage and again in *HF* 1305 *ἔπραξε γὰρ βούλησιν ἣν ἐβούλετο*, but not elsewhere in verse. It is a distinctly prosaic word and belongs mainly to the language of philosophy. In *IT* 1019 the MSS. have *ἥδε βούλησις παρά*, which is, as England says, a very weak remark and many editors accept Markland's *βούλευσις*. Here too one explanation in *Σ* implies the reading *βούλευσις*, but there seems no reason to doubt the text.

704. Τροίᾳ: i.e., as *Σ* notes, *τοῖς ἐν Τροίᾳ γεγενημένοις*.

κάθησθε: here, as often, with the connotation 'sitting back and doing nothing'; cf. 670 and Dem. 11. 17.

706–7. δείξω is here virtually equivalent to *διδάξω*, as in 1001 and Ar. *Thes.* 673 *δείξει . . . πᾶσιν ἀνθρώποις σεβίζειν δαίμονας* (though here *δείξει* picks up *ἔσται παράδειγμα* in 670 and is perhaps a condensed expression for 'his example will teach them'). This use of *δείκνυμι* is not mentioned in LSJ.

If, with Murray, we accept *ἥσσω*, the reading of MSS. other than P, the sense seems to be 'I will teach you not to consider Paris a lesser enemy than Peleus.' We should expect 'a greater enemy', and P has μείζω, but this may well be an attempt at correction; Σ evidently knew only ἧσσω, and provides two explanations: (1) μὴ ἥσσονα is merely equivalent to ἴσον. This is accepted as a possibility by Méridier, and by Paley, who observes that equality might equally be expressed by μὴ ἥσσω or μὴ κρείσσω. This is true in strict logic, but emotionally there is all the difference between them. (2) Under the cloak of ἀντίπτωσις the knot is cut by supposing that the cases are reversed and translating as though the text were τὸν Πηλέα ἥσσω . . . τοῦ Πάριδος. Kamerbeek and Méridier consider as possible a confusion on the part of Eur. between μὴ κρείσσω νομίζειν and ἥσσω νομίζειν, but the confusion seems rather gross, and S. *Ant.* 4, cited by K., is not really parallel owing to its conglomeration of negatives, and in E. *El.* 383 the text is probably corrupt.

Other editors emend. Kirchhoff's σου . . . νομίζων gives a quite different sense: 'I will show that I do not reckon Paris a lesser enemy of mine than you.' Other emendations, such as Murray's καί instead of μή and Wilamowitz's ἔγωγέ σοι instead of ἐγώ σοι μή, remove the negative from 706. We then have 'I will teach you to consider Paris a lesser foe than Peleus', which is better sense, but the choice of comparison is not happy (particularly with Murray's καί), since in the *Iliad* Paris runs away from Menelaus and later is ignominiously worsted by him. ἧσσον (with καί) would give slightly better sense: 'that even Paris was less your enemy than Peleus now is', the stress being on the bitterness of enmity rather than the formidable quality of Paris. If the ν of ἧσσον dropped out before νομίζειν the ο might then be altered to ω.

708. φθερῇ: φθείρεσθαι and compounds are used of angry dismissal in Eur. and Comedy. See 715; *HF* 1290 οὐ γῆς τῆσδ' ἀποφθαρήσεται; *Hcld.* 284; fr. 613; Ar. *Ach.* 460; *Eq.* 892; Men. *Perik.* 403. This use is probably colloquial and its appearance twice in eight lines is appropriate to the choleric old man.

710. τήνδ': see on 650. Musgrave's τῶνδ' is not necessary. Hermione is not present but inside the house (635); the deictic pronoun can thus be justified by a gesture towards the door. Garzya thinks it has a depreciatory sense. See on 735 and 1243.

711. ἣ . . . ἀνέξεται: the present tense would be more natural in a causal rel. clause, and Wilamowitz's εἰ . . . ἀνέξεται, the usual construction in threats, may be right, with a comma after κόμης; for this common corruption cf. 1051.

712. τίκτοντας ἄλλους: the reference is of course to Andromache. We should say 'other women' but in Greek the generalizing plural is masculine; see on τοὺς ἐμούς in 375. This example is more striking since τίκτειν, though it can be used of both parents, in this context clearly means 'giving birth'.

713. τὸ κείνης: here a mere periphrasis for κείνη. Cf. *Alc.* 785 τὸ τῆς τύχης; *Tr.* 616 τὸ τῆς ἀνάγκης; Pl. *Phaedr.* 230 c πάντων δὲ κομψότατον τὸ τῆς πόας; Men. fr. 410. This purely periphrastic use of the article with a genitive is found mainly in Eur., Comedy, and Plato and is probably another colloquialism.

714. ἄπαιδας τέκνων: gen. of separation; see on 612.

717. ἔπαιρε σαυτήν: a regular formula of encouragement, as in 1077; *Alc.* 250; *Hcld.* 635; Ar. *V.* 996. It is generally addressed to someone prostrate or falling and here probably indicates that Andromache is still on her knees; see 572–3.

τρέμων: another indication of Peleus' age and weakness; cf. 722–3.

718. πλεκτὰς ἱμάντων στροφίδας: 'the knotted thongs'. στροφίς, found only here, must be equivalent to στρόφος 'cord or rope', not as in LSJ to στρόφιον, which is a breast-band worn by women; ἱμάντων indicates that the cords are leathern thongs; πλεκτός normally means 'plaited, twisted' but here may perhaps refer to knots.

720. βρόχος 'noose', also used of A.'s bonds in 501, 556, is particularly appropriate here since it is often used of snaring animals, e.g. *Hel.* 1169; Ar. *Av.* 527.

ἐντείνειν: ἐλπίζειν in the sense 'imagine, suppose' naturally takes a present infinitive.

721. ἀμυνάθοιτο: for this form cf. 1079 and *IA* 910; it also occurs once each in Aesch., Soph., and Ar. See Jebb's note on εἰκάθω in S. *OT* 651.

723. δεσμόν: Murray's correction is accepted by recent editors, and the collective singular is certainly possible; in *Hipp.* 1237 the reins in which H. becomes entangled are described as δεσμόν and in 1244 as δεσμῶν. But in the sense 'bonds' Eur. elsewhere always uses the plural (29 exx.) and here we should perhaps accept Heath's δεσμὰ μητρός or Hermann's δέσμ' ἔτ' ἐν· . . . (LSJ note that the plural is usual but strangely add 'never δεσμά in this sense', though there are at least twelve examples in Eur. alone.)

723–4. ἐν Φθίᾳ σ' ἐγὼ θρέψω: he seems to forget that Neoptolemus, the child's father, is expected to return.

724–5. A grudging admission of Spartan military renown.

725. δορός and **μάχης** are defining genitives; cf. S. *Tr.* 20 εἰς ἀγῶνα συμπεσὼν μάχης. This is an example of hendiadys: 'spear-won glory and the battle's strife' (Hyslop) = glory won by the spear in battle.

726. μηδενὸς βελτίονες: cf. Pl. *Prt.* 335 a οὐδενὸς ἂν βελτίων ἐφαινόμην.

727–8. Chorus leaders are by convention strong supporters of the principle μηδὲν ἄγαν; cf. 364–5, 642–4, 954–6.

ἀνειμένον: 'relaxed, unconstrained' is the basic sense, but this adjective when applied to persons is always used in a bad sense, of those who do not show suitable restraint, e.g. *Hcld.* 3; S. *El.* 516; *Ant.* 578.

727. χρῆμα: see note on 181; this is an example of the pleonastic use;

cf. fr. 319. 4 ἐχθρὸν χ. πρεσβύτης ἀνήρ; *Or.* 70 ἄπορον χ. δυστυχῶν δόμος; Ar. *Lys.* 677; Hdt. 3. 53; Pl. *Ion* 534 b; Theoc. 15. 23.

729–46. Menelaus begins by echoing the reproach of the Chorus leader. His next few lines are halting in manner and unconvincing in matter. The combined effect of μέν in 730 without corresponding δέ, the series of short sentences, and the vague repetition of τις in 733–4 is to suggest that M. is improvising and unsure of himself. Another feature of his speech is the repeated use of juxtaposition of different forms of the same word, as in παρὼν πρὸς παρόντας (738) and θυμούμενος τεύξεται θυμουμένων (742). This is a fairly common stylistic device at this period (see Denniston on *El.* 337 for a collection of examples) but its use five times in six lines (738–43) may be significant. Perhaps Eur. is representing M. as hiding the weakness of his withdrawal behind a show of rhetoric and reason. The effect of these expressions is to stress the idea of reciprocity: 'I behave to others as they behave to me.' This is quite different from the tone previously adopted by M. and the abandonment of his former arrogance and confidence is illustrated by a comparison of 738–9 with 378–9 and 740–1 with 440. It seems to be the intention of Eur. to present the Spartan Menelaus first as a bully, then as a weakling.

729. προνωπής: only here in the metaphorical sense of being 'inclined' or 'prone' to do something.

730. πρὸς βίαν: 'not of my own accord'; see on βίᾳ in 35. (Editors cite Pl. *Phaedr.* 236 d πρὸς βίαν μᾶλλον ἢ ἑκὼν λέγειν, but the previous words of Phaedrus 'we are alone and I am younger and stronger than you' show that physical force is meant, though of course only in jest.)

μέν: this can logically be related, with Hyslop, to παρὼν δέ in 738, but the δέ is far removed and is separated from μέν by the further antithesis νῦν μέν . . . ὅταν δέ, which itself contains the antithesis πρὸ τοῦ μέν . . . νῦν δέ. This would be too elaborate, even where an involved effect is intended, and it is better to take the first μέν as *solitarium.* Denniston (*GP* 382–3) notes a tendency to begin speeches in this way in prose orators and in drama.

731. Cf. Ar. *Lys.* 1041 οὔτε δράσω φλαῦρον οὐδὲν οὔθ' ὑφ' ὑμῶν πείσομαι, which looks like a reminiscence of the Euripidean line of at least ten years before.

732. οὐ γὰρ ἄφθονον . . .: 'I haven't unlimited time to waste.'

733. The repetition of τις, confirmed by *Σ*, is probably intentional and should not be removed by emendation.

Some have assumed that there is here an allusion to Argos, and that inferences can be drawn for the date of the play, but, as *Σ* observes, it is quite possible that Menelaus' excuse is pure invention. Mantinea is less probable, since it would suggest a date after 420, which is unlikely on other grounds; see Intr., p. 19.

734. πρὸ τοῦ: 'before that', 'formerly'. This is one of the examples of the survival in Attic of the original demonstrative force of the article. It occurs again in 928 and *Med.* 696, in Ar., and in prose, but two examples in Aesch. tell against Bassi's view that it is characteristic of prose and colloquial language.

735. τήνδ': this pronoun is deictic and, though it does not necessarily refer to somebody or something that may actually be pointed to, there is always some justification for its use. Where the person referred to is not actually present, he is generally brought before the eye of imagination.[1] See A. M. Dale in a review of Bond's *Hypsipyle* (*JHS* 84 (1964), 166), where she cites *Hel.* 98–100: 'You know Achilles?' 'Yes, Helen's suitor.' 'Well, *he* (ὅδε) . . .'; but the most striking example is *IA* 72 (if the text is sound) where ὅδε is used of the absent Paris without any preparation. τήνδε is therefore appropriate, and M. deliberately uses the deictic pronoun to counteract the impression of vagueness: 'now this is the city I mean to attack.'*

737. θῶ: for this sense cf. *IA* 672 θέμενος εὖ τἀκεῖ; *Ba.* 48–9 τἀνθένδε θέμενος εὖ.*

738–9. ἥξω: 'I shall be back.'

πρὸς παρόντας γαμβρούς: i.e. Neoptolemus.

διδάξομαι: the middle is here used in a passive sense, as in S. *Ant.* 726.

740. κολάζῃ: M. no longer claims the right to deal with Andromache.

741. σώφρων must refer to Neoptolemus: 'if he behaves reasonably to us, he will find me reasonable'.

742. θυμούμενος: M. admits the possibility that N.'s anger may be directed against Hermione and himself, not against Andromache.

743. This line repeats in general terms the sense of 741–2. This redundancy and the repetition of ἀντιλήψεται hardly justify Wecklein in bracketing the line.

διάδοχ': the actions of M. will succeed those of N. in the sense of arising out of them.

744. μύθους: often merely something said, with no depreciatory force; but the contrast with deeds is always latent, and here ἔργα in the previous line brings out this connotation: 'but you only *talk*, which doesn't worry me.'

ῥᾳδίως φέρω: for the sense 'to take lightly' 'not to be perturbed by something' cf. *Ba.* 640 ῥᾳδίως γὰρ αὐτὸν οἴσω, κἂν πνέων ἔλθῃ μέγα.

745. σκιά: is a common metaphor for weakness, especially in relation to old age. Kamerbeek gives a good collection of examples, e.g. fr. 512

[1] Compare the colloquial use of the deictic iota of those not present but brought to the attention of the audience, e.g. Dem. 23. 211 Αἰγινήτας τουτουσί.

τί δ' ἄλλο; φωνὴ καὶ σκιὰ γέρων ἀνήρ; Pind. *P.* 8. 95; A. fr. 116 (Mette); S. *Ai.* 125. For the old as *vox et praeterea nihil* cf. also *HF* 229 (Amphitryon) οὐδὲν ὄντα πλὴν γλώσσης ψόφον; fr. 25.

ἀντίστοιχος, elsewhere only in prose, means 'standing opposite', e.g. in Xen. *Smp.* 2. 20 standing opposite a partner in a dance; here perhaps of the shadow standing over against a real man: 'like a shadow that attends upon reality you have no power save only to speak.' The wording is not altogether happy, since shadows do not speak, but may have been influenced by some proverbial association of φωνή and σκιά in relation to the aged. Reiske's ὢν for ὡς would be some improvement.

746. We can either, with Murray, Wecklein, and Méridier, put a comma after ἀδύνατος, which is thus used absolutely to mean 'helpless', and supply δυνατός or δυνάμενος with λέγειν, or, with other editors, take ἄλλο with ἀδύνατος and οὐδέν as a redundant negative: 'unable in respect of anything except talking'. I prefer the latter (with Bornmann and Kamerbeek), though I know no precise parallel, since in general a redundant negative is fairly common, particularly with πρίν, πλήν, μᾶλλον ἤ, and the like; cf. *Hel.* 322 πρὶν δ' οὐδὲν ὀρθῶς εἰδέναι, τί σοι πλέον | λυπουμένῃ γένοιτ' ἄν; and Pearson's note ad loc.

At 746 exit Menelaus with his attendants. Peleus contemptuously watches them file out and then turns to Andromache and the child.

747. ἡγοῦ: there is now no mention of the attendant referred to in 551, and P. asks the child and Andromache to guide him not merely into the house forming the back scene, since in 752–3 Andromache fears that they may be ambushed on the way, but presumably back to his own home in Phthia.

τέκνον μοι: cf. *Alc.* 313 σὺ δ', ὦ τέκνον μοι, ...; but here it is perhaps better (with Wecklein, Méridier, and others) to place the comma after τέκνον, μοι being then either direct object of ἡγοῦ or ethic dative 'I pray you'.

ἀγκάλαις: since motion towards is implied ὑπ' ἀγκάλας would be more usual, as in 722.

748–9. For this common metaphor cf. 891 and A. *Ag.* 900.

750. δοῖεν εὖ: cf. *Alc.* 1004 χαῖρ', ὦ πότνι', εὖ δὲ δοίης; *Or.* 667; S. *OT* 1081, *OC* 642. εὖ is probably here an old substantival use, in origin a neuter of the epic adj. ἐύς, surviving, as might be expected, in traditional religious formulae. See Fraenkel on A. *Ag.* 121 τὸ δ' εὖ νικάτω.

753. πτήξαντες: for the sense 'crouching in ambush' cf. Hom. *Od.* 14. 474 ὑπὸ τεύχεσι πεπτηῶτες; elsewhere it means crouching in fear or submission.

οἵδε: Menelaus and his men have only just departed, and Andromache looks and perhaps points in the direction they have taken.

754. They have apparently no escort.

755. σκόπει . . . μή repeats the sense of *ὅρα μή* in 752 and emphasizes her apprehension.

757. οὐ μὴ εἰσοίσεις λόγον: in Attic Tragedy and Comedy *οὐ μή* with the 2nd person future indicative is often used to express a prohibition. On the origin of this construction see Goodwin, *Moods and Tenses*, Appendix II, and, for a different view, A. C. Pearson, *Helena*, Appendix 2, on v. 437.

758. κλαίων: for the colloquial use of *κλαίειν* in threats see on 577.

759. οὕνεχ': the sense varies slightly with different nouns: 'By the grace of the gods, and with the support of the army'.

761. Wecklein brackets this line as inconsistent with 763 and 764, but *οὐ γέροντες* may here be used in the sense 'not old and feeble'; in any case the old man should be allowed some inconsistency.

762. ἀποβλέψας: in *ἀποβλέπειν εἰς* the force of the preposition is presumably 'away from other things' and the phrase always means 'to gaze at'; so here not 'with a mere glance' but perhaps 'with a single stare'.

763. τροπαῖον αὐτοῦ στήσομαι: for the metaphorical use in the sense 'triumph over' with a genitive cf. 694. Wilamowitz's *αὐτός* 'unsupported' is possible but not necessary.

764–5. The normal prose order would be *καὶ γέρων ἦν εὔψυχος ᾖ κρείσσων* (sc. *ἐστί*). Broadhead's *πολλῶν νέων γέρων γὰρ ἦν εὔψυχος ᾖ* (*Tragica*, p. 115) would avoid the hyperbaton, but I think the text can stand. Kirchhoff's *ὢν* for *ᾖ* would involve an ellipse of *εἴη*; *κἂν* is unlikely to be merely equivalent to *καί* since (except in *κἂν εἰ*) it is not so used before Menander (M. fr. 11 K.) and is mainly Hellenistic.

765. τί δεῖ; 'what's the use?' Cf. *Med.* 1046 *τί δεῖ με πατέρα τῶνδε . . . λυποῦσαν αὐτὴν δὶς τόσα κτᾶσθαι κακά; IA* 1035 *εἰ δ' εἰσὶ θεοί . . . ἐσθλῶν κυρήσεις, εἰ δὲ μή, τί δεῖ πονεῖν; Supp.* 450; perhaps *Or.* 28 and S. *Aj.* 393. Brunck's *τί λύει*, accepted by Wecklein, is therefore unnecessary.*

THIRD STASIMON: 766–801

In the epode the Chorus address the absent Peleus by name and refer to his part in the voyage of the Argonauts and other legendary exploits, but in the rest of the stasimon there is no specific allusion to anybody in the play. Some have seen in the strophe allusions to the plight and rescue of Andromache, others to Hermione and her family, but these are unconvincing and *Σ* (2) is nearer the mark with *ὁ χορὸς θαυμάζει τὸν Πηλέα*; or rather perhaps the generalized praise of noble birth, wealth, and courage is inspired by loyalty and admiration for the House of Aeacus and leads up to the specific reference in the epode. The antistrophe is also in general terms and mainly intended to contrast true and lasting honour and glory with the ultimate failure of lawless violence, but the reference to δίκας ἔξω κράτος may nevertheless be inspired by the proceedings of Menelaus. On this view the ode has unity of theme. It has no special significance in relation to the action but serves rather to mark a pause: the ordeal of Andromache is over, that of Peleus is to come, and it is appropriate enough to sing the praises of the Aeacid house at the moment when its oldest representative has just rescued its youngest. The whole ode, with its praise of wealth, noble birth, and ἀρετή, its moralizing tone in the antistrophe, and its concluding reference to heroic exploits, is reminiscent of many passages in Pindar's Epinician Odes; see notes on 773, 776, 779 ff., 789 ff., 795, 796.

Metre. As with subject-matter, so also in metre this stasimon with its triadic structure and dactylo-epitrite rhythm is reminiscent of Pindar, though this metre and structure are not rare elsewhere in Tragedy, and dactyls and dactylo-epitrites are particularly favoured by Eur. in plays of this period.

Metrical Scheme:

Strophe+antistrophe: 766–76 = 777–87

1.	– – ∪ – – – ∪ ∪ – ∪ ∪ –	iambelegus
2.	– – ∪ – – – ∪ ∪ – ∪ ∪ –	iambelegus
3.	– ∪ – ⏓ – ∪ ∪ – ∪ ∪ – –	iambelegus
4.	– ∪ ∪ – ∪ ∪ –	hemiepes
5.	– – ∪ ∪ – ∪ ∪ – – – ∪ –	anceps hemiepes anceps cretic
6.	– – – ∪ ∪ – – – ∪ ∪ – ∪ ∪ –	hemiepes anceps hemiepes
7.	– – ∪ – – – ∪ ∪ – ∪ ∪ –	iambelegus
8.	– ∪ – ∪ – –	ithyphallic

Notes:

3. On this form of iambelegus see *LM*² 179, n. 1.
6. Hemiepes+anceps here takes the form of a pherecratean.
8. This colon, which may be said either to begin or to end with an epitrite, is naturally a common clausula in this system in Tragedy.

Epode: 788–801

1.	– ∪ ∪ – ∪ ∪ –	hemiepes
2.	– ∪ – – – ∪ ∪ – ∪ ∪ – –	iambelegus
3.	– ∪ – – – ∪ –	epitrite cretic
4.	– ∪ ∪ – ∪ ∪ – – – ∪ ∪ – ∪ ∪ – –	hemiepes anceps ditto
5.	– ∪ – – – ∪ – – – ∪ –	2 epitrites cretic
6.	– – ∪ ∪ – ∪ ∪ –	enoplian
7.	– ⏕ ∪ ⏕ ∪ ⏕ ∪ –	iambic dimeter
8.	– ∪ ∪ ∪ ⏕ ∪ – ∪ – ∪ ⏕ ∪ –	iambic trimeter
9.	– – – – – ∪ ∪ –	choriambic dimeter B
10.	– – – ∪ ∪ – –	hemiepes anceps (pherecratean)

Note:

8. I prefer the reading εὐδόκιμος Διὸς ἶνις ἀμφέβαλλεν φόνῳ (see note ad loc.), which would give the following colon in dactylo-epitrite rhythm:

– ∪ ∪ – ∪ ∪ – ∪ – ∪ – – ∪ – hemiepes anceps 2 cretics.

766–7. Praise of noble birth and wealth is here expressed in the form of a first-person wish for the future that cannot in fact be realized. A similar convention operates in *Alc.* 473, where the Chorus of old men sing 'O that I may have a wife like Alcestis.' The stylized nature of the opening is also shown by the negative half of the wish: presumably the Chorus does not really mean that if you cannot have noble birth it is better not to be born at all.

ἀγαθῶν: this is the Homeric sense of ἀγαθός, which persisted in the sixth and fifth centuries, and connoted chiefly high birth, courage and skill, prestige and possessions. Here the main emphasis is on high birth (εὐγενέταις in 771) and riches (πολυκτήτων δόμων); cf. *Alc.* 600 ff., where A. M. Dale notes that οἱ ἀγαθοί practically = οἱ εὐγενεῖς. In 774 the emphasis is more on personal qualities.

769. μέτοχος: mainly a prose word, in poetry only three times in Eur. and once in Aristophanes.

770. εἴ . . . πάσχοι . . . σπάνις ⟨ἐστί⟩ or ἔσται: for the mixed conditional sentence cf. Isocr. 2. 45 εἰ ἐθέλοιμεν σκοπεῖν . . . εὑρήσομεν . . ., and see KG 2, § 576 (b). For the sense cf. *Hcld.* 302 τὸ δυστυχὲς γὰρ ηὑγένει' ἀμύνεται | τῆς δυσγενείας μᾶλλον.

773. κηρυσσομένοισι: for the metaphorical use cf. E. fr. 1 τοῦ κεκήρυξαι πατρός; *Tro.* 223. It probably derives from the practice of announcing by a herald the name and lineage of victors at the Games.

774. λείψανα: generally 'remnants' in a disparaging sense, as in *El.* 554 παλαιὸν ἀνδρὸς λείψανον 'ancient relic of a man'; Ar. *V.* 1066. In this passage only it means what heroes leave behind them, i.e. their renown. For the general idea cf. Simonides' epitaph on the fallen at Thermopylae ἐντάφιον τοιοῦτον . . . οὔθ' ὁ πανδαμάτωρ ἀμαυρώσει χρόνος.

775–6. ἀρετά: here of manly virtue as presented in heroic poetry, but see on 778 ff.

θανοῦσι: they may have in mind Achilles.

776. λάμπει: the met. use of λάμπειν and words of similar meaning is characteristic of Pindar; cf. *Ol.* 1. 24 λάμπει δέ οἱ κλέος; *I.* 1. 22 λάμπει δὲ σαφὴς ἀρετά; *N.* 10. 2; frs. 155, 214. It is less common in Tragedy, e.g. Aesch. *Ag.* 774 δίκα δὲ λάμπει.

778 ff. Bornmann notes that in the antistrophe Eur. gives a deeper ethical content to the notion of ἀρετή. It is, however, still κακὴ δόξα rather than κακία itself that is repugnant.*

μή with **ἔχειν**: it is not necessary to alter to μὴ νίκαν . . ., as Murray suggests.

780. φθόνῳ: the odium involved in overthrowing justice, reinforces the sense of *κακόδοξον*.

781. τοῦτο: i.e. *νίκη κακόδοξος*, or perhaps the general notion of unjust prosperity implied in the preceding lines.

783–4. ξηρόν: the basic sense is 'dry' 'withered', hence it comes to mean 'joyless' as in Ar. *V.* 1452 *μετέστη ξηρῶν τρόπων*. Here prosperity turns to dust and ashes.

784. ὀνείδεσιν ἔγκειται δόμων: in Tragedy *ἔγκειμαι* always seems to be used with a personal subject, e.g. *Hel.* 269 *πολλαῖς ξυμφοραῖς ἐγκείμεθα* 'I am involved in . . .'; S. *Phil.* 1318 *ἑκουσίοισιν ἔγκεινται βλάβαις* 'they cling to self-inflicted miseries'. In Pl. *Crat.* 402 e *τὸ δὲ ε ἔγκειται εὐπρεπείας ἕνεκα* the sense is 'the letter ε is included or has been inserted . . .'; so here editors take the text as it stands to mean unjust victory 'is included among reproaches against the house'. This sense is rather weak and emendations have been suggested, e.g. *νικᾶται* (Wilamowitz), from the reading of some MSS. *ὀνείδεσι νείκητε*, 'the victory is vanquished', which is perhaps rather fanciful; *ὄνειδος ἀμείβεται δόμων* (Herwerden) 'receives in exchange a reproach against the house', which gives reasonable sense but involves considerable change. The sense we should really expect for *ἔγκειται* here is 'press hard upon' 'lie heavy upon', a meaning not found elsewhere in Tragedy but often in fifth-century prose and in Ar. *Ach.* 309. Without altering the text we could perhaps supply an object for *ἔγκειται* in this sense from the previous line; 'ill-gotten victory presses hard upon him (the guilty man) with disgrace to his house', but I should prefer to read *δόμῳ* (a very slight change with the iota adscript), which would then be the object of *ἔγκειται*.

785. ᾔνεσα: this use of the aorist should be distinguished from the so-called 'instantaneous' aorist, e.g. *ᾤκτιρ' ἀκούσασ'* (421), which some editors cite as parallel. There are similarities: both refer to a state of mind excited in the past but still continuing and both are represented by the English present; but the instantaneous aorist is essentially a dialogue idiom and generally denotes approval or disapproval of some specific thing said or done in the immediate past, e.g. Ar. *Eq.* 696 *ἥσθην ἀπειλαῖς* 'I am amused at your threats'; S. *Ai.* 536 *ἐπῄνεσ' ἔργον* 'well done', whereas this use is nearer to the undefined time of the gnomic aorist; cf. *Med.* 223 (in the middle of a speech) *οὐδ' ἀστὸν ᾔνεσ' ὅστις . . . πικρὸς . . . ἐστίν*. In this passage there is a contrast between the aorist and the conative present *φέρομαι*: 'it is this way of life that has my approval (already given in the past) and it is this that I seek to win for myself.'

786. κράτος, to be taken with *δύνασθαι*, is apparently an extension of the cognate accusative.

ἐν θαλάμοις καὶ πόλει: the general sense is 'in private and in public affairs'; the Chorus presumably select the word *θάλαμος* because the relationship of Neoptolemus to Hermione and Andromache has been prominent in their thoughts.

790. πείθομαι: in *Ion* 1607 *πείθομαι δ' εἶναι πατρὸς Λοξίου* the verb indicates Ion's renunciation of his previous scepticism; here this sense seems inappropriate, hence Headlam's *πεύθομαι*. Perhaps however the Chorus mean that seeing the aged Peleus in action against Menelaus they can well believe what they have heard of earlier exploits.

σύν: 'by the side of', i.e. Peleus fought with the Lapithae against the Centaurs. This is the first extant reference to his participation. The fight between the Lapithae, a Thessalian tribe ruled by Peirithoüs, and the Centaurs is referred to several times in Homer and is portrayed on the Parthenon metopes, on the west pediment of the temple of Zeus at Olympia, and on many Attic vases. In the longest account, in *Od.* 21. 295–304, the fight was provoked by drunken Centaurs at the wedding of Peirithous and Hippodamia.

Κενταύρων: *ὁμιλεῖν* in the sense 'join battle with' governs a dative, and if *Κενταύρων* is right the verb governs *δορί* in the sense 'armed force', as in A. *Eu.* 773 *συμμάχῳ δορί*; *HF* 61 *στρατηλατήσας Καδμείων δορός*; *Ph.* 1082 *ὁ Καδμείων Ἄρης | κρείσσων κατέστη τοῦ Μυκηναίου δορός*. In that case however the descriptive epithet *κλεινοτάτῳ* is less appropriate, and it is more likely that *δορί* refers to the famous spear described in *Il.* 16. 143–4 (= 19. 390–1) *μιν οἶος ἐπίστατο πῆλαι Ἀχιλλεύς | Πηλιάδα μελίην, τὴν πατρὶ φίλῳ πόρε Χείρων*, and in the *Cypria*, according to Schol. Ven. *Il.* 16. 140: *τούτῳ τῷ δόρατι καὶ Πηλεὺς ἐν ταῖς μάχαις ἠρίστευσε καὶ μετὰ ταῦτα Ἀχιλλεύς. ἡ ἱστορία παρὰ τῷ τὰ Κύπρια ποιήσαντι.* We must thus accept, with most editors, the reading *Κενταύροις*, for which see app. crit.

792. Peleus is also referred to as one of the Argonauts in *Hyps.* fr. 1. iii (Bond, p. 27).

793. δορός: *δόρυ* 'plank' stands for the whole ship, as in *Hel.* 1611 and often. The repetition of *δόρυ* in different senses looks like rather careless writing.

ἄξενον ὑγράν: *ὑγρή* sc. *θάλασσα* is used as a noun from Homer onwards. 'The inhospitable waters' are those of the Black Sea, described as *ἄξεινος* in Pind. *P.* 4. 203; for the euphemistic term *εὔξεινος* see on 1262.

794. Ξυμπληγάδων: gen. of separation with *ἐκπερᾶσαι*: 'I believe that you sailed over the inhospitable waters away from the Clashing Rocks at the entrance to that sea.' The *πέτραι Συμπληγάδες* guarded the entrance to the Black Sea and are to be distinguished from the *Πλαγκταί* 'Wandering Rocks' in the W. Mediterranean (*Od.* 12. 59 etc.); cf. *IT* 1388 *ἄξενον πόρον Συμπληγάδων ἔσωθεν*, and see Page on *Med.* 2 for further details and probable origin of the idea of clashing rocks.

Here the MSS. have *συμπληγάδα* but Murray rightly prints

Hermann's correction. Elsewhere the plural is always used, except in *IT* 241, where Bentley's *κυανέας Συμπληγάδας* is probably right.

ποντιᾶν: the noun *πόντος* generally means 'the sea', but where the context provides sufficient indication it can stand alone for the Black Sea. The adjective is not elsewhere so used, but in this context it could perhaps be given the more specific meaning.

795. κλεινὰν . . . ναυστολίαν: perhaps a conscious reminiscence of Pind. *P.* 4. 70 *ναυτιλίας*, referring to the Argonauts.

796. πάρος: previously (as distinct from the recent destruction) Heracles had sacked Troy after the king, Laomedon, had cheated him of his reward for saving Hesione from a sea monster. In the Homeric account (*Il.* 5. 640 ff., 14. 250) there is no mention of Peleus. *Σ* notes that most authorities named Telamon, father of Aias, as the ally of Heracles (see, e.g., *Tro.* 799–807), but that Pindar added Peleus, and preserves the relevant lines (fr. 155 Bowra); but see also *I.* 5. 35–8 for an allusion to the same tradition.

797. εὐδόκιμον: with *πόλιν*; but most editors rightly keep the MS. reading *εὐδόκιμος*, agreeing with *Διὸς ἶνις* (Heracles), and (following Matthiae) omit the article.

800. κοινάν: i.e. with Heracles. The subject of *ἀφικέσθαι* is of course still *σε* (Peleus) from 790.

FOURTH EPEISODION: 802–1008

We have witnessed the mortal peril of Andromache and her rescue by Peleus; now begins a new episode, in which Hermione dreads the anger and perhaps the vengeance of Neoptolemus, and in her turn is rescued by Orestes.

802 ff. MSS. vary between *θεράπαινα* and *τροφός*; for similar variations in other plays see Barrett's *Hippolytus*, pp. 153–4. Here *τροφός* is probably right, to judge from the tone of her words to Hermione and her frequent use of *ὦ παῖ* (828, 866) and *τέκνον* (832, 874, 878). Moreover a 'Nurse', a slave woman who in this case presumably attended the child Hermione and is still in her service as personal attendant and confidante, is a useful stock character in Euripidean plays of this period, whose theme is partly passionate love or jealousy in women, e.g. in *Medea*, *Hippolytus*, *Stheneboea*, and probably *Aeolus*. Her role here is partly that of an *ἐξάγγελος* reporting what is happening within.

802. κακῷ: *κακῶν*, the reading of V, is printed by Nauck and is possible, since gen. and dat. are used with *διάδοχος*, cf. 743 above and S. *Ph.* 867 *φέγγος ὕπνου διάδοχον*. Most editors rightly print *κακῷ* (MBA) since it is usual for both nouns to be in the same number. Wecklein's *κακοῦ* is not necessary.

805. συννοίᾳ: for the causal dat. joined to a causal participle cf. *Or.* 118

φόβῳ . . . ταρβοῦσά τε. σύννοια is defined in Pl. *Def.* 415 e as διάνοια μετὰ λύπης. It is in fact used of serious but not painful reflections, e.g. the meditations of a philosopher (Pl. *R.* 571 d), but it often has the connotation of anxious thought. Here LSJ and editors take it to mean 'repentance' 'remorse'. It is not elsewhere used in this sense, and indeed it is doubtful whether the concept of remorse, as distinct from a sense of pollution or anxiety about consequences, was known to fifth-century Athens. In Hdt. 8. 54 ἐνθύμιον is also taken by LSJ to refer to pricks of conscience, but it probably denotes merely anxiety about divine retribution; similarly μετανοέω, μεταγιγνώσκω, and cognates refer to change of mind rather than remorse. In this passage the Nurse's words in 814–15 could describe repentance, but could equally well indicate realization that what she has done will look bad to others. In *Or.* 395 *Με.* τίς σ' ἀπόλλυσιν νόσος; *Ορ.* ἡ σύνεσις, ὅτι σύνοιδα δείν' εἰργασμένος, σύνεσις perhaps comes near to 'bad conscience' and it is certainly characteristic of Eur. that this concept, or something like it, should first appear in his plays.*

In this play, however, whatever sense may be attached to certain words and phrases, it is clear from the whole scene that what Hermione is chiefly thinking about is the imminence of retribution; see esp. 808–10, 856–60, 919–20.

807. κατθανεῖν: i.e. to die by her own hand rather than face execution or even disgrace.

810. κατθάνῃ: Hermione herself confirms this fear in 920 and 927, but she is surely exaggerating her danger; she has so far only ill-treated and threatened Andromache. The Nurse is more sensible in 868–75.

κτείνουσα corresponds to a conative imperfect. κτείνασα LB is also possible, since the aorist indic. and participle could be used with conative force; cf. *Ion* 1291 (where Elmsley corrects to ἔκτεινον) and 1500; S. *Ai.* 1126 δίκαια γὰρ τόνδ' εὐτυχεῖν κτείναντά με;

τούς: the article is occasionally used as a relative pronoun in Tragedy where it is metrically convenient. Except in lyrics it is rare in Eur., the only other certain examples being *El.* 279 and *Ba.* 712.

οὐ χρή: the neg. is οὐ because the reference is to specific persons. Elmsley's χρῆν would be an improvement, since the reference is primarily to an obligation in the past; it could however be held to continue into the present.

811. ἀρτῆσαι δέρην . . . ξίφη: two traditional means of suicide; cf. *Or.* 953 εὐτρέπιζε φάσγαν' ἢ βρόχον δέρῃ. In *Hel.* 299–301 ἀσχήμονες μὲν ἀγχόναι . . . the speaker asserts that hanging is for slaves and the well-born should die by the sword; but this passage is isolated and on several grounds has been regarded as spurious; in 352–6 Helen envisages both methods as equally appropriate. So also *Tro.* 1012 ἢ βρόχους ἀρτωμένη | ἢ φάσγανον θήγουσ', ἃ γενναία γυνὴ | δράσειεν ἄν. That hanging was the most common means is suggested by the colloquial use of ἀγχόνη, as in Ar. *Ach.* 125 *ταῦτα δῆτ' οὐκ ἀγχόνη;* 'enough to make one hang oneself'.*

812. φύλακες δμῶες: 'guardian slaves'. *φύλακες* seems to be adjectival, as in Eubul. 75. 7 *φύλακες 'Ηφαίστου κύνες.*

The forms *δμωή* and *δμωίς* are found in Tragedy generally; the Homeric *δμῶς* is favoured by E. (27 times) but otherwise occurs only once in S.

814. μεταλγεῖ: Nauck's correction of the MS. *μέγ' ἀλγεῖ* is accepted by most editors, but is not certain. It is not a serious objection to it that there seems to be no certain example of *μεταλγεῖν*, but the simple verb is used to describe H.'s mental distress in 836, and the emphasis given by *μέγα* would serve to justify her desperate intentions. Cf. *Med.* 291, where Nauck's *μεταστένειν* is an unnecessary correction of *μέγα στένειν.*

817. βᾶσαι . . . δωμάτων ἔσω: such an action by a Chorus would have been unique, but the appearance of Hermione is timed to save them from this unconventional procedure. Cf. S. *Aj.* 328–47, where Tecmessa begs the Chorus to go into Ajax's tent and plead with him, but a few lines later this is made unnecessary by the appearance of Ajax, perhaps by means of the ekkuklema.*

824. πόθῳ θανεῖν: *τοῦ θανεῖν* would be more usual, but cf. *IT* 1342 *φόβῳ εἰσορᾶν*; *Or.* 118 *φόβῳ προσελθεῖν.* S. fr. 953 *θανόντι . . . συνθανεῖν ἔρως μ' ἔχει* is different, since *ἔρως μ' ἔχει* can be regarded as equivalent to a verb of longing.

825 ff. Hermione, probably followed by one or more of her attendants (see on 841), appears in a frenzy of despair, which, as the Nurse tells her in 866 ff., is not justified. We heard in 811–13 that she has been restrained from simple forms of suicide; in 846 ff. she talks wildly of more spectacular methods, on which Méridier comments: 'il semble qu'E. se soit complu à faire ressortir l'exaggération et le peu de sincérité du désespoir d'Hermione.' Sometimes in this scene the thought and language recall earlier and later tragic laments (see notes on 826, 847, 861–5) and E. may at times be writing conventionally; not enough of Attic Tragedy survives to enable us to be sure of this. In any case, since Hermione's troubles are not really on the level of high tragedy, the effect of giving her language more appropriate to the tortured Io or to Oedipus overwhelmed by a fearful fate is to stamp the scene as melodramatic rather than tragic, and also to present Hermione as rather hysterical and possibly 'putting on an act', hoping that before she meets Neoptolemus he will hear of her wild grief and self-reproach. The scene also prepares us for her joy and relief at the appearance of Orestes.

Metre. 825–65 constitute an *ἀμοιβαῖον* in which Hermione expresses her despair in lyric metres, mostly dochmiacs, and the Nurse, seeking quietly to reason with her, speaks in iambic trimeters. The dochmiac metre is especially associated with strong emotions such as grief, horror, despair, and, as A. M. Dale observes (*LM* 110), in ἀμοιβαῖα the impassioned dochmiacs of the one party may beat against the other's spoken trimeters; see, e.g., *IT* 834 ff.; *Tro.* 235 ff. After 840 the metre ceases to be antistrophic.

Metrical Scheme:

Strophe + antistrophe (*a*): 825–7 = 829–31

1.	⏒ – – –	? dochmiac equivalent
2.	⏒ – ⏑ ⏑ – ⏑ ⏑ – ⏑ – ⏑ ⏑	? enoplian
3.	– ⏑ ⏑ – ⏑ –	dochmiac

Notes:

1. These exclamations may be *extra metrum*.
2. This involves resolution of the final long.

2–3. A. M. Dale prefers a different colometry which gives a known dicolon and certainly seems more probable:

σπᾰρᾱγμᾰ κŏμᾱς ŏνῠχῶν τε̆	paroemiac
δᾱῐ ᾰμῡγμᾰτᾰ θῆσŏμᾱι	prosodiac (ibycean)

Strophe + antistrophe (*b*): 833–5 = 837–9

1.	⏑ ⏑ ⏑ – ⏓ –	dochmiac
2.	⏑ – – ⏑ – – ⏑ –	dochmiac cretic
	– ⏑ – – – – ⏑ –	
3.	– ⏑ ⏑ – ⏑ ⏑ – ⏑ ⏑	3 dactyls
4.	– ⏑ – ⏒ –	hypodochmiac

Note:

2. δαΐας in the antistrophe does not correspond with καλύπτειν and, if there is strophic correspondence, must be corrupt; see note ad loc.

841	⏑ – ⏑ –	iambic metron
842	– ⏑ ⏑ – – –	dochmiac
843	⏑ ⏑ ⏑ – ⏑ – ⏑ ⏑ ⏑ – – –	2 dochmiacs
844	⏑ – – – – ⏑ ⏑ ⏑ – – –	2 dochmiacs
846	– – ⏑ –	iambic metron
847	– – ⏑ – ⏑ – –	iambic dimeter catalectic
848	– – ⏑ – ⏑ – –	iambic dimeter catalectic
849	– ⏑ ⏑ – ⏑ – ⏑ – – ⏑ –	2 dochmiacs
850	⏑ ⏑ ⏑ – ⏑ – ⏑ – – ⏑ –	2 dochmiacs
854	⏑ ⏑ ⏑ ⏑ ⏑ ⏑ – ⏑ ⏑ ⏑ – ⏑ –	2 dochmiacs
855	⏑ ⏑ ⏑ – ⏑ – ⏑ ⏑ ⏑ – – –	2 dochmiacs
856	⏑ ⏑ ⏑ – ⏑ – – ⏑ ⏑ – – –	2 dochmiacs
857	– ⏑ ⏑ – ⏑ –	dochmiac

859	∪∪∪–∪– ∪∪∪–∪–	2 dochmiacs
860	––––– ∪∪∪–∪–	2 dochmiacs
861	–∪∪––	adonean
862	∪∪–∪∪––––––	? anapaestic trimeter, with substitution of spondees
863	––––	
864	∪∪–∪∪–∪∪–∪∪–∪––	anapaestic dimeter bacchiac
865	–∪∪–∪–	dochmiac

Notes:

For a suggested emendation of 863–4, giving a different metrical scheme, see note ad loc.

863. Elsewhere this appears as a dochmiac equivalent.

865. This is also a catalectic tailpiece of 864.

826 ff. Tearing of hair and especially laceration of face and breast were traditional expressions of wild grief. So first in Hom. *Il.* 19. 284 (Briseis) *χερσὶ δ' ἄμυσσε | στήθεά τ' ἠδ' ἁπαλὴν δειρὴν ἰδὲ καλὰ πρόσωπα.* In Tragedy there are naturally many examples, e.g. A. *Cho.* 24 ff.; S. *Ai.* 633; E. *An.* 1209, *Hec.* 655, *Tro.* 280. According to Plutarch (*Sol.* 21) Solon found it necessary to forbid *ἀμυχὰς κοπτομένων* at funerals.

827. ἀμύγματα θήσομαι: for the periphrasis cf. *Or.* 833 *ματρόκτονον αἷμα χειρὶ θέσθαι.*

831. φάρος (in Hom. and Aesch. *φᾶρος*) generally means a cloak, but can be used more widely. Here, as *Σ* observes, it seems to be equivalent to *κρήδεμνον*, a kind of veil covering head and shoulders. For Hermione's action compare the mourning Antigone in *Ph.* 1490 *κρήδεμνα δικοῦσα κόμας ἀπ' ἐμᾶς.*

832–3. These lines strictly imply that Hermione's dress is torn and her breasts exposed, but there was probably no attempt at realism in such matters. The part of H. was of course played by a man.

833–5. 'What use to cover my breast when my crimes cannot be concealed.' Norwood calls this 'a fine thought finely expressed'; it seems to me rather a frigid conceit.

836. This superfluous question serves to maintain symmetry rather than, as Norwood thinks, to give H. a reason for continuing her lament; she needs no encouragement, as we see from 841–65, where she ignores the Nurse's contributions.

φόνον ῥάψασα: a common metaphor from Homer onwards; cf. 911.

συγγάμῳ: generally of a man who shares his wife with another, e.g. *HF* 149; here of a rival wife (Andromache) as in 182.

837. μὲν οὖν: according to Denniston *GP* 47 assentient *μὲν οὖν* is not found before Plato and is practically confined to him; he takes this as an example of *μὲν οὖν* indicating that the previous speaker has not gone far enough. If so *καταστένειν* must be a stronger word than *ἀλγεῖν*, perhaps because it includes the actual demonstration of grief.

δαΐας: *βιαίας* from B (see app. crit.) would give good sense and correspond with *καλύπτειν* in the strophe.

τόλμας: *καταστένειν* in E. and elsewhere is generally a transitive verb with acc., but for the intrans. use cf. *IA* 470 *ὑπὲρ τυράννων συμφορᾶς καταστένειν*, and for the gen. of cause or origin with the simple verb cf. *IA* 370 *Ἑλλάδος . . . στένω*. Hermann's *τόλμαν* is not needed.

841–4. To whom is Hermione speaking? Wilamowitz's emendation in 843, printed in OCT, places that line and probably the rest as addressed to the Nurse, and it is not really an objection that it was actually the *δμῶες* who had taken away the sword (812–13). The objection to *φίλα, 'πόδος* is that, according to Platnauer, 'Prodelision in Greek Drama', *CQ* 10 (1960), 140–4, there is no example where *α* both causes and suffers prodelision, though examples of *α* either causing or suffering prodelision do, very rarely, occur, so that the combination cannot perhaps be ruled out. *φίλ' ἀπόδος* (MAVB) is metrically difficult, but *φίλος ἀπόδος* (LP) can be fitted into the dochmiac sequence, and *ὦ φίλος* is common enough, e.g. 510, 530, 1205. In that case Hermione first speaks to one of the male attendants who have followed her from the house, and had taken away the sword; perhaps at 844 she turns to the Nurse, who in any case replies in 845.

843–50. The forms of suicide are traditional; cf. on 811; schol. Ar. *Ra.* 118–35 *τρία λέγεται καὶ κοινῶς τὰ πρὸς τὸν θάνατον συνεργοῦντα ξίφος, ἀγχόνη, κρημνός*. To these H. adds a fourth; see note on 848–9.

845. ἀλλ' εἴ σ' ἀφείην: 'what if I let you go to your death?' A conditional protasis, with an apodosis such as *τί ἂν γένοιτο* to be understood, is commonly used to express a supposition; cf. *Ph.* 1684 *ἀλλ' εἰ γαμοίμην σὺ δὲ μόνος φεύγοις, πάτερ;* Sometimes the apodosis is represented by the interrog. pronoun, as in S. *Ph.* 1405 *τί γάρ, ἐὰν πορθῶσι χώραν;*

μὴ φρονοῦσαν: 'while not in your right mind', the neg. *μή* being due to the conditional nature of the whole sentence.

θάνῃς: the mood is regular for primary sequence. Musurus's *θάνοις* is not needed, though in such sentences the verb is often attracted into the optative.

846. πότμου: causal gen., as in 394.

847. πυρὸς φίλα φλόξ: 'welcome, fiery flame'. The reference is probably to the bolt of Zeus; cf. *Supp.* 831 *πυρός τε φλογμὸς ὁ Διὸς ἐν κάρᾳ πέσοι* and A. *Pr.* 852, where Io calling upon Zeus cries *πυρί με φλέξον*.

848–9. Probably only one form of suicide is envisaged in these lines, i.e. throwing herself down from high ground, either cliffs by the sea or mountain crags; in this context *θανοῦσα* could well have the connotation 'falling to death'. The sense then is 'Where (or how) can I be raised to rocky heights, either cliffs by the sea or wooded mountain crags, that I may fall to my death and be numbered among those below?'

Bornmann and Méridier take it that H. thinks of three forms of suicide: (1) throwing herself to the ground from rocks, (2) drowning herself in the sea, (3) losing herself in the forest to die or be killed by wild beasts. It is hardly possible to extract all this from the Greek. By an extreme form of zeugma verbs for plunging into the sea and rushing into the forest have to be supplied, and if these actions intervene *θανοῦσα* can no longer be taken as 'falling to death', so that *ἀερθῶ* by itself has to mean 'rise up in order to leap down'. On this view we should also need *κατὰ πόντου*.

850. νερτέροισιν μέλω: this verb (generally middle) is several times used by E. of that which belongs to the dead; cf. *Ph.* 1303 *ἰαχὰν μελομέναν νεκροῖς*; *Hel.* 177; *IT* 183. Here the phrase is merely a poetic variant for being dead, as in *Hel.* 1161 *οἳ μὲν Ἅιδᾳ μέλονται κάτω*.

851–2. Most MSS. give these lines to the Chorus, but, as Σ observes, they are rather more in character for the Nurse, who then offers much the same consolation as her counterpart in *Hipp.* 437–9. We might indeed expect a single line from the Nurse, as throughout, and 851 could be regarded as complete in sense and syntax: 'disasters are sent from the gods'; but the lack of symmetry does not in itself justify treating 852 as an interpolation or ascribing both lines to the Chorus.

852. ἢ τότ' . . . ἢ τότε: 'sooner or later'; cf. A. *Ag.* 763–6 *φιλεῖ δὲ τίκτειν ὕβρις . . . ὕβριν τότ' ἢ τόθ', . . .*

854. ἔλιπες ἔλιπες: for the repetition, characteristic of E. though not of course confined to him, cf. 856 and many other passages; *Or.* 1426–8 is a striking example and may have suggested Aristophanes' parody in *Ra.* 1351–5.

854–5. The sense is clearly that H. is reproaching her father for having left her stranded. In English this is a familiar and now a worn metaphor, but apparently not in Greek. If *κώπας* has its proper sense 'oar' H. is comparing herself to a ship on the beach helpless without oars; for the gen. of separation with *ἔρημον* cf. 78 *ἔρημος εἶ φίλων*. On this view some word for 'ship' might have been expected, and Jacobs suggested *μ' ὁλκάδ'* for *μονάδ'*. It is however more likely that *κώπη* here stands for a ship, as often, e.g. *IT* 140, *Hel.* 1272. H. would then be describing herself as like someone abandoned on shore without a ship to take her away. *ὡσεί* is metrically intrusive and is deleted by editors following Seidler.

856. ὀλεῖ: for the shortening of the diphthong *ει* before the following vowel (epic correption) cf. *El.* 158 *κοίτᾳ ἐν*; *Alc.* 120; *Med.* 423 (with Page's note ad loc.).

After *ὀλεῖ με* the MSS. have *δηλαδὴ πόσις*, a good example of an explanatory note incorporated in the text.

859–60. Hermione may well think of Andromache taking refuge at the shrine of Thetis and remember her own cruel emphasis on the position of A. as a slave in 164–5.

861–5. The text as it stands may be translated: 'O that I might be a dark-winged bird ⟨and fly⟩ from the land of Phthia, or the ship of pine wood (i.e. Argo), the vessel which on its maiden voyage passed through the dark cliffs (i.e. the Symplegades).' The relative *ἅ* precedes its antecedent *πλάτα*, which is in apposition to *σκάφος*. For *πρωτόπλοος* cf. Hom. *Od.* 8. 34 and *Hel.* 1531. *πλάτα* 'oar' stands for the oared ship, as in *IT* 242.

The chief objection is that *ἐκ γᾶς* requires a verb of motion, which has to be supplied rather awkwardly from *ὄρνις εἴην*. Bornmann thinks that no idea of motion need be involved, the sense being 'may I be a bird far away from Phthia'. But the prep. should then be *ἀπό* (*Il.* 16. 209 is different), and the point of having wings is to be able to fly away. Moreover the desire for wings to fly away is almost a commonplace in tragic lyric, sometimes for a positive purpose as in S. *OC* 1081 and *Hel.* 1478, sometimes, as here and in *Ion* 746, to escape from an intolerable situation, and it is worth noting that in all the other examples cited, to which S. fr. 476 may be added, there is an indication of direction of flight (in *Hel.* 1478 the text is not certain, but after *ποτανοὶ γενοίμεσθ'* most editors supply a relative indicating place or direction). Thirdly the wish to be a specific legendary ship is rather odd and apparently unique.

To meet the first difficulty Murray tentatively suggests *εἴθ' εἴην*, but I should prefer (with Wecklein and Méridier) Seidler's *ἀερθείην*, or perhaps *ἀρθείην* as in *Hipp.* 734 *ἵνα . . . ἀρθείην ἐπὶ πόντιον κῦμα . . .* in a wish of the same type. This verb, however, would not suit *σκάφος*, and for this reason, as well as to meet the second and third objections mentioned above, I believe, with Wecklein, that 863–5 indicate the place, suitably remote, to which Hermione would fly; but instead of his emendation of *ᾗ* to *οἷ* I should prefer to read:

κυανόπτερος ὄρνις ἀρθείην
πευκᾶεν σκάφος ᾇ
διὰ κυανέας ἐπέρασεν ἀκτὰς

'O that I might fly away where the ship of pine wood passed between the dark cliffs.' Once *ἀρθείην* had been corrupted to *εἴθ' εἴην* the other changes might easily follow. The metrical scheme would then be:

863	– – – ∪ ∪ –	hemiepes
864	∪ ∪ – ∪ ∪ – ∪ ∪ – ∪ – –	3 anapaests bacchiac (enoplian)

866. τὸ λίαν: 'excess'; for *λίαν* as a noun cf. *Hipp.* 264 *τὸ λίαν ἧσσον ἐπαινῶ τοῦ μηδὲν ἄγαν*; *Hec.* 591; *Ph.* 584; fr. 209. It is here qualified by *ἐκεῖνο*, which means in effect 'former' as contrasted with *τὸ νῦν δεῖμα*.

869. κῆδος σόν: 'his marriage with you'.

870. φαύλοις λόγοις: the Nurse has admitted that Hermione has wronged Andromache (836, 840, 867), but cynically observes that A.'s plea will be worthless because she herself is of no account, a γυνὴ βάρβαρος and a captive of the spear.

873. ἕδνοισι: as in 2 ἕδνα is used like φερνή of the dowry that goes with a bride. It is relevant here since if Neoptolemus rejected Hermione he would be liable to return her dowry to her family.

πόλεως: not exactly parallel with ἀνδρός but gen. of origin 'coming from a prosperous city'.

μέσως: cf. *Hec.* 1113 φόβον παρέσχεν οὐ μέσως; *HF* 58; elsewhere only in prose and fourth-century Comedy.

874–5. A second line of defence, but a dubious consolation in view of Menelaus' departure, as Hermione shows in 918.

877. There are many references in Tragedy to the impropriety of women standing about outside the house where they can be seen and accosted by strangers; see S. *Ant.* 579; *El.* 518; E. *Ph.* 93; *Hcld.* 474–7; *Hec.* 975; fr. 521. In *El.* 343 the αὐτουργός is shocked to find his wife not only standing outside but actually talking to strange men.

878. This line, deleted by Nauck, is certainly superfluous but may be genuine; if so it adds a touch of fussiness to the Nurse's rebuke. Brunck's ὧδε for τῶνδε may be right, since the emphasis given by the repeated τῶνδε is irrelevant here.

879. καὶ μήν: this regularly introduces a new character; here it is also assentient, supporting the previous speaker (*GP* 353 (4)). 'You may be seen by strangers.' 'Yes, there's one coming now.'

880. βημάτων: most editors accept Brunck's correction of the MS. reading δωμάτων. Kamerbeek prints βημάτων, but thinks δωμάτων might be justified either as dependent on σπουδῇ 'zeal for the house' i.e. 'eagerness to reach it' or as equivalent to πρὸ δωμάτων (cf. *Σ* λείπει ἡ πρό), but offers no parallel for these odd usages.

881. Orestes does not see Hermione until she speaks in 891. In other passages where stage convention allows a new arrival to ignore the presence of other characters, e.g. *Ba.* 215–47 and *Or.* 356–80, he is absorbed in his own emotions, as Or. is not. Perhaps at first Hermione shrinks back among the women of the Chorus; or alternatively she may now be almost off stage, with the Nurse, and run back at 889.

882. The fullness of expression strikes a note of stateliness and formality.

886. For the oracle of Zeus at Dodona in Epirus, the oldest in Greece, see Hom. *Od.* 14. 327–8.

887–9. This pretence that he is paying a casual call on Hermione and his questions in 901, 907 are shown by Or. himself in 959–63 to be mere subterfuge, presumably adopted to avoid committing himself too soon. As Aldrich observes: 'Just as he crouched behind a rock in the *Electra*, so did he move into this scene with caution and protective falsehoods.' Even after Hermione's almost hysterical welcome in 891–5 he continues his deception.

891. λιμήν: the common metaphorical use of *λιμήν*, as in *Med.* 768 *οὗτος . . . λιμὴν πέφανται*, is here almost expanded into a simile.

χείματος: gen. of separation 'refuge from storm'; cf. A. *Supp.* 476 *λιμὴν κακῶν*.

892. πρός σε τῶνδε γουνάτων: for the ellipse of a verb governing *σε* and the separation of *πρός* from *τῶνδε* cf. *Hel.* 1237 *πρός νύν σε γονάτων τῶνδ'*; *Ph.* 923, 1665; *Med.* 324 *μή, πρός σε γονάτων*. In *Hyps.* fr. 60. 25 *ὦ πρός σε γονάτων ἱκέτις . . . πίτνω* there is no ellipse, since the last two words are equivalent to *ἱκετεύω*. So also in Latin, e.g. 'per te deos oro.'

894–5. Hermione sinks to the ground before Orestes and clasps his knees in supplication; she hopes this will be at least as effective as the formal equipment of a suppliant, an olive branch festooned with wreaths of laurel or of wool (*στέμματα*); cf. *Hcld.* 226 *ἀλλ' ἄντομαί σε καὶ καταστέφω χεροῖν* lit. 'I deck you with suppliant hands'; *IA* 1216 *ἱκετηρίαν δὲ γόνασιν ἐξάπτω σέθεν | τὸ σῶμα τοὐμόν*; *Or.* 383.

896. ἔα: Fraenkel (*Ag.* 3, p. 580, n. 4) observes that 'without exception in Eur. *ἔα* expresses the surprise of the speaker at some novel, often unwelcome, impression on his senses'; see also Page on *Med.* 1004. *ἔα, τί χρῆμα* is one of the Euripidean formulae (*Hipp.* 905; *HF* 525; *Supp.* 92; *Or.* 1583; also A. *Pr.* 298); here of course the astonishment is assumed. Fraenkel is probably right about Eur. (though there are a few dubious instances) but fifth-century usage in general is less restricted. In S. *OC* 1477 *ἔα* greets the third peal of thunder; in Ar. *Pax* 61 and *Av.* 327 surprise is not the dominant emotion; in Pl. *Prt.* 314 d *ἔα* expresses mainly disgust.

897. τήνδε is emphatic: can this desperate suppliant be the proud daughter of Menelaus? Hence the over-emphasis of Hermione's reply.

898–9. Elsewhere in Eur., where the patronymic is used, daughter of Tyndareus is *Τυνδαρίς* alone (6 times) or *T. κόρη* (6 times) or *T. παῖς* (7 times). If *γυνή* is right it should not be taken closely with *Τυνδαρίς* but in the sense 'wife'. To the question 'Is this the daughter of Menelaus?' Hermione replies: 'Yes, the only child that the daughter of Tyndareus, his wife, Helen bore to my father in his house'; she may well conclude 'make no mistake'. Hermann, with tentative support from Murray, prints *κόρη*, the reading of L, but *γυνή* is the *lectio difficilior*. Herwerden's conjecture *ποτέ* assumes that both *γυνή* and *κόρη* were glosses.

μόνην: Eur. follows a tradition going back to Homer (*Od.* 4. 12–14) that Helen had only one child. Hesiod (*Cat.* fr. 99 Rz.) gives her in addition a son, Nicostratos, and according to *Σ* on 898 the author of *Cypria* knew of a son, Pleisthenes.

τίκτει: see on 9 above. The present of this verb tends to be used even when, as here and in *Ba.* 2, there is more stress on past action than present relationship.

900. ἀκέστορ: only here as an epithet of Apollo; *Ἀκέστωρ* as a proper name is found, e.g., in Cratinus, *Cleob.* fr. 1. According to Pausanias

6. 24. 6 *ἀκέσιος* was a title of Apollo in Elis; he compares the Athenian *ἀλεξίκακος*. See Usener, *Götternamen*, pp. 158–60.

πημάτων: Norwood thinks the plural indicates the general woes of the House of Atreus, of which Hermione's plight is a continuation; but the sense may be more general, merely 'Heaven preserve us, what's the matter?'

903. ἐκ θεῶν του: a vague indication of the origin of anything for which no specific person can be blamed.

904. The conditional *μή* is due either to politeness or feigned ignorance, and *πω* softens the implied reproach.

905. Cf. *Med.* 569–70 *ὀρθουμένης εὐνῆς . . . πάντ' ἔχειν νομίζετε.*

906. τοῦτ' αὐτὸ . . .: 'that is just where the trouble lies.'

εὖ μ' ὑπηγάγου: in effect 'how perceptive you are' (Aldrich). *ὑπάγεσθαι* means to lead on or induce gradually or by guile, but Hermione needs little inducement to confess.

907. εὐνὴν: 'bedfellow'.

908. H. uses the disparaging term *αἰχμάλωτος* of her rival (cf. 155 and 932), and deliberately stresses her relationship with Hector.

909. Some MSS. have *ἄνδρ' ἕνα* or *ἕν' ἄνδρα* and Grotius's *δίσσ' ἕν' ἄνδρ' ἔχειν* is attractive. For similar antitheses cf. S. *Ant.* 12, cited on 516; S. *Tr.* 539; *Hec.* 896; *Ion* 539; *Hel.* 731.

910. τοιαῦτα ταῦτα: 'just so'; cf. the elliptic use of *τοιαῦτα* or *ταῦτα* alone, generally in answer to a question, e.g. *Hec.* 776; *El.* 645. In Comedy *ταῦτα* or *ταῦτα δή* is the response to a command.

ἠμυνάμην: her excuse is that she acted in self-defence.

911. οἷα δὴ γυνή: cf. Thuc. 8. 84 *οἷα δὴ ναῦται* 'as sailors generally do'; S. *OT* 763 *οἷ' ἀνὴρ δοῦλος*. For the ruthlessness of women, especially where their love life is concerned, see *Ion* 843–5; *Med.* 265–6.

913. *αὐτούς* is to be supplied as object of *ἔκτεινας* and *ἀφείλετο*: 'and did you kill them, or did some mischance snatch them from you'; cf. S. *Ph.* 1302 *τί μ' ἄνδρα πολέμιον . . . ἀφείλου μὴ κτανεῖν;*

914. κακίονας: 'the weaker side' (Paley) as in *Hcld.* 177–8 *τοὺς ἀμείνονας παρὸν | φίλους ἑλέσθαι τοὺς κακίονας λάβῃς*. It is more likely that here and in 932 (*κακίστην*) Hermione is as usual stressing the servile status of Andromache, and *σέβων* is sarcastic: Peleus showed respect for those who should have been beneath his notice. Hyslop's suggestion that there is a political allusion, Peleus being like one of those Athenians who to Spartan eyes *τοὺς χείρους αἱροῦνται ἐν ταῖς πόλεσι ταῖς στασιαζούσαις* (Xen. *Ath.* 3. 10), is rather far-fetched.

917. χερί: 'by force'.

918. αἰδοῖ γε: this would be more directly face-saving for Menelaus if it is a negative answer referring to *χερί*: 'no, by respect (for his age)', but in all the examples of this use of *γε* in *GP* 131 (ii) there is a negative or virtual negative. It is therefore probably a positive answer and refers to *ἡσσήθη*: 'yes, by his respect'.

919. δεδραμένοις: causal dative; so *τύχαις* in 979.

920. τί δεῖ λέγειν; 'Why talk about it'? Paley (on A. *Eum.* 826) describes this phrase as 'an Attic formula when something is suppressed which is superfluous or disagreeable to add', and compares, e.g., A. *Ag.* 598; *HF* 1270; *Ph.* 43, 761; P. *Smp.* 217 c. This is true, though he omits to note that *τί δεῖ* is also used with other verbs in what is essentially the same idiom; see note on 765.

924. δόμοι . . . φθέγμ' ἔχοντες: in this context a melodramatic touch, without the tragic quality that invests, for example, the ominous words of the watchman in A. *Ag.* 37–8. See note on 825 ff.

925. μισεῖ τε: strict correspondence with *δόμοι τ'*, where Matthiae's correction seems necessary, would require *μισεῖν τε γαῖα*, still depending on *δοκοῦσι*, but the substitution of the more direct finite verb is natural.

πάρος: i.e. before I escape.

927. κτενεῖ μ': an exaggeration; the words of the Chorus leader in 1057 suggest that they do not take Hermione to mean what she says here.

ἐπ' αἰσχίστοισιν: *Σ* explains *ἢ αἰσχρῶς ἢ ἐπ' αἰσχροῖς ἁλοῦσαν* 'condemned on a charge of foulest deeds'. The context favours the former sense: H. is thinking more of what will happen to her than of the nature of her offence. For *ἐπί*+dat. denoting attendant circumstances cf. *Hipp.* 511 *ἅ σ' οὔτ' ἐπ' αἰσχροῖς οὔτ' ἐπὶ βλάβῃ φρενῶν | παύσει νόσου τῆσδ'*, 'without disgrace or harm'; *Tro.* 315; *Ph.* 1555.

928. νόθοισι λέκτροις: for *νόθος* used of an illegitimate union cf. *Ion* 545 *ἦλθες ἐς νόθον τι λέκτρον*; here *λέκτρον* is used for 'bedfellow' i.e. Andromache; cf. 35 *λέκτρα ἐκείνης* i.e. Hermione and similarly *λέχος* (488, 592) and *εὐνή* (350, 907).

πρὸ τοῦ: see on 734.

929. This line is ascribed by the MSS. to Orestes, and Radermacher, approved by Wilamowitz, accepts this, taking the sense to be 'And how then did you come to commit this *ἁμάρτημα*, as some might call it?' i.e. Orestes tactfully deprecates the use of hard words about Hermione. Attributions in MSS. have, however, no special authority and most editors rightly follow Lenting in giving the line to Hermione. It is then an instance of the rhetorical device of putting up a question or objection to be answered or refuted (*προκατάληψις*). (H. may actually be thinking of what Neoptolemus will say and rehearsing her excuses.) Cf. Ant. *Tetr.* 3. 2. 3 *εἶεν· ἐρεῖ δέ "ἀλλ' ὁ νόμος . . ."* (then follows the refutation); E. *Or.* 665 *ἐρεῖς· "ἀδύνατον". αὐτὸ τοῦτο*; *Ba.* 204 *ἐρεῖ τις ὡς τὸ γῆρας οὐκ αἰσχύνομαι* (Teiresias proceeds to rebut the charge); *Supp.* 184 *τάχ' οὖν ἂν εἴποις· "πῶς . . .;" ἐγὼ δίκαιός εἰμ' ἀφηγεῖσθαι τάδε*; perhaps fr. 707 *ἐρεῖ τις· οὐ χρῆν*. On this view however *ὡς* hardly makes sense and the potential optative without *ἄν* is doubtful even in poetry, except in rhetorical questions such as *τίς . . . ὑπερβασία κατάσχοι;* (S. *Ant.* 604) and sentences of the type οὐκ ἔσθ' ὅπως λέξαιμι (A. *Ag.* 620); see Stahl, *Synt. der Gr. Verb.* I. 298–302 for apparent exceptions in MSS. In this passage Nauck's ὧδ' ἐρεῖ τις avoids these objections and receives some support from the predominance of the future tense in similar phrases; but the corruption is unexplained and I should prefer Pflugk's πῶς οὖν ἂν εἴποι τις τάδ'...; For the opt. with ἄν cf. E. *Supp.* 184 (cited above) and Dem. 6. 13 ἀλλὰ νὴ Δί', εἴποι τις ἂν . . .

930. According to Σ this line became proverbial, like φθείρουσιν ἤθη χρήσθ' ὁμιλίαι κακαί (Men. fr. 187 K., perh. taken from Eur.). It was parodied by the emperor Hadrian πολλῶν εἴσοδοί μ' ἀπώλεσαν.

εἴσοδοι: 'visits', which naturally imply conversation, of which we have a specimen in 932–5. Similarly in *Tro.* 651 ἔσω τε μελάθρων κομψὰ θηλειῶν ἔπη | οὐκ εἰσεφρούμην Andromache claims that she allowed no smart feminine gossip into her house. Norwood observes on 930–53 that 'Hermione speaks as an ordinary Athenian wife of the poet's own day, not as a princess of an earlier age'. Her speech is not indeed an anachronism in the same sense as Hecuba's philosophical speculations in *Tro.* 884–8, since feminine gossip about husbands and their mistresses was not invented in the fifth century, and if friends *had* called upon Hermione this is what they might have said. There is however in the circumstances, including the seclusion of the royal palace (18–19), something incongruous and improbable about these 'hen parties'; they may be thought more appropriate to the urban life of Athens or Alexandria, and certainly their appearance in literature is more in the manner of Comedy and Mime. Moreover the disproportionate length of the passage and the passionate adjuration to husbands in 943 ff. give the impression of an almost extra-dramatic digression.

934. μὰ τὴν ἄνασσαν: presumably Hera, goddess of sanctity of marriage, as in *IA* 739 μὰ τὴν ἄνασσαν Ἀργείαν θεάν.

935. βλέπουσ' ἄν: Kamerbeek and Bornmann print βλέπουσαν, the reading of most MSS. and the only one known to Σ, and explain that καρποῦσθαι is used with two accusatives on the analogy of ἀφαιρεῖσθαι; but this seems to me hardly possible and the reading in the text is surely right. Moreover the sense 'in *my* house she would not have done this and lived' is more appropriate, since it is this advice that H. actually followed. For ἄν thrice repeated cf. *Tro.* 1244, and see note on 77.

936. Σειρήνων: see Hom. *Od.* 12. 158 ff. and for this metaphorical use cf. Aeschin. 3. 228 ἀφομοιοῖ γάρ μου τὴν φύσιν ταῖς Σειρῆσιν. καὶ γὰρ ὑπ' ἐκείνων φησὶ τοὺς ἀκροωμένους ἀπόλλυσθαι.

937. λαλημάτων: abstract for concrete; neuter nouns in -μα are frequently so used, e.g. S. *Ant.* 320 ὡς λάλημα δῆλον ἐκπεφυκὸς εἶ; ibid. 756 γυναικὸς δούλευμα; *Tro.* 1106 λάτρευμα; S. *OT* 85 ἄναξ, ἐμὸν κήδευμα; *An.* 1273 ὦ γενναῖα συγκοιμήματα, . . . χαῖρε.

σοφῶν and *ποικίλων* are of course used in a bad sense: 'cunning and wily'.

The line may be a later addition. A noun in apposition is not normally qualified by a string of adjectives; the description is less appropriate for *Σειρήνων*, to which it is in apposition, than for the women themselves; the sentence runs better without it.

938 ff. H.'s line of thought seems to be 'I was a fool to bother about my husband's relations with his slave woman, since whatever happened I was a rich woman, mistress of the house, and *my* children would have been legitimate.' This is inconsistent with 32–5 and 156–8, where the charge against Andromache was that she had by magic arts made Hermione barren with the object of alienating Neoptolemus and ousting H. from her position, presumably with some chance of success. The suppressed protasis to *ἔτικτον ἄν* is not 'if I had not been barren' (Wecklein), but 'if I had not disgraced myself in the eyes of N.', and she either ignores her previous accusations or assumes that her sterility was only temporary. We should not in any case expect her to be consistent as she wistfully conjures up a vision of free-born children of her own lording it over Andromache's bastards.

939. φυλάσσειν: 'keep watch on'; cf. Andromache's criticism in 227–8.

940. ὄλβος: sc. *παρῆν*.

942. ἡμιδούλους: see on 199–202.

943 ff. This diatribe against mischief-making women (Paley calls it 'this fine passage') is not altogether irrelevant, but its elaboration certainly seems undramatic. Kamerbeek thinks that Hermione is here the mouthpiece of Eur. If he had any view he would perhaps rather agree with the speaker in fr. 1046 *μοχθοῦμεν ἄλλως θῆλυ φρουροῦντες γένος | ἥτις γὰρ αὐτὴ μὴ πέφυκεν ἔνδικος | τί δεῖ φυλάσσειν;* These passages, with *Hipp.* 645 ff., Ar. *Th.* 414–16, and others suggest some reference to contemporary Athenian life, but it is risky to draw inferences about the prison-like existence of women in the fifth century. Some Athenians may have growled 'they ought to be locked up', as some may say 'strikers ought to be shot', without really regarding this as practicable or desirable.

943. For the repetition the closest parallel is from Comedy: Ar. *Eq.* 249 *καὶ πανοῦργον καὶ πανοῦργον· πολλάκις γὰρ αὔτ' ἐρῶ*; cf. also *Hcld.* 449 *χρῆν χρῆν ἄρ' ὑμᾶς*. Repetition in lyric is rather different, e.g. *μήποτε μήποτε* A. *Pr.* 894, E. *Ph.* 190.

947. The women who corrupt others are divided into three types: (1) The woman who does it for gain, (2) the woman who has deceived her husband (perhaps for the first time) and doesn't want to be alone in this, (3) those many who corrupt others out of sheer lewdness, who take lovers as a matter of course and encourage others, perhaps even take vicarious pleasure in the adultery of others. These types, at any rate (1) and (3), are not exclusive and the old bawd in Herodas, *Mime* 1 may belong to both.

949. There is no need for dots after *μαργότητι*. The sentence is rather loosely constructed but quite clear: in 948 instead of supplying *συμφθείρει* from 947 we find substituted a main verb giving the motive for corruption; then in 949 *συμφθείρουσι* is supplied after *πολλαί*.

950. πρὸς τάδ' εὖ φυλάσσετε: *πρὸς τάδε* (or *ταῦτα*) with an imperative is a common form of expression, either to indicate defiance, as in *Ph.* 521 *πρὸς ταῦτ' ἴτω μὲν πῦρ* . . ., or, as here, a warning: 'that's the position and this is how you must deal with it.'

φυλάσσετε: she appeals to an imaginary audience of *νοῦν ἔχοντες* (944).

951. κλῄθροισι καὶ μοχλοῖσι: 'bolts and bars', but as a pair the Greek words occur only here and Ar. *Lys.* 264.

952. ὑγιὲς οὐδέν: for this colloquial expression see on 448.

954. ἐφῆκας γλῶσσαν: cf. *Hipp.* 1324 *ἀρὰς ἐφῆκας παιδί*; S. *El.* 596 *πᾶσαν ἵης γλῶσσαν*.

εἰς τὸ σύμφυτον: *Σ* explains *σύμφυτον* as *τὸ γυναικεῖον γένος*, and most editors accept this, though no example is cited of this sense of *σύμφυτος*, which normally means 'innate', 'natural'. There is, however, some support from Pl. *L.* 899 d *ὅτι μὲν ἡγῇ θεούς, συγγένειά τις ἴσως σε θεία πρὸς τὸ σύμφυτον ἄγει τιμᾶν καὶ νομίζειν εἶναι* and from the fact that *συγγενής* means both 'innate' and 'of like kind'. Some, less probably, take *τὸ σύμφυτον* to mean the innate frailty of women, and LSJ s.v. *σύμφυτος* take *εἰς* to mean 'in accordance with' and *σύμφυτον* to refer to the nature of Hermione, presumably her tendency to hysterical denunciations; but *ἐφῆκας* requires some indication of the target.

956. κοσμεῖν: from the common meaning 'adorn', 'embellish' *κοσμεῖν* sometimes acquires the special connotation (not noticed in LSJ) 'gloss over', 'disguise'. So *Ion* 833 *οἳ συντιθέντες τἄδικ' εἶτα μηχαναῖς | κοσμοῦσι*; *Tro.* 982 *μὴ ἀμαθεῖς ποίει θεὰς τὸ σὸν κακὸν κοσμοῦσα* 'dressing it up as something different'. This is probably the sense here. For the sentiment Kamerbeek compares S. fr. 679 *σύγγνωτε κἀνάσχεσθε σιγῶσαι· τὸ γὰρ| γυναιξὶν αἰσχρὸν σὺν γυναῖκα δεῖ στέγειν*, and for other references to feminine solidarity see *Hel.* 329, *IT* 1061.

The other sense of *κοσμεῖν* 'control', suggested for this passage by Bond (on *Hyps.* fr. 60. 46), is less appropriate in this context.

γυναικείας: the reading in BOP and H is *γυναικείους*; so also in Ox. Pap. 2335 (ii A.D.); cf. *IA* 233 *γυναικεῖον ὄψιν*, where the form of the adj. is certified by the metre.

957. σοφόν τι χρῆμα . . .: this is probably a compressed form of *σοφόν τι χρῆμά ⟨ἐστι⟩ τὸ χρῆμα τοῦ διδάξαντος* . . . If so it is a combination of the pleonastic use of *χρῆμα*, as in *Or.* 70 *ἄπορον χ. δυστυχῶν δόμος* and (if the OCT reading is accepted) 727 above ἀνειμένον τι χ. πρεσβυτῶν γένος, and the periphrastic use, for which see on 181.

958. τῶν ἐναντίων: this is generally taken to mean 'the opposing parties' and τοῦ διδάξαντος then refers to the unknown author of the maxim μηδὲ δίκην δικάσῃς πρὶν ἂν ἀμφοῖν μῦθον ἀκούσῃς (cf. Plut. *Mor.* 1034 e), a line which is echoed with variations in E. *Hcld.* 179 and Ar. *V.* 725, 919, and forms the substance of the ἡλιαστικὸς ὅρκος recorded in, e.g., Isoc. 15. 21 ἦ μὴν ὁμοίως ἀκροάσεσθαι τῶν κατηγορούντων καὶ τῶν ἀπολογουμένων. It is, however, hard to see the relevance of judicial impartiality here: Or. was certainly not waiting to decide the guilt or innocence of Hermione, as Paley seems to suggest. Moreover, apart from the unremarkable λόγους ἀκούειν (= μῦθον ἀκ.) there is practically no connection between 958 and the hexameter cited. The sense assumed for τῶν ἐναντίων is not impossible, since in philosophy τὰ ἐνάντια denotes 'contraries' and in a fourth-century papyrus οἱ ἐξ ἐναντίας means 'the opposing parties'; but the normal sense is 'the adversary'. Thus the Budé editor rightly takes the sense to be 'It was a wise fellow who taught men to listen to tales coming from the other side.' Then in ἐγὼ γὰρ εἰδώς . . . Or. gives the particular application: 'Thus ⟨because I listened to tales coming from the household of my enemy, Neoptolemus,⟩ I knew of the quarrel . . .' Unless then Or. is perverting the sense of the proverbial saying, the reference is to some other precept, to the effect that one should listen to what comes from the enemy camp.

One explanation in *Σ* takes the sense to be 'One should not rely on rumour but listen to what is said by those actually involved in the matter'; but though ἐνάντιον means 'in the presence of' there seems to be no example of οἱ ἐνάντιοι in the sense 'those present'.

959. It is clear that Or. can now safely admit that his presence is not accidental and that his ignorance of the situation (887, 901, 907) was feigned; but it is not obvious why he should do so.

962. φόνῳ: Lenting's correction of the MS. φόβῳ is not an improvement. φόνος would have to mean 'attempted murder', and the phrase αἰχμαλωτίδος φόβῳ in 1059 supports φόβῳ here (Lenting would read φόνῳ in both lines). With φόβῳ the genitive is not objective, but means 'fear relating to the slave woman'; Hermann compares S. *OT* 988 τῆς ζώσης φόβος. For the cognate dative cf., e.g., *Ba.* 604 ἐκπεπληγμέναι φόβῳ. Ox. Pap. 2335 gives φ]θόνῳ, which C. H. Roberts and others would accept, but, as W. Morel points out (*Bull. Am. Soc. Pap.* 2 (1965), 80), φθόνος is not an emotion that terrifies.

964. σὰς μὲν οὐ σέβων ἐπιστολάς: Norwood translates 'not respecting thy messages', and supposes that Or. had arrived in spite of messages from H. forbidding him to come. But if so there would surely have been some reference to this in the preceding 70 lines. Compare rather Hom. *Il.* 19. 336 ἐμὴν ποτιδέγμενον . . . ἀγγελίην 'expecting news of me' (which never arrived), and S. *OT* 572. *Σ* here paraphrases *οὐ γράμματά σου δεξάμενος* and the Budé editor rightly explains in a note 'il n'a pas attendu pour venir un message d'Hermione'.

σέβων is however too strong for this context, since it generally denotes reverence or respect for gods, laws, parents, suppliants, or the like. This is rather too emphatic even for Norwood's interpretation, and still less appropriate for the sense we need: it is natural to say 'I came without waiting for a message' but not 'without respecting . . .'. I should prefer, with Hermann, to accept *μένων*, the reading of P, although *σέβων* may be the *lectio difficilior* and the process of corruption obscure. I also prefer Hermann's *τὰς σὰς οὐ μένων* since *μέν* throws too much emphasis on *σάς*. (A different and to me unconvincing interpretation is given by T. Zieliński, *Tragodoumenon* I. 116.)

965. ἐνδιδοίης λόγον: 'give me a chance to talk'. For this sense of *ἐνδιδόναι* cf. Ar. *Eq.* 847 *λαβὴν γὰρ ἐνδέδωκας*; *Hec.* 1239.

The sense of 964 ff. is thus: 'I came unbidden, but in the hope that (in your present plight) you would listen to me and I should be able to take you away.'

966. ἐμὴ οὖσα: 'betrothed to me'; cf. 969 and see Intr., p. 5.

967. σὺν τῷδε: a good example of *ὅδε* used of somebody not physically present, but in the minds of those who are present; here Or. may make some gesture towards Neoptolemus' house.

ναίεις: see on 34.

κάκη: this form, metrically more convenient than *κακία*, is found occasionally in the dramatists, but in prose is confined to Plato.

972. συνέγνων πατρί: hardly consistent with 967, but there is presumably an allusion here to the prophecy of Helenus that Troy could only be taken with the help of N., so that Menelaus had good reason to propitiate him.

978. αἱματωποὺς θεάς: i.e. the Erinyes; cf. *Or.* 256 *τὰς αἱματωποὺς καὶ δρακοντώδεις κόρας*, where Benedetto compares A. *Cho.* 1058 *κἀξ ὀμμάτων στάζουσιν αἷμα δυσφιλές* and takes the sense in all three passages to be that their eyes drip or ooze blood, a strange phenomenon even for these dreadful beings. In *Eu.* 54 *ἐκ δ' ὀμμάτων λείβουσι δυσφιλῆ λίβα* (*δία* M) Aesch. appears to describe an unpleasant discharge, and in *Cho.* 1058 Burges's correction *στάζουσι νᾶμα*, accepted by some editors, would give a similar sense there. It is not indeed certain that Eur. had either Aeschylean passage in mind. Compounds in *-ωπός* are particularly common in Eur. and often refer not to eyes but to facial appearance in general, e.g. *παρθενωπός*, and often the second half loses its significance, e.g. *νυκτὸς ἀστερωπὸς σέλας* 'starry radiance'. So with the other two examples of *αἱματωπός*: *HF* 933 *ῥίζας ἐν ὄσσοις αἱματῶπας* 'with bloody streaks or veins in his eyes' 'with bloodshot eyes'; *Ph.* 870 *αἱματωποὶ δεργμάτων διαφθοραί* 'bloody destruction of his eyes' (as in S. *OC* 552 *αἱματηρὰς ὀμμάτων διαφθοράς*). Possibly *αἱματωπός* alone might refer to bloodshot eyes, a sign of madness in Heracles and perhaps also suited to creatures who cause madness. Whatever the precise sense, there is a certain incongruity, perhaps deliberate, in this casual introduction of an epithet that is more appropriate to a moment of high emotional tension, as in *Or.* 256.

980. ἤλγουν μὲν ἤλγουν: the form is almost a mannerism of Eur.; cf. *Alc.* 1017 *καὶ μέμφομαι μὲν μέμφομαι*; ibid. 1093 *αἰνῶ μὲν αἰνῶ*; fr. 285. 7 *ἀλγεῖ μὲν ἀλγεῖ.*

συμφοραῖς δ' ἠνειχόμην: for the double augment in this and other verbs see Page on *Med.* 1156 (*ἠνέσχετο*), *Gr. Gr.* 656 (c) and Rutherford, *New Phryn.* 83–7.

Editors who accept this text take *συμφοραῖς* as a causal dative, but this does not make sense with a verb meaning 'bear up', 'hold out'. Good sense is provided by *συμφοράς* (Scaliger) 'I patiently endured disasters', but since *συμφοραῖς* is supported by Ox. Pap. 2335 it is perhaps better to accept Dindorf's *συμφοραῖς ἐνειχόμην* 'I was in the grip of disasters'. Among other suggestions are Jackson's *συμφορᾶς ἵν' εἰχόμην* (*Marg. Scaen.* 215) and Broadhead's *συμφορᾶς ἵν' ἱκόμην* (*Tragica*, p. 116), which give a better line at the cost of greater change.

982. περιπετεῖς ἔχεις τύχας: the only comparable example of the adj. is Hdt. 8. 20 *περιπετέα τε ἐποιήσαντο σφίσι αὐτοῖσι τὰ πρήγματα*, and for these two passages only LSJ give the sense 'changing or turning suddenly', 'a sudden reverse'; but Herodotus is merely describing the Euboeans as having brought disaster upon themselves by mistrusting an oracle. There is no suggestion of sudden reversal, except in so far as this is inevitably involved in a disaster, and we should not read into the fifth-century adjective the special senses attached to *περιπέτεια* as a technical term of dramatic theory in Aristotle's *Poetics*. There is probably no Aristotelian *περιπέτεια* in *Andromache*, and in any case it is unlikely that Orestes here means to convey anything more than that Hermione's fortunes are in ruins. This sense of *περιπετής* could be derived from the literal sense 'falling around' (*περιπίπτω*) in Tragedy and elsewhere, leading to the metaphorical sense 'collapse in ruins'. Bornmann, taking *τύχας* in the bad sense, treats *περιπετεῖς* as active 'misfortunes surrounding you', but the Herodotean parallel supports the neutral sense for *τύχας*.

984. ἀπ' οἴκων is the reading of all MSS. and has not been questioned, but a papyrus of ii A.D. (Ox. Pap. 22. 2335) has *ες οικ[ον*, and, as Turner observes, with *οἴκων* we might expect *τῶνδε*, whereas *ἐπ' οἶκον* 'home' needs no addition; it also fits the context better.

985–6. Hermann, followed by Wecklein, assigned these lines to the Chorus. Two lines of comment might certainly be expected, and the sententious remark is entirely appropriate; in that case Hermann's *τοι* for *γάρ* must also be accepted, since brief comments of this kind by a Chorus leader are not elsewhere linked to the preceding speech by *γάρ*, and in such matters convention is strong, especially in Euripides.

For this use of *δεινός* cf. A. *PV* 39 *τὸ συγγενές τοι δεινόν*; S. *El.* 770; *IA* 917 *δεινὸν τὸ τίκτειν* 'there is strange potency in motherhood'.

987–8. Orestes has not specifically asked for Hermione in marriage, but he has implied that it would be his wish, and it is natural for her to reply that it is for her father to deal with the complications of her re-marriage (to Orestes or anybody else); these would include divorce from Neoptolemus, since she is not yet aware of Orestes' intention to make her a widow.

989. ὡς τάχιστα . . .: she could have cut down her meditations on the ways of women, but the inconsistency is sanctioned by dramatic convention.

990. προσβὰς . . . καὶ μολών: it is simplest to take this as hysteron proteron, *μολών* meaning, as often, 'return'. Otherwise we must either (with Wecklein) assume a lacuna containing a finite verb parallel with *φθῇ* or emend. Blaydes suggested *καί μ' ἕλῃ πόσις*; Palmer's *μ' ἑλών* is easier, but perhaps involves *σε* for *με* before *προσβάς*: 'lest he anticipate your action by coming and taking me'.

991. In most of the earlier MSS. the line begins at *οἴκους*; but the opening *ἢ πρέσβυς* is supplied by OD, and in *Andromache* these MSS. almost certainly copied B (in which 957–1211 are now missing), so that the opening words printed in OCT are not, as Jackson supposed (*Marg. Scaen.* 86), a Byzantine supplement, but preserve an earlier MS. tradition. They are also confirmed by Ox. Pap. 22. 2335 *η πρεσβυ[*. Jackson's *ἄλλως τ' ἄν*, keeping *μετέλθοι* in 992, might indeed be an improvement, but emendation is hardly justified.

993. θάρσει . . . χεῖρα: *θαρσεῖν* is often used with an acc., probably by analogy with *οὐ φοβεῖσθαι*, 'do not fear an old man's strength'.

994. ὅσ' εἰς ἔμ' ὕβρισε: in this idiom, rightly restored by Lobeck, *ὅσος* and *οἷος* are in effect equivalent to *ὅτι τοσοῦτος* (*τοιοῦτος*), as A. M. Dale put it, 'a kind of subordinated exclamatory construction': 'such wrongs he has done me'; cf. *Hel.* 74 *ὅσον μίμημ' ἔχεις Ἑλένης* 'so like you are to H.'; Hom. *Il.* 21. 399 *τῶ σ' αὖ νῦν ὀΐω ἀποτεισέμεν, ὅσσα ἔοργας*.

995. μηχανὴ πεπλεγμένη: the hunting-net was much used and naturally a source of metaphor; cf. 66 *μηχανὰς πλέκουσι*; *Or.* 1422 *μηχανὰν ἐμπλέκειν*. For the weaving and fixing of nets see Hull, *Hounds and Hunting in Ancient Greece*, pp. 10–18.

996. ἀκινήτοισιν: the meshes of the net were fastened to stakes fixed in the ground.

997. οὐκ ἐρῶ: i.e. I will say no more.

998. τελουμένων: sc. *πραγμάτων*; cf. S. *El.* 1344 *τελουμένων εἴποιμ' ἄν*. In A. *Cho.* 872 *πράγματος τελουμένου* we have a true present 'while the task is being achieved', and here too the sense could be 'when the deed is being performed the rock of Delphi will know'; but it would be more natural to say 'when all is done', and certainly in *El.* 1344 the sense required is 'when our task is accomplished'. Perhaps in both passages *τελουμένων* is used to denote accomplishment without any specific indication of time.

Δελφὶς . . . πέτρα: a natural periphrasis, with reference to the rocky platform on which the town and temple stood; cf. S. *OT* 463 *Δελφὶς εἶπε πέτρα*, with Jebb's note, and *Ion* 550 *Πυθίαν δ' ἦλθες πέτραν.*

999. δορυξένων: 'my friends and allies'; see Fraenkel on A. *Ag.* 880, where he cites the definition of Ar. of Byzantium *οἱ κατὰ πόλεμον ἀλλήλους φιλοποιησάμενοι.* The term is used three times in Tragedy of the relation between the house of Orestes and that of Pylades (*Ag.* 880, *Cho.* 914, S. *El.* 46); cf. also S. *OC* 632, E. *Med.* 687.

1001. δείξει: Or. refers to himself in the third person; I should have preferred Herwerden's *δείξω* 'I, the matricide, will teach . . .'; cf. *Or.* 1626 *Φοῖβός σ' ὁ Λητοῦς παῖς . . . καλῶ* (*καλεῖ* L); *Tro.* 191 *ἁ τλάμων ποῦ πᾷ γαίας δουλεύσω;* but the MS. reading is supported by Ox. Pap. 2335 ([*δει*]*ξει γαμ*[*ειν*, and should be retained. Since N. *has* married H. *δείξει* should = *διδάξει*, as in 706–7, though this involves hyperbaton and probably *σφι* instead of *σφε*.

μηδέν': a generalizing *plural* is normally masc. even when the reference is to a woman, as in *τοὺς ἐμούς* (375) referring to Hermione; here the masc. sing. form is more striking but may be right, since though Or. is thinking of Hermione he expresses himself in very general terms.

1002. πικρῶς: *πικρός* is regularly used in threats that some action will prove disastrous for the doer; cf. A. *Pers.* 473; *Med.* 339 *πικροὺς δ' ἐγώ σφιν καὶ λυγροὺς θήσω γάμους, | πικρὸν δὲ κῆδος*; *Hel.* 448 *πικρῶς ἄρ' οἶμαί γ' ἀγγελεῖν τοὺς σοὺς λόγους*; *El.* 638. For a collection of examples in Tragedy and Comedy see Fraenkel, *Agamemnon*, 2. 301, n. 1.

αἰτήσει: it appears from 52 ff. and more clearly from 1106–8 that the demand for satisfaction had been made on a previous visit to Delphi, whereas the present visit was inspired by the *μετάστασις γνώμης* of 1003. The sense is 'His demand will turn out to have bitter consequences.'

1005. διαβολαῖς: the content of these is described in 1090–5.

1005–6. ἔκ τ' ἐκείνου . . . κακῶς ὀλεῖται: a true prediction; see 1147–9, 1161–5. The notion that the gods are sometimes *μεταίτιοι*, that they may fulfil their purposes through the agency of mortals acting for their own reasons, is familiar in Aeschylus and Sophocles; but, as Norwood notes, there is all the difference between seeing in retrospect that the gods have acted thus and the cynical assurance with which Orestes predicts that Apollo will co-operate in the murder plot that he and his friends have devised.

In a modern play one might expect some indication by word or gesture of Hermione's reaction to this reference to the impending fate of Neoptolemus, or alternatively we might draw important conclusions from her silence and indifference. In Attic Tragedy I doubt whether we should be justified in doing so, though I know of no close parallel to the present situation. The absence of verbal comment has indeed led Grube (*Drama of Eur.* 210) to consider it just possible that H. retired during the speech of Or. and did not hear the last lines, and Verrall (*Four Plays of Eur.* 272) to assert with confidence that she retired at 992, that the next two lines were spoken after her, and that the rest of the speech was a soliloquy. There is no hint of this in the text, and it is more likely that Or. and H. leave the scene together. In any case the Chorus must hear the whole speech. It may be that the dramatist intended both the Chorus and Hermione to register some emotion, but this is guess-work.

1006. γνώσεται: the sense is probably 'he shall learn ⟨the meaning of⟩ my enmity', as in the fuller form in *HF* 840 *ὡς ἂν γνῷ τὸν Ἥρας οἷός ἐστ' αὐτῷ χόλος*.

1007. ἐχθρῶν: i.e. enemies of the god; but the juxtaposition of *ἔχθραν ἐμήν* may be meant to reflect Orestes' conviction that he and Apollo are united in their enmity to Neoptolemus.

μοῖραν εἰς ἀναστροφὴν . . . δίδωσι: the force of *δίδωσι* is presumably 'hands over to confusion', the whole phrase being equivalent to *ἀναστρέφειν*, used several times of similar divine action, e.g. *Supp.* 331; *Rh.* 332.

1008. Exeunt Orestes and Hermione. Orestes' speech as a whole leaves the impression that he has contrived a plot which his confederates can now be trusted to execute. There are, however, later passages which have led some scholars to think that Or. goes back to Delphi and takes part himself in the killing of Neoptolemus,[1] and this is perhaps the place to review them briefly; further details are discussed in the relevant notes.

In 1061–5 the Chorus leader tells Peleus that Or. has gone taking Hermione, with the intention of marrying her and bringing about the death of N. When Peleus asks 'Will he do so by lying in ambush or meeting him in open fight?' the reply is not 'Acting through others and not in person' but 'In the temple of Loxias, with the Delphians', from which Peleus might infer that Or. will be there. In 1074–5 the messenger reports that N. is dead, adding 'such strokes of the sword he has received from the Delphians and the Mycenaean stranger (Orestes)'. In 1115–16 a possible interpretation of the text is 'men in ambush, of whom the son of Clytemnestra was one'; so taken these lines would of course be decisive. In 1242 the words of Thetis *φόνον βίαιον τῆς Ὀρεστείας χερός* again suggest direct action by Or. Finally it has been noted that on a Ruvo amphora the artist has depicted the

[1] See Wilamowitz, *Hermes*, 60 (1925), 284 ff.; Schmid, *Ges. der griech. Lit.* 7. 1. 3, p. 404, n. 1; Ziegler, P.–W. *Real-Encyclopädie*, 16. 2, 2456.

attack on N. at Delphi, probably with our play in mind, and shows Or. with drawn sword emerging from behind the omphalos and advancing upon N.[1]

It is not of course a serious objection to this view that sixty lines after the departure of Or. from Phthia the messenger appears and announces the death of N. A choral ode intervenes, during which any period of time could be held to elapse, and there is no need to labour the point that in Attic Tragedy neither dramatist nor audience seem to have worried much about the time occupied by events off-stage. Nor does the absence of any mention of Or. in the messenger speech after 1115 seem to me to be significant: the messenger becomes absorbed in other aspects of his narrative; there is no reason why Or., if present, should take a prominent part, and no particular point in the speech at which a reference to him might have been expected. That Or. is encumbered with Hermione might be a complication, since it is hard to imagine her accompanying him to Delphi on this quest; Ziegler assumes that Or. first takes her to Sparta, as he promised in 984, and then 'hastens to Delphi to procure the death of N.'.

On the other hand the positive indications of Or.'s presence at the murder can be otherwise interpreted and are thus not quite enough to contradict the impression made by 993–1008. The evidence of vase-painting is of doubtful value here; there is no certainty that the artist had this play in mind, and in any case the inclusion of Or. in the murder scene might be merely a pictorial way of indicating his prime responsibility, which is not in question. Of the passages in the text referred to above, in 1061–5 the words of the Chorus leader do not explicitly confirm or deny the assumption of Peleus that Or. will take part in the attack; 1075 can be explained on the ground that Or. was in effect one of the killers, even though he did not actually strike a blow; in 1242 the words of Thetis are again compatible with long-range action by Or.; for details see the Commentary. In 1115–16, a crucial passage, I have referred in my note to linguistic grounds for preferring an alternative interpretation, which does not assert (though it does not actually deny) the presence of Or.

On the whole therefore I agree with Lesky[2] and others that Or. plans the murder of N. but leaves it to others to execute. I am not, however, quite as confident about this as Lesky (who does not appear to take account of 1061–5), and it seems to me odd that there should be

[1] L. Sechan, *Étude sur la Trag. grecque dans ces rapports avec la céramique*, pp. 253 ff., fig. 75; E. Vogel, *Ueber Szenen eur. Trag. in griech. Vasengemälden*, pp. 28 ff.

[2] A. Lesky, 'Der Ablauf der Handlung in der Andromache des Euripides', *Anz. Österr. Ak. d. Wiss., phil.-hist. Kl.* 84 (1947), 99 ff. (= *Ges. Schrift.* 144–55).

several prima-facie indications of direct participation by Or. I should not accept Sauer's[1] hypothesis that there was an earlier draft of the play in which Or. did not appear but was represented as taking part in the murder, and that Eur. then rewrote it in its present form but failed to remove certain references to direct action by Or. Perhaps, however, it should be admitted that in the text as it stands there *are* ambiguities about the movements of Orestes, and that the play may lack a final revision that would have resolved these, and perhaps the doubt about the presence of Andromache at the end (see note on 1047), though this would in any case be clear in performance.

FOURTH STASIMON: **1009–1046**

In strophe (*a*) the reference to Apollo as one of the gods who built the walls of Troy and in the end abandoned them to destruction may have been suggested by the same god's unrelenting enmity to Neoptolemus, as described by Orestes at the end of the preceding scene. In strophe (*b*) the allusion to Orestes and Clytemnestra is a grim reminder that Or. comes fresh from another deed of blood, commanded, it was said, by Apollo. But the function of this stasimon, as of the first, is not primarily to comment on the preceding epeisodion but to take us back once more to the Trojan War and the whole aftermath of sorrow for victors as well as vanquished, in which the action of this play is yet another episode.

Metre. Mainly dactylo-epitrite.

Metrical Scheme:

Strophe+antistrophe (*a*): 1009–17 = 1018–26

1.	– – ∪ – – – ∪ ∪ – ∪ ∪ – – – ∪ –	iambelegus epitrite
1010 = 1020		
2.	– – ∪ ∪ – ∪ ∪ – – – ∪ –	enoplian epitrite
3.	– ∪ ∪ – ∪ ∪ –	hemiepes
4.	∪ ∪ – ∪ ∪ – ∪ – –	enoplian
5.	– ∪ ∪ – ∪ ∪ – ∪	hemiepes pendant
6.	– ∪ ∪ – ∪ ∪ – ∪ ∪ – –	dactylic tetrameter
7.	– ∪ – – ∪ –	2 cretics
8.	– ∪ – ∪ – –	ithyphallic

Note:

1. In 1009 the last syllable of Ἰλίῳ is shortened by epic correption. (For a different colometry making each of the first three cola an iambelegus see A. Dain, *Traité de métrique grecque*, p. 157.)

---

[1] R. Sauer, *Untersuchungen zu Euripides*, pp. 43 ff.

Strophe + antistrophe (*b*): 1027–36 = 1037–46

1.	⏓ – ⏑ – – – ⏑ ⏑ – ⏑ ⏑ –	iambelegus
2.	– – ⏑ – – – ⏑ ⏑ – ⏑ ⏑ –	iambelegus
1030 = 1040		
3.	– ⏑ – ⏑ – –	ithyphallic
4.	⏑ – ⏑ – – ⏑ – ⏑ – ⏑ –	iambic trimeter syncopated
5.	– ⏑͡⏑ ⏑ ⏑͡⏑ ⏑ – ⏑ – ⏑ – –	iambic trimeter catalectic
6.	⏑ ⏑ – ⏑ ⏑ – ⏑ – ⏑ ⏑ – ⏑ ⏑ –	acephalous hemiepes anceps hemiepes
1035		
7.	⏓ ⏑ – – – – ⏑ –	epitrite cretic
1046		
8.	– – ⏑ – – – ⏑ – – – ⏑ –	iambic metron 2 cretics

Notes:

2. In 1038 Murray's ἄλοχοι δ' ἐξέλειπον avoids the occurrence of hiatus without period close or rhetorical pause.
5. Accepting ἐπέπεσον in the antistrophe, with most editors.
7. In 1035 Heath's ἔκτανεν for κτεάνων or Seidler's ἔκταν' ὤν, would give metrical correspondence with the antistrophe, as well as supplying the missing finite verb; but see note ad loc.
8. In 1046 Campbell's Δαναΐδαις for τὸν Ἅιδα would give resolution of the final long in the first cretic, which is fairly common.

1009 ff. The most detailed account of the building of Troy is in *Il.* 21. 442 ff., where the story is that Poseidon and Apollo were obliged by Zeus to serve Laomedon for a year, during which Poseidon built the walls of Troy while Apollo tended cattle. The more widespread tradition, followed by Eur. here and in *Tro.* 4 ff., is that P. and A. jointly built the walls; see *Il.* 7. 452; Hes. *Cat.* fr. 83; Pind. *Ol.* 8. 31; Hellanicus, fr. 26 (*FHG* 1. 113).

1010. πόντιε: a common epithet of Poseidon and of sea nymphs, but elsewhere when used of a deity it is always combined with a proper name or with θεός, δαίμων, or the like, whereas the more distinctive γαιάοχος, rarely used except of Poseidon, can stand alone. Here however the phrase κυανέαις . . . πέλαγος serves to identify Poseidon.

κυανέαις: some MSS. have κυανέοις, but ἵππος is common gender and divine horses are more often mares; cf. Pind. *Ol.* 1. 41 (Poseidon); *Ph.* 3 (the Sungod); *El.* 466; *IT* 2. This colour, perhaps blue-grey, is attributed to the sea itself, e.g. *IT* 7, and regularly appears in epithets of sea deities, e.g. *Il.* 13. 563 Ποσείδων κυανοχαίτης; *Od.* 12. 60 κυανῶπις Ἀμφιτρίτη.

1011. ἅλιον πέλαγος: acc. of space over which, διφρεύων being intrans. Hyslop compares S. *Ai.* 845 τὸν αἰπὺν οὐρανὸν διφρηλατῶν. Though πέλαγος alone has come to mean 'sea', its original sense 'smooth surface' (Latin *aequor*) may be reflected in its frequent combination with ἁλός (*Od.* 5. 335) and with adjectives such as ἅλιον and πόντιον.

1014–18. The general sense of these lines is clearly 'Why did you abandon your handiwork to destruction in war?' To this question the answer was to be found in *Il.* 21. 450 ff.: Laomedon, king of Troy, refused to pay to Apollo and Poseidon the wages agreed for their year of service, and it might be more natural to ask, as Poseidon points out, why Apollo should have favoured the Trojans at all.

There are difficulties in the MS. reading and in corrections proposed. Some details in the text are doubtful. The MSS. give ὀργάναν, qualifying χέρα. The noun ὄργανον is sometimes used (like ἔργον) to denote the product of work, but there is no other example of the adjectival form in the classical period, except in an inscription, where it is an epithet of Athena. If the MS. reading is kept ὀργάναν χέρα 'the working hand' must stand for 'handiwork', τεκτοσύνας being a defining genitive 'a work of construction'. τέκτων is properly a carpenter distinguished from χαλκεύς 'metal worker' and λιθολόγος 'mason' (Thuc. 6. 44), but in *Alc.* 348 it means sculptor, and τεκτοσύνη could presumably be extended to any form of craftsmanship.

With Murray's ὀργᾶς ἂν the sense is 'on account of what angry passion did you abandon your handiwork . . .?'. He assumes that ὅς (ἑός), properly a third-person possessive, can be used of the second person. In epic usage there is some evidence for this. Schwyzer (*Gr. Gr.* 2. 204. 7) cites three examples from Homer and one from Hesiod, though in all there is a variant, e.g. *Il.* 19. 174, where instead of φρεσὶν ᾗσιν most editors read φρεσὶ σῇσιν. See Leaf on *Il.* 1. 393, where he defends this wider usage, and Ap. Rhod. 2. 332 ἑαῖς ἐνὶ χερσίν 'in your hands' and 4. 1015 ᾧ πατρί 'my father'; for a different view see Monro, *HG* 221–4. I know of no example in Lyric or Tragedy, though there is some support from the Attic use of ἑαυτόν for a first- and second-person reflexive. χέρα τεκτοσύνας is also difficult for 'handiwork in building'. χείρ is used, generally in pl., to mean 'craftsmanship' e.g. *Od.* 15. 126; Theoc. *Ep.* 8. 5, but there seems to be no example in the sense 'product of craftsmanship'.

ἄτιμον, in agreement with Τροίαν, is used proleptically to describe the effect of the action of the gods. Jackson's ὀρκανᾶν for ὀργάναν (*Marg. Scaen.* 242) among other difficulties involves taking ἄτιμον with χέρα 'the hand cheated of its reward', which makes the question τίνος οὕνεκα pointless.

προσθέντες for the MS. προθέντες is rightly accepted by all editors; for the sense 'assign to' 'give up to' cf. *Hec.* 368 Ἅιδῃ προστιθεῖσ' ἐμὸν δέμας; *Ba.* 676 τόνδε τῇ δίκῃ προσθήσομεν.

In Virgil, *Aen.* 2. 608 ff. Poseidon is represented as himself taking part in the destruction of his handiwork.

1021. ἁμίλλας . . . ἀστεφάνους: LSJ and most editors take this to mean contests not crowned by victory, i.e. defeats, but Hyslop and Norwood rightly take the epithet as distinguishing war from athletic contests where the prize was a garland; *ἀστεφάνους* thus reinforces *φονίους* 'deadly contests where no garland is the prize'. *ἅμιλλα* is often used in Pindar and elsewhere of sporting contests, and as both Apollo and Poseidon were patron deities of games at Delphi and the Isthmus, the contrast between those contests and these is specially appropriate.

1022. ἀπὸ . . . φθίμενοι βεβᾶσιν: 'they are dead and gone'; for this use of the perfect of *βαίνω* cf. A. *Pers.* 1002, 1003; *Alc.* 392 *βέβηκεν, οὐκέτ' ἔστιν Ἀδμήτου γυνή*; *Tro.* 582 *βέβακ' ὄλβος, βέβακε Τροία*; *Med.* 439; *Or.* 971.

1025. λέλαμπεν: perhaps the only example of a perfect with present sense from this verb.

1027. βέβακε: see on 1022; the repetition stresses the identical fate that overtook both victor and vanquished.

παλάμαις: *παλάμη* 'palm' is used, like *χείρ*, to denote 'violence' (cf. *παλαμναῖος* 'murderer'), and also 'cunning' 'trickery'. Both senses are appropriate here; for the latter cf. *Od.* 3. 235 *ὤλεθ' ὑπ' Αἰγίσθοιο δόλῳ καὶ ἧς ἀλόχοιο.*

1029. αὐτά . . . θεοῦ: with Murray's punctuation the sense is 'and she herself (Clytemnestra) taking death in return for death at her children's hands, felt the power of the god', but the construction is uncertain. The rather rare compound *ἐναλλάξασα* can probably mean, like the simple verb, either take or give in exchange; for the latter cf. *El.* 89 *φόνον φονεῦσι πατρὸς ἀλλάξων*, and this sense suits the aorist participle: 'having given death in exchange (the death of Ag. is so described in anticipation of the consequences), by her own death at the hands of her children she felt . . .' For *θανάτῳ πρὸς τέκνων* cf. S. *El.* 562 *πειθὼ κακοῦ πρὸς ἀνδρός*. It would, however, be simpler to read *θανάτου* and take the aorist participle to refer to the same time as the main verb: 'exchanging death for death . . .' With a stop after *ἀπηύρα*, *θανάτου* seems inevitable, since the verb in its present sense takes a genitive: 'She met with death at her children's hands. A god, a god it was whose oracular command turned upon her.'

1030. τέκνων: perhaps a generalizing plural really meaning Orestes; or Electra may be regarded as sharing responsibility: in *El.* 1225 she actually helps to guide the sword, and in *Or.* 32 says *κἀγὼ μετέσχον, οἷα δὴ γυνή, φόνου.**

1032 ff. In these three lines there seems to be some corruption for which I know of no satisfactory remedy.

Ἀργόθεν: the MS. reading *Ἀργόθεν* is improbable, since Orestes did not go to Delphi from Argos but from Phocis, where he was sent as a child; unless of course we assume that Eur. is following some different version of the Orestes legend of which there is no other trace. Murray's suggestion is presumably that the phrase *Ἀργόθεν* (*ὁ Ἀργόθεν*) *πορευθείς* could be merely a reference to his place of origin, but in the present context this is doubtful. Lenting's Ἄργος ἐμπορευθείς 'coming to Argos' is not satisfactory either, since in the next line the Chorus are still thinking of Or. at Delphi.

1034. ἀδύτων . . . κτεάνων: if the text is sound *ἀδύτων* is here the adjective, a very rare use, and *κτεάνων*, properly possessions, stands for part of the god's temple: 'entering the secret places' i.e. the oracular shrine; but this is an odd periphrasis for *ἄδυτον* and *κτεάνων* may be corrupt; see next note.

ματρὸς φονεὺς . . .: as the text stands there is no finite verb in the *ὅτε* clause and the second *νιν* (itself an awkward repetition) has no construction. Murray assumes that the Chorus are overcome with horror and before completing the sentence break off to express their incredulity that such could be Apollo's command. As Bornmann observes, this is not strictly aposiopesis, as in *El.* 1245 *Φοῖβός τε, Φοῖβος—ἀλλ', ἄναξ γάρ ἐστ' ἐμός, σιγῶ*, where the words of condemnation are suppressed; here the accepted version is already clearly given in *θεοῦ . . . ἐπεστράφη* and *ματρὸς φονεύς*, though the Chorus go on to say that they do not believe it. In any case I know no other example of such breaking off in choral lyric, and Kranz regards it as alien to this style (*Stasimon*, p. 305, n. on p. 180). Heath's *ἔκτανεν* for *κτεάνων* or Seidler's *ἔκταν' ὤν* supply the missing verb (and improve the metre), but if either is right *ἐπιβάς* can hardly stand.

1036. πῶς πείθομαι: the indicative probably expresses a more emphatic incredulity than the deliberative subjunctive.

1037 ff. ἀγόρους: the confusion in the MSS. (see app. crit.) probably arose from *γ* miscopied as *χ*, *ἀγορ* being then written as a correction over *ἀχορους* and subsequently inserted, with different endings, in the text; see Zuntz, op. cit. 270. *ἄγορος* is an alternative form of *ἀγόρα*, found only in Euripidean lyric: *HF* 412 *ἄγορον ἁλίσας φίλων*; *IT* 1096 *ποθοῦσ' Ἑλλάνων ἀγόρους*; *El.* 723. Like *ἀγόρα* it can presumably mean either 'assembly' or 'place of assembly', but in two at least of the examples it means 'assembly' and so probably here: 'And many women in the assemblies of the Greeks sang dirges for their ill-fated children, and wives left their homes to go to another lord.'

ἄλοχοι δ' ἐξέλειπον: Murray's conjecture (actually anticipated by Burges) gives us two classes of women: mothers lamenting their children and wives going to another bedfellow. If *ἀγόρους* means 'assemblies' they must be Greek women, so that *στοναχὰς* refers to formal laments for sons fallen in war and *ἄλοχοι* are war-widows who pass to another husband. Thus strophe (*b*) deals with the fate of the Greek leaders, and the antistrophe with the Greeks in general; and in the whole stasimon the first pair of stanzas refers to the fate of Troy, the second to that of the Greeks.

1041. οὐχὶ σοὶ μόνᾳ: for this common consolatory motif in almost the same words cf. *Med.* 1017; *Hipp.* 834; *Hel.* 464; S. *El.* 153.

To whom does σοί refer? Direct address to an individual occurs elsewhere in choral lyric, but the person referred to is either present (e.g. Andromache in the parodos of this play, where in fact the whole song is addressed to her), or has been mentioned (e.g. Deianeira in S. *Tr.* 121, 126, where the reference is unmistakable). Here, of the two candidates Hermione (Méridier, Norwood) is ruled out, since in addition to being unsuitable in the context she has not been referred to and cannot be present, and Kamerbeek and others rightly prefer Andromache. If the stanza deals mainly with the distress of the Greeks it is appropriate that Andr. and her φίλοι (Hector, Priam, and her kinsfolk) should be contrasted with them; but there has been no mention of her and unless she is present (see note on 1047) the reference is unusually abrupt and obscure.*

1044 ff. In 1046 τόν, added on metrical grounds, is unsatisfactory and the improbability of Ἅιδα φόνον has been demonstrated by A. Y. Campbell in *CR* 46 (1932), 196–7. I should accept, with most modern editors, Campbell's Δαναΐδαις φόνον, but I am less happy about his interpretation. He translates (or paraphrases): 'Greece too has suffered, has suffered greatly: the storm-cloud that had so long brooded over Troy has since crossed the Aegaean; it has lowered also above fields which the war had *not* ravaged; it has drizzled blood upon the Danaans.' But, allowing for lyric compression, can διέβα Φρυγῶν mean 'it has brooded over Troy and crossed the Aegaean'? διαβαίνω does not elsewhere govern a genitive and Φρυγῶν goes more naturally with γύας. Moreover it was on the plains of Troy, not in Greece, that Greek women lost their sons and husbands. Perhaps νόσος, not an obvious word for these results of war, means rather 'war-madness', as νοσεῖν does (also with reference to the Trojan War) in *IA* 411 Ἑλλὰς δὲ σὺν σοὶ κατὰ θεὸν νοσεῖ τινα. The following words διέβα . . . γύας could then be more naturally construed: 'the war-cloud crossed over even to the fertile lands of the Phrygians'; but it brought death to Danaans as much as to Trojans.

In the last lines of this stasimon, as Aldrich puts it, 'the background motif of the Trojan legend, which has increased almost like an ominous drum beat throughout the play, reaches its fullest expression'.

Exodus: 1047–1288

Peleus is accompanied by one or more attendants (1067) and perhaps brings with him Andromache and her child (see discussion in next paragraph). If so they are all within range of the Chorus by 1041, where the reference to Andromache in σοι would be indicated by look and gesture. Peleus' reason for returning is that he has heard a rumour of Hermione's departure and has come to investigate. The real reason for bringing him back is that he must be present to hear the messenger speech, to receive and mourn the dead Neoptolemus, and finally to accept the consolations of his divine consort. It is pointless to ask how and where the rumour reached him, since Eur. was probably not interested in the time-table and other details of events off-stage.

Does he bring with him Andromache and the child? There is no indication in the text and opinion is divided. In favour of their return is that *σοί* ought to refer to Andromache, and yet it is hard to see how this could be indicated unless she is present, and that in 1246 *παῖδα τόνδε* suggests that the child is present and therefore presumably the mother too. This second point is not decisive, since the deictic pronoun can certainly be used of someone not physically present; see note on 1243. Against their return is the fact that there is no indication of A.'s presence, that from 1047 to the end she does not speak,[1] and that the only references to her, in 1059 and 1243, would, if anything, suggest that she is not present; see note ad loc. None of these points is conclusive. There is at least one similar situation, at the end of the *Ajax* of Sophocles, where Tecmessa and her son enter at 1168 and are undoubtedly present for the last 250 lines but do not speak; but at least in 1169–70 their presence and its purpose are clearly stated, and the child is directly addressed in 1180 and 1409. The only argument on either side that seems to me cogent is that in the bare text *σοί* (1041) is intolerably abrupt and obscure, and no clarification by stage business is possible unless Andromache is present. If so, no doubt even her silent presence during the closing scenes would help to give unity to the play, though only of a rather formal kind. In that case, however, it is odd that no more use is made of her. Tecmessa in the *Ajax* must be a *κωφὸν πρόσωπον* since there are three other speaking parts, but this does not apply to Andromache; there is plenty of time for the messenger to retire and return as Thetis. For Erbse's view of the significance of A.'s silent presence see Introduction, p. 10.*

1051. τῶν . . . φίλων: he is thinking of course of Neoptolemus.

1052. ἐκπονεῖν: a favourite word of Eur. (22 exx., Aesch. 1, Soph. 0) meaning exert oneself over somebody or something, e.g. *Ion* 1355 *τὴν τεκοῦσαν ἐκπόνει* 'exert yourself in the search for her'; *Hipp. τὰ χρηστὰ . . . οὐκ ἐκπονοῦμεν* 'exert ourselves to bring to completion'. Here lit. 'exert themselves over the fortunes of the absent' i.e. strive to safeguard their interests. LSJ oddly take this passage with *Ion* 1355 and trans. 'work out by searching'.

1053. σαφῶς: the adverb picks up *σαφῆ λόγον* in 1048 but has a slightly different sense: not 'clearly' but 'truly', 'correctly'; cf. Thuc. 1. 22 *τῶν γενομένων τὸ σαφές* 'the truth about the past', contrasted with *τὸ μυθῶδες*; *Or.* 1155 *φίλος σαφής* 'a true friend'.

[1] Unless some line attributions are wrong, and e.g. 1197–9 were spoken by Andromache.

1056. διαπέραινέ μοι: to fill up the line; cf. *Med.* 701 *πέραινέ μοι λόγον*; *Or.* 747 *τόδε γὰρ εἰδέναι θέλω*, completing a trochaic tetrameter, and see Gross, *Die Stichomythie*, pp. 88–9. The compound *διαπεραίνω* is a prosaic word, very common in philosophic writers and not found in Aesch. or Soph.

1057. The Chorus do not take seriously Hermione's fears for her life (810, 927).

1063. σῷ: as *παῖς παιδός* is so often treated by Eur. as a single word meaning 'grandson', e.g. 584 *οὑμὸς . . . παῖς παιδός*, *Ba.* 1327 *σὸς . . . παῖς παιδός* and perhaps *IT* 807, Murray is probably right to print Lobeck's slight correction of the MS. reading *σοῦ*.

1064–5. Peleus, not having heard Or.'s words in 995 ff., naturally assumes that *πορσύνων μόρον* means physical attack. The reply of the Chorus leader is not a precise answer, and does not explicitly reject or confirm P.'s assumption; *Δελφῶν μέτα* is ambiguous and can mean either 'in company with' or 'by aid of', 'in co-operation with'.

1066–7. τόδ' ἤδη δεινόν: 'this is terrible indeed.' For this idiomatic use of *ἤδη* to mark a climax, cf. Ar. *Ach.* *τοῦτο τοὔπος δεινὸν ἤδη*; *Vesp.* 426 *τοῦτο μέντοι δεινὸν ἤδη*; *Ecc.* 645; Xen. *Mem.* 2. 1. 14 *τοῦτο μέντοι ἤδη λέγεις δεινὸν πάλαισμα.* The phrase may have become a conversational idiom, though this use of *ἤδη* is more widespread, e.g. S. *OC* 1586 *τοῦτ' ἐστὶν ἤδη κἀποθαυμάσαι πρέπον.*

οὐ . . . χωρήσεταί τις; a common form of command implying the presence of attendants, none of whom are ever named in Tragedy; cf. *Ba.* 346 *στειχέτω τις*, and in less peremptory tone *Hel.* 892 *τίς εἶσι σημανῶν; Ba.* 1257 *τίς ἂν καλέσειεν;* S. *OT* 1069, 1154.

1068. τἀνθάδ' ὄντα: i.e. the murderous intentions of Or. described in 1061–5.

τοῖς ἐκεῖ . . . φίλοις: N. and his attendants, or possibly a generalizing plural, as in 1051, actually denoting N. himself.

1070–1165.

Introductory dialogue between messenger, Peleus and Chorus leader, followed by a messenger speech. (Strictly speaking the *ἄγγελος* of Attic Tragedy is not a messenger, since, as Barrett observes on *Hipp.* 1151, he brings news, not a message; but 'reporter' or 'announcer' have acquired special meanings and the conventional translation must be accepted.) The messenger speech is by no means characteristic of Aeschylus, but to judge by Sophocles and Euripides it became a regular ingredient in the Tragedy of their day. In Eur. there is at least one such speech in every play except *Alcestis*, *Hecuba* (where it is replaced by the speech of Talthybios 518–82), and *Troades*; in three plays there are two messenger speeches and in *Phoenissae* four. Many of these are brilliant examples of swift and vivid narration and no doubt the audience settled down to enjoy these set pieces for themselves as well as for their contributions to the plot. It is perhaps not surprising that, particularly in Eur., certain features regularly recur, e.g. there is always (except in *IA* 415 ff.) a passage of dialogue in which at some point the essential news is briefly announced (1073), and in answer to a request for details (1083) the main narrative follows. See also notes on 1070 and 1085.

1070. The messenger, who is as usual a loyal servant of the victim of disaster (1110), enters unannounced (though not unexpected by the audience). This is usual in Eur. where his entry is immediately preceded by a choral ode, but where there is preceding dialogue he is always announced, except in *IA* 415 and here; in both passages the abrupt entrance is dramatically effective and here the shock is enhanced by the opening words of lamentation.

τλήμων: here the sense is 'unhappy'; cf. the messenger's opening words in *Ph.* 1335 *ὦ τάλας ἐγώ, τίν' εἴπω μῦθον* . . . For the article cf. *Ba.* 1361 *οὐδὲ παύσομαι κακῶν ὁ τλήμων*; *Hipp.* 1066.

1071. φίλοισι: the Chorus and all loyal subjects of Neoptolemus.

1072. πρόμαντις θυμός: cf. A. *Pers.* 10 *κακόμαντις θυμός*, *Ag.* 977 *καρδίας τερασκόπου*, and Hamlet's 'prophetic soul'. In fact after the warning of the Chorus in 1063 and the opening words of the messenger no one could fail to foresee the worst.

τι: euphemistic for something disastrous; cf. S. *Tr.* 305 *μήδ', εἴ τι δράσεις, τῇσδέ γε ζώσης ἔτι*; Dem. 4. 11 *ἂν οὗτός τι πάθῃ*; Thuc. 2. 74.

1075. This line is not found in MOD, and some scholars follow Wecklein in regarding it as an interpolation, on the ground that it establishes the presence of Or., which they consider unacceptable. But after *πληγὰς ἔχει*, equivalent to a passive, an indication of the agent might be expected, and if the line as we have it is not genuine why was it interpolated in LP? At first sight this line appears to refer to participation by Or., but it is also possible that the messenger used this form of expression to link together the Delphians, who actually struck the blows, and Or., who was equally responsible.

1076. ἆ ἆ: perhaps we should not try to pin down too precisely the force of this exclamation, but it is a fact of usage in drama that *ἆ* four times repeated is used to indicate distress in S. *Ph.* 732, 739 and [E.] *Rh.* 749, whereas a single or double *ἆ* almost always, as here, expresses a protest or at least remonstrance, and is generally followed by a prohibition or indignant question; cf. *Or.* 1598, *Alc.* 526, *Med.* 1056, *Hel.* 445, *Cyc.* 565 *ἆ ἆ, τί δράσεις*, S. *OT* 1147, *Ph.* 1300. So also in four paratragic passages in Aristophanes. The schol. on Ar. *Pl.* 127 calls it *ἐπίρρημα ἐκπλήξεως*, but the only passages where this seems correct are *Ba.* 586 and 596 and possibly A. *Ch.* 1046, though there is protest as well as horror in the cry of Orestes.

δράσεις: one might expect some part of *πάσχειν*, as in a similar situation in Ar. *V.* 995 *πάτερ, τί πέπονθας; . . . ἔπαιρε σαυτόν*, but *πάσχειν* and *δρᾶν* are sometimes interchangeable; cf. *Hcld.* 176 *μήδ', ὅπερ φιλεῖτε δρᾶν, πάθῃς συ τοῦτο.*

μὴ πέσῃς: the old man first totters and then fails (*ἔπαιρε σαυτόν*) but does not actually faint. Similarly in *Hec.* 440 *προλείπω* cannot mean swoon since Hecuba does not stop talking.

1077. ἔπαιρε σαυτόν: a stock expression; cf. 717 above; *Hcld.* 635; *Alc.* 250; Ar. *V.* 996.

οὐδέν εἰμ'· ἀπωλόμην: cf. S. *El.* 677 *ἀπωλόμην δύστηνος οὐδέν εἰμ' ἔτι*; E. *Hec.* 440; *Hel.* 1194 *ὄλωλα· φροῦδα τἀμὰ κοὐδέν εἰμ' ἔτι.* The somewhat stereotyped nature of these cries does not of course either preclude or attest genuine emotion.

1078. φροῦδα δ' ἄρθρα μου κάτω: *Σ* paraphrases *ἀφανής εἰμι καὶ εἰς Ἅιδου βαδίζω* and Méridier follows with 'disparus sont mes membres; ils sont déjà dans l'Hadès!' Wecklein, less improbably, takes *φροῦδα κάτω* to mean collapsing on the ground; but perhaps the sense is not 'downwards', but 'beneath me'. *φροῦδος* is often used of failure of bodily strength or of some faculty, and in this sense elsewhere stands alone; e.g. *Hcld.* 702–3 *λῆμα μὲν . . . σῶμα δὲ φροῦδον*; *Or.* 390 *τὸ σῶμα φροῦδον*; S. fr. 949 *νοῦς φροῦδος*. So here *ἄρθρα κάτω* could go together in the sense 'lower limbs' (cf. Pl. *Leg.* 794 d *τὰ κάτω τῶν μελῶν*), but this is rather prosaic in the context.

E.'s frequent use of *φροῦδος*, sometimes repeated, as here and in *Hec.* 159, is parodied in the fivefold repetition in Ar. *Nub.* 718–22; cf. also Ar. *Ra.* 1343.

1079–80. εἰ καὶ . . . χρῄζεις: 'if you really *want* to help'. Cf. S. *Tr.* *εἰ καὶ τοῦτ' ἔτλη* (where, as Jebb observes, *καί* goes with the whole phrase, not only with *τοῦτο*) 'if he really endured this', not 'this too'; *Aj.* 1132 *εἰ καὶ ζῇς θανών* 'if you are really slain and living'. In translating emphasis may fall on *χρῄζεις* which is rather far away from *καί*, but *καί* should probably be regarded as strictly affecting the whole phrase that follows, as in the examples from Sophocles. Among emendations Jackson's *εἰ σοὶ καὶ φίλοις* (*Marg. Scaen.* 52) is the most plausible, but the text can stand.

σοῖς φίλοις ἀμυναθεῖν: *Σ* takes *ἀμυναθεῖν* to mean 'avenge' (*εἰς ἐκδίκησίν τι πρᾶξαι*); so also Méridier 'venger les tiens'. *ἀμύνειν* with dat. strictly means 'defend', 'help', but to the dead help may take the form of vengeance. In *El.* 976 *καὶ μή γ' ἀμύνων πατρὶ δυσσεβὴς ἔσῃ* the sense is hardly distinguishable from *πατρὶ τιμωρῶν σέθεν* 'avenging your father' in 974; so also *Or.* 556. If that is the sense here *φίλοις* will be a generalizing plural referring to Neoptolemus. We must not ask what action the messenger can have in mind; the real purpose of his words is to revive the old man's spirit.

1081. ἐσχάτοις τέρμασιν: for the redundant expression cf. *Hcld.* 278–9 *Ἀλκάθου δ' ἐπ' ἐσχάτοις . . . τέρμασιν*; S. *Tr.* 1256 *τελευτὴ ὑστάτη.*

1084 δ': in prose *γάρ* would be used to indicate the causal connection. For the use of *δέ* in such contexts see *GP* 169 (i); as might be expected it is far more common in verse than in prose.

1085 ἐπεί: it is an instance of the Euripidean tendency not to vary his formula that in thirteen out of twenty messenger speeches the narrative begins with an *ἐπεί* clause.

κλεινόν: a favourite epithet in Eur. for places and people, used eight times of Athens and certainly appropriate for Delphi, perhaps the most renowned spot in Hellas.

Φοίβου πέδον: for the acc. see on *ἑστίαν* in 3. The same phrase is used for the temple and precinct in *IT* 972, and in A. *Ch.* 1036 *Λοξίου πέδον* is in apposition to *μεσόμφαλον ἵδρυμα*.

1086–7. διεξόδους: apart from this passage and a zoological allusion in S. fr. 477 the word is practically confined to prose and common in scientific contexts. For the sense 'orbit' of the sun cf. Hdt. 2. 24. Here the epic form *φαεννάς* may give the whole periphrasis a more poetic tinge.

LSJ and some editors take *διεξόδους* as object of *διδόντες* and *ὄμματα* as object of *ἐξεπίμπλαμεν* in the sense 'satiate': 'devoting three bright circuits of the sun to sight-seeing we looked our fill'. But in Eur. *ἐκπίμπλημι*, which occurs eighteen times, is always used to mean 'fill up', 'complete' a space or period of time, e.g. *δέκ' ἐκπλήσας ἔτη Or.* 657 and *Tro.* 433 (except in *Ph.* 1426, where it means to fulfil a curse), and never means 'satisfy'. Thus Euripidean usage favours taking *διεξόδους* as the object of *ἐξεπίμπλαμεν* 'we spent three days', and *ὄμματα* as object of *δίδοντες*, for which cf. *Or.* 893–4 *τὸ δ' ὄμμ' . . . ἐδίδου τοῖσιν Αἰγίσθου φίλοις*; *Ph.* 462 *ὅταν . . . ὄμματ' ὄμμασιν διδῷ*.

1088. ἦν ἄρ': perhaps with a note of bitterness: 'this it seems aroused suspicion.' Sight-seeing was presumably common enough at Delphi, but in view of his previous record (51–3, 1106–7) N. was perhaps inviting suspicion if he spent three days in Delphi without informing the authorities of his desire to propitiate Apollo.

συστάσεις and **κύκλους** are virtually synonymous. Cf. Xen. *Anab.* 5. 7. 2 (of a mutinous assembly) *καὶ σύλλογοι ἐγίγνοντο καὶ κύκλοι συνίσταντο.*

1091. εἰς οὓς ἑκάστῳ: we need not ask how the messenger knows this; though he speaks in character he is also the poet's mouthpiece for convenience in narration.

1092. διαστείχει: such repetition with no special point sounds to us careless but is not rare in Eur.

1093. γύαλα: the word seems to mean a rounded hollow and so, as applied to localities, a glen or valley. In the plural it is regularly used of the Delphic precinct, e.g. *Ph.* 237 *μεσόμφαλα γύαλα Φοίβου*, though perhaps not always in quite the same sense. In Hes. *Theog.* 499 *γυάλοις ὕπο Παρνησοῖο* and *HH* 3. 396 it seems to mean the hollow in the steep mountain side containing temple and precinct; in *Ion* 76 δαφνώδη γύαλα τάδε the reference must be to a laurel grove near the temple. Here γύαλα is in apposition to θησαυρούς, which probably means the 'treasuries' set up by Greek states along the Sacred Way, and means either the precinct in general or that particular part of it. (γύαλον can also be used of a cave, as in S. *Phil.* 1081 ὦ κοίλας πέτρας γύαλον, but there is no evidence that it was ever used, as Bayfield suggested, of the prophetic cavern in the adyton, and hence came to be used of the whole sanctuary.)

θεοῦ . . . βροτῶν: the order helps to point the antithesis: the wealth of the god consists in the offerings of mortals.

1094. πάρος: on the previous occasion, referred to in 53 above, Eur. represents N.'s intention as in a sense hostile, but makes no reference to the version in which when refused satisfaction he began to plunder and burn, or that he went with the sole purpose of plundering the temple (Apollod. *Epit.* 6. 14; Schol. P. *Nem.* 7. 58; Strabo 9. 4. 21), but this tradition may have suggested the accusation here given to Orestes.

1096. ῥόθιον . . . κακόν: 'a wave of malice and resentment began to surge through the town.' The primary sense of ῥόθος and cognates seems to be a combination of noise and movement, and these words are most often used of the surge and roar of the waves, and hence also of a shouting and surging crowd, e.g. Hes. *WD* 220 τῆς Δίκης ῥόθος ἑλκομένης 'the angry tumult when Justice is dragged away'; cf. S. *Ant.* 259 λόγοι δ' ἐν ἀλλήλοισιν ἐρρόθουν κακοί; ibid. 413 κινῶν ἄνδρ' ἀνὴρ ἐπιρρόθοις | κακοῖσιν.

1097–8. Verrall's correction (merely a change of word division) printed in OCT makes ἀρχαί the subject of ἐτάξαντο, the ἀρχαί being divided into those filling the council chamber (presumably the civic authorities) and those in charge of the god's treasures. The first τε connects this whole sentence with the previous one, the second and third link together two clauses, participial and relative. For ἀρχαί = οἱ ἄρχοντες cf. *Ion* 1111 ἀρχαὶ ἀπιχώριοι 'the local authorities', and for πληροῦν in this context cf. Ar. *Ecc.* 89 πληρουμένης τῆς ἐκκλησίας; A. *Eu.* 570. We should however expect οἱ πληροῦντες for 'those filling . . .', and it looks as though ἀρχαί and ἰδίᾳ are meant to distinguish two groups.

All editors except Murray retain the MS. reading given in the apparatus criticus. In this the two finite verbs ἐπληροῦντο and ἐτάξαντο are linked by the double τε, the first of the pair being slightly postponed, and the task of placing a guard is given to the temple officials. For the absolute use of πληροῦσθαι cf. *IT* 306 πολλοὶ δ' ἐπληρώθημεν. The subjects of both verbs however are still included in ἀρχαί. Wecklein's tentative εἰς τὰ βουλευτήρια might enable ἀρχαί and ἰδίᾳ to be distinct, but if ἀρχαί τε and ἰδίᾳ τε are in correspondence either the sentence begins abruptly without a connecting particle or τε after ἀρχαί looks both backwards to the previous sentence and forwards.

In view of these difficulties, perhaps δ' has (as often) been corrupted to τ'. If we read ἀρχαὶ δ' ἐπληροῦντ' ἐς τὰ βουλευτήρια ἰδίᾳ θ' ὅσοι . . ., the sense is 'and the civic authorities flocked into the council chamber and unofficially (i.e. not waiting for the ἀρχαί) those responsible for temple treasures posted a guard'. The single connective τε is of course common in verse.*

There is no indication of what part these sentries took in the subsequent proceedings.

1098. χρημάτων: ἐφίσταμαι generally governs a dative, but the genitive is found in Hdt. 7. 117; cf. ἐπιστατεῖν, which in the sense 'to be in charge of' regularly governs a genitive, and a dative in the sense 'to be set over'.

1099. περιστύλοις δόμοις: δόμος, in sing. and pl., is often used of a god's house, i.e. temple, generally accompanied by θεοῦ or the name of a deity but sometimes standing alone where the context makes the meaning clear, e.g. *IT* 1079; *Hcld.* 695. Here we have Φοίβου ναόν in 1095, and the epithet περιστύλοις must refer to the temple, as being the only building in the precinct with columns round it as distinct from those with columnar porches. Similar epithets appear elsewhere, e.g. S. *Ant.* 285 ἀμφικίονας ναούς, but generally where there is occasion to stress the stateliness and splendour of the building, whereas here it is merely an indication of where the guard was posted. Wecklein and Méridier print δρόμοις, the reading in MO (for similar confusion cf. *Hcld.* 486 and *Hel.* 1671), the whole phrase denoting the colonnades round the temple: but I do not know any example of δρόμος in this sense and the adj. περίστυλος cannot strictly qualify anything but the temple. If this is the sense required, perhaps we should read δόμου or δόμων and the περιστύλοις as a noun.

1100–1157.

The narrative of events leading to the death of N. is vivid and exciting, but for us some details are obscure and scholars have disagreed on the relation of some parts of the narrative to what is known or conjectured about the topography of the sacred precinct. The dramatic date is of course shortly after the Trojan War, but dramatist and audience would have in mind the fifth, 'Alcmaeonid' temple, constructed at the end of the sixth century, of which we have practically no direct knowledge. The cause and extent of the damage which led to the rebuilding of the temple in 370–330 B.C. remain uncertain, but it is in any case likely that the new building was similar in plan and dimensions to the old. Some at any rate of the audience would presumably relate the narrative to what they had seen or heard of the salient features of the fifth-century temple, but they might not remember details or look for precise correspondence to what they did remember.

It is clear that at 1110–12 N. enters the temple. Wieseler (*Jahrb. f. Philol.* 1859, 690 ff.) holds that the rest of the action takes place within the temple; so also J. Fontenrose (*The Cult and Myth of Pyrros at Delphi*, pp. 213–18). Ph.-E. Legrand (*REG* 14 (1901), 62 ff.) argues that after the first attack on N. inside the temple, the rest of the action, including the actual murder, takes place outside near the Altar of Chios. There are difficulties about both interpretations, and in the latest discussion J. Pouilloux (*Énigmes à Delphes*, ch. iv, pp. 102–22) takes it that N. was first attacked as he stood near an altar close to the adyton; that he then retreated through the cella and out to the Altar of Chios, on which he made a stand; that being surrounded there and bombarded with missiles he leapt down right on to the steps leading to the pronaos and pursued some of his enemies into the temple, where he would have mastered them had not the cry of Apollo himself from the inner shrine rallied the Delphians, so that in the end N. was struck down near to the altar at which he had prayed to the god. This account is not free from difficulties and obscurities but seems with some modification the most plausible. See further notes on 1113, 1115, 1120–1, 1139, 1156–7.

Since N. goes alone into the temple (1111), the man who tells the tale apparently watches events from a position somewhere near the Altar of Chios, and some have drawn inferences from this about the scene of the action. Thus Legrand (op. cit.) argues that the messenger could not have observed what was happening unless everything took place outside the temple. Pouilloux thinks it possible to distinguish between the more exact account of events which (on his view) the narrator would see clearly and the more general impression of events within the temple, for which he would rely on sounds and occasional glimpses. All this, however, does not allow for the conventional licence of the narrator to report what in fact he could not have observed. See notes on 1091, 1152–4, *Ba.* 686–8 and 765–8 (with Dodds's notes), and *Or.* 1404 ff.

1100. μῆλα: a sacrifice was a necessary preliminary to approaching the god either for an oracular response or for any other purpose; cf. *Ion* 228 *ἐπὶ δ' ἀσφάκτοις μήλοισι δόμων μὴ πάριτ' ἐς μυχόν.*

φυλλάδος Παρνασίας παιδεύματ': provision of animals for sacrifice was perhaps a profitable line for local inhabitants. *παίδευμα* is properly used of someone who is 'brought up', as in *Hipp.* 11. For the metaphorical use applied to animals and birds cf. fr. 27. 5 *χθονίων ἀερίων τε . . . παιδεύματα.*

1101. τῶνδε: i.e. the plot of Orestes.

1102. ἐσχάραις: this must be an altar outside the temple, and Eur. probably has in mind the Altar of Chios. *ἐσχάρα* strictly means sacrificial hearth (hollowed out in the ground) as opposed to *βωμός*, a structural altar, but it is also used of that part of a *βωμός*, perhaps a hollow on the surface, on which victims were sacrificed, as in 1138 *βωμοῦ δεξίμηλον ἐσχάραν*, and, as here, for the altar as a whole considered as a sacrificial table.

1103. προξένοισι: *πρόξενοι* at Delphi were not as elsewhere in special relationship with particular states but acted on behalf of visitors generally; nobody could approach the god with any prayer or question unless sponsored by Delphian officials.

1104–5. τί σοι . . . κατευξώμεσθα; this does not seem to preclude N. from praying directly to the god; see 1113, 1117.

1106–11. N.'s profession of repentance comes too late: the slanders of Orestes have taken firm hold and N., though he does not yet know it, is thought to be insincere.

1111–12. ἔρχεται: N. now goes forward alone. His companions, presumably at least three including the messenger (1158–9, 1166), must have remained outside the temple. There is no reference to any intervention on their part during subsequent attacks upon N.

ἀνακτόρων κρηπῖδος ἐντός: *κρῆπις* in this context means the platform (stylobate) on which the pillars rested, including the steps by which it was reached. Similarly in *HF* 984 *ἀμφὶ βωμίαν | ἔπτηξε κρηπῖδ'* the sense is 'at the altar steps'. The whole phrase is a condensed expression for 'he mounted the steps and entered the shrine'.

1112. πάρος χρηστηρίων: *χρηστήριον* has three chief senses: (1) the seat of an oracle, (2) an oracular response, (3) a sacrificial victim. The third sense is possible here, but probably it means the inner shrine where the response was given; cf. Hdt. 6. 19 *ἱρὸν τὸ ἐν Διδύμοισι, ὁ νηός τε καὶ τὸ χρηστήριον*, and for the plural *Ion* 409 *οὐκ ἄπαιδά με . . . ἥξειν . . . ἐκ χρηστηρίων*.

1113. τυγχάνει δ' ἐν ἐμπύροις: for the omission of *ὤν* cf. S. *El.* 46 *νῦν ἄγροισι τυγχάνει*; *Ai.* 9; Ar. *Ecc.* 1141.

ἔμπυρα always refers to burnt sacrifice and can hardly denote the ever-burning flame on the altar of Hestia, as Pouilloux holds. Méridier refers to an altar of Poseidon in the NE. corner of the cella where certain portions of victims were burnt; but perhaps no very specific reference is intended. At any rate N. is now close to the adyton, and engaged in further sacrificial rites before his prayer to Apollo. With the expression *ἐν ἐμπύροις εἶναι* compare *IT* 16 *ἐς ἔμπυρ' ἦλθε*.

1114. †ξιφήρης ἆρ'†: the MSS. offer the unmetrical *ἄρα* and the simplest change is to read *ἆρα*, usually interrogative but well attested as equivalent to *ἄρα*, which gives a possible sense here; see *GP* 44–5, I (2). There is no objection to *ξιφήρης* and most editors print the line without obeli. On the other hand *ἄρα* indicating surprise at something that has turned out contrary to expectation is not really appropriate here, and its use to express a lively feeling of interest, though common in Epic and Lyric, is doubtful for Tragedy (*GP* 35). Among emendations the most plausible is Hermann's *ἀνθυφειστήκει*. For *ὑφίστημι* cf. Hdt. 5. 92η. 3 *ὑποστήσας τοὺς δορυφόρους*; id. 8. 91 *Αἰγινῆται ὑποστάντες*, where the intrans. tense may mean 'lying concealed'.

1115. δάφνῃ σκιασθείς: the location of the ambush has been disputed.

Wilamowitz thought the attackers were concealed in a laurel grove by the site of the temple, comparing the δαφνώδη γύαλα into which Hermes retired in *Ion* 76; but that was in order to watch events outside the temple. Others have suggested that they lurk in a corner of the main temple, concealing their presence with laurel branches. There was however a tradition that a laurel grew near to the tripod (see, e.g., Ar. *Pl.* 213, with the scholiast's comment, and Amandry, *La Mantique Apollinienne à Delphes*, pp. 133–4), and if as some think the adyton was not separated from the rest of the temple except perhaps by a low wall, the assassins may have been waiting in the adyton itself.

1115–16. There are two possible interpretations of this sentence. If we take ὧν as masculine and place a comma after εἷς ἦν, ὧν will refer to the members of the λόχος and we have a decisive reference to the presence of Or. among them. The alternative is to take ὧν as neuter, referring to the whole plot and picked up by ἁπάντων τῶνδε. For this anticipatory use of the relative see notes on 650 and 710. If the two previous examples of this rare usage are accepted it is the more likely that we have another example here. A further argument for this interpretation is the idiomatic juxtaposition of εἷς and ἁπάντων, here stressing the sole responsibility of Or. for all that happens. Lesky (op. cit. 151, n. 15) counts fifty-seven examples in Eur. alone of this juxtaposition of εἷς with words for 'all' or 'many'. Lesky also thinks that a stop after ἦν gives an abnormal and unsatisfactory rhythm, but it is not in fact particularly rare.

1117. κατ' ὄμμα: probably 'in full sight of all', as in 1064. κατ' ὄμμα at the beginning of the sentence is the antithesis of λάθρᾳ at the end, and there is again, as Bornmann observes, emphasis on the contrast between the open unsuspicious bearing of N. and the treachery of his enemies.

1118. ὀξυθήκτοις: a conventional epithet, repeated in 1150; cf. Homeric ὀξέϊ χαλκῷ. Here it may be intended to add emphasis to the contrast with the unsuspecting and unprotected victim.

1119. ἀτευχῆ: the only other example I know is *AP* 9. 320, where it seems to refer to arms offensive and defensive. Here, however, it probably means without defensive armour. In 1121 N. draws his sword and then takes down from a pillar τεύχη, presumably shield and helmet. In Homer and elsewhere τεύχη often denotes specifically defensive armour. The ordinary word for 'unarmed' ἄοπλος (ἄνοπλος) can also mean either 'weaponless' (Pl. *Prt.* 321 c) or without defensive armour (Hdt. 9. 62).

1120. χωρεῖ δὲ πρύμναν: πρύμνην ἀνακρούεσθαι was the technical term for 'to back water', as in Hdt. 8. 84, Thuc. 1. 50, and is used metaphorically of a man in Ar. *V.* 399. Hence Scaliger's κρούει, accepted by Wilamowitz; but except in Polybius only the middle is so used, and in any case *πρύμναν χωρεῖν* is a natural variant, though there may be no other example.

Fontenrose translates 'steps back' and takes 1120–3 to describe a series of almost simultaneous actions: N. steps back, draws his sword, snatches armour from a wall, and mounts an altar, all within the cella. But he has just backed away from one altar; would there be another just behind him? Pouilloux and Legrand think that he gradually retreats backwards through the cella (presumably followed by his assailants and menacing them with his sword), takes down armour when he reaches the pronaos (see on 1121–2), and finally mounts the Altar of Chios outside the entrance. Certainly *χωρεῖν πρύμναν* could refer to retreat for some distance, and we need not assume with Fontenrose that N. would have to pass through a hostile crowd of Delphians; it is perhaps more natural to suppose that they were waiting outside. How in that case he reached the altar we are not told and on this view a long retreat (in the fourth-century temple a distance of 20 to 25 yards) is compressed into a short sentence; but such omission and compression are paralleled by the absence of any specific reference to sacrifice after 1102, and in 1111–13 where Eur. moves N. from outside the temple to the adyton in a few words.

1121–2. ἐξέλκει: some editors supply *πόδα*, comparing *Ph.* 304 *γηραιὸν πόδ' ἕλκω*; S. *Ph.* 291 *δύστηνον ἐξέλκων πόδα*, but these phrases describe slow or painful movement, whereas N. though slightly wounded is evidently still strong and active. It is better to supply *ξίφος*; cf. Hec. 543 *φάσγανον ἐξεῖλκε κολεοῦ*. It may be accidental that this ellipse, familiar in English, is not found elsewhere in Greek.

παραστάδος κρεμαστὰ τεύχη: *παραστάς* probably means the side wall of the pronaos or entrance porch. For a similar borrowing of dedicated arms in a crisis see *Hcld.* 695–9.

1123. ἐπὶ βωμοῦ: if Eur. has in mind the Altar of Chios, this would certainly be a point of vantage from which N. could proclaim his innocence and defend himself, and yet might turn out to be a trap from which he must escape, as he does in 1137–40.

γοργὸς ὁπλίτης: in Ar. *Pax* 565 *γοργός* cannot have its usual sense 'grim', 'terrible', and Platnauer there takes it to mean 'bright' 'dazzling'. Here too it could be used of the flashing armour of N., as Verrall argued in his note on A. *Sept.* 523 (537); but it is more likely that it means 'terrible' and that Eur. now uses, to express the messenger's admiration of N., the same phrase that had been used sarcastically of Menelaus in 458.

1124. Δελφῶν παῖδας: a common periphrasis in Homer, e.g. *υἷες Ἀχαιῶν*, and found several times in poetry and Ionic prose, e.g. A. *Pers.* 405 *ὦ παῖδες Ἑλλήνων*; E. *Hec.* 930; Hdt. 1. 27 *Λυδῶν παῖδας*; id. 5. 49 *Ἰώνων παῖδας*.

παῖδας is governed by *βοᾷ* used transitively in the sense 'shout at'; cf. *Tro.* 587 *βοᾷς τὸν παρ' Ἅιδᾳ παῖδ' ἐμόν*, and the use of the passive in *Hel.* 1433 *πᾶσαν δὲ χρὴ | γαῖαν βοᾶσθαι.*

1127. The juxtaposition of *οὐδείς* and *μυρίων* is an instance of a common idiom.

There is something sinister about the silence in which this concerted attack is made, and the number of assailants, though *μυρίοι* is a conventional exaggeration, makes their rout by a single man the more remarkable.

1128. ἔβαλλον ἐκ χερῶν πέτροις: *βάλλειν* here, as often, means 'hit with a missile', 'pelt'.

1129. νιφάδι: cf. *Il.* 12. 156 (*χερμάδια*) *νιφάδες δ' ὣς πῖπτον ἔραζε*; ibid. 278; A. fr. 199 N.[2] (Loeb 112) *νιφάδι γογγύλων πέτρων.*

These lines certainly seem more appropriate to a scene taking place outside the temple.

σποδούμενος: *σποδεῖν* appears first (in compound form) in Aesch. *Th.* 809 *κατεσποδημένοι*, the sons of Oedipus are 'beaten down', 'destroyed', and is used in *Ag.* 670 *στρατοῦ καμόντος καὶ κακῶς σποδουμένου* of the fleet battered by wind and waves. In Eur. it is found also in *Hipp.* 1238 *σποδούμενος μὲν πρὸς πέτραις φίλον κάρα* 'smashing his own head against the rocks' Barrett. Verrall, on *Sept.* 809 (794), Fraenkel, and others take it to be a word from popular language because of its frequency in Comedy. In Ar. and Old Comedy it is used four times of beating, e.g. *Ra.* 662 *τὰς λαγόνας σπόδει*, five times equivalent to *βινεῖν*, and twice in the sense 'eat greedily'. In these met. senses it is clearly colloquial, because it is a strong word used metaphorically in trivial contexts, a common form of colloquialism, but there may be nothing colloquial about its use in Tragedy with its proper meaning.

In this line every word emphasizes the violence of the attack 'battered by missiles coming from every side thick and fast like snowflakes'.

1130–1. προὔτεινε . . . ἐκτείνων: there is little if any distinction between these verbs and if *τεύχη* means only 'shield' the two phrases seem carelessly tautologous; but *τεύχη* normally denotes armour and/or arms and might here include a sword, which would serve to deflect a missile here and there, the conduct of his shield being then more precisely indicated in 1131.

1132. ἀλλ' οὐδὲν ἦνεν: N. was successfully warding off missiles, but his efforts were vain in the sense that he could not hold out thus indefinitely.

1133. μεσάγκυλα: javelins with a thong (*ἀγκύλη*) attached in the middle for hurling them.

ἔκλυτοί τ' ἀμφώβολοι: for *ἀμφώβολος*, only found here apart from the doubtful and isolated *ἀμφώβολα* in S. fr. 1006, LSJ give 'javelin or spit with two points', but it looks as though some Delphians hurl ordinary missiles while others make use of spits they have picked up; a two-pointed spit would in effect be a similar weapon to the *δίβολος ἄκων* in *Rh.* 374. The meaning of *ἔκλυτοι* is uncertain: LSJ give, for this passage only, 'easy to let go, light, buoyant', but this sense is not easily derived from the meaning of *ἐκλύω*; see note on 1134.

1134. σφαγῆς . . . βουπόροι: LSJ and others take these words to denote a fourth kind of missile, 'knives for cutting throats of oxen', *σφαγῆς* being pl. of *σφαγεύς*; cf. S. *Ai.* 815 where *ὁ σφαγεύς* is used of a sword. In that case perhaps we should adopt the reading *σφαγῆς τ'*. This sense of *σφαγεύς* is however more appropriate to the lofty tone of Ajax's farewell speech than to plain narrative; moreover *βουπόρος* is used as an epithet for a spit in *Cyc.* 302; Hdt. 2. 135; Xen. *An.* 7. 8. 14 (where a *βουπόρος ὀβελίσκος* is used as a weapon). If *βουπόροι* is taken with *ἀμφώβολοι* (with no stop at the end of 1133), *σφαγῆς* might be taken as gen. of *σφαγή* and construed as gen. of separation with *ἔκλυτοι*: 'freed from the slaughter' i.e. from slaughtered beasts. So Hermann *e carnibus extracti*. There seems to be no example of *ἔκλυτος* in just this sense, but *ἐκλύω* means 'set free' and *ἀπόλυτος* has the sense 'freed from' in Plut. *Mor.* 426 b.

ἐχώρουν: cf. E. *Mel. Vinct.* (Page, *Lit. Pap.*, p. 114. 37) *πέτροι τ' ἐχώρουν χερμάδες θ'* . . .

ποδῶν πάρος: the missiles presumably rebounded from his shield and fell at his feet; others perhaps fell short.

1135. ἂν εἶδες: this potential use of verbs of perception in the second person draws attention to some special item in the narrative. In Homer, and occasionally in historians, this device, commended by [Longinus,] *Περὶ Ὕψους*, Ch. 26, serves to enlist the attention of each individual member of the audience, e.g. Hom. *Od.* 24. 61 *οὔτιν' ἀδάκρυτόν γ' ἐνόησας*; *Il.* 5. 85 *οὐκ ἂν γνοίης*; Xen. *Hell.* 6. 4. 16 *ὀλίγους ἂν εἶδες*; id. *Cyr.* 8. 1. 33. So also in E. *Ba.* 1085 *οὐκ ἂν ἤκουσας βοήν*, where the messenger is not addressing any specific person, unless it is the Chorus leader. The same use of the second person occurs in *Ba.* 737, 740; *IA* 432, though here the speaker may be regarded as addressing another character, and in the present example *παιδός* in 1136 confirms the direct address to Peleus. Nevertheless this usage, confined to messenger speeches, may be due to epic influence.

πυρρίχας: *πυρρίχη* (sc. *ὄρχησις*) as known in the fifth century was a lively dance in armour derived from an ancient war dance, recalling the crouching, springing, bending aside, all the movements, evasive and offensive, of actual fighting. See Plato's description in *Leg.* 815 a and cf. Ar. *Ra.* 153. According to Aristoxenus the dance was named after Pyrrichos, a Spartan, but this may be a guess. There is not likely to be in the mind of Eur. any connection with Pyrrhos = Neoptolemus,[1] since though, according to Pausanias 10. 26. 4, in the *Cypria* N. was called Pyrrhus by Lycomedes, this name never appears in extant literature until Theocritus 15. 140. LSJ translate *δεινὰς πυρρίχας* as 'strange contortions', but it is more likely to be a plural for sing. referring to the well-known dance, with *δεινάς* to indicate that this time it is deadly earnest. For another grim dance of death in Eur. cf. *HF* 978 *τόρνευμα δεινὸν ποδός* and ibid. 836, 871.

1136. παιδός is probably right. There is pathos in this reminder of the relationship to the listening Peleus of the man whose last moments are here narrated. With *παῖς* referring to a grandson cf. 632, where Peleus speaks of *τῶν ἐμῶν τέκνων* i.e. Neoptolemus. Normally the article or *σου* would be needed for 'your boy', but here the second person *εἶδες* enables *παιδός* to stand alone.

1138. κενώσας: for the sense 'make empty' i.e. 'leave', 'abandon' cf. *Ba.* 730 *λόχμην κενώσας*.

δεξίμηλον ἐσχάραν: cf. 1100–2. The epithet is perhaps slight confirmation that the altar here mentioned is outside the temple.

1139. τὸ Τρωικὸν πήδημα: the article shows that some well-known feat is referred to, and according to *Σ* a place in the district of Troy was called *Ἀχίλλεως πήδημα* after Achilles' leap from his ship to the shore. It would be particularly appropriate to use the phrase of a similarly spectacular leap by his son.[2] According to Pouilloux Eur. imagines N. leaping from the Altar of Chios to the peristyle of the temple, 'au-dessus de la masse des assailants, en pleine mêlée'. This would be a distance of some forty-five feet. This distance is exceeded by Phayllus' legendary jump of fifty-five feet (*Anth. Pal.* app. 279) but this must be a poetic exaggeration; the world record in modern times (1969) is 29 ft. 2 ins. Even if Pouilloux's general picture is accepted it is not essential that N. should leap so far. In any case the comparison with a famous leap of Achilles and the emphatic form of expression confirms that the *βωμός* of 1123 and 1138 is more likely to be the Great Altar of Chios than a much smaller altar within the cella. In the scene on the Ruvo amphora (see on 1008) N. is shown with one knee on the altar and the other foot on the ground.

1140. For the comparison with doves fleeing from a hawk cf. *Il.* 21. 493–6, 22. 139–93.

1143. αὐτοί θ' ὑπ' αὐτῶν: presumably knocked down and trampled on in the confusion, *ἔπιπτον* being equivalent to a passive verb.

[1] For a different view see E. K. Borthwick in *JHS* 87 (1967), 20 ff.

[2] E. K. Borthwick, op. cit. 18 ff., suggests that the allusion is to a 'Trojan leap' of Neoptolemus himself, when he was the first to jump down from the Wooden Horse; but the evidence is derived from late metrical scholia and the arguments in favour of this view seem to me very speculative.

Murray rightly rejects Voss's correction. In such phrases *αὐτός* in oblique cases is not rare as a reflexive in Attic Tragedy, sometimes with the rough breathing as a variant; e.g. A. *Pers.* 415 *αὐτοὶ δ' ὑπ' αὐτῶν* MAV: *ὑφ' αὑτῶν fere cett.*; S. *Ai.* 1132 *αὐτὸς αὐτοῦ* L: *αὑτοῦ* r. It is more likely that the original smooth breathing was 'corrected' to a rough than vice versa. See Tucker on A. *Cho.* 110 and Fraenkel on *Ag.* 836.

στενοπόρους κατ' ἐξόδους: these words in themselves certainly suggest that the whole scene from 1111 to this point took place within the cella, and that the Delphians pursued by N. are now trying to get out. If, however, N.'s mighty leap took him among his enemies and close to the temple entrances, many of them might first be driven inside and then in panic seek to force their way out again. Pouilloux (op. cit.) thinks that *ἔξοδοι* refers not only to the temple entrance but to other ways of escape from the pronaos; some of N.'s assailants might seek to escape among the columns of the peristyle.

1144. εὐφήμοισι δύσφημος: the juxtaposition brings out the special horror of the scene in which shouting and the clash of arms is heard where holy silence should reign.

1145. ἐν εὐδίᾳ: *εὐδία* 'fair weather' is often used metaphorically, like its opposite *χειμών*; cf. A. *Th.* 795 *πόλις ἐν εὐδίᾳ*; Xen. *An.* 5. 8. 20 *ἐν εὐδίᾳ ὁρῶ ὑμᾶς. ὅταν δὲ χειμὼν ᾖ* . . . Here the change is from the period of intense agitation and danger to the moment of calm when N. has routed his enemies and they do not yet dare to renew the attack. *πως* here adds a touch of wonder to the bare statement. It is less likely that *εὐδία* denotes a sudden shaft of sunlight in which his armour glitters.

1146. φαεννοῖς: a conventional epic epithet for weapons and armour, e.g. *Il.* 3. 357 *διὰ μὲν ἀσπίδος ἦλθε φαεινῆς*; ibid. 4. 496 *δουρὶ φαεινῷ*. Here it is reinforced by *στίλβων*, but if N. is now within the temple again, the gleam of arms is in contrast with the shadowy interior.

1147. πρὶν δή: the particle marks the decisive point.

τις: Norwood characteristically observes: 'beyond doubt Eur. wishes to hint that the voice was only that of a mortal conspirator'; but no such scepticism is implied. It is clear from 1161–5 that the narrator holds Apollo to be responsible and Eur. is not concerned to indicate his personal belief. The indefinite *τις* is used elsewhere in similar contexts either because the identity of the deity is uncertain or to add a touch of mystery, e.g. S. *OC* 1623 (of the divine voice that summoned Oedipus) *φθέγμα . . . τινὸς θώυξεν αὐτόν*; *Ba.* 1078 *φωνή τις, ὡς μὲν εἰκάσαι | Διόνυσος*; *IT* 1385 *ναὸς δ' ἐκ μέσης ἐφθέγξατο βοή τις.*

1148. δεινόν τι καὶ φρικωδές: 'uttered a strange and thrilling cry'. The MSS. have *δεινόν τε*, which is possible, the neuter adjectives being then used adverbially. Lenting's *τι* gives a more common construction, and again perhaps adds a touch of mystery.

στρατόν: not quite an army, but the word implies a large number.*

1150. ὀξυθήκτῳ: perhaps an unconscious reminiscence of 1118; the fatal blow might well be struck by one of the original assailants.

1151–2. Δελφοῦ πρὸς ἀνδρός: *Σ* gives his name as *Μαχαιρεύς*; cf. *Or.* 1656 *θανεῖν Δελφικῷ ξίφει*, where *Σ* cites Pherecydes as authority for the name *Μαχαιρεύς*. It does not appear in any other connection and is perhaps a descriptive title from *μάχαιρα* 'sacrificial knife'. According to one tradition N. was killed by a priest of Apollo (Pausanias 10. 23. 4); see Intr., p. 4. In this passage since we know the attackers are Delphians the phrase has little point, and *ὅσπερ . . . ὤλεσε* also seems superfluous. Hartung may be right to delete 1151, in which case *πολλῶν μετ' ἄλλων* will mean that many others fell too, i.e. N. fought on to the end.

1153. τίς οὐ . . . προσφέρει: another epic reminiscence; cf. *Il.* 22. 371, where the Achaeans gather round the dead Hector, *οὐδ' ἄρα οἵ τις ἀνουτητί γε παρέστη*. The messenger waiting outside would not perhaps see this happening, but this is the conventional narrator's licence; it is not necessary to suppose with Pouilloux that he merely infers all this from the state of the body when he sees it (1154–5).

1154. βάλλων ἀράσσων: perhaps a stock phrase; cf. *Hec.* 1175; *IT* 310. For participles in asyndeton at the beginning of a line cf. *HF* 602 *ἕλξων φονεύσων*; *Or.* 951; fr. 452; S. *Ph.* 11; *Tr.* 787.

1154–5. δέμας καλλίμορφον: for other examples of compound adjectives where the second part is redundant cf. *Tro.* 1194 *καλλίπηχυν βραχίονα*; *Hipp.* 827 *βαρύποτμον τύχαν*; *Ph.* 1549; *Hipp.* 669.

1156–7. Some have taken *βωμοῦ* to be the altar mentioned in 1123 and 1138, i.e. the Altar of Chios; if so this would confirm the view that N. was killed outside the temple. In that case *ἀνακτόρων* must have a wider meaning than the temple itself, as it obviously has in *Ion* 1224. On the other hand the normal meaning of *ἀνάκτορα* 'temple' is here supported by *θυοδόκων*, of which the only other examples are *Ion* 511 *δόμων θυοδόκων*, ibid. 1449 *οἴκων θυοδόκων*, both referring to the temple of Apollo. *βωμοῦ* could then quite well refer to an altar inside the temple. Thus the more natural interpretation supports the view that N. was killed inside the temple and his body cast out, perhaps near to where the narrator and his companions were waiting for their master. With all speed they take it up and depart.

1159–60. See note on 1199.

1161. τοῖς ἄλλοισι: picked up by *πᾶσιν ἀνθρώποις* in 1162. In effect mortals are contrasted with the god: he prophesies to others and is judge of right and wrong for them, but shows himself revengeful and unjust. Dobree's *τοῖς Ἕλλησι* is not an improvement.

1162–3. τῶν δικαίων . . . δίκας διδόντα: the juxtaposition emphasizes the injustice of Apollo's treatment of N., and the messenger's words confirm the particular version of N.'s death which Eur. has adopted; cf. 51–5, 1106–8 with notes.

1164–5. In *Ba.* 1348 Cadmus claims that gods should be merciful even if mortals are not. Here Apollo is censured as behaving not merely no better than a man but like the worst of men. Cherishing a grudge seems to be accepted as normal for a Homeric king, cf. *Il.* 1. 81–2 *εἴ περ γάρ τε χόλον γε καὶ αὐτῆμαρ καταπέψῃ, | ἀλλά τε καὶ μετόπισθεν ἔχει κότον, ὄφρα τελέσσῃ*, and though in *Il.* 4 Achilles is urged to relent his refusal cannot affect his *ἀρετή*. In the fifth century, however, the notion that 'magnanimity in politics is not seldom the truest wisdom' may have gained ground. In the orators and historians the absence of *μνησικακεῖν* (in diplomatic and political contexts) is at any rate claimed as a virtue (e.g. Dem. 18. 96, Thuc. 4. 74, Lys. 18. 19), and Aristotle's *μεγαλόψυχος* is not *μνησίκακος* (*EN* 1125a3). Here it is of course possible that the sentiments are those of Euripides himself and less appropriate to a common soldier.

1165. πῶς ἂν εἴη: 'how can he be *σοφός*?' This seems to be an interrogative form of the idiomatic use of *ἄν* with opt. of something that would on investigation prove to be so, e.g. Hdt. 1. 2 *εἴησαν δ' ἂν οὗτοι Κρῆτες* 'these must be Cretans'; *Hel.* 91 *τλήμων ἂν εἴης*; cf. S. *El.* 1450 *ποῦ δῆτ' ἂν εἶεν;* 'where can they be?'

σοφός: Norwood thinks that we might have expected a word for 'good', but *σοφός* is the traditional epithet for Apollo, and is often, like *σκαιός* and *ἀμαθής*, tinged with ethical meaning; thus in *El.* 971–2 when Orestes exclaims *ὦ Φοῖβε, πολλήν γ' ἀμαθίαν ἐθέσπισας* and Electra answers *ὅπου δ' Ἀπόλλων σκαιὸς ᾖ τίνες σοφοί;* the point at issue is moral rather than intellectual; so also in the words of the Dioskouroi (1246) *σοφὸς δ' ὢν οὐκ ἔχρησέ σοι σοφά.**

The loyal servant of Neoptolemus is naturally full of bitterness against the god who has helped to destroy his master; he may also be the mouthpiece of the dramatist, but it is more significant for the outlook of Euripides that he has chosen to present, if not originate, the version of N.'s death that is most favourable to him and discreditable to Apollo and Delphi.

1166 ff. The Chorus see attendants approaching from the left bearing the body of Neoptolemus. They enter the orchestra as the Chorus chant seven lines of anapaests, a metre often associated with the measured tread of a march, and set the body, lying presumably on some form of bier, before Peleus.

1167. δῶμα: *πελάζειν* in the intrans. sense does not elsewhere take an accusative, but in *Rh.* 14 we have *τὰς κοίτας πλάθουσι* and the acc. without preposition is common in verse with other verbs of motion; see on *ἑστίαν* in v. 3.

1168. ὁ παθών: euphemistic for 'the dead'; cf. Lys. 19. 51 *εἰ ἔπαθέ τι* 'if anything had happened to him' meaning in fact 'if he had died'.

1170. οὐχ ὡς σὺ θέλεις: an extreme example of understatement; cf. Hdt. 1. 16 *οὐκ ὡς ἤθελε . . . ἀλλὰ προσπταίσας μεγάλως*.

1171–2. If we accept the deletion of *πήμασι κύρσας*, the sense is 'and you yourself in your sorrows' (locative) or 'because of your sorrows' (causal) 'have become involved in one and the same fate (as your grandson)'. A papyrus of v A.D., however, has *αυτος*[. . . .]*μασι*, and we should probably read (with Garzya and Tovar) *αὐτὸς δὴ πήμασι κύρσας*. For the next line the paraphrase in *Σ συνεδυστύχησας αὐτῷ* (sc. *Νεοπτολέμῳ*) fits the MS. reading, but this is not wholly satisfactory. The repetition *κύρσας . . . συνέκυρσας* sounds to me worse than similar examples elsewhere, e.g. *HF* 153, *Ba.* 256, and some parallels cited by Garzya, e.g. *Alc.* 1103 *νικῶντι συννικᾷς* and *Hel.* 1389, are quite different, since there the repetition is rhetorically effective. For *εἰς ἓν μοίρας* cf. *Hel.* 742 *εἰς ἓν ἐλθόντες τύχης* 'united in our misfortune'; *Tro.* 1155 *τἀπ' ἐμοῦ τε κἀπὸ σοῦ | εἰς ἓν ξυνελθόντ'*. In both passages, however, there is a verb of motion, which *συγκυρεῖν* is not, and it is rather forced to say that Peleus and Neoptolemus share the same fate. The catalectic line *αὐτὸς δὴ πήμασι κύρσας* would metrically and in meaning be a suitable ending, and perhaps 1172 should be omitted, as in some MSS.

κομμός: 1173–1225

The Chorus and Peleus lament over the dead body of Neoptolemus.

Metre. The first strophe and antistrophe are separated by two iambic trimeters spoken by the Chorus; in the second iambic trimeters interspersed among lyric iambics are given to Peleus as well as to the Chorus. The purely dactylic rhythm of the first pair of stanzas is characteristic of Euripides as compared with Aeschylus and Sophocles.

Metrical Scheme:

Strophe+antistrophe (*a*): 1173–83 = 1186–96

	1.	– ⏑ ⏑ – ⏑ ⏑ – ⏑ ⏑ – ⏑ ⏑	dactylic tetrameter
	2.	– ⏑ ⏑ – ⏖ – ⏑ ⏑ – –	dactylic tetrameter
1175 = 1188	3.	⏑ – – – – –	?
	4.	– ⏑ ⏑ – ⏑ ⏑ – ⏑ ⏑ – ⏑ ⏑	dactylic tetrameter
	5.	– ⏑ ⏑ – ⏑ ⏑ – ⏑ ⏑ – ⏑ ⏑	dactylic tetrameter
	6.	– ⏑ ⏑ – –	adonean
	7.	– ⏑ ⏑ – ⏖ – ⏑ ⏑ – ⏑ ⏑	dactylic tetrameter
1180 = 1193	8.	– ⏑ ⏑ – – – ⏔ – ⏖	dactylic tetrameter (with substitution of spondees)
	9.	– ⏑ ⏑ – ⏑ ⏑ – ⏑ ⏑ – ⏑ ⏑	dactylic tetrameter
	10.	– ⏑ ⏑ – ⏑ ⏑ – ⏑ ⏑ – –	dactylic tetrameter
	11.	⏑ ⏑ – ⏑͡⏑ ⏑ – –	? ionic a minore+bacchiac

Notes:

3. The metrical form of these exclamations is uncertain, and the antistrophe seems to be corrupt here.
8. In 1180 *βάλλων* gives a dactylic colon with spondees in place of the second and third dactyl. Correspondence with 1193 is sufficiently close, except that the final dactyl *τέρψομαι* is not normal in responsion to the final spondee of 1193. Wecklein's *δὴ φίλον αὐγὰς τέρψομαι ἄρας* gives exact correspondence, but the process of corruption is obscure. The MS. reading *βαλών*, accepted by Kamerbeek and Bornmann, gives a choriambus followed by two cretics, interrupting the dactylic movement and not corresponding with 1193, which looks sound.
11. The resolution is doubtful, and in any case ionic a minore is somewhat incongruous here. Perhaps, as T. B. L. Webster suggests, the following colometry would be preferable:

ε̄ῐθε̆ σ' ὕπ' Ἰλῐῶ ἦνᾰρε̆ δαῖ-	dactylic tetr. catalectic
μῶν Σῐμο̆έντῐδᾰ πᾰρ' ᾱκτᾱν	dactylic dimeter + bacchiac

Strophe + antistrophe (*b*): 1197–1213 = 1214–25

1.	– ⏑⏑ ⏑ – ⏑ – ⏑ – ⏑ – ⏑ –	iambic trimeter
2.	⏑ – –	bacchiac
3.	– ⏑ – ⏑ – –	ithyphallic
4.	⏓ ⏑⏑ ⏑ – ⏑ ⏑⏑ ⏑ – ⏑ – ⏑ –	iambic trimeter
5.	⏑ – –	bacchiac
6.	– ⏑ – ⏑ – –	ithyphallic
7.	⏑ – ⏑ – ⏑ ⏑⏑ ⏑ – ⏑ – ⏑ –	iambic trimeter
8.	– ⏑ ⏑⏑	cretic
9.	⏑⏑ ⏑ ⏑⏑ ⏑ – –	ithyphallic
10.	– – – ⏑ – – ⏑ ⏑⏑	spondee + 2 cretics
11.	⏒ – ⏑ – ⏑ – ⏑ –	iambic dimeter
12.	⏑ – ⏑ – ⏑ – ⏑ – ⏑ – ⏑ –	iambic trimeter
13.	– ⏑ – ⏑ – ⏑ –	lekythion
14.	– ⏑ – ⏑ – ⏑ –	lekythion
15.	⏑ – ⏑ – ⏑ ⏑⏑ ⏑ ⏑⏑ ⏑ – ⏑ –	iambic trimeter
16.	⏑ – ⏑ –	iambic metron
17.	– ⏑ – ⏑ – –	ithyphallic

Note:

10. The first part of this colon is scanned by some as a dochmiac and the rest as a choriambus ending in brevis in longo; but a lone dochmiac is less likely, and it is better to scan as spondee (here = syncopated cretic) + 2 cretics. As 1206 has no corresponding line in the antistrophe some editors reject it, but see note ad loc.

1174. χερί: instrumental dative; Peleus perhaps lays his hand on the body. *δώμασι* is locative.

1176. πόλι: the vocative form is here required by the metre; see note on 1 above. The reference is probably to the city of Phthia rather than Thessaly as a whole.

1177. μοι τέκνα: if these words are omitted, with P and O (here = B), the sequence of dactylic dimeters is preserved; they may have been added by someone who thought another noun was needed after the second *οὐκέτι*. Nauck suggested *οὐ τέκνα* in place of the second *οὐκέτι*, but the repetition is pathetic; cf. *Med.* 976 *νῦν ἐλπίδες οὐκέτι μοι παίδων ζόας, οὐκέτι.*

1179. παθέων: causal genitive with *σχέτλιος*.

1180. αὐγὰς βάλλων: 'casting my eyes'; cf. *Ion* 582 *πρὸς γῆν ὄμμα βαλών. αὐγαί*, generally the rays of the sun, is used elsewhere with *ὀμμάτων*, e.g. S. *Ai.* 70; E. *HF* 132, *Ph.* 1564. The only other example of *αὐγαί* alone in this sense is [E.] *Rh.* 737 *κατ' εὐφρόνην ἀμβλῶπες αὐγαί.*

1181. Peleus probably caresses the dead body, naming each part as he touches it. So Hecuba, mourning over the dead Astyanax, *Tro.* 1178 ff. *ὦ χεῖρες . . . ὦ . . . φίλον στόμα*; *Med.* 1071 *ὦ φιλτάτη χείρ, φίλτατον δέ μοι στόμα.*

1182. *ἐναίρειν*, a regular verb in Epic for to slay in battle, is appropriate here. The notion that it was a better fate to fall in battle before the walls of Troy than to perish later by some more obscure or sordid death goes back to Homer, e.g. *Od.* 1. 236 (Telemachus is speaking of his father) *οὔ κε θανόντι περ ὧδ' ἀκαχοίμην, | εἰ μεσὰ οἷς ἑτάροισι δάμη Τρώων ἐνὶ δήμῳ*, and appears again in Tragedy e.g. A. *Cho.* 345 ff. *εἰ γὰρ ὑπ' Ἰλίῳ πάτερ . . . κατηναρίσθης.*

1184. ὡς ἐκ τῶνδε: 'arising out of that', i.e. 'in that case'; cf. S. *Aj.* 537 *τί δῆτ' ἂν ὡς ἐκ τῶνδ' ἂν ὠφελοῖμί σε; Med.* 459; Thuc. 4. 17. 1 *ὡς ἐκ τῶν παρόντων*. It is perhaps a rather prosaic expression, but the text appears to be sound. (The emendation ascribed to Wilamowitz in the apparatus criticus was later withdrawn by him[1] in *Hermes*, 60 (1925) 293.)

The correspondence *τε . . . δέ* is not rare; see *GP* 513 (6) (ii).

1186. γάμος: the marriage of Neoptolemus and Hermione. The text of the antistrophe is corrupt, but it seems clear that Peleus is proclaiming as causes of disaster the marriage with Hermione, which roused the enmity of Orestes, and the feud with Apollo (1194–6), which enabled Or. to invoke the help of the Delphians and of the god himself.

1187. ἁμάν: Murray's emendation of the MS. reading *ἐμὰν* restores correspondence with 1174 and is a simpler alteration than that of Hermann.

---

[1] W. observed: 'Radermacher was once pleased with *ὡς Προῖτός τις* (929) as I was with *ὡς Ἕκτωρ*. I hope we now know that our conjectures were only soap-bubbles.'

1188. The MS. reading does not correspond with that of most MSS. in 1175 but the precise form of such interjections is uncertain in both lines and cannot be restored with any confidence. Murray's tentative *αἰαῖ ὦ Λήδας παῖ* is very speculative and implies that *σῶν λεχέων* and *ὦ γάμος* is the marriage of Helen, which is unlikely in this context.

1189–93. These lines are also difficult and probably corrupt, though there is metrical correspondence with the strophe. Taking the text as printed Bornmann interprets thus: the subject of *ὤφελε* is *ἐμὸν γένος*; *σῶν λεχέων τὸ δυσώνυμον* = *τὸ σὸν δυσώνυμον λέχος* 'your hateful marriage' (cf. S. *OC* 528 *δυσώνυμα λέκτρα*, and for similar phrases S. *Ant.* 1265 *ἐμῶν ἄνολβα βουλευμάτων*); on this phrase depends the gen. *Ἑρμιόνας* and to it *Ἀΐδαν* is in apposition. The sense is then: 'My son, would that my race had never burdened itself with that hateful marriage of yours in the hope of children and home, marriage with Hermione that brought death to you, my child; would that she had perished ere that by the lightning's stroke.' No convincing improvement of the text has been proposed.

1194–5. *ὤφελες* must be supplied from *ὤφελε* in 1190 and Barnes's correction *Φοῖβον*, accepted by all editors except Murray, seems to be necessary. 'And would that you, a mortal, had not fastened upon Phoebus, a god, the death (lit. blood) of your noble father, by reason of the fatal archery.' The epithet *διογενής* properly belongs to *πατρός*, but is attached by hypallage to *αἷμα*; cf. 399 *σφαγὰς Ἕκτορος τροχηλάτους*.

1198. δεσπόταν: *γόοις κατάρξω* is regarded as equivalent to *γοήσομαι* and governs an accusative; cf. *Ph.* 1549 *ἄλοχος . . . πόδα σὸν θεραπεύμασιν ἐμόχθει* = *ἐθεράπευε*.

νόμῳ τῷ νερτέρων: *νόμος* probably in the musical sense: 'in the strain consecrated to the dead'. The lack of traditional laments was almost as bad as lack of burial and the two things are regularly linked together, e.g. Hom. *Il.* 22. 386 *ἄκλαυτος ἄθαπτος*; S. *Ant.* 29 *ἄκλαυτον ἄταφον*; S. *El.* 867 *οὔτε τοῦ τάφου ἀντιάσας οὔτε γόων*; cf. also 1159–60.

1200. διάδοχα: neut. pl. of the adj. used adverbially: 'in my turn'.

1203. θεοῦ αἶσα: probably in a tone of pious resignation: 'God's will be done.' Individuals may speak bitterly, as Peleus does in 1213, but a Chorus tends to be resigned.

1206. There is no corresponding line in the antistrophe, where the sense is complete. If, following Matthiae, we bracket 1206 we lose *ἐμέ*, which is needed with *γέροντα*, and Hermann accordingly reads in 1205 *ὦ φίλος, ἔλειπες ἐν δόμῳ μ' ἔρημον*, giving an iambic trimeter catalectic. For 1206 he substitutes a parenthetic *ἰώ μοί μοι*, repeated after *κεῖται* in the antistrophe. There is, however, nothing objectionable about 1206 and Murray, followed by modern editors, may be right to keep the MS. reading and assume a lacuna of one line after 1219.

1207. νοσφίσας: LSJ take the meaning to be 'deprive me (of yourself)', but elsewhere there is always a second acc. of the thing removed, and it is more likely that the active is here used, like the middle elsewhere, in the sense 'forsake'. For the notion of death as abandonment of the living cf. *Alc.* 250 *ἔπαιρε σαυτήν, ὦ τάλαινα, μὴ προδῷς*; ibid. 275 *μὴ . . . τλῇς με προδοῦναι.*

1209–11. These are the ritual manifestations of grief. Cf. A. *Cho.* 24; *Tro.* 279–80; *Hec.* 652–6; *Hel.* 372–4; S. *Aj.* 631–4.

1209. οὐ σπαράξομαι . . .; formally a question but in effect an exhortation, as often with the 2nd person; cf. *Med.* 878 *οὐκ ἀπαλλαχθήσομαι | θυμοῦ;*

1211. ὦ πόλις: P. is not, as Σ takes it, apostrophizing the city of Troy, ultimate cause of his sorrows, but appealing for the sympathy of the citizens of Phthia. So Oedipus in S. *OT* 629 cries out in anger and distress *ὦ πόλις, πόλις*, and Polyneices in *Ph.* 613 *ὦ πόλις.*

1217. ἐς Ἅιδαν: 'till my death'; cf. *Alc.* 13 *ᾄδην τὸν παραυτίκ' ἐκφυγεῖν.* Perhaps here too the initial capital is not needed.

1218. ὤλβισαν θεοί: the festivities at the wedding of Peleus and Thetis were unique in that the gods and goddesses came and, according to Pindar *Nem.* 4. 67, gave him *δῶρα καὶ κράτος*; see also *P.* 3. 93. The wedding is a theme of the third stasimon of *IA* (1036–79). For *ὀλβίζω* and cognates as the regular term for wedding congratulations cf. Hes. fr. 81 (Rz.) *τρὶς μάκαρ Αἰακίδη καὶ τετράκις, ὄλβιε Πηλεῦ*; Sappho, fr. 112 (L.P.); *Alc.* 918; *Hel.* 640; Theoc. 18. 52.

1219. ἀμπτάμενα: a fairly common metaphor for what is lost and gone; cf. *HF* 69 *ἐκεῖνα μὲν θανόντ' ἀνέπτατο.* In some examples, e.g. *Med.* 440 *αἰθερία δ' ἀνέπτα* (*χάρις* and *αἰδώς*) and *IT* 843 *πρὸς αἰθέρα ἀμπτάμενος* it does not sound like a worn metaphor, so that *κεῖται* has been thought incongruous, and Musgrave conjectured *ἀνεῖται.* The metaphor may, however, only come to life in certain contexts, and the text can stand.

1220. κόμπων μεταρσίων: this is generally taken to mean 'proud boasting', i.e. his fortunes are now nothing to boast about. It would, however, suit the context better if there were some reference back to *ὤλβισαν θεοί*, and *κόμπος* could perhaps have the sense 'praise', 'commendation', which is the meaning in all three occurrences in Pindar (*Nem.* 8. 49; *I.* 1. 43, 5. 24) though it may not be found elsewhere: 'Gone with the winds are all my fortunes; they lie in the dust . . . unworthy now of high acclaim.' (If a line is missing it probably amplified *κεῖται*, as in the supplement suggested in the app. crit., and would not affect the meaning of the next line.) Whatever the sense of *κόμπος*, *μετάρσιος* probably has, as often, the connotation 'out of touch with reality'.

Peleus and Cadmus are linked together in Pind. *P.* 3. 86 ff. as having achieved in their marriages the highest bliss and been then brought low by the fate of their offspring; Peleus suffers the double bereavement of son and grandson.

1222. οὐκέτ' εἶ, πόλις, πόλις: the reading of most MSS. is *οὔτε μοι* πόλις πόλις, which is accepted by Kamerbeek and Bornmann, but the repetition is perhaps more likely in adjuration, as in S. *OT* 629; for the death of N. as the end of the πόλις cf. 1187. On the basis of the reading of AP οὐκέτι μοι πόλις πόλις, which is unmetrical, Jackson, *Marg. Scaen.* 79 suggests a combination of haplography and dittography οὐκέτ' εἰ⟨μ', οἴ⟩μοι, πόλις [πόλις]. For the false repetition of πόλις he compares *Hipp.* 884.

1223. σκῆπτρα: the plural is common when σκῆπτρον is used as a symbol of royalty, e.g. S. *OC* 425 ὃς σκῆπτρα καὶ θρόνους ἔχει; *HF* 213 ἔχειν γῆς σκῆπτρα τῆσδε; *Ph.* 514; *Or.* 437; cf. A. *Ag.* 1265–7 (where Cassandra throws down her prophetic wand) σκῆπτρα καὶ μαντεῖα . . . στέφη . . . ἴτ' ἐς φθόρον.

[ἐπὶ γαῖαν]: an unmetrical addition. If this was originally a stage direction (Page, *Actors' Interpolations*, pp. 112–15) the form of the word has been changed.

1224. On this cue Thetis prepares to enter.

1225. ὄψεαι: this uncontracted form from ὁρᾶν is elsewhere found only in Epic.

[πρὸς γᾶν]: if this is a stage direction the form is again poetic and the direction is mistaken, since πίτνοντα is surely metaphorical here.

1226–30. As in 1166 ff., the anapaests spoken by the coryphaeus mark the transition to a new scene and, as often, herald the appearance of a new character.

1226. τί κεκίνηται; LSJ translate 'What motion is this?' Perhaps rather, with Norwood, 'What is it that moves?'

τίνος αἰσθάνομαι θείου: the speaker presumably now glimpses a figure approaching through the air and therefore apparently some divinity, θεῖόν τι being more indefinite than θεός or δαίμων. She bids her companions look too, and then, at the words δαίμων ὅδε, the figure is more clearly seen. As Denniston observed on *El.* 1233: 'When gods appear at the end of a tragedy their divinity is always recognized at once, their identity never.' Here the speaker does not yet distinguish the sex of the deity (ὅδε, πορθμευόμενος). It seems to me improbable that αἰσθάνομαι here refers to hearing sounds, as is suggested by Hourmouziades, *Production and Imagination in Euripides*, pp. 164–5.

1228. λευκὴν αἰθέρα: acc. of space over which. αἰθήρ is masculine in Attic prose and generally in post-Homeric poetry, but Eur. often reverts to its Homeric gender. λευκός is perhaps not elsewhere used of αἰθήρ (λαμπρός is a regular epithet in Eur.), but in Homer and Eur. it is used of water in the sense 'clear, limpid', e.g. *HF* 573, *IA* 1294, and in *El.* 730 of the 'bright face of dawn'. Wecklein's λευράν, from A. *Pr.* 410 λευρὸν . . . οἶμον αἰθέρος, is not necessary.

1229. πορθμευόμενος: in the active this verb merely means 'convey' e.g. *IT* 735 τάσδε π. γραφάς, and I cannot agree with Hourmouziades (loc. cit.) that the passive implies here anything more than the μηχανή, some sort of crane by which an actor could be swung through the air and suspended in the air, though here ἐπιβαίνει suggests that he is deposited on some platform, perhaps the θεολογεῖον; this is in any case more likely here and elsewhere than the delivery of long speeches by an actor suspended in the air. Only this passage and *El.* 1253 directly refer to movement through the air, involving some mechanical contrivance, and Barrett (on *Hipp.* 1283) suggests the possibility that they were interpolated to suit the practice of the later (fourth-century) theatre; but, as he notes, a μηχανή was certainly used in fifth-century comedy, sometimes apparently in parody of scenes from Eur.; see also Webster, *Greek Theatre Production*, pp. 12–13. There seems no reason to doubt the use of the μηχανή in this scene.

EPILOGUE: 1231–end

Thetis appears as *dea ex machina*, but not to cut a knot: there is no impasse, no dilemma, as for instance in the *Philoctetes* and the *Ion*. The main action of the play is finished, but there are loose ends, especially the future of Andromache and her child, left stranded in Phthia, and the burial of Neoptolemus. These matters could have been arranged on the human plane, but not with the ease and simplicity of a divine fiat. Thetis, then, comes partly to offer some consolation to the shattered Peleus, and thus to end the play on a quieter note, but mainly (1238) to adjust the outcome of this play to established legend. As usual she declares her identity at once, and the appearance at the end of the play of the goddess round whose shrine the action of the first part was centred helps to convey some sense of formal unity.

1235. ἄκλαυτα: the gods are essentially μάκαρες and exempt from sorrow as well as death; yet by their unions with mortals they may be drawn into the circle of human sorrow. Zeus weeps for the death of Sarpedon (*Il.* 16. 459–60) and Thetis weeps in sympathy with the distress of Achilles (*Il.* 1. 413 and 18. 94). She could not really expect that children by a mortal would never die (though she is said to have tried hard to achieve this), and Norwood takes her to mean that as a goddess she might have expected to marry a god and have immortal offspring 'children who would never have cost me a tear'. Certainly according to one tradition (e.g. in Pi. *I.* 8. 36–8) Zeus and Poseidon had once been rivals for her love, and in *Il.* 18. 429 ff. she speaks of herself as forced by Zeus to marry a mortal against her will; but it is rather hard that her words of consolation to Peleus should begin with a reminder that she married beneath her. Possibly it is not merely the death of Achilles of which she thinks but his untimely death in the flower of manhood.

1240. Πυθικὴν πρὸς ἐσχάραν: that N. was buried at Delphi was an established fact (Pindar, *Nem.* 7. 43–8; Pherecyd. fr. 64 Jacoby) and visitors to Delphi might have seen his burial place; Peleus is accordingly bidden to take his body there. It seems to be assumed that the Delphians will accept the divine mandate.

1241. Δελφοῖς ὄνειδος: a final solemn affirmation of Delphian responsibility, though the moving spirit was Orestes.

ὄνειδος is acc. in apposition to the sentence *τὸν μὲν . . . ἐσχάραν.*

1243. γυναῖκα . . . Ἀνδρομάχην λέγω: the third-person reference is not incompatible with the presence of Andromache, though examples cited by H. Erbse (*Hermes*, 94 (1966), 295, n. 1) of a *deus ex machina* using a third person of those present are not relevant, since there the third person is inevitable (e.g. *El.* 1249 *Πυλάδῃ μὲν Ἠλέκτραν δὸς ἄλοχον*), whereas here Thetis could have addressed her prophecy directly to Andromache. Nevertheless the reason why she continues to address Peleus may be not that A. is not there, but that the main point is not her future but that of the house of Peleus. Some positive indication of Andromache's presence is provided by *παῖδα τόνδε* in 1246, since mother and child are likely to be together, and though the deictic pronoun does not necessarily imply physical presence, it normally does so unless there is some other justification for it; see notes on 710, 735, 967.

1246–7. μόνον λελειμμένον δή: *δή* emphasizes *μόνον*; for the order cf. Hdt. 9. 27. 5 *οἵτινες μοῦνοι Ἑλλήνων δή.*

1247. χρή: in 1250 Eur. writes *δεῖ*; both are used of what is fated and there appears to be no distinction in meaning; cf. *El.* 1264 *δεῖ* and 1273 *χρή*. Barrett (on *Hipp.* 41) observes that *δεῖ* tends to stress mere inevitability, *χρή* an accordance with the divine order; in this passage, however, *χρή* is used to indicate what must happen, but in the reason for it (1249–51), where the stress is on the divine purpose, we have *δεῖ*.

1248. ἄλλον δι' ἄλλου: 'one after another' is the sense required by the context, but there seems to be no parallel. Hyslop compares S. *Phil.* 285 *ὁ μὲν χρόνος δὴ διὰ χρόνου προὔβαινέ μοι*, but there the line grows from the common phrase *διὰ χρόνου* 'after an interval'.

Μολοσσίας: some editors and LSJ keep the MS. reading *Μολοσσίαν* and take *διαπερᾶν* to mean 'reign through all Molossia', but there is no example of this sense, nor can it be derived from the basic meaning of the verb. It is better to accept Lenting's correction, in which case *Μολοσσίας* depends on *βασιλέα* and *διαπερᾶν* is used absolutely: 'and descended from him one after another as king of M. shall pass through ⟨life⟩ in prosperity'. *διαπερᾶν τὸν βίον* occurs in Xen. *Oec.* 11. 7 and the verb might well be used, like *διατρίβειν* and *διάγειν*, with or without an object; cf. the absolute use of the simple verb in Xen. *Cyr.* 7. 2. 20 *σαυτὸν γιγνώσκων εὐδαίμων, Κροῖσε, περάσεις.*

1249. εὐδαιμονοῦντας: *ἄλλον δι' ἄλλου* is equivalent to a plural.

1251. καὶ γάρ: no need to emend. *καί* here means 'indeed', 'in fact' (*GP* 108. 1 (2)).

κἀκείνης: 'Troy too' i.e. as well as the House of Aeacus.

1252. προθυμίᾳ: cf. *Ion* 1385 *τοῦ θεοῦ προθυμίᾳ*; *Hipp.* 1417 *Κύπριδος ἐκ προθυμίας*; ibid. 1329. *προμηθίᾳ* 'forethought', the reading of LP, is elsewhere used only of mortals.

1254. The line is rightly bracketed in OCT and regarded by Page as an expansive interpolation. It is however unlikely, as Jackson observes (*Marg. Scaen.* 51), that anyone would interpolate such a line at this point, and I prefer his suggestion that it originally followed 1235, that it was at some stage accidentally omitted and inserted after 1253 because this was at the end of a page, and was subsequently left there because the sign indicating its true position was not noticed. If so, a scribe probably 'corrected' *θεὰν γεγῶσαν* to the nom. case, though a nom. in agreement with *κἀγώ* would not be impossible after 1235.

1256. Thetis speaks as though she had the power to transform a mortal into a *θεός*, ageless and deathless and, as her words in 1258–9 imply, on a level with herself; but it appears from 1269 that she is acting in accordance with the decrees of Zeus. So too it was from Zeus that Eos won the gift of immortality for her bridegroom Tithonus, but forgot to ask exemption from old age (*HH* 5. 220–4). Eur. here assigns to Peleus a more exalted destiny than mere translation to the Islands of the Blessed, which in Pind. *Ol.* 2. 78–80 he shares with Cadmus and Achilles.

1258. τὸ λοιπὸν ἤδη: 'from that (this) time on', generally in solemn utterances; cf. S. *Tr.* 168 *τὸ λοιπὸν ἤδη ζῆν ἀλυπήτῳ βίῳ*; ibid. 921 *τὸ λοιπὸν ἤδη χαίρετε* 'now and for ever'; *Med.* 1128; Pl. *Ap.* 41 c *ἤδη τὸ λοιπὸν χρόνον*.

1259. ξηρὸν. . .πόδα: his divinity will protect him as in the *Iliad* it protects Thetis and Poseidon (*Il.* 8. 65, 13. 29).

1261–2. The tradition that Achilles, with other specially favoured heroes, was transported to the Islands of the Blessed (alternatively known as the Elysian Plain) goes back to Pindar (*Ol.* 2. 78–80), Ibycus, and Simonides (Sch. Ap. Rh. 4. 814), and probably became the standard version; cf. Pl. *Symp.* 179 e. Eur. here follows a tradition earlier than Pindar, since according to Proclus' summary Arctinus in the *Aethiopis* recorded that Thetis snatched her son from the funeral pyre and bore him to Leuce. The same version is alluded to in Pind. *Nem.* 4. 49 and *IT* 435–7. For reasons given in antiquity for the name 'White Island' (the modern Phidonisi) see Platnauer's note on *IT* 435.

1263–4. A repetition of the command already given in 1239–40, now with a complimentary epithet for Delphi, *θεόδμητον*, used of the towers of Troy (*Il.* 8. 519), of Delos (Pind. *Ol.* 6. 59), and bestowed by Attic dramatists on Athens (S. *El.* 707; *Hipp.* 974, *IT* 1449).

1265. χοιράδος . . . Σηπιάδος: according to *Σ* *χοιράς* properly denotes a rock rising from the sea, and presumably presenting a 'hog's-back' appearance. It was also more widely used, e.g. *χοιρὰς Δηλία* 'the rocky isle of Delos' (A. *Eu.* 9). Here the reference is to the Sepias promontory near Iolkos, called *Σηπίας ἀκτή* in Hdt. 7. 188, 191. According to *Σ* on Ap. Rhod. 1. 582 it was so called because to escape Peleus Thetis changed into various creatures and finally into a cuttle-fish (*σηπία*). This part of the coast was sacred to Thetis as the place where, according to one tradition, Peleus won her as his bride by holding her fast through all her transformations. See note on 1278 below.

1267. πεντήκοντα: so in A. fr. 285 (M) Thetis is *δέσποινα πεντήκοντα Νηρῄδων κορᾶν*.

1269. Ζηνὶ γὰρ δοκεῖ τάδε: for the repeated *γάρ* see *GP* 64–5; Murray's tentative *τοι* is not needed.

It is common form in Eur. for the *deus ex machina* to ascribe to Zeus or Destiny the ultimate responsibility for the arrangements; see *Hipp.* 1331, *El.* 1247–8, *IT* 1486, *Hel.* 1660, *Or.* 1634–5, *Ba.* 1349; Athena in *Ion* is perhaps the only exception. So also Heracles (virtually a *deus*) in S. *Phil.* 1415. Sometimes, as here, the reference to Zeus is probably conventional; elsewhere it may have deeper significance, particularly in *Ba.* 1349, where the authority of Zeus is claimed with special emphasis and in answer to direct criticism.

1272. ψῆφος: see on 496 and cf. A. *Supp.* 943 *ψῆφος κέκρανται*; *Tro.* 785 *ψῆφος ἐκράνθη* referring to an Argive decree; I know no other example of *ψῆφος* used of a divine decree, but *κραίνειν* is regularly used of decrees of gods and fate; see Fraenkel on A. *Ag.* 369 and cf. *θεόκραντος* and *μοιρόκραντος*.

κατθανεῖν τ' ὀφείλεται: Eur. uses the same phrase in *Alc.* 419, 782; fr. 10; cf. S. *El.* 1173 *πᾶσιν γὰρ ἡμῖν τοῦτ' ὀφείλεται παθεῖν*.

1273. συγκοιμήματα: *συγκοίμημα* 'bedfellow', not found elsewhere, is an example of an abstract noun used of a person; see note on *λάλημα* in 937. The combination of this usage with plural for singular perhaps makes the form of address a little more ceremonious. For the same combination cf. *Hipp.* 11 *Ἱππόλυτος, ἁγνοῦ Πιτθέως παιδεύματα*.

1278. Cf. Pind. *N.* 3. 75 *ποντίαν Θέτιν κατέμαρψεν (Πηλεὺς) ἐγκονητί*. Eur. does not actually refer to transformations of Thetis, but no doubt he is alluding to that version of the story. In *IA* 707 he follows a different version in which Zeus gives Thetis to Peleus in the house of Cheiron. The two accounts are not irreconcilable, since a formal betrothal could follow the initial encounter, but in fact the transformation story must presumably be earlier and belong to folk tale; the more dignified version was the main, if not the only one known to epic tradition (*Il.* 18. 431–4; Hes. *Cat.* fr. 81). See Robert, *Bild und Lied*, pp. 22–3; B. Schweitzer, 'Mythische Hochzeiten', *Sitzb. Heidelb. Ak.* 6 (1961), 13–19.

1279. κᾆτ᾽ . . . δῆτ᾽: *εἶτα* is often used to denote consequence, especially with an emotional connotation such as surprise or indignation; *καὶ δῆτα* adds further emphasis (*GP* 272–3), so that these lines should follow a striking demonstration that birth is more important than wealth in marrying and giving in marriage. Peleus himself certainly married someone of very high birth indeed, and as a result he is to become a *θεός*; but it would be rather absurd to base a general maxim on this peculiar experience. It is also true that Neoptolemus married a wife with a large dowry and met with disaster; but Hermione was well-born as well as rich, and whatever the final outcome it is hard to see how *κακῶν λέκτρων ἐπιθυμία* can be ascribed to N. In any case it was not the dowry, lineage, or character of his bride that led to his death, but the ill-will of the injured Orestes. The whole passage 1279–83 seems to me to betray a perverted sense of relevance that one would more happily ascribe to an interpolator than to Euripides, though there is no external evidence that 1279–82 belong elsewhere. 1283 is bracketed in OCT because it is cited by Stobaeus 70. 10 as from *Antiope* (fr. 215), except that the last three words are *εἰς τέλος κακῶς*, but it is not more appropriate there than here, and such a line, with or without modification, might be repeated.

1284 ff. These concluding anapaests also appear at the end of *Alc.*, *Hel.*, *Ba.*, and (with a different opening line) *Med.* This tail-piece is most appropriate where it first appears in the *Alc.* and may have been composed by Eur. only for that play. As a comment on the play as a whole it is not particularly appropriate to any of the others (least of all to *Med.*), except in the vague sense that in most dramas the unexpected occurs somewhere, though in all these plays except *Med.* it has a more direct relevance to the divine arrangements announced by the *deus ex machina*; e.g. in this play the arrangements for the future of Andromache and her child and the immortality of Peleus are *ἄελπτα* and *ἀδόκητα* to those concerned. For a good discussion of tail-pieces in Eur. see Barrett's note on *Hipp.* 1462–6.*

ADDENDA

INTRODUCTION

Page 24, *l.* 7. For a full codicological description and discussion of relationship to other manuscripts see now *The Jerusalem Palimpsest of Euripides*, edited with commentary by Stephen Daitz. Berlin, 1970.

Page 24, *l.* 33. Cf. Daitz, op. cit., Appendix A, p. 27: 'Each manuscript must be regarded as a composite entity whose components, the plays, were often taken from different sources.'

COMMENTARY

22–3. Another example is Theseus, who in E. *Hipp.* reigns in Troezen, though Pittheus, his grandfather and the former king, is still living.

159–60. Cf. also E. fr. incert. 913 (Snell, Supplement to Nauck) *τίς . . . οὐ προδι[δ]άσκει ψυχὴν αὑτοῦ θεὸν ἡ[γεῖ]σθαι;*

299. The best example is Dem. 19. 282 *ποῖος γὰρ ἵππος, ποία τριήρης, ποία στρατεία, τίς χορός, τίς λητουργία, τίς εἰσφορά, τίς εὔνοια, ποῖος κίνδυνος;* See also Pind. *P.* 9. 335.

321. Cf. also fr. 484 *τῆς ἀληθείας ὕπο.*

375. ἡμᾶς τε πρός: this adverbial use of *πρός* 'besides' is not found in Sophocles, and in Aeschylus only in *Pr.* 73, 929, and perhaps *Cho.* 301. It occurs 10 times in Eur. and in Aristophanes, Herodotus, Plato, and Demosthenes, and perhaps has a colloquial flavour.

379. For *φαῦλος* in the sense 'ineffectual' cf. *Med.* 807 *μηδείς με φαύλην κἀσθενῆ νομιζέτω.*

433. For *ἀλλ' ἕρπ' ἐς οἴκους* in Eur. add *PSI* xiii 1302, 1 (= Austin fr. 150), cited by Diggle on *Phaethon* 54.

437. See also *Hel.* 124, 162, 1492, and for other examples of a river standing for the country fertilized by it see Kannicht on *Hel.* 1–3.

439. On the ground that there is no parallel for *ἔχειν δίκην* in the sense required here, J. Diggle, in *Proc. Camb. Phil. Soc.* No. 195 (N.S. 15), 1969, p. 41, would read *οὐ Δίκην ἡγῇ Δίκην*, with a comma after *θεῖ'*, in the sense 'Have you no belief in divinity, no belief in justice?' This suggestion, the phonetic equivalent of the reading in the text, is the most plausible I have seen and may be right. Though, if the Greek *can* bear this sense, the explicit affirmation that divine powers both exist and are concerned with δίκη seems to me more likely in this context.

440. J. Diggle, loc. cit., finds the reference of τάδε impossibly obscure and the verb ᾖ unacceptable, and proposes ὅσ' ἂν δοθῇ ποτ' οἴσομεν. I still think that the context suggests a reference for τάδε, and though we might indeed expect, for example, γένηται rather than ᾖ, I am not sure that the latter is impossible in the sense 'Whenever in the future this situation (i.e. the gods punishing injustice) exists, I shall not flinch.'

497. Cf. also *Med.* 111 ἔπαθον τλάμων ἔπαθον μεγάλων.

530. See A. *Ag.* 1272 φίλων ὑπ' ἐχθρῶν, with Fraenkel's note, and E. *Ph.* 1446 (Polyneices speaking of Eteocles) φίλος γὰρ ἐχθρὸς ἐγένετ', ἀλλ' ὅμως φίλος.

637. Cf. also E. *Ph.* 648 βαθυσπόρους γύας; fr. 7 πλούτου καὶ βαθυσπόρου χθονός.

735. See H. Hunger, *W.S.* 65 (1950), pp. 19–24 for further examples illustrating the circumstances in which ὅδε can be used of someone not physically present.

737. For the active verb cf. fr. 287, 3 τὰ πράγματ' ὀρθῶς ἢν τιθῇ.

765. For other examples of τί δεῖ in the sense 'what use?' see frs. 112, 221, 757.

778 ff. See Adkins, *Merit and Responsibility*, ch. 9, 'The Infiltration of Morality'. He notes (p. 191 n. 12) that this passage and *Hipp.* 409 ff. 'both show tension, but adhere to traditional usages'

805. The possibility of 'remorse' in the strict sense depends of course on the belief that some actions are wrong in themselves, irrespective of their consequences. To what extent such a belief was established before the end of the fifth century cannot be discussed in detail here, but I should have noted that in 409 B.C., the year before *Orestes* was produced, there is in S. *Phil.* 1270 an example of μεταγνῶναι in the sense 'repent'. Neoptolemus has succeeded, but feels remorse because success has been achieved by means that are in themselves αἰσχρά.

See also M. Class: *Gewissensregungen in der griechischen Tragödie* (1964), and earlier literature to which he refers.

811. There is a detailed discussion of ancient views on suicide in three papers by R. Hirzel in *Archiv für Religionswissenschaft* 11 (1908). On p. 256 n. 4 he asserts that in the fifth century hanging was considered ignominious, but, apart from *Hel.* 299–301, the only evidence cited is Neophron, fr. 3 τέλος γὰρ αὐτὸς αἰσχίστῳ μόρῳ φέρεις βροχωτὸν ἀγχόνην ἐπισπάσας δέρῃ, where the text is not certain and the disgrace need not depend on the manner of death, and Homer, *Od.* 22. 462 ff., where there are special circumstances, and the reference is to execution, not suicide. Certainly a number of tragic heroines killed themselves by hanging (Antigone, Iocasta, Phaedra), and in this play the Nurse and Hermione between them speak impartially of four methods: hanging (811, 816, 844), the sword (813, 841), fire (847), and falling from a cliff (848).

817. The departure of the Chorus at the end of a scene in S. *Aj.* 814 and E. *Hel.* 361 (or 374) is rather different.

1030. In *Or.* 1235 the half line *ἠψάμην δ' ἐγὼ ξίφους* is given to Electra in OCT, but should probably be given to Pylades; see V. di Benedetto's note ad loc.

1041. See also Wolf Steidle, *Studien zum antiken Drama* (1968), pp. 118–21, who supports the view that *σοι* refers to Hermione. It is not possible to include here a proper discussion of the reasons why I do not find his arguments convincing.

1047. In suggesting the possibility that Andromache may be approaching with Peleus before the end of the second antistrophe, and that in their last lines the Chorus include a direct address to her, I should have added that I know no exact parallel. In *Phoenissae* 258–60 before the end of the second antistrophe the Chorus see Polyneices approaching and in the last lines describe his appearance, but do not address him.

1097–8. J. Diggle (op. cit., p. 43) suggests a slight change to *ἀρχαῖά τ' ἐπληροῦτο βουλευτήρια | ἰδίᾳ θ'* . . . comparing for *ἀρχαῖος* A. *Pers.* 141 *στέγος ἀρχαῖον* and E. *Ion* 1322 *τρίποδος ἀρχαῖον νόμον*. This is tempting in its simplicity, though it may be worth noting that in the passages compared, in A. *Pers.* 141 there is a special point in the anxious elders resolving to take counsel 'beneath this ancient roof', and in *Ion* 1322 the words *τρίποδος ἀρχαῖον νόμον σῴζουσα* are part of a solemn affirmation by the priestess of her sacred office, whereas in our passage *ἀρχαῖα*, which gains some emphasis from its position, has no special point.

1149. στρέψας πρὸς ἀλκήν: 'rallying to battle'; cf. *πρὸς ἀλκὴν τρέπεσθαι* used by historians, e.g. Thuc. 2. 84, always of those getting the worst of an encounter.

1165. Adkins, *M. and R.*, p. 256 n. 4, takes *σοφός* to be used here 'in a persuasive definition to commend quiet behaviour'.

1284 ff. For a similar sentiment, apparently in a dialogue passage, cf. fr. 101 (*Alcmena*) *πολλά τοι θεὸς | κἀκ τῶν ἀέλπτων εὔπορ' ἀνθρώποις τελεῖ.*

INDEXES

I ENGLISH

Numbers in italics refer to pages; other numbers refer to lines as indicated in the commentary.

II GREEK